EARLY MODERN ITA

MW00777427

Early Modern Italy, 1550–1800

Three Seasons in European History

GREGORY HANLON

EARLY MODERN ITALY, 1550–1800

St, Martin's Press, Scholarly and Reference Division,
175 Fifth Avenue, New York, NY 10010

First published in the United States of America in 2000

Printed in China

ISBN 0–312–23179–2 (cloth)
ISBN 0–312–23180–6 (paper)

Library of Congress Cataloging-in-Publication Data

Hanlon, Gregory.
Early modern Italy, 1550–1800 : three seasons in European history /
Gregory Hanlon.
p. cm. – (European studies series)
Includes bibliographical reference and index.
ISBN 0-312-23179-2 (cloth) – ISBN 0-312-23180-6 (pbk)
1. Italy–History–16th century. 2. Italy–History–17th century. 3. Italy–History–18th century. I. Title. II. Series

DG540 .H36 2000
945'.07–dc21   99-055573

Contents

List of Maps and Plates

Maps

vii

Preface

The origin of this book lies in my failure to interest an English-language publisher in translating Jean Delumeau's *Italie de Botticelli à Bonaparte*, which at the time of its publication constituted the only textbook to span the entire early modern period of Italian history. Unlike French, British, Spanish, Polish or even German history, where good textbooks have always been available for every period, the lack of an Italian equivalent was striking. A few years later, the Longman series helped fill the gap, but the piecemeal and uneven nature of its volumes, and the prior knowledge it assumed of its readers made it difficult to use in an undergraduate setting. Even good students in North America have little background in the mechanics and the problems of pre-industrial societies, and the relentless dechristianization of Western culture renders early modern religion almost unrecognizable. Not having the textbook I wanted, I wrote my own.

I should confess, however, that I did not begin with the conclusions placed at the end of this book. Only after years of both reading studies and pursuing archival work in Tuscany have I come to believe that Italy's seventeenth-century decline was broader and more durable than historians generally write. If Italian history never strays from a general European norm, it is difficult to argue that Italian societies evolved with anything like the continuity found in France or England, important reference states. This has long been accepted by economic historians, like Carlo Cipolla, who used the term "Indian summer" to describe Italy's lingering pilot role in European civilization, until 1620. Its splendid precociousness then faded quickly with the onset of terrible storms, and one could argue that winter set in for the better part of two centuries. Italians, who see their past over the longer duration than most others, more readily admit cyclical analogies.

This book could not have been written without the quiet efficiency of the Killam Library Document Delivery Service at Dalhousie University, whose net pulls in books and articles from all over Europe and North America; and from Kelley Hawley and Marlyn McCann in particular. While Halifax is isolated from the mainstream of Italian studies, I have benefited from other viewpoints. Dr Sheila Zurbrigg has kept me honest on problems of agriculture and population, while two former graduate students, Peter Cullen and Elmar Henrich, focused my interest on the indocility of Italians. Edward Michalik provided invaluable assistance in scrutinizing the text, catching stylistic infelicities and gallicisms. I wish to express my gratitude as well to the Italian scholars and archivists in Tuscany whose amiable patience aided my reconversion from French history in the early 1990s, and Oscar Di Simplicio, to whom I owe more than anyone. Carla Zarilli and Giuseppe Chironi in Siena, and Don Aldo Franci in Pienza revealed to me some of the finer points of archival science that no amount of theory can offset. Loretta Roghi, Giovanna Piochi and Blandine Duclap, in Torrita di Siena, Montefollonico and Paris, respectively, helped this study in countless ways. By funding research on my forthcoming book on social relations in the Sienese countryside, the Social Sciences and Humanities Research Council of Canada indirectly made this project possible. Finally, I do not forget my wife Anne, and my little girl, Ariane, who have allowed me to indulge this passion. To all I express my heartfelt gratitude.

G. H.

Table of Monetary Values

The following currencies of account have been measured against the value of the Italian lira of 1866, itself based on the French franc. Moneys of account were never entirely stable, but they varied much less than in the twentieth century. These values were all derived from Angelo Martini, *Manuale di metrologia, ossia misure, pesi e monete in uso attualmente e anticamente, presso tutti i popoli* (Turin, 1883).

Italian money		value in Italian lira (1866)
Genoa	scudo d'argento (1713)	8.18
Rome	scudo d'argento (1650)	6.83
	scudo d'argento (1675)	6.48
Venice	scudo d'argento (1773)	6.69
	ducato d'argento	4.18
Milan	scudo d'argento (1588)	6.66
Florence	scudo or ducatone (1571)	6.65
Parma	ducatone argento (1676)	6.55
Naples	scudo (1689)	5.63
	ducato (1689)	5.10
Modena	scudo (1739)	5.54
Turin	scudo of 6 lire (1690)	5.46
Lucca	scudo d'oro	5.32
Palermo	scudo (1735)	5.16

Other European currencies

London	guinea of 21 shillings	26.48
Paris	ecu of 3 livres (1641)	5.6
Madrid	ducado de cambio	5.58
Vienna	thaler of silver (1753)	5.20
	gulden	2.60

Introduction

Mention Italy's baroque heritage to educated Italians even today, and they will often repeat time-worn clichés. Baroque is excessive and encumbered. It expresses irrational impulses in individuals and obscurantist ideas in society.[1] The values the age exalted – aristocracy and monarchy, militant Catholicism and dolorist piety, regionalism and local loyalties – were the ones that nationalist and secular Risorgimento thinkers considered inimical to the modern age. A strong current in Italian cultural life considers the epoch of the city-states (roughly 1200–1500) as a kind of Golden Age. The long early modern period became a mere parenthesis before the progress of the Risorgimento. Underlying this view is the premise that history celebrates the progress of humankind, and that only innovative achievements and edifying events are worth recording and pondering. The idealist assumptions of traditional Renaissance scholarship are partly responsible for the longevity of this attitude, which is more aesthetic than critical. Since Italians and foreigners both accepted this interpretation, few studied the early modern era from the end of the wars of Italy in 1559 to the French Revolution more than two centuries later. Researchers can still call the Baroque age, when Italian influence on Europe was at its height, the "forgotten centuries".

Nineteenth-century historians hoped the Risorgimento would break completely with the baroque legacy. However, the long period between the onset of the Counter-Reformation and the French Revolution still weighs heavily on contemporary Italy. Socio-cultural historians have shown that if the early modern age did not make the modern unitary state, it was the formative period for making modern Italians. The Council of Trent forged modern social discipline, sharpened individual consciences and applied Rome's rules consistently to society for a prolonged period. Other aspects of the period's legacy haunt Italians still. Separatist and autonomist sentiments are increasingly widespread, in the nostalgia for regional states that a dose of federalism may not satisfy. The Catholic Church's impact on the way Italians view social relations and values endures despite the collapse of traditional religious practice, particularly with regard to the traditional family, less eroded than elsewhere. The baroque *bella figura* exists in Italy as nowhere else in the Western world.

The period was never entirely ignored by excellent scholars. Historical scholarship does not merely replace one interpretation by another, equally relative, glossing of reality. Much of the old "kings and battles" genre of events history, now out of fashion, is still useful. Cast an eye on the political and diplomatic histories of Italian questions by Camillo Manfroni, Romolo Quazza, Luigi Simeoni, Franco Valsecchi, Emile Laloy and Ludwig von Pastor and one will see that perceptive historians working on substantial archives achieved results not inferior to our own time.[2] The period after World War II witnessed the exhaustion of the Risorgimento tradition, and a shift of interest from political questions to intellectual and economic ones.[3] Italians, and Gino Luzzato in particular, helped pioneer economic history after 1920. Much of the evidence pertaining to Italy's place in the European economy accorded with the earlier view of a long decadence after a Renaissance Golden Age. In the wake of Fernand Braudel and the *Annales* school, economic historians analysed and described the underlying processes, structures and conjunctures that conditioned events. Braudel proclaimed the long sixteenth century, lasting until 1620, as an era of great achievement. In two or three decades, Braudel and his French and Italian disciples, Ruggiero Romano, Giuseppe Galasso, Carlo Cipolla, Domenico Sella and Marino Berengo among others, completely transformed our understanding of the Mediterranean economy. Italy's economic decline after 1620–30 became a problem worthy of attention and rich in implications for the history of the entire western world.

Further along the *Annales* path, Italian historians moved beyond socio-economic history to underlying cultural structures, the history of what used to be called *mentalités*. Older forms of cultural history combined with a new sensitivity to social context, permitted scholars to approach old problems with new depth. The place of the aristocracy in Italian society became a central problem, manifest in the work of Rosario Villari and Elena Fasano Guarini, among many others. How the great Tridentine Church shaped Italian culture and behaviour became apparent after Mario Rosa's work on institutions appeared alongside Ernesto de Martino's ethnological inquests. Cultural historians also invented a format of historical analysis with international resonance – *microhistory*. Carlo Ginzburg, Judith Brown, Raul Merzario were able to show how singular incidents cast light across a wide arc of attitudes and activities. By the 1960s, the early modern period became one of the most innovative and exciting fields in Italian historiography, animated by the knowledge that there was much to be discovered. Italian periodicals appeared to elaborate new questions and new methods, of these *Quaderni Storici* is the best known; but it is now only one among many publications of national and international scope and ambition. Historians are showing that baroque Italy was neither less interesting nor less crucial to the development of the modern age than the same period in other countries, and that even crisis and decline offer lessons of general value. The vigour of Italian historiography makes it one of Europe's most fertile "laboratories".

Italian historiography has a few flaws too. One is its overwhelming regionalism. One could argue that the unitary Italy is Garibaldi's and Cavour's creation of 1860. There are strong reasons for arguing that there were at least two Italys: that of the north and centre: and that of the Mezzogiorno and the islands. Italian historians take as their empirical framework the particular territorial states of the time. Emilian history rarely embraces Parma, Modena and the Papal territories simultaneously. Historians of central Italy will study the Florentine state, or Siena, or Umbria, or the Marches, but not all of them together. Historical research also appears in numerous published conference proceedings, not widely distributed. A multitude of slender monographs treat very localized subjects. Attempts to write a history of Italy in the 1970s and 1980s underscored the difficulty in grasping a common experience. The Einaudi *Storia d'Italia*, published in the mid-1970s, embraced the contemporary Italian space, but did so in generalizations. The initial series consecrated only a fraction of one of its five volumes to the early modern period, and then dealt with specific questions in subsequent volumes without attempting to weave them into a coherent whole.[4] The UTET series of Italian history, of twenty-five volumes, preferred to consecrate specific volumes to each state, without ever attempting a national synthesis.[5]

The superlative and now abundant scholarship, in Italy and France particularly, and increasingly in the United States and Britain, cries out for both a general assessment, and a deployment of the tools necessary for students to grasp the basics. Introductory texts usually embrace too much, that is, they pass from the early Renaissance to the French Revolution in a few pages, generally focusing on selected topics, or remain content with broad overviews that are miserly with specific information.[6] Those dealing with the emergence of modern Italy, like the book by Stuart Woolf, still very useful for the relation between intellectuals and government, see little interest in the period before 1700.[7] An early volume in the Longman series on Italian history from antiquity to the present, was a republication of an Italian work on the Enlightenment by Dino Carpanetto and Giuseppe Ricuperati, which begins in the eighteenth century. The publisher then commissioned Eric Cochrane to cover the century after 1530. Neither work glances long at issues beyond the relation between intellectual life and political institutions. The first had already gone out of print before the gap between them was filled by Domenico Sella's fine volume on the seventeenth century, which places greater emphasis on economy and society.[8]

This book has several purposes, then. First, it attempts to weave structural and conjunctural history into a general narrative, embracing the period between the end of the wars of Italy and the French Revolution, as one in which a set of coherent structures, institutions and values predominated. Such an extended period can be articulated in epochs placing Italy in a broader European context. The framework remains only loosely chronological, since thematic cohesion is sometimes better served by embracing an ongoing process to its apparent conclusion. Second, the book attempts to signal much exciting work coming from Italy, ahead of more accessible European and American scholars. Finally, the work is a convenient tool for students, concentrating more on basic information than on differences of approach and opinion among historians, which tend to converge over time as archival research yields fuller explanations. Consequently, the passages concerning agriculture and industry, demography and society, politics and institutions, culture and religion, seek to be as descriptive and didactic as possible. The student and lay reader will judge if I have succeeded.

This one's for Ariane

1 *Italy* circa *1700:* a *Geographical Expression*

Defining "Italy"

Italy's cartographic configuration, a great boot, changed little from Roman antiquity to our own times. I exclude the northern alpine valleys of the Alto Adige, or South Tyrol, which were ethnically German and formed an integral part of an incipient "Austria". Over the western Alps, francophone Savoy lay subject to the dynasty based in Piedmont; but it gravitated towards France, as did the Mediterranean district of Nice. Conversely, I include Corsica and the Istrian coast in the north-east corner of the Adriatic sea, with its Venetian population. Malta was a special case, a Catholic but Arab-speaking adjunct of Sicily and totally dependent upon it for its sustenance. The whole territory under consideration, over 300,000 square kilometres, stretching 1,500 kilometres in length, shares few basic geographical features. While the Romans unified Italy politically, subsequent invasions overlaid Greek and Arab traits in the south, and Germanic influences in the north. The population spoke such a variety of dialects in 1700 that Venetians needed interpreters in Naples. Nevertheless, the Latin framework persisted in a network of interrelated cities. Another element of unity was the early christian-ization of the peninsula, which was accomplished by the fourth and fifth centuries. Rome and Latin prevailed everywhere. Preindustrial cultures adapted like wildlife species to an ecological niche. Regions are ethnic, ecological and historical. They form a framework for the very long duration, and are more durable than nations, which are

relative latecomers. They impinged on the identities of early modern
Europeans and Italians, and they weigh heavily still. For the sake of
convenience, one can delimit three zones in the Italian area: north,
centre and south, with the great islands belonging to the last. I wish
to examine each region in turn, as it appeared around 1700, when
we have statistics that are broadly reliable.

Northern Italy

The map reveals a vast horseshoe of mountains encasing a great alluvial valley some 400 kilometres long from east to west. The coastal
plain along the northern Adriatic shore extends the valley by
another 200 kilometres. The high Alps to the north often reach
heights of 4,000 metres. Alluvions flushed down the slopes gradually
filled the shallow seabed, and silt continues to push the shoreline
into the Adriatic by 70 or 80 metres every year.[1] These lowlands, with
their rich soils and abundant water have always been disproportionately important economically. Glacial runoff allowed boats and
barges to ply the Po and its major tributaries, the Ticino, the Adda,
the Oglio and the Mincio, in addition to the Adige below Trento. A
few rivers fed by Apennine streams were navigable too. A glance at a
map of navigable rivers and canals of Italy underlines how much this
advantage is particular to the great northern plain (see Map 1).

Lombardy

At the centre of the great Po river valley, Lombardy's diverse districts
compounded its advantages. Alpine lake-shores, bordered with olive
and citrus trees, enjoy a microclimate like the Riviera. Mountains
and hills provided woods and pastures, and mineral resources like
iron, that provided city manufacturers with meat and raw materials.
The lush alluvial plain, irrigated by summer rains, springs and alpine
glaciers, produced vast amounts of hay for livestock, in addition to
grain and fruit.[2] Such lush agriculture supported a number of great
towns, which were considerable by the standards of 1700. Milan, the
most important crossroads since Roman times, contained about
124,000 people. Several other manufacturing towns counted over
20,000 inhabitants, like Bergamo, Brescia, Cremona, Mantua and
Pavia. Como, Alessandria, Lodi, Monza, Novara, Vigevano and

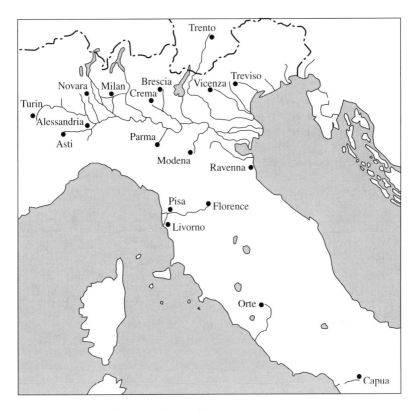

Map 1   Navigable rivers and canals

Crema each contained near or over 10,000.[3] By 1700 much of that industry had withered away, or dispersed into rural zones.

Veneto

East of Lombardy and north of the Po, the plain continues uninterrupted around the top of the Adriatic sea, a waterlogged district under the suzerainty of Venice, which gave its name to the region. The economy and geography look not so much to the sea, as to that single port. The zone between Lake Garda and the Venetian lagoon was the most intensively cultivated. This part of Italy was reclaimed from the marshes, not unlike the Netherlands. There was still plenty of bog near the delta and along the Adriatic shore.[4] The plain north of the Adriatic enjoyed a sunnier climate. Runoff water filled its great rivers, the Piave and the Tagliamento, to the brim in winter, but they were empty, dusty ditches in summer. The foothills were best adapted to manufactures, since water flowing from the mountains turned the mills' wheels all year around. The sharp-peaked mountains to the north were often buttressed by high plateaux used for grazing. Despite some manufactures in the cities, the Veneto was mostly rural, preoccupied with providing food for the great capital which, with its 138,000 inhabitants, was the largest city in northern Italy.

Venice was built on millions of wooden piles pounded into the tiny islands in the lagoon. Its trading vocation in the Greek and Arab world during the late Middle Ages made it fabulously wealthy. Venice claimed the whole Adriatic as its "gulf", before becoming the great intermediary between Europe and Asia, via the Middle East. Venice conquered the towns of the *Terraferma** only around 1400, in order to preserve its control over the routes to Germany and its access to food and fuel. The subject cities near it were in relative decline in 1700, although Vicenza, Verona and Padua each contained more than 20,000 inhabitants, and Treviso and Chioggia more than 10,000.

Friuli

On the eastern frontier, Friuli consisted of a coastal plain, waterlogged nearest the sea, and an alpine district behind it, whose eastern passes led into Austria and Slovenia. This rural region sustained a single town, Udine, with 14,000 people in 1700. Near the Isonzo river, the first Slovenian villages announce the Slavic regions of Balkan Europe under Vienna's rule. The Austrian Empire was a potential enemy, and two wars between Venice and the Empire left the border uncertain. Ottoman possessions in Bosnia were not far away, and Turkish cavalry raids in the late fifteenth century probed as far west as Vicenza. There was otherwise not much movement towards the east. The Italian-speaking port of Trieste belonged to the Empire; since no convenient road linked it to the Danubian basin beyond the mountains, it could not rival Venice.

---

* This and other important terms presented for the first time in italics are defined in the Glossary.

Emilia-Romagna

South of the Po, occupying the plain and the north slope of the Apennine mountains, from Lombardy to the Adriatic, is Emilia-Romagna. Despite the double appellation, the region is an integrated whole of a plain, the hills behind and the mountains above. The Apennine peaks are only 1,500 to 2,000 metres high, but their ruggedness and sterility make them an obstacle. Parallel ridges descending towards the plain become more amenable to grazing and cultivation, but they are nowhere fertile. Deforestation and erosion scar the slopes everywhere, and rain washes the landslip debris, the *frane*, into the stream-beds, choking the channels and causing overflowing. A great zone of bog and lake still remains behind Comacchio. The silting up of the estuary has stranded Ravenna, once a Byzantine seaport, eleven kilometres inland. An extensive *bonification* of the waterlogged river-beds by hydraulic engineers permitted dense settlement in the plain, where intensive agricultural techniques permitted large cities. Rimini, Forlì, Faenza, Imola, Bologna, Modena, Reggio Emilia, Parma and Piacenza, connected close to 200,000 city-dwellers along a single road, the Via Emilia, connecting central Italy to Milan. Added to Ravenna and Ferrara on the edge of the delta, these constituted an urbanized pole of northern Italy. Different political entities belied Emilia-Romagna's geographical unity. The duchies of Parma, Modena and a segment of the duchy of Mantua shared part of it, while Rome ruled Bologna and Ferrara as autonomous territories. A cluster of Imperial fiefs were only gradually incorporated by the duchies around them.

Piedmont

Mountain walls surround Piedmont on three sides, rising right out of the plain to attain a height of between 3,000 and 5,000 metres in a single chain about 30 or 40 kilometres deep. Above 2,000 metres pastures for sheep and cattle predominated. The forest below provided chestnuts to help feed a dense population scraping an existence off smallholdings. The Val d'Aosta, an autonomous zone north of Turin, and a few Alpine valleys south of it spoke French or Occitan. Although the mountain passes to France and Savoy were not accessible to wheeled traffic, convoys of mules plodded their way up and down the slopes. The hilly territory south of the Po, in the Monferrato and the Langhe districts, was thickly settled in small villages, whose fields, vineyards, pastures and woods sustained them. Only 20 per cent of the region consisted of plain, and some of it was sterile scrub south of Vercelli, recently (in 1700) converted to rice-growing. Piedmont's cities played only a minor role in comparison to the feudal lords living in rural castles, and Turin only gradually surpassed Chieri, Asti, Mondovì, Vercelli and Cuneo, which contained less than 10,000 people.

Liguria

Another "natural" region identifiable since Roman times, Liguria forms the grand arc of the Apennines plunging down into the Mediterranean. For over 300 kilometres, it consists almost wholly of mountain slopes, valley bottoms and a thin, intermittent coastal strip. Because of the multitude of small ports and the lack of a viable rural hinterland, this coast was home to the most maritime people of Italy. The Riviera climate of the western half (Ponente) allowed peasants to cultivate citrus and olive trees, clinging to mountain walls in *terraces*. The eastern, or Levante districts of Liguria were better adapted to vines and grains, and its chestnut groves provided a staple for the population. Three or four major routes led north to the Po valley, but Genoese merchants, whose port constituted the natural maritime outlet for Milan and the Lombard cities, rose to a commanding position by 1200. Medieval Genoa rivalled Venice in the Middle East, but by 1500 it looked westward to Spain, and south to Spanish possessions in Italy, where its merchants played the leading commercial role. Past its peak prosperity in 1700, Genoa still contained more than 60,000 inhabitants, active in commerce and industry.

Trentino

The northern periphery of the Italian world, where the Alps descend into the south, belonged to the Holy Roman Empire, and the Habsburg dynasty ruled it from Vienna. In some ways the Trentino was an Italian-speaking frontier of Germany, and the local aristocracy combined German and Italian bloodlines. A carriageable road

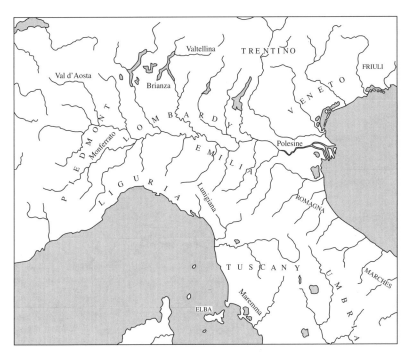

Map 2   Regions of northern Italy

to the Brenner pass, which was the easiest point of entry into Italy, connected Brixen (Bressanone) and Bozen (Bolzano) to the Danubian heartland of Austria and southern Germany. The gentle descent of the Adige, nourished by glaciers between Bozen and Verona, made it navigable. A fairly dense population planted the lower slopes in vines and pastured their cattle on the plateau above. Since Trento did not reach 10,000 inhabitants, the mountains remained overwhelmingly rural.

Central Italy

Mediterranean Italy is a mountainous peninsula lying between the Tyrrhenian and the Adriatic seas, where the Apennines consist of sandstones, clays and limestones, covered with trees on the higher slopes, and planted at lower altitude in a garden-like, *promiscuous culture*. Deforestation and overgrazing everywhere flushed the soil

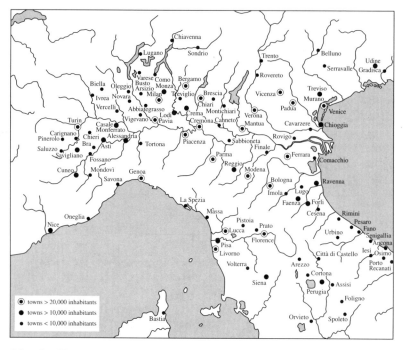

Map 3   Towns and cities, North

into the streams. Today we see lake basins and wetlands as a precious resource; in the days before malaria could be cured, wetlands inhibited human habitation. During summer, anopheles mosquitoes carried the *Plasmodium falciparum* that laid low with intermittent fever undernourished hosts, and well-fed Italians too. Since malaria was endemic in lowlands, people preferred perched hilltop villages and cultivated higher land instead. The four "historic" regions of central Italy shared all of these features.

Tuscany

Tuscany took its name from an ancient but largely forgotten urban civilization, that of the Etruscans. Most of the northern half formed the watershed of the river Arno, which was navigable between Florence and its mouth just below Pisa. Tuscany's eastern frontier lay open to the depression of Lake Trasimene, and the wide Val di Chiana (ancient lake-beds). The Apennine mountainsides overlooking them offered resources of chestnuts and pasture.[5] The valleys, the Lunigiana, the Garfagnana, the Mugello, the Casentino and the Val Tiberina, were so densely populated that they forced thousands of workers out towards the cities and the agricultural estates in the lowlands. Central Tuscany was a complex region of hills cloaked in forest, or covered by extensive brush or *macchia*, when not put under extensive grain cultivation. Along the coast lay a marshy zone of coastal lowlands extending over 200 kilometres between the mouth of the Arno and Rome. This was the *Maremma*, a semi-wilderness that migrant labourers and shepherds exploited for short periods each year. Apart from a few hilltop villages, and the tiny town of Grosseto, the zone was inhabited by exiles, bandits, adventurers, rootless peasants and itinerant traders. Attempts to intensify agriculture by draining the Maremma and the Val di Chiana marshes were all failures.

The complex geography and the segmentation of the region by ranges of low mountains gave birth to a large number of medieval city republics. Florence subjugated those in the Arno valley (Pisa, Pistoia, Arezzo) by the fifteenth century, and the Sienese-controlled south a century later. Only Lucca survived in the north-west corner, thanks to its massive fortifications. Tuscany remained deeply marked by its cities, their industries (not completely dead by 1700), their elites and their cultural institutions, the universities, the academies and their colleges.

Umbria

Umbria was not a historical region, since the very term only dates from the Renaissance. Like Tuscany, it combines cultivated hills and swampy valleys, drained by the central course of the Tiber river. Rome gradually extended its rule over the autonomous towns there, from Città di Castello in the north to Rieti in the south. Only Perugia surpassed 10,000 inhabitants in 1700. Umbria was the land of the hillside olive tree. The valley floor and the high plateaux were reserved for grain cultivation. Soldiers, bandits and malaria pushed the inhabitants into perched fortified villages, called *castelli*, often dating from Roman or Etruscan times. Promiscuous culture aided soil retention by integrating trees and vines with cereals and legumi-

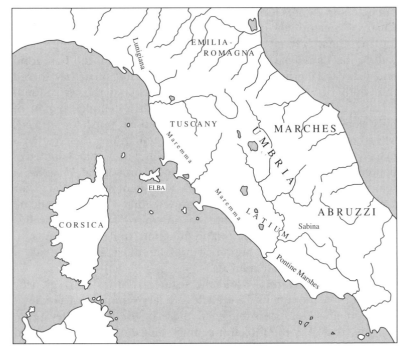

Map 4   Regions of central Italy

nous crops.[6] The landscape resembled a giant garden, lush with as
many types of crops and animals as household autonomy required. A
special government department in Rome, the Congregation of the
Waters, supervised never-ending work on building dykes, clearing
ditches, and planting trees to keep the marshes at bay. Despite their
labour, the hills remained more heavily settled than the plains.

Marches

Across the Apennines from Umbria, only 1,500 metres high, and
pierced by numerous passes, lay the Marches. Their parallel ridges
descend to the Adriatic for almost 200 kilometres, with a valley every
ten kilometres. The low rainfall and the mediocre soils supported a
modest agriculture organized in countless farms cultivated in
promiscuous culture. In the fifteenth century, the Marches were as
politically fragmented as Umbria and Emilia, but Rome gradually

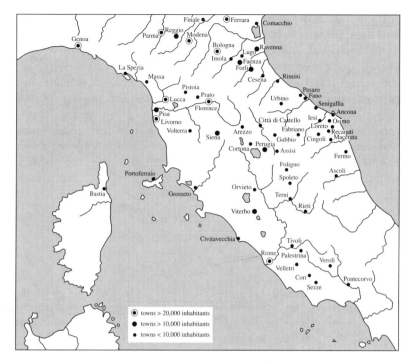

Map 5   Towns and cities, centre

imposed its rule by extinguishing urban autonomies and suppressing the largest fiefs. Only the duchy of Urbino, annexed in 1631, was ruled as a separate legation. None of the towns surpassed 10,000 inhabitants.[7] The overwhelmingly agricultural economy of the region impeded the development of its only significant port, Ancona.

Latium

More than the other regions of central Italy, Latium is not so much a territorial entity defined by its topography, as it is the zone of attraction of a single great city, Rome. The coastal lowland was for vast sectors virtually uninhabited, even within sight of the walls of the ancient metropolis. South-east of the mouth of the Tiber lay the deadly coastal wetlands of the Pontine marshes. Behind the plain, migrant labourers toiled on scattered estates on the low plateau of volcanic tuff and ash soil. Low volcanic peaks rise from its surface and their bowls contain small lakes. In order to maximize the tax on hides and wool and economize on scarce manpower, the popes encouraged grazing on large *latifundia* estates.[8] Just east of Rome lay the vine-covered slopes of the Colli Albani, where cardinals and princes built palaces and villas. The arid Sabine massive of the Apennines is broken into several disjointed chains bordering densely inhabited valleys, rich in flowing water and lush in vegetation. Apart from the capital the area is devoid of cities save for Viterbo, which counted about 12,000 people. The papal administration, the prestige of the Church, the lure of the Roman Empire, and the attraction of charity and cheap food for workers, combined to turn Rome into an important European city, which in 1700 counted 138,000 people.

Southern Italy and the Islands

Political unification in 1860 and even more so, economic development and mass migration in the later twentieth century brought northern Italy closer to the south. Many argue that in all important aspects, the two are separate countries. In 1700, the disparity between north and south was less noticed because nothing forced these peoples to live together. The south was a separate kingdom, with Naples as its capital; indeed, contemporaries spoke of *the* kingdom, without specifying further. Sicily and Sardinia were kingdoms too, but the latter was just barely considered Italian. The south possessed distinctive features – drought, seismic activity in zones of dense settlement, active volcanoes, the absence of autonomous cities, and above all, its feudal system. Until 1600, only neighbouring Latium contained similar baronial jurisdictions with uninhibited sway, but the popes were reining them in. Perhaps the principal burden on the south was summer drought. Aridity fostered monocultures and latifundia in the driest regions, where large holdings were put under wheat. Over much of the Mezzogiorno, peasants journeyed far to work in the fields, when there was work, and when they were not too debilitated by the pervasive malaria which affected most of the region. Even the mountains were less hospitable. Much of the soil is covered only by *macchia*, a drought-resistant scrub growth that has replaced forest. Pasturing sheep and goats on it reduced vegetation to evergreen shrubs, or low bushes and grass-like plants called *garrigue*, of cistus, rosemary, lavender, gorse and broom.

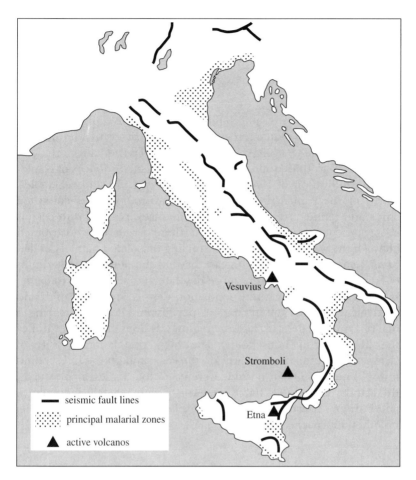

Map 6   Malarial zones and seismic activity

Mezzogiorno regions pay another heavy toll to seismicity and volcanic activity. Tectonic fault lines run through north-eastern Italy, in the Alps west of Lake Garda and on the northern fringe of Friuli. Intense and frequent earth tremors shake the Apennines for their entire length, but with special severity in all the Mezzogiorno provinces. Periodic earthquakes have shattered major cities, such as L'Aquila, Potenza, Catanzaro, Reggio Calabria, Messina and Catania. Volcanoes have long been dormant in Tuscany and Latium, but they are extremely active near Naples and Catania in Sicily. One ancient city now in Naples's suburb, Pozzuoli, has been virtually abandoned as volcanic forces push up underneath it (see Map 2).

Campania

Geography commands and bullies in the Mezzogiorno, but not everywhere with the same ferocity. *Campania felix* forms a fertile crescent between the western Apennines and the Tyrrhenian shore. Rich volcanic ash around Mount Vesuvius in the distant suburbs of Naples permits cultivation of a marvellous variety of fruits and vegetables. North of the capital, in the Terra di Lavoro, peasants cultivated citrus and tender fruit orchards and vineyards, planted with cereals in promiscuous culture. Settlement there was evenly distributed between the walled towns and a sprinkling of isolated hamlets, called *casali*.[9] The lands to the south-east, beyond the densely planted hills of Salerno and Amalfi, were more desolate and arid, given to extensive cereal crops. The rural population density around Naples and Vesuvius was about 160 inhabitants per square kilometre, making it one of Europe's densest, and the region was home to over a third of the Mezzogiorno households. The high population density of Campania and the ring of towns on the coast and on the hills behind it would not have been possible were it not for Naples, a colossus by the standards of 1700. Italy's largest city with 300,000 inhabitants, and Europe's fourth-largest after Paris, London and Constantinople, no other approached it.

Abruzzo

One often speaks of the Abruzzi in the plural, for in addition to constituting two administrative provinces of the kingdom, it shared characteristics of both central and southern Italy. The Apennines reach almost 3,000 metres at their highest, snowcapped peak, the Gran Sasso d'Italia, overtowering thick woods and well-watered valleys. The high chains separate swampy depressions that were once lakes, from which narrow gorges and river valleys lead to the Adriatic. Rugged hills descend in steps down to the sea. Mediocre soil precluded the promiscuous culture sharecropping in *poderi* like the Marches to the north. Molise formed the south-east part of the Abruzzi, drier than the hills to the north, with more uneven water-flow. The sandy Adriatic coast allowed little maritime commerce. Since maritime raids from Islamic pirates based in Albania and Greece made the coast unsafe, people preferred to live on the ridges well back from shore. Most of the habitat consisted of tiny hamlets. With about 13,000 inhabitants, the sole important town was L'Aquila, a medieval commune looking more to Rome and to Umbria than to Naples. Chieti, Teramo and Lanciano were large *agrotowns* facing the Adriatic. Feudal lords still held sway over most districts, sometimes still living in castles. Hamlets were ringed with walls, because forests and mountains harboured bandits who thrived in the region, dodging across the papal border whenever pressed.

Apulia

Apulia forms the heel of the Italian boot jutting into the sea towards Albania, in a flattish slab 350 kilometres long. Much of it was rock, covered by sparse vegetation. The Tavoliere plain was desolate and almost uninhabited save for the sheep-market towns of Foggia and San Severo. The crown kept this district unpopulated in order to allow for mass sheep *transhumance* every winter.[10] Combined flocks totalling over a million head scampered down from the highlands where the grass ceased growing, and were confined in great pens. About a third of the zone was placed under the plough every summer to grow grain for Naples, and soil enriched by sheep manure gave miraculous yields. South-east of the Tavoliere was the Murge, a tableland of rock leading down to the Adriatic in abrupt steps. Closer to the sea a rich red soil allowed intense cultivation. The Adriatic coast was indented with dry stream-beds creating natural ports of some importance: Barletta, Trani, Bari, Monopoli, Molfetta and Brindisi each counted between 10,000 and 15,000 inhabitants. Southeast of the Murge in the pointed heel of the Italian boot, lay the flat, fertile Salento plain, with its wheat, olives, vines, mulberries, figs, almonds, flax, hemp and citrus fruits. In 1700 it sustained a large peasant population (often Greek-speaking) living in agrotowns. Despite the lack of surface water, and a constant struggle against the stones in the fields, grain yields here were among the highest in Europe. The main alternative to grain was the olive tree, grouped in great plantations. Many aristocrats still lived in the region, in commercial port cities like Gallipoli, Otranto and

Taranto, or in the regional capital of Lecce, the kingdom's second
city with 18,000 people.

Basilicata, or Lucania

The Campanian Apennines descend towards the "instep" of the
Italian boot in a tortuous sea of hillcrests, of unstable, eroded clay
soil suitable for cereals but not much else. The Basilicata, or
Lucania, as the Romans called it, was a zone overgrazed by sheep
and goats since ancient times, to such an extent that it retains a
squalid aspect. Unlike Apulia, it rains there. Parts of the Basilicata
contrast a continental winter of paralysing rain and snow with long
months of heat and drought that bake the soil. The coastal district of
the Metaponto was an uninhabited malarial swamp, devoid of ports.
The inhabitants (often Albanian and Greek refugees) took refuge in
hilltop agrotowns, separated from each other by the rugged relief.
None could claim the status or the population of a significant city.
Simple transit across the region was an adventure rendered perilous
by rural banditry. Frequent earthquakes destroyed houses, roads and
bridges, while drought, deforestation and overgrazing kept the agriculture poor and marginal.

Calabria

The "toe" of the boot is articulated entirely around the Apennine
chain, 250 kilometres long, subdivided into several massifs. Two of
these are crystalline rock plateaux over 2,000 metres high: the Sila,
and the Aspromonte, both of which are subject to seismic shocks.
The region's plains were narrow bands of malarial marsh. As in
Basilicata, there are only two seasons, a wet one in winter, and a
long, parched summer. During the rainy period, water gushes
down the mountain slopes in torrents. The obstinate cultivation of
tiny sloped fields by Calabrians worsened the deforestation and
erosion.[11] Apart from large cereal-growing estates close to the
coast, the commercial crops were raw silk and olive oil. Only the
capital, Catanzaro, and the ports of Tropea and Reggio Calabria
contained more than 10,000 people. Possessing most of the landed
wealth, the feudal nobility had long abandoned the region in
favour of Naples. Coastal districts were subject to corsair raids of

Map 7   Regions of southern Italy

great violence, often guided by former inhabitants who had converted to Islam.

Sicily

Sicily was separated from the continent by a strait only two to five
kilometres wide. People and goods travelled by sea more than by

Map 8   Towns and cities, South

road, since Calabria was difficult to traverse. Curiously, none of the
Italian islands or seacoasts, except for Liguria, developed the seafaring habit to a degree comparable to the Portuguese, Basques,
Bretons, English or Dutch on the Atlantic shore. Sicily and the
adjoining mainland supported some tuna-fishing from small boats,
but little else. Sicily is broken into several zones connected by a spine
of mountains along the northern shore. The east coast contains

excellent ports, such as Messina, Catania, Augusta and Siracusa. Europe's most fertile soil rests at the base of Mount Etna, whose cone reaches 3,269 metres. Commerical crops brought by the Arabs, such as sugar, rice, citrus fruit and silk complemented the traditional Mediterranean trilogy of cereals, olives and vines. Endowed with ample trading privileges, Messina was one of the largest cities in the Mediterranean, with close to 100,000 inhabitants in 1674. The loss of its privileges reduced it to only 40,000 people in 1700, still more than its nearest rivals, Siracusa with 17,000 and Catania with 16,000.

   Thanks to the fertility of its soil and its central position in the Mediterranean, Sicily has always been an important granary. The drought-resistant durum variety of wheat grown on the clay hills gave a hard grain with high protein content, which kept for years without spoiling. The treeless wheat-producing interior was marked mainly by ravines chiselled by erosion. A strong, dusty wind originating in the Sahara desert, the *scirocco*, worsens the drought occasioned by the high temperatures and long periods of sunshine. The western tip of the island and the north coast were more densely settled, with ter-raced gardens of citrus trees and vines. Where water was available, crops could be grown throughout the year because of the absence of frost. Two-thirds of the island's population lived in large communi-ties of more than 5,000 people.[12] Trapani, with 17,000 people, was a major link with Spain and North Africa. Palermo, with 100,000 inhabitants was the political hub, place of residence of most of the nobility, and principal seat of the viceroy.

Malta

Although not strictly speaking Italian (for its population spoke an Arabic dialect), Malta was a feudal dependency of Sicily. Its two islands, Malta and Gozo, consisted of almost barren rock, and people subsisted on meagre cereals and sparse tree crops. Like some smaller islands around Sicily, Pantelleria, Formentera, Ustica and the vol-canic Lipari islands, it was exposed to Barbary pirate raids. In 1530, the emperor Charles V granted the island to a crusading order of fighting monks, the Knights of Saint John of Jerusalem, who had been ejected from Rhodes by the Turks in 1522. After an epic Turkish siege in 1565, the knights turned their port capital Valletta into a modern fortress city of imposing strength.[13] Profits from plunder quadrupled the population to about 50,000 people.

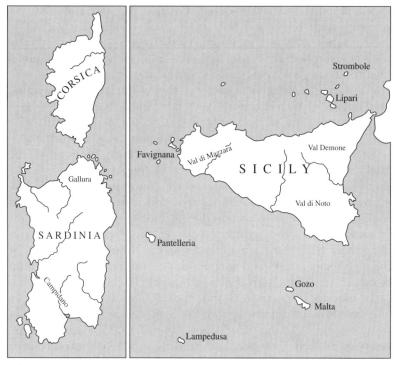

Map 9   Regions of the Islands

Although half the knights of Malta were French, Italian served as the lingua franca for the island.

Sardinia

Sardinia was a great granite plateau, 270 by 100 kilometres, astride the sea lanes between Italy and Spain, Tunisia and France. Ideally placed to exploit links with the lands around the great interior sea, Sardinia was paradoxically one of the most isolated places in Europe. Sardinians spoke an archaic Latin dialect quite different from Italian, and their manner of living was similar to that prevailing in North Africa.[14] Sardinia was an island without ports or seafarers, and its only plain was a lowland marsh. Inland Sardinia was fragmented into multiple zones living in autarchy, whose peasants retained primitive agricultural techniques. Where there was land for the taking,

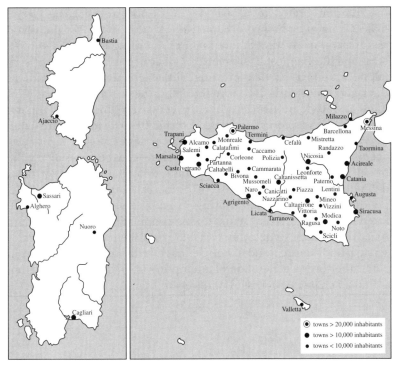

Map 10   Towns and cities, islands

households envisaged agriculture primarily as a support for a pastoral economy. Sardinians produced neither wine nor olive oil of
commercial quality. Neither of the two mediocre towns, Sassari in
the north, and Cagliari in the south, surpassed 15,000 inhabitants, or
produced any exportable manufactures. Only a few salt-pans and
tuna fisheries along the coast provided goods for export besides the
sheep-milk cheeses.

Corsica

By its location, the island of Corsica belongs to central Italy, its population receiving continual replenishment by seasonal workers from
the continent. Corsicans were also numerous in the cities of central
Italy, from Genoa to Naples, serving as soldiers and labourers. Its fortified ports, characterized by social and ethnic diversity not found in

the interior,"wished to be Genoese".[15] Corsicans spoke a Tuscan
dialect long after France occupied the land in 1768. Yet the island
was apart in many ways. A mountain massif rising out of the sea to a
crest height of almost 2,700 metres, Corsica consisted mostly of crystalline granite rock that provided little agricultural soil. With its
thick chestnut stands, the more fertile northeastern district was most
open to outside influences, while the centre and the south were isolated "zones of eternal resistance".[16] Its 100,000 inhabitants cultivated only a small portion of it, with pastures, forest or *macchia*
occupying most of the remainder. Sheep- and goat-raising in the
brush coexisted fitfully with the cultivation of tiny plots of land,
defended by a ferocious sense of property. Corsica's fiercely independent extended families, living in easily defended hamlets, suffered little control from Genoa. Bastia (population about 4,000) and
Ajaccio sustained some commercial life and sheltered a bureaucracy
serving both church and state. Genoa sold the island to France in
1768, after over a generation of attempting to quell revolts there, but
its Italian character persisted until recent times.

2 Family and Sociability

Writing of aristocratic families competing for posts in the Roman Curia, Renata Ago described Italy as a commonwealth of autonomous houses, each plotting its progress through complex strategies of marriage and preferment.[1] Her observations on aristocrats extend to everyone. While organizing principles of families varied considerably over space, they seem stable from the sixteenth to the eighteenth century. We must make a special effort to understand that individuals defined themselves, and were defined by others, primarily as members of a set of kin, rather than autonomous "atoms" striving for self-fulfilment.

Kinship and Residence

In the Middle Ages, most rural and many urban Italians lived in close proximity to their kin, in large houses subdivided into apartments, or in hamlets where almost everyone bore the same names. Neighbours were also relatives because families were rooted in communities where they tilled the land over generations. The stem-family household is a "museum", an archaeological layer over which more outward-looking patterns of family life developed. Widespread across Italy until the late sixteenth century, it gradually receded into mountain districts.[2] Giovanni Levi shows that in Piedmont, even when kin lived in separate dwellings (hearths), they often pooled their assets or their labour. Until after 1700, nuclear families recognized the existence and the authority of a family *capo* who governed a group of kin commonly numbering twenty to thirty adults.[3]

Research on southern Italy derives in considerable part from the work of Gérard Delille, who reveals how different types of agriculture spawned specific family organizations.[4] In the countryside around Salerno (Campania), adjacent properties belonged to different households bearing the same family name. Members of a *casale* lived adjacent to their male relatives in a large multi-unit dwelling or group of attached dwellings, and sometimes shared tools and livestock, or woods and chestnut groves with them. They aimed to achieve the autarchy not so much of each component household, as of each "house". A large family was less vulnerable: it might boast a literate son, or a cleric, or a nobleman's servant among its members, which further bolstered its standing. Age at marriage for men was high, and permanent celibacy of many males resulted. Dowries usually took the form of long-term debts or mortgages, and might never in fact be paid, but be compensated by a future reciprocal marriage. For peasants as for aristocrats, arranged marriages and alliances with cousins maintained estates intact over generations. Land or houses were preferably sold to cousins of the same name, for a price much lower than market value.

The nuclear family, composed generally of only four or five persons, predominated in the grain-growing zones. In Apulia, Delille found peasants buying and selling small plots as part of dowry arrangements. Women often inherited their parents' house, and attracted men to live with them. In contrast to the areas of "tree demography", with their large families and late ages at marriage, the zones of "wheat demography" (including Sicily) devoted to cereal agriculture used day-labourers hired intermttently. This encouraged smaller, younger, households with low standards of living and high mortality. Girls married younger, and children soon worked for salaries too.[5] As in Campania, people preferred to contract matrimony with the closest relative available, between the fourth and sixth degree of kinship. Double marriages of brother and sister marrying a sister and brother were consciously promoted as a way of settling dowries with a minimum of disruption, and simultaneously tightening kinship bonds. Marriage arrangements all over Italy reveal that people cherished ongoing relations with kin who did not reside with them.[6]

Wealthier families everywhere tended to be larger and more complex. The ideal patriarchal household was best achieved by the nobility, whose extended families shared an ancestral *palazzo*. In Siena and Parma (*circa* 1570), multiple and extended families accounted for half of the city households.[7] The poorer the house-hold, the smaller the number of individuals in it. Peasant sharecrop-ping families on larger, consolidated farms, called *poderi*, were largest of all.[8] The principle of the *mezzadria* household was that the family had to be large enough, and distributed between both sexes and by age, to exploit the *podere* at an optimum level (see Chapter 7). Where nuclear households comprised four persons or less on average, *mezzadria* families counted over six persons, and sometimes over ten. In the classic *mezzadria* system, fathers never retired, and married sons lived with them and obeyed their commands. Most adult men did not become heads of households until later in life, towards age 40.

Marriage and residence in most regions of Italy were patrilocal, that is, the bride joined her husband's family, who considered her an outsider. The strong cohesion among members of the masculine line, between paternal uncles and nephews, is striking. Marzio Barbagli uses the term "patriarchal" to denote this extended family, in which strict roles were allotted to each, according to their age and their sex. Fathers were legally responsible for their sons and daugh-ters, whatever their ages, and interceded for them with authorities. Children did not systematically leave their families as servants in ado-lescence, as they did in other parts of Europe, but remained with their parents and siblings. Brothers frequently continued working in common once their father died (an arrangement known as the *fratel-lanza*), although typically only one brother married. If ever children acquired property of their own before the death of the patriarch (through a dowry, for example), they formed a new household. The common thread through these different systems is how family, prop-erty and residence were closely related. As Giovanni Levi argues, the family has to be understood as a whole, not only with respect to the combined income, but also to the transmission of social skills and the array of occupations open to its members. Those living under the same roof enjoyed a web of assistance and support from those related by blood or by godparentage. The proximity and alliance of kin conditioned one's whole life and fortune. These solidarities were extremely powerful, and until recently impeded the breakdown of society into "individuals" governed by an impersonal state.

Agonistic Sociability

No region was as much a museum of Italian social practices and customs as Corsica, whose families displayed a strong sense of dynastic identity and behaved like sovereign states. The patriarchal father "ruled", sometimes with the aid of a council composed of male kinfolk, to decree the family's own laws and apply them.[9] Relatives often constituted kin-hamlets closed to the outside. The erection of a chapel, with its graveyard, tended by a priest belonging to the lineage, made these hamlets virtually independent. Marriage was a "loving alliance" not between individuals, but rather families or lineages. Marriages to kin in the third and fourth degree were not rare, despite being prohibited by canon law without a prior dispensation. Oral culture kept track of who could marry who, and parents often conferred names on their children in advance of their conception, following rules that made it easier to determine filiation.[10] Marriage was also a political alliance, and children were often promised at a tender age to strengthen it. Both sons and daughters required parental consent to marry, and fathers did not easily reconcile themselves to their offspring's disobedience. Unauthorized courtships were fraught with danger. Family honour compelled the patriarch to guard the chastity of his womenfolk ferociously. Youths could not court girls openly; a young man might place himself on the road by which she fetched water, or make himself visible in other subtle ways. At most, he could serenade a girl below her window, but in the company of others. Once accepted, he made himself scarce again until his father-in-law signed the marriage pact. Publicity surrounding the courtship discouraged the man from changing his mind, and compromising the girl's reputation as a virgin. A man who breached an understanding to marry a girl committed a capital offence in Corsica, liable to be punished by her relatives, to the third degree (common great-grandparents) inclusive.

Elsewhere, this "private" conception of marriage endured until decades after the Council of Trent. It was the father who "married" his daughter to someone he designated. Lucia Ferrante sees this custom weighing more heavily on boys than girls; the bride could challenge the legitimacy of the marriage if her parents coerced her, and church officials responded to her laments with increasing sympathy. If boys were generally not beaten into submission, they risked exheredation, for they represented the continuity of the family name, and its public face, so that their disobedience shamed their parents in a public way.[11] Rites of courtship were not as stern as those in Corsica, and usually entailed the complicity of the whole community. Girls and women of nubile age were held vulnerable to the wiles of men, who might impregnate them after promising marriage and then abandon them. Not only did the family network close ranks to protect its womenfolk from predatory males; other youths kept their eyes open and passed around information, consenting or warning potential partners of what to expect. While the initiative was the man's and exposed his honour, the woman assessed how well he measured up to her expectations before consenting to sexual relations. As elsewhere, the "rules" allowed for a wide latitude of individual behaviour, and honour proved more flexible than in Corsica. Even giving birth to an illegitimate child did not definitively compromise a woman if the father owned up to it, conferred his name on the child and paid for his or her upbringing, as was generally the case before 1650.[12]

Honour also required men to demonstrate their ability to provide for their family and protect it from insult, to sire children by their spouse, and to support their sons and daughters honourably.[13] There was a complex hierarchy between men and women in the family, based on a radical division of tasks and separate spheres of competence. Although men boasted superiority over women, and the law of both the Church and the state sanctioned this, gentle birth gave women command over men of lower rank. The role and the authority of mothers has not been much studied, yet the modern stereotype of the influential but discreet "mamma" has deep roots. There existed specific tribunals in Italian cities dealing with the fate of orphans, minors and families damaged by the death of fathers. Maternal lines were more important than legal discourse or folk wisdom allowed. Widows with children enjoyed both prestige and authority; magistrates usually sided with the widow when her late husband's kin contested the succession. One sign of a widow's control was the difficulty her children had in emancipating themselves from her decisions, for girls to leave a convent, and boys to get access to their father's tools or assets.[14]

Relatives were expected to help one another at the risk of incurring dishonour, although the more remote the degree, the less their assistance was obligatory. Society was thus divided between kin and non-kin, the latter being potential enemies and at best certain to put their own families' welfare first. Each person strove to maintain their own and their family's capital of honour, the defence of which could entail long-term hostilities with neighbours and other adversaries in the form of vendetta. Italians long regarded war and peace between families to be a matter as "private" as marriage, but hostilities mobilized kinship solidarities and often pitted hamlets against each other, or rent villages into competing, homicidal factions. Hence the imperative to counterbalance agonistic behaviour with more conciliatory practices. Formal master–servant relationships forged strong bonds across social classes. Servants not only attended to fieldwork and transport (men), or household chores (women), but showed off the power of the family. The female servants especially were poorly paid, but were lodged, fed and protected. Boys residing in other people's households after 1550 comprised a third of those between the ages of 16 and 20 in Verona, and almost half in Parma. Over time, household service was feminized, and the numbers diminished.[15] Barbagli sees domestic service as a powerful tool of integration and acculturation in Italian society, transmitting language, knowledge, ideas and practises, while giving youths a bit of experience in the world before marriage. Domestic service was not widely practiced in the Mezzogiorno by either men or women. Earning the money to form a new family was the responsibility of the groom and of the girl's father and brothers.[16] Only notables employed a servant or two, and rather than being a succession of nubile girls building a dowry, domestic servants tended to spend their whole lives in that function.

Communal standards were keenly felt and self-conscious shame cut very deeply. In Italy, as in other Mediterranean cultures, shame was a feeling that one had breached the community's view of what was proper and good. For men, honour signified their trustworthiness, their freedom from menial dependency and their courage in challenging any affront. For women honour was more closely tied to their chastity and their diligence in raising children. Honour and shame were not individual assets or liabilities, for they were shared by the members of the family, or the groups to which one belonged. It was possible to deprive someone of his honour in a way that put him to public disadvantage. This implies that there was only a fixed quantity of honour to go around, and not quite enough for everyone. Therefore, men and women asserted themselves in order to keep their neighbours from rising above them. Since one's good reputation was paramount, people were tyrannized by gossip, and were on their guard not to give ammunition to their neighbours. There was indeed a culture of insult and malicious gossip in early modern Italy that was rooted in honour and shame. There were multiple ways of showing contempt, from finger gestures; to contradicting others in public (giving them the lie, or *mentita*); or smearing their door with excrement. Every slur was a challenge which could not be ignored on pain of losing face, of being held as a coward.[17] Shameful behaviour in Italy included public drunkenness. Wineshops were more likely a place for playing cards than for serious drinking. Public begging was also rare in face-to-face communities, and was extremely rare in Corsica.[18] Most communities were small enough that individuals knew their neighbours well from daily contact. Even today Italians practice the *passeggiata*, the stroll up and down a square or main thoroughfare in the view of, and in company of neighbours. Men were required to spend their time outdoors, with other men, in competetive games and tavern sociability. When their interests or their words were openly challenged, they usually sought some equitable solution, by resorting to arbiters and seeking satisfactory solutions. Before the "arbitrary" behaviour of their neighbours, and their "challenging" words and gestures, they "faced" them.[19] Neighbours scrutinized any cross-gender sociability with extreme suspicion. One of the few occasions for women to socialize with men outside the family was the *veglia*, a winter evening by the fireside with neighbours and friends. This was a time for storytelling, music, supervised courtship, while accomplishing tedious chores in common to save firewood.

No problem preoccupies modern Italy so much as the persistence of this behavioural regime, the deficiency of commitment to public institutions. In 1958 the American sociologist Edward Banfield reformulated this resistance to public-spirit organization as a "pathological trait", expressing itself as a "syndrome" called *amoral familism*.[20] Social action was based on the premise that everyone would act in the immediate short-term interest of themselves and their family without regard for the "general" or public good, knowing that other families would do the same. Members of the village assembly constantly invoked the "public good" in their proceedings, but their preoccupation with it belied a deep insecurity about their neighbours' motives. Since social relations were based on envy, mistrust and fierce competition, it was difficult to motivate people to act in concert. Those who governed were universally assumed to be out for their own interests.[21]

While respectability was everyone's aim, no one pretended that all people were equal, as they saw this being daily contradicted by experience. Rank was explicitly recognized in law in every European state. Only substantial differences in rank compelled formal recognition of it. Many village nobles lived in fear of the slurs and challenges from low-born neighbours that they might not be able to punish, and treated them with concern for equity. The powerful cultivated, protected and promoted their subordinates in exchange for service and solidarity. This was not so much a relationship of domination as one of reciprocity of services.[22] People situated low in the social scale sought out protectors, *padroni*, and friends, who could benefit their family. The protection of a powerful patron could also be used offensively in actions against one's peers and other neighbours. Since other people were expected to resort to patronage as well, this justified one's own recourse to it. Patronage was also "the lubrication that made it possible for early modern institutions to function".[23] It was a form of social and political interaction that mobilized "influence" to get things done. Creating and maintaining effective patron–client relationships was important for both parties. Underlings spontaneously showed proper respect for their superiors, using the correct titles and proper deferential posture. Patrons enjoyed the opportunity to show their liberality, goodwill and clout, which they needed to weigh and measure continually. Both sides acted in their own interest, but by doing so this form of social action afforded greater harmony. Patronage reversed the vicious circle of insult and vengeance and cemented Italians into larger communities of interest.

Part I

High Summer, 1550–1620

Introduction to Part I

The period from the end of the Italian wars until 1620 corresponds to the period of Italy's greatest impact on western civilization. Every European country contrasted more developed and more archaic zones, with great disparities of wealth, population and social diversity, but no other exported its expertise and taste with as much effect. Overall, Italy could boast the highest population density in Europe, and one of the highest levels of urbanization anywhere. Italy of the cities, embracing a large third of the country from eastern Piedmont to the Veneto, to Naples and Campania, was remarkable for its bustle, the array of goods and services on offer, and the high prices it commanded for food and labour. Italian urban governments were as efficient as those anywhere, and political prerogatives were shared by a broad swath of the upper class. Everywhere the cities reined in and controlled feudal jurisdictions, seducing rural lords into electing residence there. Princes and republics exercised ever greater control over the countryside and placed weapons in the hands of peasant militiamen to keep the peace. Even in the zones where feudal jurisdictions held sway, lords and their retainers flocked to the capitals and replaced their hilltop castles with more genteel palaces on the urban model.

Neapolitan and Sicilian aristocrats readily admitted the necessity of a strong foreign monarch who served as a safety valve against overbearing members of their own group. Spain held out many rewards for their compliant obedience; autonomy at home, influence in Madrid and a vast international theatre in which to display their *virtù*. Italians almost everywhere enjoyed access to the Spanish imperial theatre that drew on their expertise, their talent and their treasure. Spain also kept the peace in Italy, by barring the way to invaders on land and sea and mediating and arbitrating the tensions arising between Italian states. Far from importing archaic cultural references to the peninsula, Spanish rule in southern Italy yielded an important "peace dividend", which added to the relative prosperity and tranquillity of the age.

This prosperity was ubiquitous during the "long" sixteenth century, for it was the outcome of a number of cultural advantages Italy had accumulated since the Middle Ages. Armed with Arabic numerals, widespread numeracy and commonplace recourse to paper transactions, Italians developed the most sophisticated financial and lending mechanisms anywhere. Italy's high-quality urban manufactures were as yet unmatched, because skills protected by each city and an unceasing investment flow swelled up from a broad social base. The decline of some industries, like wool, was compensated by the rise of others, as innovation flourished. By virtue of their access to the Spanish imperial system and its voracious appetite for loans and supplies, Genoese financiers commanded the top levels of international commerce until the onset of the Thirty Years War. Italians sustained this burgeoning urban economy by innovating in agriculture too, by adopting more rational utilization of scant resources. Where geography and urban markets permitted, they fashioned the early tools of the agricultural revolution, judiciously integrating livestock-raising and grain cultivation to eliminate fallow. Ruling elites simultaneously evolved complex administrative tools to avert urban famine, reflecting both a political instinct to maintain order, and a religious and moral imperative that emphasized cooperation and the common good.

The powerful movement to regenerate the Catholic Church and to recover ground lost to the Protestant threat introduced religious and cultural reforms lasting until the 1960s. The Italian Church spearheaded changes in deportment, inculcated self-control, defined breeding, promoted learning and brought its message more forcefully to a largely animist civilization. A literary vernacular united educated Italians across different regions without simultaneously subjecting them to political hegemony. Venice inundated the continent with millions of books, while the country's universities laid the groundwork for a new way of looking at the world. Italian urbanism gained new mastery over space, rendered in scores of projects and thousands of new monuments. Rome in particular defined modern urbanistic principles by combining the practical and the monumental. A new urbanity, stemming from an aristocratic ethic that infused elites with a sense of creativity and accomplishment, and a social purpose beyond war and government, blossomed in the urban hothouse. Italian baroque aesthetics swept Europe. The models and structures of artistic creation defined in this period lasted and flourished until the twentieth century. If there has ever been a true Golden Age in Italian history, this was it.

3   The Renaissance Origins of Modern Italy

Renaissance of the Humanists

There is no need to diminish the achievements of the Italian Renaissance, roughly the period between the Black Death after 1350 and the early sixteenth century, in order to rescue the succeeding periods. It is more difficult to determine what the Renaissance was. The term applies to trends in intellectual life that transformed medieval Christian values. Cultural historians emphasize the rise of secular thinking and the celebration of individual achievement that typify the modern era. While the Middle Ages never quite "forgot" ancient Greece and Rome, Christianity focused on sin and salvation, emphasized passive contemplation and prayer, and encouraged flight from a sinful and corrupt world. Only the existence of a single, jealous God reigning in the heavens, who destined the wayward majority to eternal torment, could temper humankind's innate perversity. Christianity saw death as a liberation, as the "goal" of life. The spread of Franciscan monasteries in late medieval Italy revived this sentiment, but the Black Death undermined its allure. The Tuscan poet Francesco Petrarca (Petrarch, 1304–74) and the Florentine writer Giovanni Boccaccio (1313–75), joined by a number of influential Florentine writers, expounded very different virtues from those of St Francis of Assisi. They argued that ancient philosophers advocated a more civilized behaviour and self-awareness that could liberate contemporaries from the barbarian, albeit Christian, past.[1] Antiquity taught that mankind was noble and the measure of all things. Man's action in this world was preferable to retreat into the "desert", and his perfectibility through education and self-knowledge could attenuate the consequences of original sin. In place of humility, philosophers praised *virtù*, a non-Christian nobility of spirit and action. Humanists encouraged leaders to cultivate generous and altruistic actions in order to acquire *fama*, and the esteem of fellow men, a kind of eternal life focused on this world rather than the next.

The Ancients were held to have discovered universal rules governing the arts and letters, which they derived by carefully observing nature and by copying it. This belief, and the rules based on it, have been characterized as *classicism*. Petrarch advocated a return to arts and letters as the Ancients had perfected them, and developed models of rhetoric based on Cicero that systematized grammar and vocabulary. Human beauty was the outward sign of inner qualities, and all sublime beauty in its perfection, by virtue of analogy, led to God. Worldly and powerful Italians rejected the asceticism that the clergy had cultivated for a millennium.[2] The enthusiasm for the works of antiquity incited people to collect manuscripts, statues, inscriptions and coins. Such collections formed the first European museums, which, although private, were on display to notables, tourists and other visitors. Greek artefacts figured increasingly alongside Roman ones, while refugees from the fall of Constantinople (1453) disseminated new versions of Aristotle and above all, Plato, whose idealism fitted the period perfectly. Plato posited that there was a hidden, divine unity in all Creation that human minds could comprehend. Astrology, alchemy and even mathematics presupposed that celestial truths expressed themselves in earthly forms that scholars could "read".

Scholars figured as secretaries in Italian chanceries, drafting documents for public use. Because literature was primarily poetry, those with an active muse and rhetorical verve found employment at princely courts. Humanists laboured to establish the "definitive" texts from the fragments of ancient writings in multiple versions recovered from monasteries. *Humanism* was *philological*: that is, it strove to elucidate the meaning of words in ancient texts as their creators understood them and to gloss them. They revived all the secular genres used in antiquity: the epic, the satire, lyrical or didactic poetry, tragedy, comedy and the philosophical dialogue.[3] Books were no longer overwhelmingly religious in subject, although such books still constituted the large majority.[4] Deference to antiquity elevated the pre-Christian world and its thought. One view held that philosophers like Plato "anticipated" Jesus Christ, and that ancient stoicism prefigured and prepared Christian values. The influential philosophers Pietro Pomponazzi (1462–1525) and Marsilio Ficino (1433–99) were only marginally interested in Christianity. Italian humanist circles gave birth to freethinkers and philosophical atheists by the mid-sixteenth century.[5] But humanist striving for self-knowledge and perfection coloured Christianity too. Erasmus of Rotterdam, who influenced sixteenth-century Italian philosophers considerably, criticized the worldliness of the Church, and the prevailing archaic and unreflective habits of devotion.

A disregard for Christianity permeated another branch of revived ancient learning. Medieval historians viewed time as a continuum, beginning with Adam and Eve and progressing to the Last Judgement. History unfolded as a demonstration of divine providence and the struggle between good and evil. Around 1400, Florentine humanists infused history and political action with classical virtues of civic altruism, extolling the public good to which it was the duty of citizens to sacrifice themselves.[6] Historians thereafter embellished their accounts with edifying, but perfectly imaginary, speeches depicting historical figures personifying high ideals. Despite this stylistic fancy, humanists adhered to the Ciceronian claim that history was the main font of knowledge applicable to practical ends.[7] After 1500, Niccolò Machiavelli peeled the rhetoric away to reveal an understanding of human actions and motivations unembellished by noble sentiments or Christian scruple.[8] Francesco Guicciardini did as much in his *History of Italy*, by explaining the catastrophes befalling Italy after 1494 in terms of secular *realpolitik*. The emphasis on history as an illustration and a school of the ways of the world led to new consideration for the historical document, subject henceforth to philological clarification. Renaissance scholars laid the foundations of modern textual criticism, intent on producing an authentic version and elucidating its exact meaning. They supported this textual labour with reference to archaeology, epigraphy and numismatics, which all became new disciplines.[9]

The humanist moment mobilized a masculine elite living in central and north Italian cities, although Naples figured prominently too.[10] Serious scholarship in law, medicine and philosophy would be predominantly expressed in Latin for another two centuries. Latin, which few women read, remained the language of the Church and much of the daily state administration, although Italian made increasing inroads. Scholarship seeped into broader society, though, for the vernacular benefited from the greater grammatical consistency that humanists applied to Latin. This vernacular was in fact Tuscan, which elites used increasingly as a common idiom after 1450.[11] The central role that Tuscans played in the Roman Curia counted more than anything to elevate their dialect to the status of an "official" language. The most successful Renaissance literary works were all in Italian: Baldassare Castiglione's *The Courtier*; Machiavelli's *The Prince*; Guicciardini's *History of Italy*; Giorgio Vasari's *Lives of the Artists*; Andrea Alciati's *Emblemata* and, above all, Ludovico Ariosto's chivalric romance *Orlando Furioso*. The audience of these works ranged far beyond the narrow circle of humanists preoccupied with fidelity to ancient models. Chivalric romances were not works to read and contemplate quietly, but were written with recitation in mind, to listeners eager for the grandiose and the exotic.

The manner of writing became an object of study too, with the aim of simplifying it, and manuals appeared to that effect in Rome in the early 1520s.[12] The multiplication of professional letter-writers gave a larger proportion of city-dwellers access to the written word. The trend was pan-European, but the peninsula's cities were nurseries for modern pedagogical methods and educational institutions. Humanists and ecclesiastics felt that spiritual deficiencies and ignorance were social problems, and they prescribed new teaching methods to cure these ills. The number of children and adults learning the rudiments seems to have swelled after 1500. A combination of independent, communal and church schools brought basic literacy and numeracy to a significant proportion of the urban population. Paul Grendler estimates that a third of males and a tenth of women in late sixteenth-century Venice could read and write, a proportion attained in other Italian capitals.[13]

Renaissance of Abstraction

Europe never ceased to make technical improvements over Antiquity. Renaissance Italy spawned a large number of "inventors", part artist, part architect, part tinker and part humanist, of whom Leonardo da Vinci was the most illustrious example. He surpassed all others by careful attention to the theorizing of his observations. The most revolutionary invention was no doubt Gutenberg's mechanical printing press with movable metallic type, which Italians rapidly adopted. Around 1500 there were 73 presses operating in Italy as opposed to 51 in Germany, 39 in France, 24 in Spain and 15 in the Low Countries.[14] By 1500 this technological bent received fresh impetus from the publication of the treatises of classical antiquity, of Vitruvius, Vegetius, and Archimedes. From physics interest shifted to mathematics as Euclid, Pythagoras and Diophantes emerged from the Greek. Generations of Italian mathematicians, such as Luca Pacioli, Niccolò Tartaglia and Girolamo Cardano prepared the scientific revolution of the next century by advancing the discipline. Italian universities, particulary Padua, Bologna and Pisa, attracted practitioners from all over Europe.

Closely associated with mathematics, the sciences of divination also received fresh stimulus from the diffusion of ancient texts. Hermes Trismegistus and Zoroaster, drawn from Arab science, Hebraic culture and late Roman Neoplatonic thought, posited astrology as an indispensable tool for celestial investigation.[15] Before the general adoption of materialism as an exclusive explanatory principle in physics during the eighteenth century, no clear boundary separated religion from science, rational from mythological thought. Astrology involved complex calculations derived from the movement of heavenly bodies that explained events on earth. The Church's doctrine of free will held that astrological "influences" did not *determine* the outcome of events, but Catholic scholars could still assume that they predisposed to a given outcome. Even popes and cardinals commissioned astrologers to devise their horoscopes, which "predicted" their rise.

Mathematics found a pragmatic outlet in architecture and urbanism. Medieval towns were not "beautiful" according to Renaissance criteria for they developed unplanned. Romanesque and Gothic monuments rose over extended periods, with little concern for unity of conception, and all kinds of houses and stalls crowded the access to them. Renaissance architects set their projects in a showcase of squares and boulevards, rendering in stone the elegant receding lines of perspective.[16] Medieval communal halls constituted most of the early projects, but the vogue for an imposing aristocratic *palazzo* soon multiplied the building sites. Princes began to invite architects to build monumental residences to display their grandeur. The greatest project was, nevertheless, the refashioning of Rome, which emphasized the Church's grandeur. Pope Nicholas V sought to attach the basilica of Saint Peter to the dense quarters of

medieval Rome via the Castello Sant' Angelo, and invited dignitaries
to erect palaces worthy of princes of the Church along that route.[17]
An essential element of the project was to tear down the Roman
basilica of Saint Peter, dating from the fourth century, and to
replace it with a monument conceived as a unified whole that would
be the world's largest religious building. The regularity and geomet-
rical symmetry of this new urbanism impressed contemporaries by
the "order" it projected. Popes and princes built and rebuilt palaces
and towns elsewhere to complement one another. Scores of
improvement projects were realized as cities expanded after 1500
along preplanned avenues marked with palaces and villas. Alongside
these realizations, figured scores of projects that remained on paper,
such as the great designs that Leonardo da Vinci elaborated for
Milan.

Architects also redesigned town fortifications to withstand modern
artillery, which could topple the high and narrow medieval walls by
battering their base. In the process architects became engineers.[18]
By 1500, Giulio Sangallo and Francesco di Giorgio Martini invented
the bastion; an angular projection from the wall, packed with earth
rather than stone, with casemates deep in the interior where soldiers
lived. Its thickness allowed cannon to be placed on top of it to keep a
besieger's artillery at a distance. Setting these walls and bastions
deep in a moat reduced the wall's profile to the besieger's artillery.
Early bastions were built singly, attached to the most vulnerable part
of the medieval defences. By 1520, engineers were erecting bastions
at regular intervals around the perimeter of towns in order to create
supporting fields of fire. City fortifications suddenly acquired geo-
metrical forms, conceived in relation to firepower. This system of
defence, which was not fully obsolete until the mid-nineteenth
century, took the name *Italian trace*. It rendered towns and cities virtually invulnerable to artillery in the sixteenth century. Nevertheless,
it took over half a century for this revolution in design to become
widely adopted, due to the great building expense incurred. Three
great projects marked the century's end: Valletta in Malta after 1565;
Livorno on the Tuscan coast in the 1570s; and above all Palmanova
in Friuli in the 1590s, a great octagon symmetrically articulated
around a web of straight streets. Italian engineers, architects and
stonemasons were exporting their expertise across Europe by the
1530s and 1540s. Manuals of fortification and military engineering
enjoyed a wide circulation in Italy itself, attesting to the technical
interests of many people.

The science of business, born of numerical calculation, evolved over a much longer period. Double-ledger bookkeeping allowed merchants to keep track of both assets and liabilities at one glance. Replacing Roman numerals with Indo-Arabic ciphers in the fourteenth century made numerical operations infinitely simpler, although this Venetian innovation spread slowly to the rest of Europe. Widespread numeracy hastened the development of the laws of probability, so vital to maritime insurance, which soon became an Italian monopoly. Italians invented two other mechanisms facilitating commercial expansion: the cheque and the letter of exchange, both of which permitted payment in distant cities in foreign coinage without having to transport precious specie.[19] Italian city states soon consolidated lending and borrowing into permanent credit institutions, to soften the chain effect that one company's bankruptcy could unleash upon others without warning. Banks also administered the public debt and facilitated taxation by placing large sums of money at the government's disposal. Large family merchant firms themselves took on an institutional character, by associating with allies or relatives in easily renewed contracts of several years' duration. The stability and perenniality of these "companies" attracted the savings of hundreds of investors great and small, and enabled them to wield great sums of capital. Employing family members and trusted agents as factors in distant branches across Italy and Europe, Italian merchants coordinated buying, selling, shipping and lending across Europe on a scale hitherto unimaginable. Already by 1300 these "Lombards" or Florentines were creditors of the popes and European monarchs, their initiatives held together by a continuous flow of letters. We once viewed this phenomenon as the rise of a bourgeoisie, whose values differed from those of the nobility, but inside most Renaissance merchants lurked a Mediterranean patriarch obsessed with lineage, status and honour.

Renaissance of the Aristocracy

Neither modern science nor modern industry emerged full-blown from the Renaissance, which was too transfixed on "quality" to care much about "quantity". Perhaps most Renaissance writers were noblemen, either from feudal houses or the urban patriciates of northern and central Italy. Several decades ago, historians speculated that a "bourgeois" ethic was displacing a feudal culture, as one social class toppled another. Perhaps the opposite happened. By combining valour and virtues, humanism and chivalry in a great, urban theatre of self-presentation, humanist writers offered attractive and accessible models of nobility to social elites.[20] Renaissance ideals of "purity", "dignity", "honour", the "sublime" are judgements concerning quality and excellence, a *virtù* diametrically opposed to the "vulgar" or the "coarse". This more ethereal concept of nobility survived until the nineteenth century. Italy enjoyed a vogue for the chivalric romance, imported from France and Spain, whose armoured knights contested predominance with grim resolve.[21] Ariosto's epic romance, *Orlando Furioso*, applied the trappings of French chivalry to plots lifted straight out of Virgil, to produce the most successful literary work of the century. A runaway bestseller with 183 printings between 1516 and 1600, it heralded a wave of similar poems, culminating with the works of Torquato Tasso in the second half of the century.[22] Along with the enchanted swords, the naked princesses, the winged chargers and fire-breathing dragons, literary imagination seized upon the emblems its heroes sported. Visual conceits and emblems expressed correspondences found between objects: they were symbolic representations of a purpose, or a line of conduct. Alciati's *Emblemata* (1531) furnished a reference catalogue of hundreds of such concepts.[23]

As the wars receded from experience, elites played at war in public arenas. Never was the taste for tournaments, more theatre than combat, so pronounced as after 1560.[24] Este productions in Ferrara were particularly lavish, perhaps because the dynasty was especially close to France. Alfonso II (1559–97) carefully choreographed whole jousting pageants along preset themes exalting himself and his dynasty, enacted by a star-studded cast of titled gentlemen. Participants knew that conspicuous consumption was part of the programme, and displayed gorgeous armour, silks and precious stones as prominently as possible. The major cities boasted companies of "gendarmes", display warriors who graced pageants and processions into the 1620s.

The visual arts were not far behind. Aristocratic patronage ignited the creative explosion of the fifteenth and sixteenth centuries, manifest in countless palace and chapel frescoes and paintings.[25] The Florentine and Venetian governments hired artists to illustrate the glory of the city and the heroism or piety of its leaders. The artist himself rose in status as humanists exalted his genius and his *virtù*. After Raphael Sanzio of Urbino, who illustrated humanist ideals in papal Rome, the Tuscan Michelangelo Buonarroti represented the artist as a genius searching to express an "idea" in stone or paint. The pope ennobled Michelangelo by virtue of his talent. The Venetian painter Titian lived like a prince, and monarchs all over Europe sought their portraits by his hand. Once artists were recognized as possessing *virtù*, nobles could dabble with its genres without fear of losing status. Noblemen practised all of the virtuoso arts, and sometimes made an honest living by painting, writing poetry or music, or designing buildings or theatre productions. Nobility of birth and nobility of talent were not irreconcilable notions. Italian nobles' urbane manners were soon imitated all over Europe. As judicial and mercantile families became *de facto* and increasingly *de jure* nobility, they sought models of deportment that proclaimed their social and cultural superiority. In this context appeared the work of Baldassare Castiglione, *The Courtier* in 1528. It was not so much a description of aristocratic behaviour as a model of bearing, conversation and behaviour to which social elites might aspire. Castiglione fused traditional noble values such as military valour, fidelity, piety and altruism, to more recent notions of civility which stressed eloquence, taste, bearing, beauty, politeness and social ease.[26] This urbanity flowered in the court atmosphere of Urbino (where Castiglione wrote) and gradually elsewhere. Young noblemen acquired the bearing that distinguished them from the common sort, just as they learned to speak *cortegiano*, a precious dialect of Italian that set them apart from the lower classes. Under the influence of this ethos, urban factional rivalry quickly began to lose its savagery and opened the nobility to political domestication.[27]

4   From Communes to Principalities

The Communal framework

For Renaissance Italians, modern history began in the early ninth century when Charlemagne subjugated the Lombards and created the Holy Roman Empire. Northern Italy recognized the ultimate suzerainty of the emperors, his successors in Germany. The popes challenged and diminished them in a centuries-long conflict between the advocates of papal primacy (the Guelfs) and Imperial overlordship (Ghibellines). By 1450, the principal role of the emperor was to redistribute fiefs falling vacant when a direct line was extinguished. There were still two to three hundred Imperial fiefs in north-central Italy, whose sixty-odd holders could appeal to the Aulic Council in Vienna if their larger neighbours threatened them.[1] Although the emperors loosened their grasp over northern Italy, the papacy waned too. After a long exile in Avignon, disputes over electoral procedure after 1377 resulted in a schism where two rival popes competed for the allegiance of prelates and princes. Only after 1447 was the papal tiara restored to a single head in Rome.

The centuries-long absence of a coherent institutional framework in northern and central Italy threw power into the hands of city councils, whose committees administered the rural hinterland and its infrastructure of public utilities. They watched over staple food prices; controlled weights and measures; stored up grain reserves; inspected bread; decreed hygienic norms for slaughtering animals and tanning hides; and posted guards during epidemics. Municipal governments minted coins, created protectionist taxes and tariffs and restricted access to "foreign" goods. They regulated the *guilds*, and colleges of experts such as notaries, judges and medical doctors.

Urban nobles served terms as *podestà* or magistrate in subject towns and villages, dispensing rudimentary justice. Notables thus served in numerous capacities throughout their adult life.[2]

The lack of an overarching political framework unleashed two processes. Municipal councils dissolved into feuding factions competing for power, that often bore labels like Guelf and Ghibelline, or Black and White for convenience. Nobles built castles in the city centre with battlements and high towers, controlling whole neighbourhoods. Elites often consented to appoint the head of a major family to "tyrant" status to crush division and unrest.[3] Second, as city states competed for control over food supplies and raw materials, larger towns bought the services of professional commanders, *condottieri*, supplying ready-made armies. Large cities submitted smaller ones to their overlordship. In 1300 about a hundred city-states competed for existence in northern and central Italy. By 1454 only about a dozen "territorial states" remained, under the sway of a single capital city, the *dominante*. These states belonged to one of two models; the city-republic, or the principality.

The Republics

Venice

Contemporaries almost universally admired the constitution of the Venetian republic, whose particular institutions developed without external interference. As an *aristocratic republic*, Venice combined principles of monarchy, aristocracy and democracy. Sovereignty resided in a large assembly of citizens belonging to recognized dynasties. In 1328 members entered their names into a register, the *Golden Book*, giving their direct descendants monopoly over high office. This created a class of *de facto* nobles, whose number reached a peak of about 2,500 individuals around 1570.[4] No patrician could serve a foreign state or even receive distinctions from other princes, under penalty of losing political privileges at home. This required them to marry other Venetian nobles in order to avoid contracting other loyalties. Religious power, too, was subordinate to civilian government, for the Senate selected the head of the Venetian Church, the Patriarch, and lay patricians drew up the list of nominations for cardinal that it submitted to the pope. After 1540, fearing that the spread of Lutheranism might give Rome or the emperor a pretext to

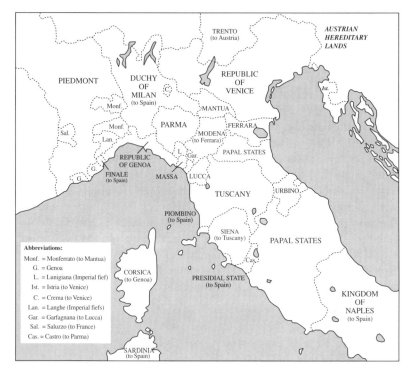

Map 11   Political boundaries after 1560

intefere, the republic established its own Inquisition, separate from the Roman one.

This regime built on fear of ambition, typical of republics, distributed power to a broad segment of the upper class. After the Great Council and the smaller Senate, patricians served the state on a number of interlocking executive committees. Complicated electoral mechanisms and short terms of office prevented influence-peddling and cosy arrangements, but senior patricians repeatedly won high office. Election costs, entertainment expenditures and "representation" made it easier for the wealthy to participate disproportionately. The Senate directed daily government and nominated officials to serve on all the councils. It also elected a duke, or *doge*, to lifelong figurehead status at the head of the Republic. This prestigious elder was literally kept prisoner in his palace and subjected to constant vigilance, while members of his family lost their offices and their church benefices. This prevented the "monarch" from consolidating power on the strength of his family connections and outside alliances. If the members of the judicial Council of Ten held sweeping powers in the sixteenth century, executive power eventually gravitated to a larger college of twenty-five members emanating from the various executive commissions, operating like a council of ministers. Disputes were relatively rare. According to Grendler, "Venetian ethos prized seniority and continuity, great age over youth, wisdom over brilliance, and stability over innovation."[5]

Over time the patrician families entered into prolonged decline, with the largest houses maintaining their numbers best.[6] As economic crisis, restrictive inheritance practices, and brutal wars with Turkey scythed the number of young patricians with means, the eight hundred positions open to nobles of the city became gradually too many.[7] Nobles served as judges and accountants, supervised confraternities and schools. While Venetian army commanders were usually not subjects of the republic, Venetian patricians usually commanded the galleys, oversaw provisioning and determined strategy.[8] They were rectors, or *rettori* of Venetian subject cities, watching over their administrations in Venice's interest.[9] To assist the patricians, there existed a separate and inferior class of "citizens", who staffed the republic's legal and administrative machinery. Recruited by examination in 1600, they filled the minor magistracies, and functioned as lawyers and notaries.[10]

Venetian patricians governed subject territories too, sometimes with a heavy hand. The population of their Greek and Croatian "empire" rarely exceeded 400,000 people, but it included some large territories. Cyprus came under its control at the end of the fifteenth century, and Venice retained it until the Turkish conquest of 1570. Crete was ruled by Venetian patricians residing there as feudal overlords. To stamp out its vicious feuding culture, the republic periodically took hostages, burned villages and deported unruly clans.[11] Venice transformed Corfu into a great fortress with a naval base and a large garrison. There, the Orthodox Greeks and Sephardic Jews, the latter constituting a quarter of the population, flourished and prospered.[12] The Dalmatian coast and the islands produced little in the way of grain and livestock for Venice, but their ports were necessary stopovers for merchant galleys, and the Croats who lived there served the republic loyally in its fleets and armies.[13] Venice ruled a large section of northern Italy behind the lagoon, the Terraferma. It was careful to leave local nobles in charge of town affairs, such as the establishment of tax rolls. Each subject city (there were eleven), was overseen by two functionaries, a military governor with a small garrison, and a rector, who coordinated local concerns with the overall policies of the republic, and arbitrated quarrels. Faction-wracked cities like Brescia required considerable diplomatic skills.[14] In all the Empire, however, there was no representation at Venice, which did not need to build citadels to keep its subject towns in check. Dependent cities rallied generously when the republic was in danger, although their taxes were lower than in the capital.[15] In 1700 the population of the Venetian republic exceeded 2 million people, of whom about 1.7 million lived in Italy. That was comparable to the Netherlands, or about a quarter of England.

Genoa

Genoa competed with Venice for Middle Eastern predominance and its merchant colonies flourished around the Black Sea and in the Aegean until the Ottoman advance forced it to relocate into the Spanish world and southern Italy. Some Genoese patricians were feudal lords with fiefs along the coast and in the Apennine mountains; others were merchant-bankers, but over time the two elites merged. This patriciate lacked unity of vision and wide diffusion of power throughout the political system. It also lacked Venice's invulnerability to invading armies. Competition for pre-eminence characterized nobles not only in the capital, but also in towns along the Riviera. In 1528, when Genoa passed from the French to the Spanish alliance, the senate decided that only those families serving before 1506 should hold senior offices. These noble houses then regrouped themselves into twenty-eight *alberghi*, that is, associations of great families with their extended kin, incorporating minor allied families in their clientèles.[16] More fractious was the split between "old" noble families, with the greatest wealth and the longest political pedigrees, and the ambitious "new" families desiring access to civic office. In 1575–6 tensions between them erupted into a brief civil war, until King Philip II of Spain arbitrated an accord which stipulated that 300 new families join the ruling oligarchy, and that as many as ten families, including three from Riviera towns, be admitted annually thereafter. The promise was never kept, as the new families joined the old in closing off access to office. The patriciate still numbered 2,000 to 2,300 adult male nobles around 1600.

This constitution remained in place for over two centuries and while plotting still rippled the smooth surface of institutional life, deep civil strife abated. Genoese nobles governed towns and fortresses, the galleys and militia companies. Minor offices like notaries, customs officials, secretaries, or health officials went to non-noble residents, or to notables from subject territory. Where the Venetian nobility was ferociously independent, Genoese patricians acquired fiefs, offices and honours in Madrid, Naples and Sicily, becoming willing vassals of the Catholic king. This resulted in a diaspora of Genoese patricians, which no other Italian city experienced to the same extent. In 1608, a third of the members of the new noble families, and half of the old ones resided outside Genoa: 154 lived abroad permanently, three-quarters of those in Spanish-held lands. They purportedly possessed almost 1,200 of the 2,700 feudal communities of the kingdom of Naples in 1631.[17]

Ligurian and Corsican notables remained mere subjects. Genoa wrecked the port of Savona, its only potential rival for maritime commerce, and kept it poor deliberately. Genoa's hold on Corsica was periodically tenuous. France seized the island during the latter part of the Italian wars, and fighting there resulted in tremendous slaughter, especially since all bloodshed was regarded as "private" and therefore subject to revenge killings. When Genoa recovered the island, it reconciled feuding families, and knocked down scores of towers that encouraged private wars.[18] Corsica rose in revolt against Genoese rule in 1564, led by Sampiero Corso, a nobleman supported by France and Constantinople. Philip II sent Spanish veterans to crush the guerrillas who "fought like Arabs" in hit-and-run skirmishes. By 1569, Genoese and Spanish troops and treasure had killed Sampiero and suppressed all resistance. Thereafter, the island enjoyed a century and a half of peace without precedent, although remaining a colony without much say. "Citizens" and "subjects" did not mix.

One non-governmental institution fundamental to the republic was the *Banco di San Giorgio*, originally set up to manage colonial trade. Its loans later kept the state solvent, but in return, the bank managed the public debt, the customs revenues and *gabelles*. While the members of its board were Genoese patricians and government officials, the head of the bank managed the institution for the benefit of its shareholders. There was a saying in Genoa: "*pauvre public, riches sujets*".[19] Valsecchi calls the republic of Genoa a great "shareholder's corporation" via the Banco di San Giorgio.

Lucca

History ignored the republic of Lucca, and this was the ardent wish of its citizens. Tucked into a corner of the Apennines, the medieval commune barely escaped absorption by its powerful Florentine neighbour. Despite their pro-French leanings and their profitable business dealings in Lyons, Lucca's rulers made the switch to the Spanish alliance in the 1520s and held fast thereafter. Factional infighting in the early Renaissance led to a consensus by 1530 that collective harmony was the supreme good. Power was wielded collegially by families of long residence that became *de facto* and then *de jure* noble after 1628, when a Golden Book on the Venetian model ennobled 224 houses.[20] As in Venice and Genoa, fear and envy were dominant sentiments governing republican political life. Lawyers and judges were eligible to participate in the Great Council, but not in the *Anziato*, the executive of elders, because of a widespread mistrust of their technical expertise. The republic safeguarded its independence by erecting massive ramparts, still intact today. This commitment to defend its "liberty" maintained Lucca independent until 1796.

Siena

Siena's fate is an excellent illustration of the weakness of medieval republics. It was not rich enough to protect itself or to be indispensable to great powers; not remote enough to be ignored; not harmonious enough to defend its independence.[21] Thirteenth-century Siena rivalled Florence in wealth, population, and the extent of its dominion. After the Black Death, it retained its grip over southern Tuscany only with difficulty. Factional infighting endured until well after 1500, which the Italian wars only exacerbated. Siena's congenital weakness convinced the emperor Charles V of the need to build a *citadel* in the city with a Spanish garrison. Citadels were anathema to republics, however. Their unpaid garrisons, the belligerence of soldiers towards civilians, and the "pride" of foreign military commanders grated on every republican value. In 1552 the Sienese rose up, stormed and then demolished the fortress. French help came in the form of an army under a Florentine exile, Filippo Strozzi, sworn enemy of the Medici dynasty, which spurred duke Cosimo de' Medici to join the emperor. A combined Imperial-Spanish–

Florentine army laid siege to Siena, which resisted for over a year until it capitulated from hunger in 1555. Siena and most of its territory was given to duke Cosimo in 1559, while Spain retained the ports along the Maremma coast in a presidial (garrison) enclave governed from Naples. The Medici ruled Siena as a principality, with two concessions to its republican past. First, it would remain a separate entity from Florence, a *stato nuovo*. Second, most republican offices survived the conquest, as the monopoly of Sienese patricians. The chief positions went to non-Sienese appointees of Cosimo, who became Grand Duke of Tuscany in 1569.

Principalities

Florence

Florence exemplifies the way in which a leading family, the Medici, gradually imposed its pre-eminence. Directors of a consortium of wealthy families, the Medici were careful not to upset established institutions, and "ruled" the republic from 1434 to 1494. The French invasion upset everything. The dissolution of this consensus pushed Piero de' Medici into the French alliance, but the city revolted and exiled the family. When French armies returned as conquerors in 1512, they restored the dynasty, which ruled with the complicity of two Medici popes, Leo X and Clement VII. When an Imperial army besieged, stormed and sacked Rome in 1527, Florence rose up again to restore the republic. While the new regime proclaimed universal liberty, factional infighting quickly alienated many of the most influential families, leading to plotting, banishments, confiscations and imprisonment. The Medici turned to Charles V to point out the city's instability; and republican Florence called for French aid. Charles V decided to lay siege to the city in 1529, and when it surrendered, he restored it to Alessandro de' Medici as "duke" of the republic.[22]

Both Charles V and Pope Clement VII de' Medici gave Alessandro *carte blanche* to rule as an absolute monarch. A distant relative assassinated Alessandro in 1537, but his supporters immediately designated his adolescent cousin Cosimo de' Medici to succeed him. To shore up his regime, Cosimo murdered opponents at home and replaced elected magistrates with appointees, legislated, named and revoked judges, and modified court sentences at will. A functionary supervised church jurisdiction, and the duke distributed church benefices to loyal clients.[23] Erecting no fewer than three stout citadels around his capital, each commanded by a non-Florentine, Cosimo integrated elites from the periphery at the expense of the *dominante*. His policy committee the *Pratica Segreta*, served as a kind of privy council. Cosimo also took care to remain in the Habsburg alliance. This yielded him Siena in 1559 and the title of grand duke of Tuscany a decade later.[24]

Tuscany under the Medici grand dukes (1530–1737) enjoyed peace and stability for two centuries. The state was small enough (750,000 inhabitants in 1600, about half the population of Portugal) for the prince to follow daily business in detail. All the grand dukes turned out to be competent and conscientious rulers. Under Cosimo's successor, his son Francesco (1574-87), the aristocracy entered the prince's entourage.[25] Even Siena's republican nobles let the dynasty tame them.[26] Cosimo I cautiously inaugurated a policy of creating new fiefs and selling them to his courtiers, whose titles set them apart from "ordinary" aristocrats. The grand dukes' rationale was that by conceding villages as fiefs in remote districts, they encouraged the beneficiaries to develop them at their own expense in order to draw revenue from them.[27] Feudatories agreed to administer justice, respecting existing statutes and the autonomy of local assemblies. The commissioners they dispatched did not always respect these clauses, but the grand duke retained rights of interference and appeal. Not enough investigation has been done into the actual practice of local administration to determine whether vassals suffered from this regime. The number of fiefs was never larger than a few dozen, and included no significant towns, unlike southern Italy.

Ferrara-Modena

Just as Florence's destiny was tied to a single family for centuries, other cities grew accustomed to their rulers. Ferrara submitted to the Este family when, in 1264, the papal Guelf party proclaimed Obizzo II lord. Ferrara became a lively centre of humanist culture in Italy, and the ducal house flourished too. The last duke of Ferrara, Alfonso II (1559–97), kept a brilliant court but sired no heirs. In 1567 Pope Pius V proclaimed that fiefs would devolve to the papal domain when a ruling lineage was extinguished. Alfonso bought

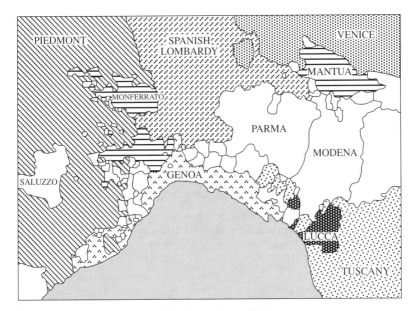

Map 12   Principalities and fiefs in northern Italy

imperial permission to pass Modena and Reggio to his cousin Cesare d'Este, descendant of an illegitimate branch. Cesare d'Este raised troops in order to retain Ferrara, and when the pope raised an army too, Europe braced itself for a war in northern Italy. When France declined to back the duke, he quit Ferrara and transferred his capital to Modena.[28] The loss of Ferrara was a great blow to the house of Este. Part of the Ferrarese nobility removed to Modena as well, and links between the two cities remained solid for another half-century. The transformation of Modena into a proper capital took a few decades to accomplish. Francesco I built a citadel there in 1635; then a palace that assembled the territory's aristocracy around the throne.[29]

Mantua

The Gonzaga emerged as tyrants of Mantua in 1328, and gradually solidified their regime as a fief of the Empire. If princes elsewhere sought to agglomerate diverse jursidictions into a coherent whole, the fractiousness of the house of Gonzaga resulted in the contrary.

In 1478 a pact sanctioned a division whereby the senior branch governed Mantua and the district around it. Minor branches retained a number of large fiefs (Guastalla, Busseto, Sabbioneta, Castiglione, Solferino), which they ruled autonomously as Imperial vassals.[30] In the sixteenth century both Sabbioneta and Guastalla were transformed by their princes into secondary Renaissance capitals with their separate courts. With its extravagant palace, Mantua was one of the showcase cities of the Italian Renaissance. The duchy's profile rose when the marquisate of Monferrato passed to it in the 1530s, through marriage to a Paleologo princess and heir to the defunct Byzantine throne. Mantua flourished under the miserly hunchback duke Guglielmo (1560–87), a gifted administrator. He pruned back the court, eliminated patrician tribunals, and centralized justice and finance for his personal advantage. He tried to control the principal benefices of the Church too, to keep Roman jurisdiction at bay. Suppressing tax privileges and exemptions of towns sparked a revolt in Casale Monferrato, which Guglielmo repressed with Spanish support. Guglielmo's successor, Duke Vincenzo (1587–1612), was the antithesis of his father. In his youth he was wild and given to bad company, which was not infrequent amongst Italian princes. Vincenzo never outgrew his propensity for ostentatious display, lavishing honours, administrative functions and tax privileges on court nobles. By 1608, the Mantuan court consisted of 800 mouths again.[31] The other great drain on the treasury was the erection of a great fortress, with its citadel at Casale Monferrato as a symbol of ducal sovereignty. Mantua required Spanish permission to communicate with the Monferrato across Lombardy, however, so the dukes never strayed from the alliance. The duchy remained a prosperous and populous little state of 300,000 inhabitants in 1600.

Urbino

The duchy of Urbino consisted of territories conquered by the Montefeltro dynasty around the Marches town, which the dukes held as a papal fief with the right to grant sub-fiefs. Too small to constitute a secondary power, with only about 150,000 inhabitants around 1600, the Della Rovere dukes submitted themselves first to Venetian dominance and then to Spain. To the towns, they dispatched zealous functionaries to defend and extend the ducal prerogative. Guidobaldo II's new taxes, which he imposed on Urbino in 1573 without consultation, ignited a revolt there. When city nobles sent delegates to negotiate with their prince in good faith, he crushed them brutally. Typically, the revolt led to deep tax cuts under Guidobaldo's son, Francesco Maria II (1574-1631), who led the life of a private lord in Pesaro.[32] Like their counterparts in Florence, Parma, Ferrara and Turin, the dukes gave a high profile to feudal lords. The fiefs brought little if any revenue to those who bought them. Nevertheless, they conferred titles and status, and judicial and fiscal autonomy. These lords were the duke's faithful servants, who helped solidify an amalgam of city territories and their mountain hinterland into a coherent territorial state.[33] However, the papacy made it clear that Urbino would return to direct papal rule upon the extinction of the ducal line. Francesco Maria's delinquent son predeceased him. At the duke's death in 1631, the territory passed to Rome, although a papal legate continued to administer it separately. The courts at Urbino and Pesaro simply vanished, and the courtiers removed to Rome or Florence.

Parma

The junior princely dynasty was the Farnese, a warrior house from northern Latium. A papal conclave elected cardinal Alessandro Farnese pope in 1534 at the age of 67. He married his illegitimate son Pier Luigi to Margarita of Austria, illegitimate daughter of Emperor Charles V in 1545, and granted them Parma and Piacenza under both papal and Imperial tutelage. Charles V warned Pier Luigi to rule Parma's urban and feudal aristocrats cautiously. His overt centralizing, his dismantling of feudal castles, and his citadel in Piacenza kindled widespread dissent against him. Leading aristocrats assassinated this upstart bastard in 1547, with the complicity of the duke of Mantua and perhaps too, his imperial father-in-law. Pier Luigi's son Ottavio clung tightly to Parma, however, and recovered the duchy entirely in 1556 as a Spanish client. Ottavio's more prudent policies towards the nobility yielded results until after his death in 1587. The dynasty's greatest asset was the talent of Alessandro Farnese, raised in Madrid as a cousin to Philip II, and close companion to Philip's illegitimate son Don Juan. Alessandro became commander-in-chief of Europe's largest force, the Spanish army of Flanders after 1578. His considerable military and political skills almost recovered the entire territory for Spain, and he remained in Flanders until his death, even after becoming duke (1587–93).[34] Both Alessandro and Ranuccio (1593–1628) mistrusted the aristocracy. Mindful of Pier Luigi's end, Alessandro paid for Parma's citadel out of his own revenues, drawn not just from the duchy, but also from estates held in Latium, in the Abruzzi and Lombardy. Ranuccio enticed the barons to live at the court in Parma, which he transformed into an aristocratic capital. He also created a large peasant militia, whose captains he chose among the nobles he trusted.[35] In 1611 Ranuccio crushed a plot against his life (which may have consisted only of idle talk), and watched with grim satisfaction while the executioner decapitated prominent nobles in Parma's city square.[36] The property he confiscated from families accused of conspiring against him, eventually gave him the money and power his dynasty craved. Ranuccio was unloved by his subjects, but the duchy prospered, and the state with its 350,000 or 400,000 inhabitants counted in the Italian world.

Piedmont-Savoy

The state straddling the Alps between Italy and France bore more resemblance to the feudal monarchies in north-western Europe than to the heirs of medieval communes. Its territories formed the western fringe of the Holy Roman Empire, and the dukes attended the Imperial diets in Regensburg. In the 1530s France simply ejected the duke and annexed both Savoy and Piedmont, and created institutions resembling French Parlements in both Chambéry and Turin, while Geneva embraced the Protestant Reformation and broke away to join the Swiss confederation. The heir to the duchy, Emanuel Philibert, took refuge at the imperial court and recovered his state – except for Geneva – by the treaty of Cateau-Cambrésis (1559). The Savoy dynasty was initially a docile Spanish satellite. In 1560 the duke enjoyed no permanent taxes and maintained no army. The court was small and soldierly in manners. Unable to fix local nobles there in any numbers, Emanuel Philibert preferred the counsel of non-subjects, principally from Spanish territories, but also of other Italian nobles.[37] He gradually increased his control by obliging feudal investees to serve him. Further, the duke instituted a direct tax, the *taille*, on the French model. Finally, in addition to the temporary feudal levies provided by the seigneurs, or professional mercenary soldiers, he created a large, unpaid peasant militia. Militias existed in most Italian states, and Piedmont's differed only in that its members fought more frequently. Militiamen were usually substantial peasants who enlisted in order to enhance their village status.[38] Their privileges were many: they were exempt from torture or arrest for debt, which was common; their lands and chattel were exempt from seizure in case of litigation, which was also common; they were exempt from compulsory service in parish or village offices; they could wear finery reserved for nobles. Cavalry militiamen who provided their own horses could hunt like nobles with dogs and falcons, and could legally fight duels with each other and with nobles to defend their honour. Petty nobles loyal to the duke mustered them.

The magistrates and courtiers at Turin, the new Italian-speaking capital, played a more active role too. Charles-Emanuel I (1580–1630) used the court, its entertainments, its sinecures and offices to tie the aristocracy to his person.[39] In return for fiefs or employment, nobles obeyed their prince, ornamented his throne and laid their swords and personal fortunes at his disposal. This bargain enhanced their status, but simultaneously it deprived them of political autonomy. Most gentlemen serving there, including the pages, were soldiers. Alongside the Savoyards and the Piedmontese, the court attracted Italian military aristocrats from Brescia and Ferrara, Milan and Parma. French-speaking courtiers played a lesser role after the loss of the Bugey and Bresse districts to France in 1601, and the Piedmontese increasingly found in the court a source of employment and influence. Charles-Emanuel I was bent on glory, that is, to acquire a royal title, or at least expand his state. His obsessive desire for fame nourished the most imprudent and treacherous foreign policy of his age. The myth of the warrior destiny of the house of Savoy was given free rein at the court. This megalomania curiously tied the aristocracy more tightly to his service.

Papal States

The Papal States also fell outside the norm of Italian principalities. The monarchs were unmarried priests, responsible for the welfare of the Universal Church, elected from a college of cardinals after lengthy negotiations. The medieval Papal State was a patchwork of different jurisdictions, over which the pontiff had limited control, declining further during the long exile in France and during the schism. Rome gradually submitted Umbria, Romagna, Emilia and the Marches and dispatched a network of urban governors to dispense justice and manage provisioning.[40] The suppression of a salt-tax revolt at Perugia in 1540, followed by the building of a citadel there, marked Rome's decisive victory over the regional capitals.[41] The state's increased taxing power compensated for the loss of remittances from countries that had embraced the Reformation or which had, like France, negotiated a *concordat*.[42] Simultaneously, Rome submitted feudal lords to central authority and abolished their jurisdictions in favour of urban tribunals. Rome annexed fiefs whose lineages fell extinct, and in 1578 recovered some fifty castles in one swoop by "verifying" feudal titles. Popes granted offices and privileges to families building Roman palaces and fixing their residence there, while governors and legates in provincial cities contained centuries of factional infighting. None of this was easy, for the most turbulent nobles were usually clients of powerful cardinals, who interceded for them.[43] The papal interregnum was often a period of near anarchy, when the prisons emptied and pardons were given out indiscriminately. Nevertheless, by 1600 the popes had eliminated all the great jurisdictions with wide autonomy.

The Roman Church in full reforming zeal after 1560 consolidated the institutions governing the temporal state. The college of 70 cardinals served as a kind of senate, separate from the administration, or the *Curia*. In 1586, 80 per cent of the cardinals were Italian. A few foreigners and members of Italian dynasties were informal ambassadors for their princes, when and if they resided in Rome. For the rest, however, popes appointed diligent bureaucrats out of the ranks of the middling and minor nobility of north-central Italy. Most were rich enough to maintain their own clientèle in Rome and in the territories of their posting.[44] The popes circumvented this by retaining the cardinal legate close to Rome, and designating a vice-legate to whom most of the power devolved. Even the vice-legate's power was limited, for none held the post for very long. Any initiative which required a firm hand over the long term was doomed to falter because of the high turnover of people at the top of the administration.[45]

The pope was in theory absolute ruler of the Catholic Church and of the Papal States, with both spiritual and temporal jurisdiction. As the head of the Church he had to emit an aura of charity, impartiality and generosity. Papal government was nevertheless guided by sterner principles. The pivotal head of government was the pope's nephew, chosen either from the paternal or maternal line, and raised almost immediately to cardinal status. Other cardinals were frequently in the pay of foreign governments, and could not be trusted with sensitive political posts. The *cardinal-nephew* supervised the distribution of patronage and *nepotism* to numerous kin for the duration of his uncle's reign. He also established the list of new cardinals, taking care to place his own creatures and supporters of his uncle's policies, who would control a large block of votes in the next conclave.[46] The cardinal-nephew also supervised the papal bureaucracy and corresponded with the nuncios abroad, the legates and town governors. The college of cardinals acquiesced in this power, because no papal nephew retained power after the death of his uncle, and the pope's ultimate power was never contested. Sixtus V fused political and religious power even more, by creating in 1588 the system of Cardinal congregations. There were eventually fifteen of these, each consisting of a committee of several cardinals governing an area of competence. The cardinals themselves moved from one committee to another, from administrative functions to religious ones, and back again, rarely holding a position for more than a few years.[47] With a pope's death the system was ended. If several successive popes lived for only a short time, confusion set in. Before 1600, the system was not noticeably more archaic than other forms of government. Its most curious aspect was the practice of popes, especially in the wake of Sixtus V, to supplant lay administrators, whatever their birth or pedigree, with simple tonsured, celibate clerics, many of whom were ineligible to say mass or administer sacraments.[48] But gradually this temporal government of priests resembled a relic from medieval times, and the papal prince could no longer rival his lay counterparts, the foremost of whom was the Catholic King, monarch of Spain and much of Italy.

5 Spanish Regimes in Italy

Genealogy of Spanish Rule

Like Italy and Germany, "Spain" was also a geographical expression
whose modern shape still lay in the future. Italy's Iberia was initially
the kingdom of Aragon, whose merchants and barons seized Sicily
and Sardinia in the thirteenth century. King Alfonso of Aragon eventually ejected the troubled Angevin ruler from Naples in 1442, and
distributed fiefs there to his followers. Alfonso projected such a positive image of order and magnificence that Naples had its admirers in
central and northern Italy too.[1] With Alfonso's death in 1458 the
Iberian possessions, Sardinia and Sicily, passed to his son Ferdinand,
while Naples passed to his illegitimate son Ferrante. At Ferrante's
death in 1494, King Charles VIII of France declared himself the
lawful heir to the Angevin line and set forth with a large army to
conquer his birthright. The invasion unleashed a Pandora's box of
calamities lasting for over half a century. Charles occupied Naples
only briefly because an Imperial–Italian alliance ejected the "barbar-
ians". His successor Louis XII invaded Italy in 1499, and laid claim to
Milan too, on the pretext that his grandmother was a Visconti. As the
French army tramped southward, Ferdinand proposed to split the
kingdom of Naples between them. In 1503, when the conquest was
complete, the Spaniards turned on the French and drove them from
their share. The wars ignited again in 1508 to challenge Venetian
ambitions in the peninsula. Quickly defeated, the republic aligned
its former enemies against the French and expelled the latter from
Milan in 1512. In 1515, the next king of France, François I, returned
to Milan, which he held for a decade. A stalemate had emerged

which left France with mastery over the Po valley, while Spain set up its governing institutions in the south.

When Ferdinand of Aragon died in 1516, his mentally unstable daughter was already a widow of the Habsburg heir Philip. Their eldest son Charles was raised at the Habsburg court in Brussels. Charles united in his person the separate administrations of Castile and Aragon, but also of Naples, Sicily, Sardinia and the growing Spanish Indies, attached to Castile. In 1519 Charles inherited the Habsburg possessions from his grandfather Maximilian: the Low Countries; the Free County of Burgundy (Franche-Comté to the west of Switzerland); the "Austrian" lands between the upper Rhine and the edge of the Hungarian plain; and the crown of Bohemia, including Moravia and Silesia. Charles's subsequent elevation to the imperial throne made him master of Greater Germany, with suzerainty over northern Italy. His crowns combined the greatest collection of territories since the Roman Empire, and these would increase again in 1528 when the parts of Hungary not in Turkish hands – principally Croatia and Slovakia – acclaimed Charles king.

A French offensive to drive the Hispano-Imperial forces out of Lombardy failed utterly at the battle of Pavia in 1525, where King François and his Italian allies fell prisoner. After François I paid his ransom, he invaded Italy anew in 1526 with papal backing. An Imperial army besieged and sacked Rome in 1527, and papal power momentarily vanished. Genoa abandoned the French alliance in 1528, and Charles entered Milan. The wars of Italy between France and the Habsburg monarchy continued for another generation. Charles was beset by other crises too. One was the rise of Lutheranism in Germany, which undermined his authority there. The most urgent task was to stop Ottoman progress. In 1526, the Turkish host under the young sultan, Suleiman the Magnificent, destroyed Hungary's army and the king with it. The Ottomans laid siege to the Imperial capital at Vienna, without taking it (1529). In the Mediterranean the Ottomans occupied the Barbary coast, what is now Algeria, Libya and eventually Tunisia. From there they exerted intense pressure by sea on Spain and Italy. Charles tried with varying degrees of success to capture North African ports with great galley fleets, but the inconclusive operations consumed much treasure.

Because it proved too unwieldy for a single monarch to govern, in 1555 Charles V decided to split his colossal empire into two parts. Thereafter, until 1700, there would be *two* Habsburg Empires: the Spanish portion ruled from Madrid included Spain and the Indies, the Low Countries and Franche-Comté, and Sardinia, Sicily, Naples and Milan in Italy. This lion's share went to his son Philip II, who was raised as a Castilian. The "German" portion, consisting of the Imperial crown and the hereditary crowns of Austria, Bohemia and Hungary passed to his brother Ferdinand I. Each branch of the house of Habsburg ruled its own realms, but the dynastic ties united them against common foes.

Philip II's forty-year reign constitutes Spain's Golden Age. Part of the glory is owed to the conscientious monarch himself, the "paper king" who collected information from around the globe and pondered action.[2] Philip decided policy through a small Council of State, composed of trusted councillors that he chose himself. In 1558 Philip added to their number the Supreme Council of Italy to act as the ultimate court of appeal for Sicily, Naples and Milan. Sardinia remained under a similar Supreme Council of Aragon. Each of the three regions was represented by two regents, both lawyers, one native and one Spaniard, who sorted through business and compiled memoranda for the king to read and sign. The viceroy (and his detractors) transmitted "mountains of paper" in the form of causes, petitions and appeals to officials in the Council. On Philip III's accession in 1598 little of the mechanics changed. The sovereign, who cared little for business, confided it to a powerful prime minister, or *valido*, the Duke de Lerma, who made decisions in his place. Viceroys and the principal Italian subjects struggled for influence in Madrid. There was no collective sense of purpose among the Spanish possessions in Italy; each territory, and each city looked out for its own interests.[3] Even the viceroy could be subjected to criticism, scrutiny and occasionally even recall. Madrid subjected its administrators to periodic inspections of *visitadores*, who dealt with a wide range of problems.[4] Seven "general" visits took place during the two centuries of Spanish rule. They did not always proceed without obstacle: officials blocked the visitor, criticized him to the king, or appealed to the Council of Italy to disregard his recommendations. Nevertheless, they were an integral part of the mechanisms by which Italians accepted Habsburg rule.

Sardinia

Sardinia's institutions resembled those of other constituent kingdoms in the Empire. At the apex was enthroned the viceroy, an aristocratic appointee originating from another Spanish dominion, whose normal tenure lasted for several years. As the highest political authority, he kept close watch over the baronage and town councils, nominating islanders to key judicial and fiscal offices. It was in his career interest to be held impartial. Daily administration fell to the regent of the royal chancellery, tax officials, and a panel of judges deciding controversial civil and criminal cases. Royal officials periodically consulted the Sardinian parliament, which like Catalonia's consisted of three "arms", the nobility, the cities, and the clergy. It enjoined the king to uphold the land's traditional liberties and autonomy; in its view, the king had to negotiate with his subjects if he wished to extract money from them. Philip II was careful not to dispute this contractual concept of power. However, the parliament was rife with internal divisions and rivalries, among the barons themselves, between Cagliari and Sassari, and among the different branches of the church. The Spanish crown gradually enhanced the viceroy's powers with respect to the island's institutions, for the crown needed *servicios*, or tax money.

Over three hundred feudal jurisdictions shared about a third of the island in the seventeenth century, but half of those were possessed by seven great lords living in Spain. Feudal power in the countryside probably fell short of that exercised by barons elsewhere in southern Italy, due to the sparse population. Baronial judges seem to have administered justice with a light hand, and did little to reduce the local penchant for feuding. Such loose government of an impoverished land left Sardinia vulnerable to all the dangers presented by the Mediterranean, although sterner control would probably have succeeded no better. The kingdom's Spanish garrison, the *tercio de Cerdeña*, rarely surpassed a few hundred effectives. Spain was unable to aid Sardinia in any meaningful way, and Sardinians did little to aid Madrid. Sardinian elites were nevertheless deeply attached to the Spanish connection, and continued to write and speak Castilian long after the end of Spanish rule.

Sicily

Baronial power in Sicily predated the Spanish regime, which was content to maintain what it found. Two-thirds of the kingdom's communities lay under feudal jurisdiction, whose barons designated officials of the *università*, the chief of police, the public prosecutor and the magistrates of both civil and criminal tribunals. Feudal lords in Sicily, as elsewhere in southern Italy, held the monopoly of many economic services and activities. Denis Mack Smith castigates Spanish rule for being too respectful of established powers.[5] Spaniards shared a dim view of Sicilians. They considered them "vengeful and passionate, with infinite capacity for perjury and bribery". The natives often freely admitted these faults. The corrective was a strong foreign monarch, above the interests of local politics.[6] Viceroys preferred to use foreigners (Spaniards, "Belgians" and Italians from the mainland) in many capacities to check corruption in government and the judiciary. Spaniards served as aides to the central government, as members of the episcopate and the Inquisition, and as commanders of the fortresses. The viceroy's power was circumscribed by the Spanish Inquisition, and the occasional *visitador*. His powers were nevertheless considerable, for he commanded the army and issued decrees and regulations within the framework of existing laws. A "good" viceroy was the Spanish duke Osuna, who launched a vigorous campaign against Barbary corsairs; summarily executed bandits; demonstrated paternalistic solicitude towards the city poor; attempted to recover royal revenue alienated to Messina; made showy gestures of great generosity, and held splendid festivities in the capital Palermo. While individual viceroys like Osuna might humiliate and mortify barons, they were obliged to appoint Sicilians to high offices. The chief difficulty was finding an adequate number of capable officials for these posts.[7]

Peculiar to Sicily was the king's status as "Apostolic legate". This permitted him to tax the clergy and to confer church benefices without interference from Rome. This *Monarchia Sicula* (Sicilian Monarchy) implied that "there was no pope in Sicily". The viceroy dealt with the pope directly over ecclesiastical matters, and authorized papal briefs and decrees. He was aided in some ways by the Spanish Inquisition, which investigated every suspicion of heresy. Charles V introduced the tribunal to Sicily in 1519, without any religious pretext, for the kingdom lacked the Jewish and Moorish populations that Catholics feared in Spain.[8] Thousands of middle-class Sicilians soon joined it as familiars (spies and agents), in order to be protected by its jurisdiction and immune to other tribunals. It was very much a separate entity within the state, out of the hands of barons and state officials.

The Sicilian parliament sat almost continually. Its three "arms" – the barons, the clergy and the representatives of the royal towns – met separately and issued one vote each. Parliament's function was to give assent to tax requests from the crown. Revenue also derived from the sale of grain export licences, the *tratte*. Pressed to find more money, the viceroys sold baronies and jurisdictions of *mero e misto imperio*, or the right to judge appeals.[9] The Messinese patriciate offered huge lump sums in order to appropriate the proceeds of particular customs duties. Messina's aim was to separate itself from the rest of the island, like a city-state, answerable directly to the sovereign.[10] It also paid to require the viceroy to reside half the year in the city, to deprive rival Palermo of its status of capital. Many Spanish aristocrats lived in Palermo and intermarried with local families, while Sicilian aristocrats spent long periods at Madrid.[11] Castilian was the language of the island's central government, even though Italian or Sicilian dialect was the medium of communication at lower levels. Viceroys lured barons away from their fiefs and used them to ornament the court in Palermo, sold titles to them, offered them offices and sinecures, and stayed seizures of their property to pay debts. Spanish policy in Sicily was on the whole remarkably successful, helping Madrid achieve its Catholic and Imperial aims, while preserving the institutions and privileges of the kingdom.[12]

Naples

In Naples Spanish policy was never so single-minded. Alfonso I established a modern tax system and brought the judiciary more under royal control.[13] But he conceded to barons the *mero e misto imperio* that underlay feudal power in the countryside. Don Pedro de Toledo, viceroy from 1532 to 1553, established absolutist principles in political and jurisdictional matters at the barons' expense.[14] Only the Spanish Inquisition was rejected outright by Neapolitans in two great riots in 1510 and 1547. The viceroy in Naples, as elsewhere, was most often a Spaniard. Many of the members in his governing circle were Spaniards too. A Collateral Council was the custodian of the laws and interpreter of legal custom: half its members were Neapolitan and the other half Spaniards. The viceroy named Neapolitan judges to the benches in the capital and the provinces, but at subalternate levels, the crown sold offices to candidates with the requisite legal qualifications, as was the practice elsewhere in Europe. These judges, termed collectively *togati*, derived their power not just from a single office, but by virtue of mutiple office-holding and through their tight endogamy with magistrates of similar rank.[15] A parliament was convened every few years until 1642 in order to vote tax increases and new levies. While it debated political problems with considerable liberty, the parliament never effectively opposed policies decided in Madrid.[16]

In contrast to Sicily, where the king assumed the papal role, Naples was a fief of the Church, like Ferrara and Urbino. In the 1550s, Pope Paul IV Carafa declared that Philip II had forfeited the throne and called on subjects to overthrow him. A brief war resolved the crisis in Philip's favour, but the Council of Trent sometimes challenged royal authority in areas of church jurisdiction. Every year the king made a present of a white horse to the pontiff as a token of his fealty. This *chinea*, as it was called, symbolized a submission rendered concrete by Rome's heavy taxes on the Neapolitan church and the liberty with which the pope nominated prelates to the kingdom's benefices.[17] In the last resort, Spain's rule depended on its armed muscle and on the consensus of the inhabitants. The first was notoriously weak, at least *in situ*. The Spanish *tercio* of Naples amounted to only a few thousand effectives. They were usually sufficient to keep banditry within bounds and to deter Barbary pirate fleets from raiding the major cities, although soldiers were prone to plundering the inhabitants and disturbing public order.[18] Behind the garrisons stood a large peasant militia, the *battaglione*, mobilized only locally to meet crises.

The great majority of jurisdictions in the kingdom were feudal. Around 1590 there were only 76 royal jurisdictions in the entire kingdom, usually the largest towns, as opposed to 1,974 feudal ones. In the Abruzzi the crown held only 4 towns out of 470; in Molise, only 1 jurisdiction of 104.[19] Although serfdom had disappeared, the feudal institution itself was still powerful and its jurisdiction gradually expanded. Provincial authorities counted on the barons to capture suspects and hold them for trial. Feudal lords also monopolized commercial activities in the village, such as the mill, the oven, the butcher's stall, the wine press or the inn. They levied tithes and tolls on all the merchandise passing through the fief, on livestock and textiles. Castles crowned nearly all of the feudal communities, sometimes flanked by a more modern palace. These strongholds were sometimes stocked with cannon, arsenals and munitions, and served by soldiers in the lord's pay. Some great seigneurs owned several of them, giving them great leverage over large districts.[20] Their power was such that barons and their retainers violated laws with impunity. Aurelio Lepre exaggerates only slightly to affirm that in his fief, the feudatory was king.[21]

Don Pedro de Toledo enticed the barons into the more urbane atmosphere of Naples where he could watch them more closely. By 1620, 800 noble families living in the capital rivalled each other in conspicuous consumption.[22] Each great family posted members close to the viceroy and in Madrid too, to exploit opportunities for profit or advancement. They cultivated the viceroy with splendid presents, just as he patronized them.[23] This "generosity" gave rise to great debts and noblemen depended upon Madrid's goodwill to stave off their creditors or pardon their crimes. In exchange for their continual collaboration, the crown rendered fiefholding more stable. By extinction of a lineage, or felony, fiefs returned continually to the monarch who was free to concede them to another client. Gradually, the Spanish crown allowed feudal families to buy and sell fiefs, divide them, and sub-infeud them; allowed collateral lines to inherit the fief; and extended the jurisdiction of barons over their vassals. In 1500 only a few enjoyed the right to inflict capital punishment, but by 1600 almost all of them had bought appeals jurisdictions from the royal domain.[24] Habsburg monarchs sold fiefs and titles to the highest bidders, regardless of the pedigree of the purchaser. Genoese financiers collected them avidly, but they could not match the great families. They deployed much of their energy competing against each other, so were never capable of forming a united front against the viceroy. The Habsburg monarch, the object of real loyalty on the part of both the barons and the people, cemented the system in place. The monarchy saw as its mission the prevention of *prepotenza*, the abuse of authority.[25] The crown's ministers were not forgetful that the king entrusted them with the public interest, which they invoked whenever they chose talent over influence. Although never intending to compromise feudal authority *per se*, viceroys could be very harsh with delinquent nobles, torturing and imprisoning them for their crimes (vendetta, harbouring bandits, counterfeiting) to set an example for others. Nevertheless, the nobility of southern Italy rallied to the crown, for it offered them a theatre of vast proportions in which to deploy their talent and energy.

Naples held a special place in the Spanish regime on account of its size. Early modern cities were usually distillations of a region's elites. A huge market, Naples also produced both luxury goods for the upper class and a broad range of ordinary products for the entire kingdom. Naples monopolized large-scale commerce with the rest of the kingdom, and held all the capital reserves. Conversely, its huge concentration of urban poor, the *lazzaroni*, constituted a turbulent crowd always ready to riot at price increases.[26] Given the extraordinary dimensions of the capital city, the Naples civic government acquired special importance. Representatives of six electoral districts, each holding a seat, or *seggio*, directed city affairs. Of the six, five belonged to nobles, and just one to a representative of the "people", picked by the viceroy. It ran the city's main tribunal, controlled grain provisioning and managed the "physical plant" of the capital.[27] Unlike parliament, the city government sat permanently and noble representatives in civic government claimed spokesmanship for the entire kingdom. The main issue on their agenda was taxation.

More than Sicily or Milan, Naples was a pillar of the Spanish Empire.[28] The monarchy had no central administration entrusted with assessing taxes individually. As in other countries, state officials imposed direct taxes on communities, or else levied duties on a host of articles or rights accruing to the royal domain, known collectively under the term *gabelles*. Both forms of taxation were hampered by the absence of an honest and efficient civil service, which was beyond the means of every European state until the eighteenth century. Each large village or town was a corporate entity, a *università*, collectively responsible for paying a tax order. They were generally run by the small group of professionals or wealthy peasants, who were not always on good terms with the baron.[29] These administrators leased (or farmed) out what revenues they could, and for the rest established the tax bill of each household, levied it, and after deducting their own expenditures, sent the remainder to a provincial official. The royal tax administration, the *Sommaria*, preferred direct taxes established on the wealth of each house, like the hearth tax introduced in 1510. Although paid proportionately to household wealth, this tax was not levied on the clergy, or on the inhabitants of Naples, or on the elderly or the poor, or on those without land or houses. Crown officials would have preferred to add new direct taxes, or increase the old ones, and submit the privileged groups to them, but the parliaments refused.

The privileged classes preferred to base taxation not on wealth, but on consumption, through the gabelles. They were levied on products consumed primarily by the well-off. But they also weighed on essential items, like salt or flour, the *macinato*. The crown imposed duties on the export of manufactured goods, foodstuffs and raw materials, such as silk and olive oil. The *Sommaria* offered the gabelles to the highest bidder in secretive negotiations. A consortium of financiers advanced the money after assessing the probable value of the tax against the cost of its collection. With the backing of the state's coercive power, they then collected the money using their own agents and pocketed the surplus. *Tax farming* was a means of rapid wealth for financiers, and perhaps too for poorly-paid officials, subject to great pressure from the financiers and their high-born associates. The single most important tax administration was the *Dogana of Foggia*, which levied duties on the wool, meat, cheese and hides from the million or so sheep grazing on crown land around Foggia every winter.[30] Officials working in that administration bought their position, and were intent on recovering their investment. Illegal kickbacks were the norm, not the exception. When economic crisis made it more difficult to levy the amounts stipulated, the financiers exacted more stringent guarantees that they would recover their investment. Before the 1620s the privatization of the indirect tax system was neither systematic nor permanent.[31]

"Extraordinary" taxes usually entailed some alienation or diminishing of the crown's rights, property or "domain". Forms of it were the sale or resale of fiefs, alienation of towns in the royal domain, or of jurisdictions, rights or monopolies. Yet tax revenue was always inferior to expenditures. The difference had to be made up by borrowing, and this pried money from taxpayers to pay interest to financiers. Throughout Europe, the state took money from the rich in the form of taxes, and gave it back to them in the form of interest paid on bonds. Around 1600, lending money to the crown was, at 8 per cent interest, a good investment in a period of agricultural and manufacturing uncertainty. The crown always met the interest on its debts. This "deficit financing" gradually enriched the wealthy, and drove the crown to more desperate measures to find money in the short term. In Naples the king of Spain provided order, stability and opportunity for advancement and enrichment; the kingdom's elites repaid the monarch with their fidelity.

Milan

Charles V's accession to the duchy of Milan was not a long-held ambition, and he hesitated before adding it to the Habsburg domain in 1535. He retained the recent French-style parliament, renamed the Senate. This supreme court had wide discretion over the interpretation and application of laws, with the right to register royal decrees before they took effect. The Senate was one of the few overarching institutions of Lombard government, which is a good example of what Domenico Sella calls the "city-state system".[32] The duchy was subdivided into nine autonomous districts, (Milan, Pavia, Cremona, Lodi, Como, Novara, Alessandria, Tortona and Vigevano) each with its own economic policies and tax lists. The citizens of the *dominante* exploited the countryside through myriad taxes and corvées (compulsory labour details) from which city-dwellers were exempt. Citizens were also not subject to rural or feudal courts. This privilege extended to their servants and workers on their country estates.

In Milan the great council of the medieval commune gradually shrank to an elite of two hundred noble families, in a tight assembly of just sixty members, but it retained a great deal of power and autonomy.[33] The professional bodies of lawyers and physicians also tended to close ranks to exclude non-Milanese from exercising these functions. The craft guilds wielded influence over economic policy. The Church was largely off-limits to royal patronage, due to the intransigence of Saint Carlo Borromeo, archbishop and papal nephew. His nephew and successor Federigo Borromeo almost excommunicated the *visitador* in 1608, after royal constables mishandled a cleric. The Council of Italy warned the governor to proceed with caution wherever he might run counter the Church's interests.[34] Papal taxation and rights of nomination were greater in Spanish Milan than anywhere else in northern Italy.[35] The duchy of Milan also contained a patchwork of 1,600 feudal jurisdictions. Most fiefs resembled those of Tuscany or Piedmont more than their homonyms in the Mezzogiorno or Sicily.[36] The baron held only local jurisdiction and power of sentencing minor offences. Feudalism in Spanish Lombardy, as in contemporary France, was not so much a manner of lordship, as a tax on the vanity of those who possessed or purchased the title.

Madrid's chief functionary was the governor of Milan, usually a senior Spanish soldier, subject to periodic inspections from *visitadores* and to constant scrutiny by the Lombard patricians. Advising the governor were hand-picked military and political advisers who constituted his secret council, with jurisdiction over general politics, war, alliances, edicts and legislation. It watched over the tax cases

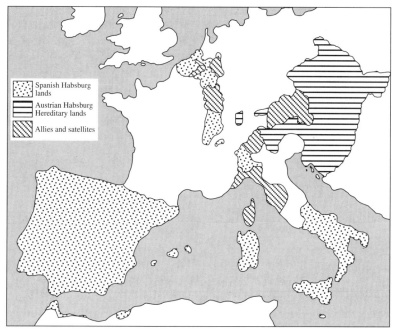

Map 13   Habsburg territories and their allies

and criminal trials before the magistrates. It selected candidates for offices, awarded pardons, gave assent to decisions made in the king's name, and received oaths of fealty from feudatories. Most of its participants were "foreigners", that is, Spaniards and Italians not native to the duchy; but about 40 per cent of its members were Milanese or Lombard subjects.[37] Their strenuous objections foiled two attempts to install the Spanish Inquisition, in 1547 and 1563. The Senate retained its supremacy over civil and penal causes. Equally important, the Milanese patriciate could lobby the Council of Italy directly, sending "ambassadors" to plead its case. Lombard patricians were also entrusted with important missions for the king of Spain and occasionally commanded his armies.[38]

Fortress Lombardy blocked French designs on Naples and impeded communication with its Venetian ally. Milan was the main staging point for Hispano-Italian troops destined for Flanders after 1566.[39] Governors were given great latitude to make military preparations and negotiate alliances.[40] Spain established a treaty with Catholic Swiss cantons in 1587 in order to recruit soldiers there and

keep the passes open to Flanders, but Venice and France sought to
close off these routes by wooing the Swiss away from Madrid. The
governors of Milan also wielded their authority to mediate border
tensions between other Italian states, their clients; such as between
Lucca and Modena, or Parma and Mantua. The Spanish garrison in
Lombardy, only 5,000 men in 1605, was therefore the key to peace in
northern Italy. Behind it was a net of alliances between Spain and its
north Italian satellites that bound them to assist the Catholic King if
his domains were attacked.

Spanish Preponderance in Italy

The king of Spain ruled directly over 5 million of Italy's 13 million
inhabitants in 1600, through institutions that varied a great deal
from one territory to another. The combined Spanish European possessions totalled about 18 million people, about the same as France,
but they were dispersed across half a continent. Spanish hegemony
stemmed in part from the collapse of the French threat in 1561,
when that kingdom descended into religious civil war that continued
intermittently until 1629. A constant flow of American treasure was
another pillar of strength for Madrid. It never constituted more than
10 per cent of the monarchy's revenue, however.[41] Spanish ascendancy depended on more than a strict accountancy of people and
economies. The martial spirit of the Spanish *tercios* permitted the
king to maintain a constant threat over wavering allies. The minus-
cule Tuscan presidial state consisted of four separate fortresses on
Elba and the coast, halfway between the Campanian naval base of
Gaeta and Genoa. They protected the vital sea lane along the Italian
coast and simultaneously intimidated the grand duke. Spanish
muscle also assisted individual states too weak to defend themselves.
Troops in Spanish pay helped recover parts of Savoy for Duke
Charles Emanuel. They restored Genoese control in Corsica in the
late 1560s, and enabled Rome to break up large bandit companies. It
was in Madrid's interest to enforce a *Pax Hispanica* in the peninsula.
Spain subsidized Piedmont, Genoa and Tuscany's efforts to maintain
galley squadrons, a collective effort to protect the coast from corsair
raids. Madrid subsidized Duke Francesco Maria of Urbino by
awarding him recruiting contracts. Italian princes at the court in
Madrid were not merely hostages to their fathers' good conduct, and
they were instrumental in introducing the more punctilious Spanish

etiquette into Italian courts. Charles V and Philip II cultivated the peninsula's great families, called *los Potentados*, by granting them fiefs in Spanish Italy and sundry honours and privileges.[42] These clients counted heavily in the college of cardinals, where the Catholic king could influence papal policy.[43] He honoured important families by granting them membership in the prestigious Spanish chivalric orders. The most select was the Order of the Golden Fleece, the highest rank to which a noble could aspire. Philip II and his son awarded it sparingly to Italian princes, as a reward for their docility. Below the Golden Fleece were the orders of Santiago, Alcàntara, Calatrava and Montesa, the "habits" of which were distributed to members of select nobility in Genoa, Florence, Mantua, Parma, Turin and Bologna. Such distinctions established the recipients as "friends" of the king of Spain who would lobby for his interests. Italians became frequent recipients after 1560, and constituted 11 per cent of the total number in Europe.[44]

Spain also championed a Catholic *reconquista*, ardently desired by the papacy and indeed by most Italians.[45] Italian elites seized the opportunity to participate in the great religious struggles convulsing Europe. Flanders attracted aristocrats from all over the peninsula, serving either as commissioned officers in Spanish or Italian *tercios*, (infantry units equivalent to regiments), or as simple adventurers. Likewise, the great maritime struggle against the Ottoman Empire and the Barbary pirates was organized under the Spanish banner. This too was a crusade, sanctioned by the Church as a pious cause, for the greater glory of God. Italians were active partisans of this world-view.

Spanish power reached its zenith in the age of Philip III (1598–1621), a king of limited intelligence and weak character. Spain's hold was never absolute. Italian princes made occasional attempts to shake off its domination, creating sometimes considerable tension. The Este, Medici and Gonzaga dynasties were never entirely supine. Piedmont could not be trusted, and Venice was a declared adversary. King Henri IV of France revived Hispanophobe sentiments in 1610 as he prepared to make war on Spain, but his assassination destroyed those projects. And while Spain focused the energies and the ambitions of the military aristocracy abroad, Italy enjoyed a long period of peace. The *Pax Hispanica* of Philip II and Philip III paid an important peace dividend.

6   The Great City-economies to 1620

Buying and Selling

The buoyant sixteenth-century economy established regular trade between Europe and the rest of the world for the first time.[1] Carlo Cipolla has called this period the "Indian summer" of the Italian city-economies, still the most advanced in Europe. In this chapter I will not address the largest sector, that is, the production, transport and sale of agricultural products, which is the object of the next chapter. The exchange economy entailed buying and selling articles brought to market. Moreover, a multi-layered manufacturing economy produced goods for both the rural population, and an international clientèle. The profits derived from the first two activities nourished the trading of money itself, an activity in which Italians possessed a technological advantage well into the seventeenth century.

No region ever achieved the state of autarky to which it aspired. Some goods were exchanged on a market, which was a physical place with rules specific to it. Individuals who went there to buy were able to compare merchandise, to pick up and examine the articles that interested them, to look for flaws and to haggle over prices. Fairs, which were great markets extended over several days, connected city merchants with pedlars hawking minute quantities of merchandise off the backs of their mules to villages and farms. Merchants moved from one fair to another, carrying the bills of exchange necessary for large-scale purchases. Towns boasted shops in addition to the market. Large cities contained thousands of them: 2,200 in mid-sixteenth century Florence, and over 5,000 in Rome in 1600, in addition to throngs of street vendors. The fairs and village markets

76

busied a dense network of rural merchants. Even in the deep Mezzogiorno, these tended to be northerners, who bought up raw materials for distant places.[2] Every spring the roads came alive with merchandise on the move. On the well-travelled road connecting Naples with Rome, great convoys of horses, mules and wagons needed beefy armed escorts to protect the precious cargoes from bandit attacks.[3] Poor roads and the threat of attack limited the quantity of goods moving about the interior, but no place was ignored. North Italian princes built canals, which made it possible to ship heavy cargoes like wheat, iron and wood to cities more cheaply.

Italian firms pioneered the use of representatives in foreign locales. The improved letter-post system made it quicker and safer for commercial correspondence to reach distant destinations. Long-distance trade was a "balancing act" (Braudel), connecting a place where merchandise was plentiful with another where it was dear. Merchants passed several large commands simultaneously with results they could not entirely predict. What they lost on one deal, they recouped on another.[4] Merchants often banded together in companies (mercantile, industrial and financial, rarely specialized) in which the profits and losses were borne equally. In the *commenda* association, which Venetians invented, investors could finance other people's companies in exchange for a share of the profits, without the responsibility of managing the money. Capital invested this way irrigated business across much of Europe. Michel Carmona sees the success of this form of investment as a weakening of the entrepreneurial spirit, but it allowed families not interested in business to keep their capital active.[5]

The manufacture and the transhipment of precious goods was the basis of the prosperity of northern Italy and Naples. Paradoxically, few Italians were seafarers like the Basques, the English or the Dutch. Most traded from small ships tramping the coast, buying and selling in the tiny ports and the *marina* beaches. Small ships then converged on a large port, where they exchanged their cargoes for metal currency. Large ports possessed naval supplies and repair yards, tradesmen, shipping offices, insurance agents, and merchants who could cash bills of exchange that were used increasingly in place of coin. Braudel points out that "all ports face two ways, where land and water meet".[6] Genoa's importance derived from the easy passes through the Apennines just behind the city, traversed by great mule-trains. Venice connected the Po valley and the alpine passes into Germany with the Adriatic. Precious goods often travelled overland, departing northward from the cities close to the edge of the Alps, into Germany and Switzerland across any of 23 passes. Carts were common only around the largest cities where the road network was better maintained. Elsewhere the mule was indispensable.

Fernand Braudel, who was influenced by Immanuel Wallerstein's vision of world-economies in the modern period, placed Venice at the centre of a network of global dimensions with its heart in the Mediterranean.[7] A world-economy "seizes the market-economy and directs it from above, collecting and organizing exports, in an unequal exchange". The concentration of great wealth pushed prices up until they attracted goods over a vast space. Alongside the north Italian axis appeared a northern European economic zone centred in Antwerp. Its emergence was the first sign of a shift in European trade patterns, but Italians were well represented there, divided into their different "nations" with their own personnel of clerks and correspondents.[8]

Venice moved into the declining Byzantine sphere after 1200. Trading families constituted colonies sometimes numbering hundreds of individuals, in centres such as Constantinople, Aleppo, Tripoli, Cairo and Alexandria. Their factors purchased spices, cotton, silks, carpets, precious stones and other goods, and sold off stocks of European goods; woollen textiles, paper, metal products, glass, soap, sumptuous silk fabrics, and coarser English or Dutch cloth.[9] Venice was also the conduit for silver specie towards the Middle East, for its commerce with the Levant was always in deficit. To thwart Adriatic corsairs and to compete with its rival Ragusa (modern Dubrovnik, a commercial city-state), Venice developed Spalato (modern Split in Croatia) as a trans-shipment point through the Balkans. Its customs houses, warehouses, quarantine stations for people and for merchandise arriving from Constantinople by caravan regulated the flow of goods. Venice also unilaterally declared a monopoly over trade in the Adriatic sea, and obliged ships trading there to bring their cargoes to the lagoon. Venice's Adriatic rivals avoided compliance whenever they could, but they needed its insurance brokers, cheap credit, abundant specie, and its transit facilities to markets beyond the lagoon. Venetian ships assuring this commerce then re-exported these products and others throughout the western Mediterranean and the North Sea. Shipping made Venice a great *emporium*, or warehouse, where foreign merchants could find products in large quantities at low prices. The

Portuguese discovery of a route to the Indies around Africa *circa* 1500 made Lisbon the chief centre of the spice trade for several decades, but after 1530 the Mediterranean route flourished again.

Venetian patricians reasoned that commerce required organizational talent, technical knowledge, and a taste for risk and adventure that constituted a form of noble *virtù*. Many non-nobles participated too, primarily in the "citizen" class, whose sons learned the art of long-distance commerce in the Levant.[10] Foreign colonies of traders in the lagoon city governed themselves through their own councils. German merchants frequented the *Fondaco dei Tedeschi*, a Venetian complex of storehouses and dormitories from which they organized shipments over the Alps. Florentines, Spanish and Portuguese *marranos*, or converted Jews, Greeks and Armenians, lived among their own in tight trading communities. While each merchant tried to maximize his own profit, he was bound by tacit conventions, because non-conformity undermined the assumption of good faith inherent in the bargaining process. Merchants possessed their own tribunals and arbiters. They abhorred legal chicanery, and needed special jurisdictions to sort out conflicting interests quickly. Jewish merchants expelled from the Iberian peninsula played a noteworthy role. Spanish and Portuguese marranos formed dynamic business networks from Morocco to Turkey. Both Sephardic and Ashkenazi Jews peopled Venice's ghetto, the largest in Italy. They played a dominant commercial role in Italian centres such as Ancona, Ferrara and Mantua.[11] All these foreigners bought Venetian products with the proceeds of their sales.

Until the Dutch seized the Indian Ocean after 1620, the balance of trade between the lagoon and northern Europe was favourable to the Mediterranean. The volume of traffic in Venice remained stable until about 1625, although it declined relative to Holland in the previous generation. Venetians gradually withdrew from the carrying trade, under the impact of damage inflicted by pirates of every nation.[12] English ships of the Levant Company first appeared in 1573, seeking raisins, wine and oil. Their first guides were Italians resident in London who sought healthier profits by excluding other Italian intermediaries. By 1600 they possessed more than 30 ships operating in the zone. By 1605 the English began to compete with Italians in the Levant itself. Tired of crippling attacks on their ships by *Uskoks* and Barbary pirates, Venetian merchants began to freight out northern vessels. They soon relinquished much of the carrying trade and its attendant profits to the northerners.

Genoese merchant colonies were hardly less dynamic. Squeezed out of their position opposite Venice in the Levant, Genoese round-hulled merchant vessels assured the liaison between the Mediterranean, Iberia and the Atlantic coast. There was a conspicuous colony of them in Seville, which was the base of the Indies fleets and the economic capital of Spain.[13] Genoese merchants transported cargoes from Italy and Spain to Antwerp and London, and brought back the Flemish, French and English textiles and other manufactured goods consumed by Spain and the Indies colonies. They soon controlled the market for American products like sugar, hides, drugs and cochineal. Genoese merchants in Seville, who tried to assimilate by intermarriage and naturalization, dominated the financing of voyages from Spain to America until 1568, when they redirected their capital into royal finance. Their emporium was not Genoa, but rather Antwerp, the distribution centre for northern Europe. The great Genoese vessels, often more than 1000 tons, were the largest ships in Europe, but they too lost out to the cheaper North Sea vessels after 1590. Genoese financiers disembarked in Sicily as moneylenders and shopkeepers, but soon controlled grain exports from estates they managed. Raw silk became the staple of the flourishing economy of Messina, where Genoese patrician families intermarried with the island aristocracy, exempting them from taxes and duties applying to their foreign competitors.[14] Virtually any enterprise requiring substantial capital came into Genoese hands.

Tuscan merchants were familiar figures in northern European and Iberian cities too. Florentines and Luccans were travelling through Poland by the late sixteenth century, selling their luxury fabrics in a grain-rich economy. Tuscans were numerous in Antwerp and Marseilles, and helped found the banking sector and the stock exchange in Lyons. Florentines were prosperous intermediaries between Spain and Italy. Until the onset of the Thirty Years War in 1618 they were especially numerous in the principal German cities.[15] What Tuscany lacked was a natural port, once the Arno silted up below Pisa. The Medici developed Livorno just south of the Arno's mouth. Cosimo I then linked it to Florence via a barge canal to Pisa.[16] Grand Duke Ferdinando I invited non-Christian and Protestant merchants to settle in Livorno, since English and Dutch Protestants, and Levantine Jews were considered likely to develop commerce with the Levant. The idea was to turn the city into a *free port*: products brought there would be free of taxes until they entered Tuscan territory behind it. English and Dutch ships soon deposited great quantities of Baltic wheat, smoked herring and salt cod after 1590. Livorno benefited from the buoyant Mediterranean economy of the early seventeenth century, growing from 3,000 inhabitants in 1601 to 12,000 in 1642.

Making Things

City-states exercised their authority over the surrounding countryside in order to ensure a supply of food and raw materials. Everywhere the *dominante* concentrated the "noble" professions within its walls. Cities were the seat of the skilled trades that produced luxury goods for the wealthy. Their *guilds* regulated production in order to keep standards high. Peasant industry, producing coarse goods for everyday local consumption, resided primarily in the countryside. What made Italy special was its dense network of cities producing luxury goods for all of Europe, situated in a zone from Chieri and Asti in the west, to Vicenza and Venice in the east; from Verona and Como in the north to Naples and Salerno in the south. Luxury industries were *manufactures*; that is, made by hand. Instead of factory workers producing great quantities of standard goods on machines, craftsmen, and to a lesser extent, craftswomen, made them individually in family-based shops employing a handful of apprentices and journeymen. The possession of technical secrets played an important role in the success of a city's manufactures. Goods for a European market had to be outstanding in their design, in the rarity of their raw materials, and the exquisite workmanship, all of which was reflected in the high cost of the article.[17] This concern for quality is understandable in a civilization where people expressed their status through appearance. Each state issued sumptuary laws imposing limits on finery, but prohibitions were not often successful. One means of displaying ambition, success, taste and dignity was to dress like one's superiors, in the "Spanish" fashion of dark fabrics, close-fitting vests, padded hose, short capes and high collars.

City guilds inspected the level of expertise of the workers and monitored new admissions to the trade. They determined the entire manufacturing process; which products to make, the raw materials used, the procedures to follow, the duties of the masters and the journeymen, the duration of the working day. They fixed the wages of the workers, the price of the article, and often channelled its distribution too.[18] Guilds sought to implement a certain culture of work in which cooperation prevailed over competition.[19] Many ran their own benefit schemes for their members. In Venice guildsmen moved easily from producing into retail, and the boundary between the two activities was not always clear.[20] There were so many guilds in the lagoon city, about 120, that it was impossible for a cartel of patricians to control them and impose hard bargains.[21]

Venice was possibly the most industrial city of all Europe, but most of it was of fairly recent creation. The city's population of workers was considerable: about 3,000 toiled in the *Arsenal*, 10,000 more worked wool and silk, in addition to the stonemasons, canal dredgers, fullers of cloth, millworkers, the glassmakers of Murano, those employed in the sugar refineries, leatherworkers, coppersmiths, blacksmiths and goldsmiths, and hundreds more in the new printing industry, of which Venice was Europe's largest centre. Venice claimed a whole range of luxury manufactures for itself, such as wax, soap, sugar-refining and, above all, glass and mirror manufacture for which it is still famous. Venetian artisans developed lead crystal around 1480, and then plate glass for mirrors. Sixteenth-century growth proved a great stimulus to manufactures, whose unit cost relative to food tended to decline. Venice's medium-quality products used second-grade Spanish and Neapolitan wool, worked to the tastes of the Levant. Many wool-workers earned 144 ducats annually, equivalent to the income of petty nobility in central Italy, although the cost of living in Venice was one of the highest in Europe.[22] Only continual rural immigration kept labour costs down, although this was more the case of unskilled labour rather than the skilled craftsmen. Food costs in Italian cities constituted a floor on wages. Urban and state taxes on exports also tended to inflate manufacturing costs. As long as the international economy remained buoyant, and consumers preferred high quality over considerations of cost, this was not a problem.

Venetian rectors watched over the Terraferma manufactures closely. Territorial states subjected the cities in their dominion to regulations protecting the advantages of the capital, sometimes to obtain the most efficient distribution of tasks. Entrepreneurs in subject cities were forced by law to buy their raw materials in Venice, even when they could buy them more cheaply elsewhere. There was continual tension between the *dominante* and the subject cities over the production of wide and narrow woollen cloth, silks, cottons and linens. Woollens suffered competition from England and Holland as consumer tastes passed from a preference for heavy, high-grade broadcloth (*panno alto*) made of fine carded wools, to new worsted textiles produced in different colours and patterns. As the woollens sector declined, Venice converted to luxury silks. Arabs brought silk-worm-raising to Sicily in the eleventh century, and by 1500 Tuscany, the Veneto, Piedmont and Lombardy were all silk-producing regions. By 1600 the urban and rural middle classes also began to wear silk, as technical innovations made it accessible. We find the first "factories", around Bologna at the end of the sixteenth century, powered by water-mills, employing hundreds of women and children producing silk thread.[23] To Venice went the monopoly on exquisite silk brocades and damasks; Vicenza and other subject cities produced lower-grade silks.

The Venetian *Arsenal* was Europe's largest industrial complex in 1600. Its docks, storage sheds, workshops and yards for laying keels and building up hulls employed 4,000 craftsmen and labourers at its peak.[24] It pioneered the line-production system, whereby teams of workers built standard components of vessels, and then assembled them later. Under a hundred technical and supervisory managers, and under close scrutiny of the Senate, teams of shipbuilders could assemble a galley hull in a single day. Workers there enjoyed lifetime jobs and benefits for their families, such as preferred employment, and invalid workers and widows benefited from pensions.

Milan and the cities surrounding it, such as Cremona, Pavia, Como and Lodi formed the hub of the most active manufacturing pole in Europe. Lombard cities produced silk, fine woollen cloths, "fustians", or blends of cotton and wool, ceramics, soap and paper, and leather goods of high quality. Milan also manufactured arms and armour of fine steel, and decorated, chiselled armour for parades and tournaments. The endless wars of the king of Spain stimulated production of muskets, arquebuses, pistols and cannon.[25] Nearby Brescia in Venetian territory produced firearms as well. At its height, the sector boasted 200 arms workshops, each employing several workers. Others toiled at the ovens, the forges and the water-wheels; while others extracted ore from the mines, and transporters hauled it to smelters.[26] Domenico Sella attributes the success of Lombard manufactures abroad (in France particularly) to the pioneering development of superior techniques that foreigners found difficult to imitate. Alongside the urban manufactures, peasants toiled at handicraft industries, often to compensate for the poor soil.

Paper-making was located along water-courses near wooded areas. The production of low-quality woollens and cotton and linen weaving occupied peasant households north of Milan. Textile towns thrived around the central and western Po valley outside Spanish control. Chieri, near Turin, was "rich in work". Peasants with plots of land too small to be viable helped to produce the cotton "fustians" exported to France in large quantity. The city guild members tended to be merchants who parcelled out work to over a thousand weavers, who toiled at home with their families.[27] In Mantua, as one textile production waned, another rose to take its place. Knitting work reached peak activity about 1565, after which silk looms took its place. Needleworking occupied ever more hands until 1615, although it too gradually moved to the rural zones. There was no overall decline in manufacturing until the catastrophes of the late 1620s wrecked both urban industry and the "putting-out system".[28]

Urban economies tended to function best in the larger states, with ample hinterlands or easy access to foreign markets, but few large cities in northern Italy lacked manufactures for export. Genoa established its own manufactures in the fifteenth century. Silk weaving was almost entirely confined to the city, where there were about 250 silk entrepreneurs, with 15,000 weavers among the city's 50,000 inhabitants in 1575. Women, who were not guild members, produced the thread in rural Liguria. They unwound the cocoons, combed them and spun them, selling them back to the urban merchants who controlled the commerce. Northern Tuscany also possessed a cluster of manufacturing towns and cities producing a range of articles. There was a diversified mountain industry, based on iron mines and foundries, paper works and sawmills working from water power.[29] The hubbub produced by looms and forges in northern Tuscany stimulated commerce of all kinds. Most Tuscans wore woollen garments woven on small-town looms using low-grade domestic wool. In the district of Prato, which has always been a busy textile town, one family in four owned a loom. Florence's fine woollen industry produced a record 30,000 pieces in the 1570s and perhaps more than half the city's population of 60,000 drew income from it. The merchant-entrepreneur distributed fine Spanish and Apulian wool to peasants who produced the yarn. Fulling, carding and spinning thread were the only activities allowed to go on outside the city. Finished cloths were exported to France, Spain, the Levant, and later to Rome and southern Italy. As the woollen cloth industry stagnated and declined after 1600, Florentine capitalists converted to silk production, sustained by the continual spread of mulberry planting and cultivation. Cosimo I issued many regulations on the quality, prices and distribution of goods manufactured in Tuscany. Grand Duke Ferdinando I, who wished to compensate Pisa for its loss of independence, established silk-weaving there too, albeit of lower quality so as not to compete with Florentine workshops. This was typical of *mercantilist* legislation which saw competition as a waste of precious resources and energies. In an era of poor communications and weak infrastructure, it was considered better for the state to organize production and distribution. The other silk manufacturing city was Lucca, whose patricians frequented Antwerp, Lyons, Augsburg, Nuremberg and Cracow. As elsewhere, there was considerable concentration in the industry. In 1600, there were about 75 enterprises, but fewer than 10 of them controlled most of the activity.[30] The pieces they produced were of very high quality, and the guilds punished those who tampered with the finished product to lower production costs. Artisans were always willing to cut corners, to make it cheaper, but the merchants who commissioned the work and who commercialized the product were on the lookout for such practices.

Guilds everywhere actively inhibited competition, and prevented master artisans from having more than one shop. Master weavers located their shop on the ground floor, and lived with their family, apprentices and helpers in rooms rented above it. A silk loom and its harness cost the equivalent of a year or two of steady work, that a weaver often acquired in his wife's dowry. Artisans rarely worked to full capacity, and depended upon a merchant who supplied them with the thread. The master weavers enjoyed the highest status and standard of living. Apprentices received only food, lodging and clothing during the years they acquired their trade. Other workers gravitated around the masters for a couple of scudi every month, when there was work. In Chieri, where two-thirds of the weavers were peasants also, children began to work the loom when aged about 10 to 12. Marriage allowed the weavers to diversify their activity, buy some land, and save some money for their old age. Not many weavers were still active after the age of 45, save a small percentage of those who became masters.[31] Giovanni Vigo has attempted to calculate the living standards of workers in quantities of bread they could purchase with their wages. Their purchasing power dropped considerably from the 1520s to the 1590s, and stabilized thereafter.[32] Merchants often forced workers to accept merchandise from their store as part of their remuneration, notwithstanding regulations to the contrary.

The kingdom of Naples produced a wide array of objects: leather for shoes, boots, saddles and harnesses for military and domestic use. Industrial establishments existed in the mountains wherever there was water. Woollen-spinning and dyeing expanded in Naples and in Salerno, fed by fleece from Apulia. Calabrians raised silkworms, spun and sometimes wove silk into lower-quality velvets in Cosenza and Catanzaro, before sending them to Naples for finishing. Work like this was the mainstay of the region's commercial economy. The output of the silk industry doubled until 1620, and Naples was still considered a strong competitor in 1640. Naples produced a broad range of luxury goods: laces, braids, frills, trimmings, light fabrics, fine linens in addition to the silk cloths sold across Europe. The dynamic textile economy tended to stimulate other sectors. An expanding urban population and the urbanization of the aristocracy were powerful stimuli for the construction sector. Pressure on nobles to compete stimulated a whole range of manufactures, from fine furniture to musical instruments, where Italy still led Europe.

Making Money

Commerce created industry. The profits of both produced enough money to make money-dealing an activity in its own right, although entrepreneurs often combined all three activities. Before the nineteenth century, "real" money contained some quantity of precious metal. The cheaper, smaller coins of feeble value wore down in usage, making them easy to counterfeit.[33] Good coins were relatively rare and were usually reserved for wholesale business and international exchange. Merchants who had ready access to them held an advantage over their competitors and were able to avoid long delays or cumbersome operations in order to acquire them. Moreover, there were two precious metals, gold and silver, and the value of each relative to the other fluctuated constantly. The different national units of currency (Venetian ducats, Neapolitan ducats, Roman scudi, Florentine florins, Piedmontese lire) were not expressed in coins of that designation. Rather, mints struck many different coins representing odd fractions of those amounts. Money changers, who attended fairs with their little weighing scales, knew the metallic content in a specific coin. One way to circumvent the scarcity of good coin was to pay one's debts with paper, a bill of exchange that the recipient signed and could sell to a third party as an instrument of credit. Bills of exchange circulated widely along with other fiduciary papers, allowing merchants to make purchases in distant locales without transporting specie.

The sixteenth-century world underwent what has been called a "price revolution", a long period of steady inflation from 1500 to about 1630, stoked by the massive arrival of silver from the Potosì mines in Spanish Bolivia after 1560. Silver lubricated commercial life everywhere, and greater availability of coin also served to stimulate credit transactions. Price increases undermined any dues, tariffs, taxes or rents that were expressed in a fixed amount of money. Inflation of 4 to 5 per cent annually discouraged *thesaurization*, that is, the accumulation of a treasure of good coinage. Inflation forced individuals to keep most of their assets active in order to avoid them losing value over time.

Moneyed people confided their fortune to bankers, who borrowed coin and paid interest on it before restoring the principal. The Catholic Church condemned lending money for interest, which it called usury, but it tolerated the practice. People of all classes needed credit on occasion, and sometimes they paid dearly for it. In Chieri, a wide variety of lenders practised usurious interest rates of up to 50 per cent per annum. Jews were the most notorious of them, but were not the most frequent. Usury often took the form of short-term loans on food to peasants in the critical weeks before the harvest.[34] Unlike usurers, public bankers were city notables who accepted deposits in addition to lending. At Venice bankers set up their tables in the open air on the Rialto, near the Doge's palace, where they helped fix interest rates on public loans. Court financiers lent money to princes for their wars, their buildings or their marriages. It was a risky business, and private bankers frequently collapsed and sought shelter in debtors' prisons. Public banks multiplied after 1580, when the *Banco di San Giorgio* in Genoa resumed common banking functions. Between 1587 and 1593 others appeared at Messina, Venice, Milan, Rome and Naples. Banks were already taking over the administration of indirect taxation, that is, the purchase and distribution of monopoly items, auctioned off by governments for periods of up to nine years. The papal government instituted a series of loans using the *Monte di Pietà* as collateral. The bonds it issued bore interest paid out of general tax revenues. The shares, or *luoghi di Monte*, brought annual returns to their holders.

They were usually sold to a bank, or to a syndicate of bankers, who in turn distributed them retail. The rate of interest fluctuated occasionally and the shares gained or lost value according to the laws of supply and demand. The popes also allowed select noble families to issue bonds in their own names. These developments constituted a revolution in sixteenth-century money markets, as states learned to use credit on an unprecedented scale.[35] The stable Venetian republic had no trouble emitting public bonds worth millions of ducats, snapped up at 6 per cent tax-free interest. There were two ways to invest: by buying bonds, the interest of which was payable at fixed dates, or by purchasing the revenues of tax offices. The latter was widely practised by Spain, and since the income derived from the offices was often unpredictable, they required some expertise on the part of investors.

The real specialists of finance were the Genoese, who dominated international banking from the decline of Antwerp around 1550 until after 1620. The Spanish crown forbade the free export of specie from Castile. But even with this bullion, which amounted to about 200,000 kg annually after 1580, Spain needed financiers with access to private money.[36] The Genoese were the best-placed bankers from the time they joined the Spanish alliance in 1528, and they worked hard to consolidate their position thereafter.[37] Genoese expertise made them fearsome competitors for *asientos*. These were money transactions between the Spanish monarch and businessmen who advanced provisions or services to the crown in exchange for profits that were stipulated in the contract.[38] By 1600, the Genoese were lending hundreds of thousands or millions of scudi in a single operation. Because of their influence at Madrid, Naples and Milan, wealthy individuals all over Italy and Spain were keen to place their own money with Genoese financiers. They were experts in the working of gabelles and the administration of public entities in both Iberia and Italy. Much of the precious silver coin they smuggled out of Spain in galleys and cargo ships headed for Italy. Merchants also took goods to Spain in order to acquire specie. They inserted clauses into *asiento* contracts permitting them to export currency equal to the amount of their loans. Specie left Spain for Naples, Palermo and Genoa in millions of ducats per shipment, along with huge sums in bills of exchange to be drawn on Genoese merchants. Venice used Spanish silver in its payments to Turkey and the Levant, provoking a price rise there that was simultaneous to the one in Europe. Italy was the centre of a great traffic in precious metals and bills of exchange, organized by Genoese capitalists. Since real, sound metallic money was at a premium, they lent it at more advantageous rates of interest than did anyone else. Theirs was mobile capital, a bit like the petrodollars or "hot money" of modern times, which moves from place to place seeking the best advantages. Spain was only one outlet. Bankers bought bonds in Rome, Florence, Venice and elsewhere to diversify their holdings. They sought to diversify from public finance as well, since the interest rate declined from 5.5 per cent around 1550 to about 2 per cent in 1620, when Italy was awash with capital seeking worthwhile investments.

There were two instruments of financial business. The first was currency exchange itself. Businessmen met in fairs dedicated exclusively to exchange operations for the whole of Europe. These first took place at Besançon in Franche-Comté, but they moved to Piacenza soon after. Exchange fairs were held four times a year and functioned according to regulations decreed by the Genoese senate, which resolved disputes. The principal protagonists were a few dozen bankers, great merchants or their agents who came from Genoa, Milan, Florence and Lucca to determine the exchange requirements of their own companies and those they represented. They fixed the official exchange rates. The fairs observed a money of account established on a gold standard. Alongside the principal bankers were exchange merchants or money-changers who followed the fairs and presented their books. Other firms sent brokers to arrange international payments. In all there were about two hundred participants. The transactions involved a series of cancellations or compensatory payments where assets and debits were redistributed in the group. Any leftover sums which could not be reallocated there were to be paid in gold, but the creditor often accepted an extension of credit until the next fair. These operations reached their peak in about 1600 or 1610, when the sums changed amounted to between 40 and 50 million scudi, equivalent to the tax revenues of Spain, France, England and Italy combined![39]

The second financial activity was the *asiento*, which was a contract with multiple clauses drawn up between the government of Castile and a consortium of businessmen usually headed by a Genoese financier. The *asiento* was usually a short-term loan, repaid from the bullion arriving in Seville, or some other revenue. These loans met current expenditures of government, or entailed transfer of money to other places. In case they were not repaid, they could be transformed into long-term bonds. Their clauses usually included the right to export specie from Seville, or fixed high rates of interest on unpaid balances after the contract's term. *Asientos* enabled bankers to rake in savings available on the major trading places in Europe and to unite huge amounts of lending capital.[40]

The quickening pace of economic exchange and the busy manufactures of the sixteenth century produced vast new wealth in Italy. The limits of the system lay in the strategic overreach of the Catholic king, whose wars against numerous enemies required him to draw upon credit as never before. Spanish bankruptcies in 1559, 1608 and 1627 (amongst others) shook the banking houses hard, although they usually recovered their money in hidden ways. Nevertheless, the appeal of public finance proved irresistible as the king of Spain, the popes and other states offered rates of interest that were higher than the profits financiers could derive from trade and manufactures. Historians have considered this kind of investment a net drain on the economy, since expenditure on war was hardly a productive investment, but Luciano Pezzolo considers this too simplistic, because good alternatives were not always available. It was increasingly difficult to place money advantageously in an economy with a high manufacturing output and a monetary flow already the most intense in Europe. Competition from northern Europe, where prices and wages were much lower than in urban Italy, began to make inroads on the Italians' market share. Italian detachment from industry has been criticized by economic historians as short-sightedness. However, there was no way that Genoese, Venetian or Florentine capitalists in their "mature" economy could have guessed that there would be an industrial revolution two hundred years later. A capitalist's aim was to make a profit, and he was not tied to a specific economic sector. Moving from one sector to another which showed more promise was a sign of flexibility, not sclerosis. Only one sector showed more promise than government finance at the end of the sixteenth century, and that was agriculture.

7 Feeding the Cities

Producing from the Land

Most Italians lived in rural communities, scraping a meagre living from the soil. Travellers were struck by the intensity of cultivation in the vicinity of the towns, where urban dwellers possessed patches of land cultivated by gardeners.[1] Suburban "farming" produced delicacies for affluent city-dwellers, and experimenters introduced and acclimatized exotic plants like tomatoes. This variety sometimes deceived foreigners into thinking that Italy was a land of plenty. In fact, what struck most northern Europeans, more corpulent meat-eaters, was the frugality of diets.[2]

The mechanics of food production differed little from other European countries. European diets were based on carbohydrates delivered in the form of cereals, supplemented by animal proteins in the form of cheese and meat. The quantity of meat one ate was largely determined by social status. Aristocrats consumed the most animal proteins, while village and town notables bought more sparingly from butcher-stalls and *pizzicherie*, or delicatessens. Rural labourers and shepherds ate meat only rarely, even though animal husbandry was their chief occupation. Early modern Italians ate bread above all else. Citizens ate a white bread of wheat flour, in addition to modest quantities of pasta. Wheat was the most nourishing cereal, but it was unsuitable for rugged climates or poor soils. A biennial rotation, where wheatfields were left fallow for a year before being replanted, underlay the low productivity. Hardier and

91

less nutritious cereals like rye, millet, barley, sorghum and oats were secondary crops, and the bread of peasants was usually a dark mixture of wheat flour with other ingredients. Protein-rich leguminous vegetables like beans, peas, lentils and chick peas could also be dried and stored. Chestnuts were a peasant staple, either dried and ground into flour that could be baked into a heavy loaf or cooked like porridge as *polenta*. The tree provided food, wood, and the dried leaves served as fodder for animals. All of these were collected every autumn.[3]

We know little about those peasants who lived in virtual autarky. No village, and no family lived entirely outside the realm of commerce and exchange. Salt brought even the most isolated rustics to the local town, and its market square. Peasants were blacksmiths, coopers, joiners, wheelwrights, shoemakers and woodcutters when they were not in the fields.[4] In Montaldeo, on the hilly confines of Liguria, peasants worked mostly for their own consumption, with hoes and shovels that city-dwellers identified with menial status. Local yields were only half those obtained in the nearby plain of Alessandria, generally 2.5 grains for each seed, but there were considerable fluctuations and the return was often less. Peasant bread included at least a third of flour obtained from legumes and beans, whose yields were also low, about 2 to 3 for every grain, compared to modern yields of 10 or more.[5] In the hills around Montaldeo subsisted the peasants' various livestock. Few could afford oxen, a pair of which cost a fortune, but many owned a donkey, a pig and some sheep or goats. Giorgio Doria has calculated that they ate only about a quarter the amount modern stock eat, and lived in constant hunger, often sterile from malnourishment. On a diet of chestnut leaves, the average sheep yielded only 2.6 kilograms of wool annually, and a mere 20 litres of milk, enough to make 3 kilograms of ripe cheese. Hens raised for their eggs scrounged what they could; their average weight did not reach 1 kilogram. The meat animal was the pig, prized for its choicest part, the lard.

Everywhere in Europe, the law distinguished between ownership of land and access to it. Villagers in Montaldeo enjoyed gleaning and grazing rights on common lands and harvested fields that were essential for their survival. These rights were often restricted to those families residing in the jurisdiction for many years.[6] Peasants placed great pressure on the surrounding *coppice* woods to feed themselves and their livestock, and to produce charcoal. Much of the deforested land they replanted in vines, the only cash crop suitable to the area.

Not possessing grape presses, many peasants sold their harvest to the baron, and contented themselves with watered wine or *vinello* for their own consumption. Famine was a constant nightmare. Hungry peasants could not work the fields energetically, and the earth yielded less food to them. In bad years peasants ate acorns to survive.[7] They badgered the lord's agents to loan them seed, and hinted that they would steal what he would not give them. In Montaldeo, nine out of ten people had to work for others, or were constrained to migrate temporarily to seek work. Almost all the men devoted three or four weeks a year harvesting and threshing grain in the Po valley, which provided a few weeks' income. Landlords hired women too, to gather forage, rake manure, bind and fertilize the vines, pick grapes, make faggots and collect leaves and straw for animal stalls.

Montaldeo seems typical of mountain communities away from axes of communication. Montaigne was amazed at Bagni di Lucca where vines and chestnut groves seemed to extend to the mountain tops, planted on *terraces*, to which earth was carried up in small baskets and banked with stone retaining walls. These steps up the mountainside required continual, backbreaking maintenance against erosion. Mountains also furnished grassy summer pasture for livestock, and their forests supported woodcutters and timber merchants. Lower slopes not subject to frosts could be planted with olive trees or mulberry bushes for silkworm-raising. Valley bottoms yielded rye, beans, squash, cabbage and other vegetables alongside hardy fruit and nuts. The mountains therefore sustained a dense population by balancing fieldcrops, tree cultures and grazing, but regularly forced their manpower down towards the plains in search of work and money.

Economic historians commonly invoke the Anglican clergyman Thomas Malthus, who smugly predicted that populations unable to control their reproductive instincts would be subject to famines, epidemics and wars that would brutally reduce numbers to the level that the economy could sustain. Following the demographic catastrophe of the Black Death and its aftermath, the commercial economy soared after 1450 and the population rose with it. Despite archaic techniques of food production, Italy as a whole in 1595 contained 44 persons per square kilometre, the densest population in Europe. Fertile France supported 34 persons per square kilometre; Spain and Portugal only supported 17.

Esther Boserup has recently challenged the pessimistic Malthusian

view, arguing that population growth forces people to find new techniques to produce food.[8] Noblemen, merchants, wealthy artisans,
monks and nuns owning the land required the services of peasant
families to produce the harvest, in exchange for a portion of it. This
reflex of hiring peasants to work the land extended down to the
village level too, where widows or elderly peasants hired neighbours
where kin were not available. Peasants worked the land under different kinds of contracts, the main one being *emphiteusis*, by which
they paid a fixed annual rent in kind over generations. Prime commercial land was almost invariably owned by a wealthy town-dweller.
Over much of north-central Italy, landlords replaced the *livello* or
emphyteusis contract with the *mezzadria*, or sharecropping agreement.
In Emilia, after 1550, peasant families began to plant vines, elms and
mulberry bushes in widely separated rows in the fields, in a pattern
of *promiscuous culture*.[9] This raised ground temperature by several
degrees in winter, and sheltered the cereals or legumes from the
sweltering summer sun. It was also an excellent protection against
erosion. *Mezzadria* polyculture allowed the peasantry to work the
land more intensively and for a longer period of the year. In fall the
peasants ploughed and planted, harvested grapes and olives, and
pressed them for their oil and wine. In winter they pruned the vines
and trees, shovelled the earth, sowed the winter wheat, beans, peas
and vetch, dug ditches and bordered the fields. In spring they
seeded the fields with grasses, weeded the cereals, raised silkworms
and sowed hemp seed. In summer it was time to harvest the grain
and dry it, separating the kernels from the chaff. The vines required
attention for most of the year.[10] With cheese being a staple in rural
diets, animal husbandry was an important sideline for all regions,
the poor pastures notwithstanding.[11] At Finale Emilia promiscuous
culture occupied only 6 per cent of the useful surface in 1574, but
fully 62 per cent in 1610. Population density in this part of the Po
valley, already a crowded 60 peolpe per square kilometre in 1550,
rose to 120 in 1610. *Mezzadria* spread in Umbria simultaneously.[12]
This more intensive culture was everywhere a product of urban
demand, and eventually resulted in the urban expropriation of the
peasantry.

Promiscuous culture and *mezzadria* became the dominant form of
rural exploitation from the Veneto and Emilia to Tuscany, Umbria
and the Marches, and endured until the appearance of the tractor.[13]
Landlords allotted a farmstead, or *podere*, providing virtual self-suffi-
ciency to an individual family. Sharecropping pacts required the

peasant householder to live on that land, maintain drainage and irrigation ditches, harvest the grapes and olives, and keep the house in
repair. The landlord lent the seed and livestock and the family provided the labour; the crop was then divided between them.[14] One is
struck by the extreme variety of a *podere*'s production: wheat, wine,
oil, beans, barley, oats, spelt, chick peas, green beans, vetch, lupin,
lentils, flax, hemp, saffron, and a whole range of beekeeping, fowl
and livestock produce. Tree crops included mulberry bushes,
almonds, chestnuts, figs, olives and fruit trees, whose planting and
maintenance were costly undertakings. Elm trees provided wood for
tools and leaves for forage, and their branches could be pruned
without much damage. Acorns and oak leaves in the adjoining scrub
were forage for pigs. The sharecropper sometimes took on larger
flocks of sheep under a separate pact. Their wool was generally poor
– used for peasant homespun – but the lambs and milk were an
important source of income. Pigeons gave high-grade manure for
industrial crops like hemp and flax. The house was usually a substantial building of brick or stone, with a room and a loom for spinning,
an oven for treating flax, another for baking bread, and a wine
cellar, as well as quarters for animals on the ground floor or in separate stalls, with a threshing floor nearby. The family produced wine
and oil, extracted saffron, treated silkworm cocoons, or macerated
hemp to separate the fibres, spun them into thread and wove them
into rough cloth. What could not be processed on the *podere* was
taken to a *fattoria*, which was a large estate capable of transforming
and storing the produce of the *poderi* depending on it.

The *mezzadria* contract could be harsh, and the increasing detail in
their clauses was a sign of the declining status of peasants.
Sharecroppers were forbidden to work off the *podere*, or take its oxen
to work elsewhere, or take on other livestock not owned by the landlord. They were not to cut any wood, or sell anything without permission. They had to supply chickens and eggs on holidays, help in
hauling and carting produce and materials, or help stonemasons
undertake repair and construction work without pay. The landlord
or his estate agent arrived punctually at each critical moment of the
harvest. Each side eyed the other warily as they tallied up their
respective portions, for the contract was rarely generous. The size of
the *podere* was not always ideal from the peasant family's perspective
and they frequently went into debt to the landlord. Some future
study of rural debt based on the seizures by bailiffs in the homes of
sharecroppers will shed better light on these relations. One should

not exaggerate the tensions, for landlords, too, were saddled with credits they could not collect, and forgiving such debts was a frequent clause in their testaments.[15] The system was remarkably stable. It ensured the survival of the peasant family, fixed it to the land, and turned peasants into a class of semi-independent farmers with multiple skills.

The Business of Agriculture

No sector of the economy was as important as agriculture, and no issue attracted as much continuous government attention as the supply of affordable grain to the cities. The grain trade was the foremost sector in every European country before 1850, with the largest numbers of buyers and sellers. Not all were on an equal footing. Small producers usually sold their surplus at the moment of harvest, when the price was low. Prices rose slowly over the winter, as reserves were used up. The well-to-do could wait until the spring to release their stocks, when prices were much higher. This market mechanism maximized the advantages of the wealthy over the long term.

Producing grain on a large scale could be extremely lucrative in the sixteenth century. With inflation and population growth, the price of grain climbed relentlessly and more quickly than the wages of most workers. Landlords sought ways of producing grain efficiently for urban markets.[16] Direct exploitation, in which superintendents hired labourers daily, was profitable close to a large city. In Lombardy commercial farms fed the great cities and adjacent regions, such as Switzerland, while supporting simultaneously a rural population of a hundred persons per square kilometre. Helping hands spilled out from the mountains at every harvest, for wheat takes four additional days to ripen for every 100 metres of elevation. Mountain-dwellers had time to work the fields in the lower plain, and return home to harvest their own tiny plots. At Soncino, near Cremona in fertile Lombardy, only 1 per cent of the land was uncultivated in 1600. Irrigation there made for abundant pasture, and hay was mowed three or four times a year from the meadows. This made it possible to feed numerous livestock that produced both cheese and manure. Crop rotation eliminated the need for fallow.[17]

Landlords sought to produce a large surplus while employing few men. The Tuscan Maremma and the Roman Campagna were empty zones owned by city nobles, where tens of thousands of labourers, organized in armed companies resembling militiamen on the march, descended from the hills to plant and harvest grain. Most lived in straw huts and bought their food from taverns. Their earnings were dearly bought, for a large portion of them fell sick from malaria, and many died.

Cereal culture was practically the only "industry" in regions like Basilicata and Apulia.[18] Conditions there were radically different from central and northern Italy. Wherever heavy clay soils predominated, *latifundia* flourished, for only large landowners could afford to feed the powerful oxen that ploughed the fields.[19] Peasants lived grouped in "proletarian dormitories" (Labrot) of the *agrotowns* for protection and sociability, and spent hours daily walking to the fields, just as women could walk for hours with clay jugs on their heads to fetch water. Peasant property often consisted of simple gardens near their rudimentary houses. Large "food factories" called *massarie*, contained magazines and warehouses for grain, oil and wine, with pens for livestock. Stout walls often surrounded these *massarie* as protection from bandits. Few peasants lived there. Superintendents managed an extensive cereal culture that could be expanded or curtailed by hiring or laying off labourers. In Sicily landlords extended the planted surfaces at the expense of vines and olives. From 1583 to 1653, barons created 88 new villages, conceding franchises and privileges to attract inhabitants there.[20] These estates still lacked water and infrastructure like roads. The scrub nourished considerable numbers of sheep that descended annually in transhumance from the mountains. The entire system was characterized by low productivity, even by the techniques of the period. The feudatory and his men controlled directly 20 or 30 per cent of the production on their fiefs, a larger proportion than most landlords claimed anywhere.[21] Seigneurs often exploited their tenants with tolls and taxes, and brutalized indocile individuals. Peasants were not attached "amicably" to the land like the *mezzadria* family. They were hired hands needed to grow grain, not gardeners and vintners skilled in agriculture. Nor were they aided by a resident local nobility, whose measured agromania gave a certain dynamism to the local economy, as in central Italy.[22]

Sicily's grain fed much of the Mediterranean. It has been described as "the Canada or the Argentina of the Mediterranean world" (Braudel) for its ability to produce substantial surpluses every year.[23] At most, these exports equalled the annual consumption of about 200,000 people, or less than 2 per cent of the population of

Italy.[24] Nevertheless, it represented a much larger portion of the wheat which cities consumed. As long as they could afford to import it – until about 1620 – the entire Sicilian economy remained buoyant, fuelling an extraordinary building boom of palaces, churches, fortifications and public works all over the island.

Large-scale production in the Mezzogiorno and Sicily usually entailed a pact between a "farmer" (often a merchant or official with administrative competence) and a noble landlord. At Melfi in the Basilicata, the Genoese Doria family rented out its land to numerous farmers large and small, in exchange for about 10 per cent of the crop. This was not the full extent of their agricultural revenue, since the lords extracted considerable income from feudal and pasture rights.[25] Anyone who wished to produce for the market needed at least two expensive oxen (worth the annual wages of several men, and expensive to feed), a heavy plough, tools, seed and money to pay employees. Grain production required a lot of labour. Once it was harvested, it was necessary to beat the grains with a flail or crush them to detach the husk; then to air them every two weeks, sift them every month, and finally take them to mills to grind into flour. Few farmers were wealthy enough to pay all their costs in advance, and they usually borrowed money. If the demand for grain remained strong, these entrepreneurs could make a fortune. Should there still be a surplus from preceding years, or an economic slump with low prices, or if interest rates were too high, the loss could be just as significant. Governments intervened during harvest shortfalls, when farmers could make a killing, to prevent the price of grain from reaching levels it judged too high. Provisioning magistrates broke speculation by seizing reserves of grain in storehouses and attics and selling it at low prices. Given the unpredictability of harvests, many landlords preferred to convert to livestock-raising which was less labour-intensive and less dependent upon good weather or political interference. Such was the case around Rome after the 1570s, where the region ceased entirely to export grain by the 1570s, and reverted to grazing land.[26]

Stimulated by both population growth and the development of manufactures, the pastoral economy flourished. Every community reserved part of its commons for grazing local livestock, the *bandite*, which it could apportion to every household, or rent to notables in larger parcels.[27] At Foggia a variant of capitalist agriculture produced meat, wool and wheat. King Alfonso reorganized the traditional transhumance between the Abruzzi and Apulia on fiscal lines in the 1440s. The Dogana of Foggia rented winter pasture in the Tavoliere plain to sheepowners. A vast network of compulsory sheep-walks from the Abruzzi, Basilicata and Molise converged on the zone to speed the arrival of over a million sheep and 6,000 shepherds every autumn.[28] These avenues had connecting tracks and side pastures along the way, like great parking lots, to sustain the sheep *en route*. Foggia was the obligatory point of sale for the cheese, wool, hides and meat, on which tax officials levied an array of duties. The Dogana then allocated the land on which the sheep grazed, on a regulated system of rotation, to farmers for six-year periods to produce wheat for Naples. Land enriched by sheep manure produced very high yields (15 grains for 1 seed) that made the zone the kingdom's granary. Pastoralism was an essential part of supplying cities with their sustenance. There were 37,000 individuals owning or herding sheep under the Dogana of Foggia's administration. Families with only 80 sheep or goats could not afford to hire a shepherd to move them down to the plain, so they pooled their flocks. The shepherds themselves appear to have been the most literate category of the peasant population, and sheep-raising on a large scale usually brought a decent return. The shepherds' and grazers' own organization negotiated pasture rights with the Dogana, although the nobility, possessing the largest flocks, enjoyed predominance in it. Important in sheep-raising was the quality of pasture and the amount of water available to the animal. Fleece varied considerably in colour, length, thickness, texture, strength and flexibility. The finer grades from the Spanish merino sheep in the Mezzogiorno fetched high prices. Their wool was the staple of the luxury manufactures in the cities of the north, and after Castile, southern Italy was Europe's largest supplier. Proper flock management kept the sex and age ratios at an optimum. Most of the males were castrated, fattened and then slaughtered for their meat. Competent management of the system was vital to Spanish finance, for the taxes levied on it constituted the largest single slice of the kingdom's revenue. Notwithstanding occasional accidents, the system expanded until about 1620. At 6°C, grass stops growing. Harsh winters could kill sheep by covering the grass with snow, or by retarding its growth. Up to 70 per cent of the stock perished from starvation in 1612 and a similar catastrophe struck again in 1622.

Italy recovered fairly quickly from the great famine of the 1590s and subsequent climatic accidents to reach its previous population of thirteen million inhabitants. That number stagnated at the level of 1600 for another generation. Neither promiscuous culture nor more aggressive commercialization of agriculture could resolve the basic problem: that of insufficient and inelastic food supplies during bad years, which tended to become more frequent as the cooling trend of the climate produced what has been called the "little ice age". Additional agricultural land would have to be reclaimed from steep hillsides and from marshy river beds and shallow lakes. The forest became an object of contention between rich and poor peasants, and between established families with grazing rights and disenfranchised newcomers. Everywhere there was pressure to convert them to grain-producing farms. Plains and marshlands gave much higher yields than hillside plots, provided they were drained. Massive projects reclaimed coastal marshes and lake and river beds in the lower Po valley, and in the Arno and Tiber river basins. Around Venice this *bonification* required hydraulic pumps, dykes, canals, entry points for water, irrigation streams and trenches, and a permanent flotilla of small boats for transport and maintenance, to clear the channels of debris. Huge investments mobilized by consortia of patricians and city governments absorbed much of the profit from trade and manufacture. They were not all successful. Local communities were generally incapable of working in harmony on large projects, and required compulsion by state officials to further the general good. In 1588 Pope Sixtus V established the Congregation of the Waters to organize and oversee these projects in his states. Over 2,000 workers toiled to reclaim part of the Pontine marshes south of Rome in 1586, but heavy rains in 1589 and 1590 wrecked the work.

The impact of the price of grain on the urban poor weighed more heavily on the conscience of rulers than did the interests of the aristocrats, who owned most of the land from which commercial crops were extracted. After all, if famine in the countryside was a tragedy, famine in a large city was a *problem* of major proportions. In Naples the viceroy spent heavily from tax resources to keep the public peace. Princes and magistrates were all landowners themselves, but from a conscientious paternalism and a desire to avoid trouble, they intervened continually to prevent market forces from wreaking the full extent of their negative consequences. Government intervention to block price increases and forbid exports may have prevented growers from reaping the rewards of their risk, and discouraged them from intensifying production that would have ensured more prosperity for all. This is at least the position of liberal economic theory. Their intervention, on the other hand, probably spared the population the apocalyptic famines of the sort that strike modern Africa, or China and India of recent memory. Italian cities presented the greatest array of provisioning systems in Europe, generically referred to as the *annones*. Supplying the city market legitimized the governing class in the eyes of the poor, who measured the stocks and assessed the quality of bread every day.[29] Mechanisms were often complex, for it was necessary to prevent imported grain from doing harm to local suppliers. In time of famine, purchases were arranged by top levels of government, at exorbitant prices. Even if grain arrived too late, at least the government was seen to be doing its utmost to aid famished subjects. High grain prices by themselves were not enough to unleash popular disturbances. It was the hint of speculation or government indifference that provoked an uprising. This was indeed a "moral economy" aiming to maintain the public good, similar to that obtaining in guild manufactures. In Modena every July and August, magistrates issued decrees on grains, forbade their export, and ordered landlords to bring their harvests into the city. During bad years they ordered hoarders to declare their stocks. The decrees notwithstanding, landlords and grain traders hid as much as they dared, and fed contraband, which usually consisted of escorting a grain-laden donkey outside the city's jurisdiction. Official grain prices were always political. The city would discourage speculation by dumping reserves on the market at opportune moments.

Annonary legislation received fresh impetus across Italy from the onset of the famine of 1590–3, the worst subsistence crisis in almost three centuries. In Modena, 5,000 people died in the city and its district, about one person in eight. Dearth became famine when bad weather damaged the grapes and fodder crops, which deprived the population of money to buy grain. In 1593 there was grain available, but the two preceding famine years had drained all the city's cash reserves. In Naples the viceroy simply fixed the price of grain at what he thought the population could accept, but this tended to stop the supply of grain into the city. Landowners and farmers hoarded stocks of grain and waited for prices to climb. In Rome the popes, who had restricted imports from the Marches and Romagna to foster grain production in Latium, suddenly reversed their policy. The difficulty of supply became such that the Papal government took over the provisioning of Rome from the municipal authorities. The curial Congregation of Abundance (the *Abbondanza*) and the finance ministry (Apostolic Chamber) together fixed the price of foodstuffs.[30]

We have good studies on the workings of the Tuscan

mechanisms.[31] The grand dukes permitted exports in the abundant years between 1566 and 1577; from 1591 to 1599 and again from 1604 to 1607. In other years they simply forbade or limited the *tratte* to keep the grain at home. Peasants and landlords were obliged to declare how much grain they planted and harvested. Individuals were prohibited from buying more foodstuffs than were necessary for family consumption. In 1602 Ferdinando I ordered landlords and peasants to contribute 5 per cent of their harvest to public store-houses administered by the magistrates of the *Abbondanza*. These officials could force whoever held reserves to sell them to the com-munity at a low price, and scores of inspectors visited the granaries and the attics of the duchy to estimate available stocks. Paradoxically, when annonary regulations were efficient, the countryside experi-enced worse hunger than did the cities, and famished peasants con-verged on urban charitable institutions.

The *Abbondanza* sent emissaries abroad – to Sicily or France, for example – to buy large quantities of grain. In 1590 the grand duke himself bought grain in Danzig and Amsterdam. Purchasing grain from Poland in times of emergency was a desperate measure. So was the practice of using warships to seize foreign grain ships on the high seas. In Venice, where the needs of the city came before those of the Terraferma, no food could move without government approval. Even though cereal traffic remained in the hands of private merchants, urban markets were never allowed to be "free", and government kept watch over movements of grain until its final sale and consumption.[32] Magistrates protected consumers against fraud by supervising all the stages of fabrication, regulating and stan-dardizing the product. In Bologna, the different kinds of flour, pasta, minor grains and legumes were all regulated. Negotiating with the food guilds, magistrates decreed official prices for beef, mutton, goat, salt and fresh pork, so that consumers might choose among many products. Pork was shared between lower-class favourites such as hams and sausages, and elite consumption of mortadella, "Bologna" sausage and salami, with the respective quantities fixed by decree.[33] Measures like these managed to diminish social tensions.

Land hunger and high food prices destabilized both urban and rural communities. In 1500 peasant diets consisted of bread, meat, milk and cheese, eggs and vegetable soups, relatively rich in proteins and fat. A century later they subsisted on porridges, dark breads and a bit of raw wine. Most of the meat, poultry and cheese produced was sold to city-dwellers to pay new taxes. Deforestation quickly led to a deteriorating environment. In Sicily, avalanches sometimes killed hundreds of people at a time and wrecked the fragile system of roads and tracks that connected the grain producers with the outside world. In the cities new impetus was given to charitable institutions designed to alleviate poverty. But the picture is not all sombre, as peasant marriage contracts and post-mortem inventories are beginning to reveal. If they enjoyed fewer culinary satisfactions, many peasants handled more money than ever before. A full world in 1600 afforded ever more occasions for work at the loom.[34] So Italy was still at the apex of its wealth at the end of the extraordinary sixteenth century.

8 Traditional Catholicism and its Persistence

The Universal Church in Italy

In our times of gradual but sweeping dechristianization it is difficult to imagine the profound importance of religion in early modern civilization. Before the Enlightenment or Darwin there was no clear boundary between the sacred and the profane, the material and the supernatural, the living and the dead. It is not enough to point out that Italians were Christians and Catholics and loyal adherents to the doctrines defined and taught by Rome, for Catholicism accreted beliefs, liturgies and traditions over many centuries. Here I survey the basic structures and doctrines of Catholicism as they preceded and survived the Council of Trent, and also the complex body of beliefs that, although unorthodox, formed part of the "system of the sacred" in Italy. Before commencing, it is worth while to signal some of the basic tenets of Catholic Christianity at the end of the Middle Ages.

Christianity holds that a historical person, Jesus Christ, one of the three "persons" of God, came to earth incarnated as a man, and after he had spread a body of moral and ethical teaching in Palestine, the Roman authorities reluctantly crucified him. His sacrifice redeemed the sins of the people who recognized this suffering by embracing the tenets of the Christian faith. Those who earnestly believed might be admissible to eternal life with God in heaven after their deaths. Meanwhile, the world's destiny unfolded until God decided to end it.

Ecclesiastical tradition held that Christ designated the apostle Peter to found an organized cult with its seat in Rome, where he was martyred. After several centuries of periodic persecution, Christianity became the official religion of the Roman state. Rome and Constantinople each claimed primacy. The bicephalous organization of the religion made schism a *fait accompli*, between a Latin Church under the pope in Rome, and a Greek Church under the patriarch in Constantinople. The spread of Islam in the east placed the Greek Church in a position of inferiority before long. Christianity spread by occupying the sites of pagan devotions, without ceasing to be Christian, for it still focused upon the central theme of a god-man who sacrificed himself to redeem humanity. This sacrifice, the Eucharist, was re-enacted in the liturgical ritual of the mass. By the elevation of the host over the altar, and the pronouncement of the phrase *Hoc est corpus*, the communion wafer became the body of Christ, which believers swallowed. Easter was much more important than Christmas in the religious calendar, although traditional religion focused on God the father, a punisher, more than Christ the son and redeemer. Medieval thought assumed that each individual's destiny would be settled at the moment of their death. An important twelfth-century innovation was the concept of purgatory. Unwilling to admit that the vast majority of humanity would be cast eternally into the fiery pit of hell, theologians postulated that there existed a temporary hell, where sins would be burned off the soul until it was pure, at which point it would gain admittance to heaven. Another central concept was that people could carry the cross for someone else in order to shorten the time the beneficiary spent redeeming their sins in purgatory. Individuals could say prayers or have masses said to this intention for their late kin. Anyone who voluntarily made some sacrifice, earned a "credit" for their own redemption, but they could transfer this benefit to another person or an entire community. This trait of carrying the cross for someone else made Catholic Christianity a helping religion.

The Church's ordained clergy administered a number of "sacraments" that marked one's belonging to the group of believers. The ritual of baptism brought babies into the Christian community at birth, and it gave the newborn a godparent or two who became spiritual kin. The sacrament of confirmation at the onset of adolescence strengthened this sense of belonging. Confession of sins and acts of penance were obligatory purification rites before receiving annual

Easter communion. To be eligible to partake of it, Christians had to make peace with their enemies. The sacrament of marriage was conceived as an alliance of families to bring them into peaceful relations. While families or spouses themselves selected their marriage partners and arranged dowries, the priest enhanced the ceremony's efficacy by blessing the couple at the church door, blessing the ring and the marriage bed. Finally, the sacrament of extreme unction which was administered to the dying, prepared the soul for its journey, possibly to hell, but presumably to the delayed gratification of purgatory.

We speak of the Church as a single monolithic institution, weathering centuries of change from its size and inertia. It was only because Rome was a centralized authority that such an immense institution could retain its cohesion. Since papal elections required a two-thirds majority in a secret vote, it was difficult for outside powers to select their clients. European monarchs found the uninterrupted election of Italians to the head of the Universal Church to be an acceptable compromise, for they rarely took sides in conflicts between Catholic powers. Italy's disadvantage with respect to European States gave it an advantage when governing an international institution.

Cardinals managed the affairs of state and church simultaneously. Candidates to the prelature needed to be noble, to have studied law for five years, and practised it for another five, and have established a substantial income.[1] Sixtus V fixed the number of cardinals at seventy, although there were never that many in Rome, because vacancies might take years to fill, while foreign cardinals did not always reside there. Although more than 60 per cent of the cardinals came from outside the Papal States, a good portion of those came from Tuscany, Genoa, the Po valley duchies or the Veneto, all neutral states. Reaching the cardinalate was usually the reward of a long and fitful journey, as few prelates spent a long time in any one office. Despite some role for talent and application, no one could climb the church hierarchy without the support of relatives or compatriots in higher echelons. Prelates saw their career in the Curia primarily as a political, not a religious one, until they advanced in years and gave more thought to the afterlife. Having a cardinal in the family was an enormous asset. He usually resigned part of his income to his family, who invested it in real estate and bonds that could be passed along to heirs. Cardinals played an important patronage role in Rome and in the territories from which they came.

They served as godparents for their clients, dowered girls and distributed school bursaries to boys, offered legacies to shrines, commissioned artists, intervened in judicial proceedings, and assigned
ecclesiastical benefices and minor offices to their compatriots.[2] But
cardinals did not act differently from kings, princes and barons anywhere else in Europe. Unlike other elites, this one exalted virtues of
self-control, of moderation, of abstinence and piety.

Why appoint legists and "politicians" to head a religious organization designed to secure entry into heaven for the multitudes?
Exceptionally pious men were rarely capable of organizing the salvation of Christians scattered across the globe. The Roman Curia's first
concern was to safeguard the extensive rights of the Church everywhere. Clerics were often exempt from taxation, although northern
Italian states gradually tapped into their private property.[3] Clergy
were exempt from death duties, value-added taxes or government
monopolies, contributions in wartime, or billeting soldiers. They did
not answer to state tribunals, except by the bishop's permission, and
could only be tried by church courts, which were disinclined to shed
blood. Anyone who harmed a cleric could be excommunicated.[4]
Pope Urban VIII set up a Congregation of Immunity in 1624 to
watch over these rights, and Italian princes hesitated to provoke it to
action. Roman power was bolstered by an apostolic nuncio, who
watched over the Church in each of the Italian capitals and served as
a papal ambassador to the prince.

The Church was anything but monolithic, and rivalries festered
among different groups of clerics. There were two clergies, each with
a specific programme.

Secular clergy

Secular clergy were those who lived in their "century", or *secula*; that
is, they lived among laypeople and administered the sacraments to
them. They embraced many different states, from bishops to canons,
to *pievani* (parish priests) and parish curates, to chaplains in
churches at altars and oratories. Not all of them were full-fledged
priests, eligible to celebrate mass. About 40 per cent were unordained clerics, generally titled *abate*. Most secular clerics who
achieved ordination were assigned a *benefice*, a secure revenue
attached to a clerical function, permitting a comfortable standard of
living for the holder. A great many benefices were of lay nomination,

or *giuspatronato.* Families detached part of their property and placed it in their cleric son's name, removing it from state taxation. Many of these entailed no corresponding cure of souls. Powerful families or individuals might nominate priests to benefices, but corporate entities could do so also. Barons sometimes resorted to threats or violence in order to control the nominations. Obtaining a good benefice was often the point of departure for the social rise of a whole family. In the cities they tended to be numerous, along with the endowments for masses and chapels. It was different in the countryside. Priests there were often constrained to alienate their benefice to families or relatives through perpetual leases or unfavourable contracts. Benefices remained in families over generations through the practice of resignation, whereby uncles resigned their position (usually in exchange for a portion of the income, called a pension), and nominated their successor. Bishops' quizzing of these candidates on their qualifications was frequently cavalier and *pro forma.*[5]

The person who watched most closely over the administration of these benefices was the bishop, each in his diocese. Italy had about 315 dioceses in 1600, compared to 130 in France, which was much larger and more heavily populated. Many of these, especially in the centre and south, were small and consisted of only a few dozen parishes or less. The bishop was not everywhere selected by the pope. In Sicily the king of Spain enjoyed such patronage rights by virtue of the *Monarchia Sicula,* and his influence was considerable elsewhere. Bishops confirmed children, consecrated holy oil and church buildings, ordained and tested the clergy, visited parishes, watched against heresy, and reported to Rome. Bishops were also continually issuing licences and dispensations (allowing relatives to marry, or married couples to separate, for example, or for people to eat meat during fast days and Lent), or commending devotions or pilgrimages. Bishops generally did not nominate priests to benefices. Before the introduction of seminaries after 1560 they had little control over the training of their clergy either. Bishops often resided elsewhere than in their cathedral seats, especially the capital cities. In the absence of the bishop, the vicar-general would govern the diocese in his name.

Canons were elite priests with substantial benefices and good family connections, whose chapter administered the property of the cathedral church. This celebrated mass with more pomp than elsewhere, with organs and choirs of professional singers and musicians.

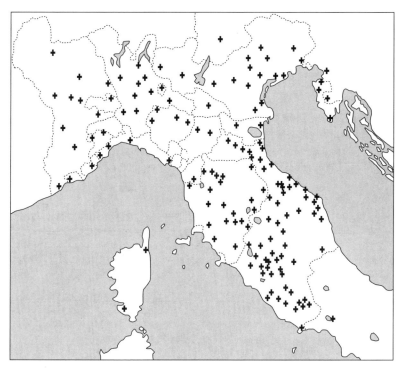

Map 14   Dioceses in north-central Italy, circa *1700*

Large dioceses also contained one or several collegiate churches, large, well-endowed structures whose canons administered the property and the cult. When the bishop died or retired, they took over his function in the interim. Relations between bishops and chapters were often stormy. They argued over who should pay for costly repairs to church buildings, for example, or over the suitability of candidates to benefices. Bishops nevertheless drew from their ranks to help administer their diocese.

Italy was covered by a network of parishes. One medieval survival was the *pieve*, a parish church which dominated nearby parishes by possessing the baptismal font. Parish priests were influential persons who performed rites of supplication and exorcism for laypeople. They were supposed to hold themselves above the infighting that rent every community, withholding communion from embittered parishioners who harboured hate towards a neighbour. They also fulfilled secular tasks, such as drafting wills and marriage contracts,

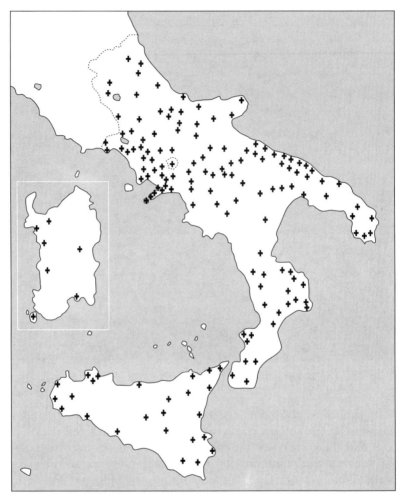

Map 15   Dioceses in southern Italy, circa *1700*

formulating petitions, assessing taxes and treating the sick.[6] Although towns employed a plethora of secular priests, only a fraction was attached to the parishes. Non-residence of the curates was a serious problem in sixteenth-century Italy, as it was in neighbouring countries. Where they did reside, they often did not adhere to canonical requirements. In the mountains of Lombardy, as in rural Sardinia, priests were neither tonsured nor did they wear the cassock, and many of them kept women and sired children. While such customs disappointed bishops, local communities had their own criteria of what constituted a good priest, and they tolerated married or non-celibate priests as long as they did not cause scandal with virgins or married women, and as long as they performed their functions well. Parishioners expected them to reside in the parish, administer baptism and communion, to be moderate in their demands for offerings, and to be available for the problems of their flock.[7] Parishioners were more upset that priests gambled, haunted taverns, practised usury, carried weapons, worked illicit magic, danced and masqueraded during carnival. When parishioners denounced priests to their bishops for keeping concubines it was usually for ignoring the wishes, traditions and standards of their communities.[8]

In the Mezzogiorno almost a third of the parishes were *chiese ricettizie*, communities of secular priests living on a common patrimony, and collectively exercising the cure of souls. Only local sons would be accepted into them, notwithstanding their insufficient preparation for the task. These churches usually enjoyed a wide array of immunities restricting interference from the bishop. Administration of sacraments to parishioners was often delegated to junior members.[9]

Regular Clergy

From very early in the Christian period, the Church encouraged people to seek their salvation and that of others by personal penance, mortification and contemplation. These anchorites were forerunners of a different kind of clergy, who congregated in little communities on the margins of the civilized world and lived according to a rule, the *regula*. By virtue of the rule, monks lived apart from and in opposition to the outside world, century after century. The early regular orders possessed lands and revenues, and they lived a comfortable, contemplative existence in rural abbeys. Popes increased their privileges by extricating monks from the bishops' supervision, and referring them directly to Rome. More clearly an abuse of the original intention of monastic founders, many monasteries were subject to the *commenda* system, by which a powerful absentee patron pocketed most of the revenues and reduced the monastery to an empty shell.

In the thirteenth century, Saint Francis of Assisi renounced the world, gave away his possessions, and cultivated penance in a little hut below the Umbrian city. Not content with the hermitic life, Saint Francis wandered from town to town, exhorting people to abandon their sinful ways and to cultivate poverty. The wealthy medieval Church hesitated a moment, and then embraced the movement by granting it a rule. Preaching friars were usually not priests, and only a portion of them were eligible to say mass, but their sermons had an enormous impact on Catholic towns. Franciscans became the first *mendicant* order, that is, begging friars who depended upon the generosity of the faithful. Over time they competed with the parish clergy for the attention and the alms of parishioners. Their houses were generally not large, with an average of fourteen brothers in each, performing liturgical celebrations, praying in the choir, submitting themselves to ritual mortification, including flagellation, and other ascetic practices, such as extenuating vigils, long silence and frequent fasting. The prayers friars recited had protective and preservative effects and, moreover, most monks distributed talismans in exchange for alms. Monks brought a whole arsenal of spiritual reinforcements to local communities. They also employed many people for their daily welfare.[10] Whatever the revenues of their houses (and in the case of the mendicants, they were often meagre), they devoted part of them to feed the poor.

Nuns worked for the salvation of their neighbours and their families by their prayers. Girls placed there were taught that the outside world was evil, that marriage was disappointing and that husbands were brutes. Convent dowries were certainly more accessible to parents than marriage portions, and those who had several daughters and no sons were hard pressed to establish them all. The age rules and conditions of voluntary entry were not always respected. While there were still nuns living outside walled and cloistered convents in the sixteenth century, the hierarchy considered this an "abuse" of their vocation. Bishops always retained more ample authority over nuns inside and outside the convents than they did over male regulars.[11] The intellectual training of nuns was generally less strict than that of the monks, and they were not universally literate, even if well-born. Usually it sufficed for the nuns to memorize their breviary, obey the abbesses and pass on their traditional devotions. The collective recital of sacred dramas made the female convents the depository of medieval lore. Nevertheless, what feminine learned culture existed, flourished in these convents. Nuns were also musicians and singers, who gave pomp to the mass on feast days and attracted a distinguished audience.[12]

One would misrepresent Catholic religiosity if one dwelled strictly and exclusively on the role of the clergy, who often mediated a demand for the sacred that swelled from below. Stressing the cleric's point of view often unduly intellectualizes religious life, and modern historians are apt to depict early modern religion in almost rationalistic terms. Religion was an affair of "devotion", which placed an emphasis on outward rituals. Individuals had their own concepts of eternal life. The doctrine of purgatory created a veritable "death industry" whereby Catholics would leave money to be spent on masses for their soul by priests in churches, chapels and altars of their choice. One cannot exaggerate the importance of the Catholic commemoration of the deceased, especially in Mediterranean lands. Those who could afford it purchased space at the foot of altars, in chapels, under the floors and in the walls of churches, particularly those of monks to whom they had a family affinity. Wealthy houses erected chapels, or decorated them with elaborate altarpieces bearing their coats of arms. Lay testators often controlled the rights to nominate chaplains, and ensured family sinecures for future generations. Legacies for masses created a demand for priests that grew unchecked until the second half of the eighteenth century. Rome was disinclined to allow bishops or religious orders to discontinue these masses, for they might anger the families who donated money for them, or delay the beneficiary's deliverance from purgatory.[13]

The impetus for these good works came from the faithful, who understood salvation as a kind of bargain to be struck with God.[14] Pious people joined together in voluntary associations called confraternities, which existed to feed, clothe, house, visit, redeem and bury poor people. The greater part of their alms went towards dowries for girls from poor or from large families, so that they could make an honourable marriage and avoid the temptation of easy money that prostitution promised. Although peasants and workers belonged to these also for purposes of sociability, confraternities were the embodiment of the charitable imperative in Christianity. Every substantial village boasted at least one, and cities had many. Women often joined too, although they never mixed with the men. Confraternities multiplied religious ceremonies outside the parish, at altars they established on their own. These altars were not neutral places, since they were provided with revenues and focused the loyalties and rivalries of village notables.[15] Setting up chapels in outlying

hamlets was not so much an expression of piety as of a local separatism, expressed in religious terminology. They often enjoyed a
wide autonomy with regard to the priests, whom they hired episodi-
cally for their services, or whom they selected from the ranks of the
foremost families. Bishops inspecting their finances often found
fraud or favouritism benefiting the powerful.

Confraternities also provided spiritual alms, in the form of prayer
for souls. The fifteenth century witnessed the spread of devotional
groups, such as the Rosary and Marian societies, whose members
accompanied funerals, and who confessed and took communion
more frequently than once a year. Established first by the
Dominicans, and later fostered by Jesuits, these companies aimed to
inculcate an individual religious conscience into their members. The
Penitents accompanied funerals, and were instrumental in spreading
monastic forms of devotion throughout the upper reaches of lay
society. In so doing, they were combating ancient modes of dying
that survived from the age of Magna Graecia in the seventh century
BC, like the "wailers" who led funeral dirges. In southern Italy, and
especially in communities of Greek rites, hired mourners led family
and relatives into paroxysmal states of lamentation and self-mutila-
tion, screaming, clapping their hands, scratching their faces, and
uttering ritualized dialogue with the deceased, dwelling upon his or
her qualities or exploits. Instead, the modern funerary companies
celebrated daily masses for the souls of those recently departed, and
did their best to give their members a "decent" send-off.

Holy People in Traditional Catholicism

The Church mediated salvation in the next world. Its clergy administered bits of divine power to the living to aid them in this world too.
The ritual of liturgy, including the mass, was an elaborate ceremony
intended to capture benevolent power for the benefit of the community, and to avert or repulse evil. Liturgy, like all magic, manipulated
words, symbols and gestures to effect some concrete result. This
form of technology was almost universal in pre-statistical civilization.
People expected clerical intercession to placate divine anger.[16] The
gestures of clerics and faithful alike solicited supernatural power, by
kissing a relic, or crossing oneself, or kneeling before an image.
Many of the rituals were exorcistic, that is, they warded off evil. The
Rituale Romanum of 1612 contained ceremonies for blessing water,

palm fronds, candles, church bells and images, houses, crops, domestic animals and the marriage bed. It contained exorcisms against insects and storms. The Church promoted elaborate protective rituals for crops, such as the rogation processions, in which priests paraded the consecrated host and saints' statues around the boundaries of the village and before each of the local landmarks. Processions with miraculous images were a common response to disasters like plague, famine, drought, earthquakes and invasions of locusts. Priests and people often advanced barefoot, scourging themselves with whips, carrying heavy crosses, wearing crowns of thorns, exteriorizing their suffering and their despair to invoke God's mercy. Most homes possessed their devotional images like the saints' pictures, called *santini*, pinned to the walls or to the door frames to keep evil spirits at bay. Standing in corner shrines, statuettes of Christian saints or the Virgin Mary looked very much like those erected to pagan divinities in ancient Rome.[17]

Clerics were not all equally charismatic, despite the doctrine that held that the personal shortcomings of ordained priests had no effect upon the efficacy of the ritual they performed. The laity had other ideas. They conceived Christ to be someone who had particular friends, whose charisma proclaimed their election. Saints ascended directly to heaven at the instant of their death, and could intercede directly with God in favour of their supplicants. Officially there was no "adoration" of saints, but rather a simple "veneration" of their heroic status and their virtue as "role models" for individuals on earth. People hoped the saint would work some cure for themselves or someone in their family. A miracle was often preferable to medical treatment. Monks often mediated this search, in blessings, prayers or through written *brevi* that contained names of saints.[18] The Virgin Mary was by far the most important intercessor. Her shrine at Loreto, in the Marches near Ancona, was the most important in Catholic Europe, but there were many hundreds of shrines to the Virgin in Italy, of variable power and influence. Shrines to medieval saints were powerful attractions too. Saint Gennaro, patron saint of Naples, drew great crowds to watch his solidified blood liquefy in its reliquary in an imposing annual ritual that presaged good times or bad for the city. Cities were arsenals filled with relics accumulated over centuries.[19] Supplicants made a special vow or a prayer to the saint, promising an offering if their prayers were answered. It became common in the Mezzogiorno, according to a practice popularized by Jesuit missionaries, to approach the altar on their knees, or lick the floor or beat their breast in self-abasement.[20] Miracles were extremely commonplace occurrences, and everyone would have known a beneficiary personally. In thanks for a positive outcome, people left a gift, called an *ex voto*, to commemorate the event. Silver ornaments could be sold or melted down to maintain the shrine and its keepers. Frequent too were small paintings evoking the circumstances of the miracle, which are precious documents portraying ordinary people in their daily surroundings and routines. Others left a donation in wax, in the form of the body part that was stricken, which could be reshaped into candles as they accumulated week after week. *Ex votos* advertised the past prowess and the future likelihood of the Virgin Mary or the saint performing a miracle there. Before returning home, people could acquire holy images, statuettes, blessed oil, gourds of holy water to keep in their homes or to give to friends and relatives. Whether or not the cult of saints was a survival of ancient polytheism, the century after 1550 witnessed its revival all over Catholic Europe.[21] This was not popular religion in the sense that it was peculiar to the illiterate masses, but a belief holding near-universal appeal. Such devotion was nourished by a constant production of *hagiographic* literature, the *Lives of the Saints*, eagerly collected and read.[22]

Veneration was not restricted to mythological figures long dead. Sainthood itself was on the rise all across Italy, and most vigorously in the Mezzogiorno. No holy people had been canonized between 1523 and 1588, during the era of the council of Trent. In the interim a number of prophetic figures, mostly women called *sante vive*, attracted followers with their prodigious insights. The Council of Trent returned these women to their convents and appointed confessors to control their enthusiasm. Later in the century hundreds of more orthodox figures revived the traditional holy man or woman. In the kingdom of Naples alone, Sallmann encounters 105 candidates for the status of beatification and canonization in the two centuries after 1550, of whom a score were eventually canonized after lengthy investigation. Hundreds of others lived exemplary lives and died "in the odour of sanctity". Saints belong to a widespread archetype of the holy person, not specific to European civilization, sometimes called the "shaman". Their ecstasies and raptures brought them into direct contact with the other world. Nuns, who cultivated mysticism and prophecy in their cells, were not less adept than the monks at mortifying the flesh. By the supernatural powers that God bestowed upon them to make prophecies and work miracles in His name, they cured their followers by the laying on of hands, or reciting prayers. The Dominicans, Franciscans and Jesuits, who provided most of the candidates, did not have to search far for the proper path, being voracious readers of hagiography. Their sainthood was recognized by the population well before their death. The moment of their funeral was usually a dramatic illustration of their creditworthiness, as people without any clerical mediation pressed forward for clippings from their hair and their habit. People commonly visited the tomb of a holy man to approach the sacred aura that emanated from it. Monks and nuns promoted the cult of saints in all of their activities. The Church and the Inquisition were on the lookout for feigned holiness, and self-serving hypocrisy among the crowd of candidates for eternal glory. They occasionally investigated and imprisoned suspicious individuals without solid institutional backers, like the religious orders.[23]

Priests and monks had no monopoly on negotiating with the other world, although all the forms of communication that escaped their control they banned as "superstitious" or diabolically inspired. People ascribed an illness to sorcery when the malady seemed strange, or when they believed themselves to be victims of aggression. Magical ailments were characterized by a slow wasting away, a halting of development in children, or a general malaise in adults that we call depression. Where a ritual action was believed to cause an illness, only another ritual, like an exorcism, could cure it. If the priest's ritual attempt to alleviate suffering failed, one could go elsewhere. About a quarter of the trials for magic before the Inquisition in Modena between 1580 and 1600 involved ecclesiastics, whose unauthorized magic Rome considered especially pernicious, even if it was performed in good faith, as was usually the case.[24]

Many laypeople, observing the clerics, performed exorcisms themselves. Laypeople practised all manner of divination, but just as holy men and women possessed additional insights and mysterious powers, every village contained wise women and occasionally wise men whose powers could heal or harm. It has often been associated with southern Italy, but what we see there can easily be found in central and northern Italy, and indeed, in most of its forms, in all European countries.[25] Witches operated much like the priests, and referred to the same cosmology, exorcizing the malady with a narrative formula evoking a brief episode in the life of Jesus, the Virgin or the Saints. Witches in Friuli treated stomach and womb ailments, fever, headache, measles, sunstroke, bleeding wounds, broken bones, skin diseases, gout, coughs, worms, eye problems, epilepsy, depression and melancholy, wasting and digestive diseases in babies and children.[26] People feared generic evil spirits carried in the wind, or flying priests or magicians bringing storms. People recounted hallucinations, impulses from dreams, paroxysms, paralysis, loss of strength, or stupefaction at critical moments. In these cases, the witch sought to recapture the "stolen soul" and return it to the victim. Witches generally had secret knowledge and formulae they muttered *sotto voce*, as they made some secret gesture. Like priests and friars, they also employed amulets, charms and other objects that depicted saints and symbols of crosses. One form of these trance states was tarantism. Victims attributed their malaise to a bite from a mythical tarantula, to be exorcized by music. The victim danced compulsively to crush the spider, and participants in the ritual attempted to draw out the poison by waving cloths of particular colours. De Martino's interrogation of tarantism's mostly female victims in the 1950s revealed stories about poverty, insecurity and frustrating sentimental or marital situations.

In addition to curative powers, women had recourse to witches for love philtres and soothsaying, such as identifying a future spouse. Women were likely to indulge in erotic plots, using menstrual blood, feminine secretions, pubic and armpit hairs as ingredients in a mixture intended to bind a man.[27] Mothers fretted about other women using love magic to enchant their sons and gain control of their estate. Inversely, if he should spurn her, a suitor had reason to fear the curse of a girl. Everybody could have recourse to witches to accomplish vendetta, so every neighbourhood needed one. They used the altars, the Mass, holy oil and holy water, the host, consecrated or not, and blessed candles. Hearth chains, pans, beans, salt and other witchcraft paraphernalia appear in the Inquisition proceedings against them.[28]

The witch could deliberately harm people too, conceivably so that the victims would come to her for a cure. People of all social classes believed them capable of harming others by their gaze, called the "evil eye", or *malocchio*. In Naples, even noblemen and bourgeois wore talismans inside their clothes to ward off its effects.[29] Pregnant women and infant children were considered especially vulnerable to *malocchio*, cast upon them by a witch out of simple envy. Envy was a sentiment that came easily in early modern Italy, towards nursing women, or people of exceptional beauty or good fortune. Witches could also strike at marital concord by causing impotence. Spouses and relatives were always on the lookout for favourable or unfavourable omens during the marriage ceremony, and erected propitious phallic objects at the door of the wedding chamber and underneath the bed to enhance the success of the consummation. People knew who to blame when misfortune struck, and they could ascribe a motive – envy – that was plausible.

Paradoxically, with its rich magical universe, and the imposing presence of the institutional Church, Italy escaped the bloody repression of witches that claimed tens of thousands of lives north of the Alps. Almost everyone believed in their powers and their potential malevolence. But apart from some scares in Lombardy, spilling over from German-speaking Tyrol and Switzerland, witches were only infrequently executed.[30] The Inquisition in Italy was much less disturbed by the female, garden-variety witch, than by the male, ecclesiastical practitioners of learned occult sciences, who frequented the professional classes and the monasteries. The archaic magic, with so many links to Mediterranean Catholicism, survived and flourished until the modern era.

9 The Tridentine Church

The Council of Trent

Italy was not immune to the deep religious revival sweeping western Europe, which destabilized the apparently timeless structures of traditional Catholicism. Humanists echoing Erasmus criticized popular "superstitions", and advocated a stripped-down evangelism that could satisfy pious but educated people. Martin Luther's doctrines of justification by faith and universal sacerdocy rejected both good works and the papal hierarchy, so Pope Leo X Medici dismissed his reform call out of hand. Only after German soldiers sacked Rome in 1527 did the papacy confront the spread of Protestantism with urgency. Yet in the initial decades many theologians on both sides of the Alps hoped that an irenic compromise could be worked out. Italian evangelists favourable to reforms in the liturgy and in Catholic tradition were influential within the highest reaches of the Roman Church.[1] Cardinals Pole, Contarini, Sadoleto and Morone led these reformers in a battle for influence in the Curia.

A consensus emerged in favour of traditional positions after 1542. Paul III Farnese founded Ignatius Loyola's new Jesuit order, and reorganized the Roman Inquisition under the zealous Gian Pietro Carafa. The urgency to do something was highlighted by the appearance of Protestant groups in Lucca, then Ferrara and Modena, and finally Siena, all states with close links to France. When the pope moved against them, with the blessing of the emperor Charles V, they had no choice but to flee. Paul III sidelined cardinals who sympathized with reform ideas. Cardinal Carafa, founder of the Theatine order, became cardinal archbishop of Naples and head of the Inquisition. On becoming Pope Paul IV, he imprisoned prelates who opposed him by accusing them of heresy. On his death in 1559, the Roman crowd demolished the palace of the Inquisition and liberated its prisoners. While Carafa had gone too far, the Catholic Church now intended to fight the challenges to its doctrine and its organization. This tendency was confirmed with the election of another former head of the Inquisition, Michele Ghislieri, to the papacy as Pius V in 1566. By 1570, heretical groups in Friuli, Istria and Calabria were all uprooted and there were no longer any Protestants in Italy.

The emperor called for an ecumenical council to address the crisis. After lengthy hesitations, Paul III ordered the prelates to deliberate on church reform at Trent in 1545. The city was a compromise choice between the pope and the emperor, who had great stake in the outcome. It was located in the Empire, but was an ecclesiastical principality and ethnically an Italian city. In 1547, the pope transferred it to Bologna in the Papal States where he could control it more closely. When the Imperial bishops refused to follow it there, the pope suspended the council. Pope Julius III reconvened it in Trent in 1551–2, but it was suspended again until after the death of Paul IV Carafa, who would not abide it. After much wrangling with Catholic monarchs, Pope Pius IV reconvened it, until its conclusion in 1563.

The council was attended rather fitfully by most participants. It was not a debating forum, which would have created public winners and losers. Roman theologians dominated the private sessions by defining orthodoxy from the outset and imposing their views.[2] Once determined, the position was read out to the several hundred prelates in attendance, who uttered "Amen". From its first sessions in 1546, the prelates addressed fundamental questions of dogma. While the Bible remained central to Catholic teaching, the council recognized a whole corpus of canonical literature as being divinely inspired as well. This legitimized purgatory and all the practices of mediation and supplication associated with it. The council also confirmed the place of good works, which validated the sacrifices of monks and nuns, pilgrimages, charity and mortification. They conceded that individuals could have a direct, personal relationship with God, but that sacraments administered by priests were also indispensable. Finally, the council reiterated the doctrine of *transubstantiation*, whereby God's body and his blood become one with the wafer and the wine when the priest elevates them over the altar. Later sessions dealt with organizational and disciplinary matters, reaffirming papal supremacy over the council, and the pope's role as sole interpreter of its decrees. The council forbade secular clerics from holding more than one benefice at a time, and bound them to perform their functions and reside in their cures. It reaffirmed the bishops' obligation to reside in their dioceses, holding the clergy to their task.

In subsequent decades, the Curia worked in its various cardinal congregations to tie up the loose ends. One project established an authorized Bible, the Vulgate, which separated those scriptures that were divinely inspired from the apocryphal texts, and fixed a proper translation (1592). Clement VIII Aldobrandini carried forward the revision of liturgical texts: the Pontifical (concerning episcopal functions), the Breviary (governing the traditions of the saints), then the Missal (the different masses), elaborated under the supervision of two controversists and scholars, cardinals Cesare Baronio and Roberto Bellarmino. The *Rituale Romanum* (1614) standardized practices of administering the sacraments.[3] Baronio produced a multivolume history of the Church (1588–1607) that refuted Protestant charges that Catholic rites and doctrines perverted Christ's message. Roberto Bellarmino, a Tuscan Jesuit, produced both a long scholarly summary of Catholic doctrine, and, more importantly, a small catechism for mass indoctrination, suitable for memorization.

Decrees emanating from the Council of Trent became church law in 1564. Successive popes then applied the decrees by appointing a number of apostolic visitors in strategic cities, often Inquisition personalities with sweeping powers of inspection. Within a decade after the council's conclusion, church reform was in full swing.

The Century of Saints, 1550–1650

Many reformers held monks and nuns in low esteem, despite the fact that the mendicant orders still enjoyed considerable prestige. Monks mobilized urban crowds during their impassioned sermons, and brought people to confession in ever greater numbers. The mendicant orders gradually produced a vast array of confession manuals and related devotional literature for both priests and laity.[4] The examination of conscience, refined by Ignatius Loyola and Carlo Borromeo, launched the profession of the director of conscience and the science of casuistry, or moral reasoning.

The stirrings of new developments began around 1530 in
Lombardy, with the creation of the Barnabite order, the multiplication of hospitals belonging to the new Somaschi order, and the
spread of Holy Sacrament confraternities. Capuchins split from the
Observant Franciscans, the stricter branch, which they considered
too soft (1528). Like Saint Francis, their bookish knowledge was
usually slight, seeking as they did a more emotional faith. They spent
much of their time helping celebrate mass in the monastery chapel.
The brothers reunited each day in prayer and for meals. Once a
week they met for culpability sessions, where they berated themselves
for their shortcomings.[5] Flagellation was a mandatory practice three
times a week, and daily during Holy Week preceding Easter.[6]
Because of their intransigence, Capuchin numbers exploded. By
1650, they numbered almost 11,000, the largest religious order in
Italy, and about a third of the various Franciscans.

Medieval orders like the Carmelites received fresh impetus too;
the number of their convents quintupled in Apulia after 1530.
Noblemen and the *università* notables enjoyed the obit masses, sacraments, confession and predication the monks offered. Carmelite life
was articulated around individual and collective prayer, spiritual
readings, Bible study and casuistry. Friars kept regulation silence in
the dormitories, the refectory, the cloister and garden, and practised
long and frequent fasts. Although their constitution called for flagellation once a week, there was a widespread desire to harden the
rules after 1600. The monks lived off the income of the houses and
land they owned, bequeathed in tiny fragments in the wills of the
faithful. Luxurious church decorations contrasted with the sparse
furnishings of the monks' cells, which consisted of just a table and
chair, a bed and a chest for personal effects. Monastery libraries contained books of theology and philosophy, but also of law, literature
and history. They nourished the sermons of preachers, who learned
their written texts by heart, and delivered them from the pulpit with
robust voice and theatrical flourish to fix the attention of the audience and compel it to consent. Pulpit oratory was a pillar of learned
culture the impact of which is hard to assess.[7]

The mystical revival affected women too. The Brescian Angela
Merici wanted to create a group without convent walls or a habit,
whose purpose was to teach Christian doctrine to girls and women.
They were given a rule in 1546, and Saint Carlo Borromeo accelerated their metamorphosis into a conventional teaching order by
steering them away from unsupervised devotions, mortification,

fasting and seeking trance states. Their schoolmistress role for the daughters of the elite had less impact on Italy than on France, however, where female literacy was more widespread.[8]

Rome became the centre of this monastic revival when the Spanish Basque mystic, Ignatius Loyola, an ex-soldier, enlisted in the popes' crusade against heresy. Paul III established the Society of Jesus, or the Jesuits, in 1542. Unlike other orders, the Jesuits were all priests, ordained after very lengthy schooling that set them apart from every other order save the Dominicans. Loyola considered them to be the pope's soldiers, intelligent, learned and disciplined, but active in the world. Jesuit spirituality avoided mystical transports; they preferred discretion, prudence, moderation.[9] Before long, they directed the most famous cultural institutions in Rome, such as the Collegio Romano and the Roman seminary. The Jesuits were not created as a teaching order, but after opening their first college in Messina (1547), they rapidly stepped into that role. Rome's ability to promote new religious agencies appears even clearer with the Oratory. Filippo Neri was a poor son of a Florentine notary, who attached himself to shrines in Rome. Before long, he had become a priest, confessor and director of conscience to young men attracted by his saintly reputation. By 1567 there were 18 priests residing next to his church, called the Oratory. Two of their members, Tarugi and Baronio, who were made cardinals in 1596, gave a much higher profile to the group. The community was soon imitated elsewhere, and there were 35 houses in Italy before 1650, and some 150 set up after the Roman model in Europe.[10]

Each order, new and old, interpreted Catholic activism in a slightly different way. Both urban and rural populations revered these men who wore hair shirts and tied chains around their necks, placed a sharp pebble in their sandal and slept on straw in order to reduce their body to obedience and their spirit to submission. In order to "moralize" the Roman Curia the popes promoted many religious to cardinal status after 1560.[11] In addition to their example, monks established or supervised confraternities on a large scale; the members of these were obliged to proselytize, teach or admonish their comrades, relatives and landlords. They turned out in force to solemnize missions, and also attended funerals, as an act of Christian charity. Capuchin confraternities went further. In addition to promoting frequent communion, they sponsored "discipline" confraternities where brothers whipped themselves and each other in churches. This was a male activity, but their womenfolk could wail or beat their breast at the church door. The religious orders also invented some of the more theatrical, masochistic behaviour at shrines, which expressed the dolorist conception of religious life underlying monastic vows.[12]

The monks' greatest impact was in the realm of missions. It was a missionary maxim that the operation had to impress the minds and the hearts of rustics. They focused on the emotional moment, the meditation on the Passion, the great processions, and the excitement of a series of fire and brimstone sermons aimed at provoking a "rebirth". Preachers used emotive metaphors and figurative language that brought forth laughter and tears; they used scenes from the Bible and recent events in order to instil a deep fear of God's retribution, to try and provoke repentance and conversion, tallied in the form of full confessions.[13] Monks knew how to adjust the level of their sermons to their audiences, by studying their presentation and delivery. During their exhortations, some of the faithful might mortify themselves with stones, ropes and twigs. The monks would then burn books, playing cards, ribbons and other vanities. Even in the mid-eighteenth century, Saint Alfonso Liguori, founder of the Redemptorist missionary order, preached with a standing portrait of the Madonna by his side, lashing himself with a scourge. With bell and candle, he laid curses on impenitent sinners, blasphemers and men of vendetta. Missions were occasions to bury feuds, convert sinners and criminals, and hold alms-giving competitions. How much this catharsis modified people's long-term behaviour is difficult to assess.

The best measure of monastic piety was the soaring recruitment into the orders. In 1650 Italy counted over 70,000 male religious, scattered in over 6,300 separate houses.[14] Monasteries and convents multiplied in southern fiefs, where the barons helped them build and gave them revenues and protection. Piety and the desire for prestige combined in these foundations, for nobles fixed their coats of arms in prominent places and often elected for burial there.[15] Despite the ambient poverty, the churches of religious orders were often opulent monuments decorated with altar and ceiling paintings of high quality by urban masters. Numerous religious statues in them, frequently painted or gilt, were carried around on feast days, touched, kissed and caressed by the devout. The friars were often too few to accomplish all the rituals specified by the rule. They lent crucial support to the understaffed parish clergy in remote rural districts. By the mid-seventeenth century the saturation point had been reached.[16] Italian princes petitioned Pope Innocent X to reduce the number of monasteries in the public interest. In 1652 the pope decreed the suppression of more than 1,500 male religious houses, particularly in provinces like Calabria with its dense network of tiny houses with only three or four monks. Some of them were restored in the following years because of the disruption their closure created for local communities, but in the subsequent century, only the Capuchin and the Jesuit orders continued to swell.

The female orders experienced the same heady growth as their male counterparts. Bishops imposed a new respect for the rules by which admission was to be strictly voluntary and the result of mature reflection. The bishops also saw to it that each convent followed its order's constitution, wore the habit and observed the same regulations. Counter-Reformation zeal put nuns back behind high walls, and forced them to restrict access to the outside world through the grille.[17] Although Italian elites did not accept reclusion without resistance, monastic values had deep resonance and families used these convents to house and educate their daughters, widows, and a variety of women and girls in irregular circumstances. Nobles founded many new convents for their daughters' convenience and their descendants' opportunity, while noblewomen frequented the monastery to be sociable.[18] While forced internment was a serious problem, many nuns showed early signs of vocation, and their "election" by God cast glory and renown upon their house. At the Theatine convent of Pescia, in Tuscany, nuns practised fasts, mortifications of the flesh, rigid obedience, attendance at communion once a week (most Italians took it annually), confessing sins in the presence of all, remaining secluded in their house and their cell, and attending mass at the nearest church. Books in these convents were primarily intended to be read aloud in common. Convents were not centres of study as they were for Dominicans, Benedictines or Jesuits. Notwithstanding the similarity of Franciscan dolorist practices of both monks and nuns, the latter emphasized the mystical ravishings and ecstatic visions popularized by the writings of the Spanish Carmelite, Saint Theresa d'Avila.[19]

Convents rarely lived up to the ideals outlined in their constitution. Many sisters spent a good part of their life doing manual labour, like reeling silk, which was officially undertaken to instil humility and discourage idleness. Many convents existed in straitened circumstances, and abbesses needed good administrative skills to keep them out of debt. The atmosphere was often tense due to a kind of "cabin fever" that exploded in factions and jealousies. Nuns found consolation by collecting personal objects, such as paintings, or gilt devotional objects. Wealthier communities competed for the title of the most beautiful convent, with lavish expenditure for rebuilding and redecorating.[20] By 1650 the number of forced vocations was on the rise again, as noble families in economic decline could no longer find money for dowries. Nevertheless, the nuns were the impetus for spiritual reflection among elite laywomen, who procured crucifixes, prayer-stools and rosaries, read or listened to pious literature, and sought out directors of conscience. This transformation of pious practices from public devotional acts to private prayer spread through the middle and upper class just as the mystical surge began to wane and recruitment into the convents began to taper off.[21]

Rise of the Secular Church

The greater self-discipline noticeable in elite behaviour after about 1650 was a consequence of a vast expansion of colleges for adolescents.[22] Religious concerns guided education everywhere in Europe. The number of Jesuit teaching schools in Italy grew from 18 in 1556 to 80 in 1630, and 111 in 1700. Most of them counted a few hundred pupils, weighted heavily in the lower years. Their competition in Italy, from the Barnabite and Somaschi orders principally, never menaced them. By the 1580s, Jesuits ran paying colleges exclusively for nobles with the same general curriculum.[23] The Jesuits developed pedagogical doctrines and methods arguably more effective than those practised today, laid out in a constitution known as the *Ratio Studiorum* (1592). Much of it involved rote learning in Latin, sitting at a bench before a serious-looking priest with a stick. A prefect administered corporal punishment (caning across the buttocks) if the good fathers coldly judged the lesson worthwhile. In addition to the discipline, however, they sought ways to harness the good will of their charges, inculcating self-control, and self-monitoring relayed by confession.[24] In a society where speaking well in public was an essential skill, sacred theatre was an integral part of the programme. Jesuit fathers applied concepts of monastic discipline and corporeal control to their young charges in order to teach them "modesty". Pupils had to learn how to behave at school, during religious services, at the table, in the latrines and the dormitories. They had to walk, not run, avoid laughter, not stick their finger up their nostrils or in their ears in public, not to spit in front of someone, not to stare, or gawk around them. Humanists like Erasmus added precepts on how to walk with dignity in the street, in church and at home; to say prayers morning and evening; to dress decently; to wash hands, and to say prayers before meals; to eat and drink with moderation; avoid swearing, and to use correct language; to say a prayer or make the sign of the cross before a church, a statue or a religious image; to doff one's hat out of deference to a priest; to be polite to one's elders, and so on. There was another code for girls, taught in convents, stressing modesty and courtesy in order to protect one's good reputation.[25]

With an effective Jesuit pedagogy it mattered less that the development of seminaries to train priests was much more gradual. Carlo Borromeo established the first important seminaries at Milan and Rome in 1565, each with a hundred students under the Jesuits. There were only 128 established between 1550 and 1600; 70 more in the seventeenth century, and 40 more in the next, still less than the requisite one per diocese. Some were merely residences for priests in training, not proper schools.[26] Seminaries were considered adequate if they imparted Latin to their students, good manners, elementary doctrine, basic moral theology, how to say mass and chant.

Ecclesiastical authorities did not envisage these institutions as complementing primary schools.[27] In the minds of primary education promoters, basic literacy was synonymous with catechism instruction. The schools of Christian Doctine spread from Milan into the Po valley towns in the 1540s and the 1550s, operated by lay confraternities. The numbers of pupils in these schools was often considerable, and must have matched the most advanced regions in Europe. Children learned the rudiments of Catholicism and had more than passing acquaintance with the world of print culture.[28] In addition to these catechism schools, the Spaniard Giuseppe Calasanzio launched his *Scuole Pie*, or Piarist schools in Rome in 1597. They adopted a novel programme of instruction more complete than catechism schools, dispensed in Italian. But Italy soon reached a plateau of urban literacy just as England, Germany, the Netherlands and northern France were encouraging mass instruction.[29]

In 1540, eighty bishops complained of the obstacles they faced in their dioceses: exemptions of people and corporate bodies from episcopal decrees; patronage rights that prevented them from excluding unfit candidates to benefices; the monopoly of mendicant orders over public preaching and confession in the cities; the ability to circumvent the bishop's court by appealing to Rome or to lay judges. Bishops were stymied by chapters of canons allied with local notables, by religious "powers" like the great abbeys, or commanderies of the orders of Malta or Santo Stefano.[30] Frustrated bishops needed a reference guide to reform, and a papacy that would support them. Their model was Saint Carlo Borromeo. Nephew of Pope Pius IV, the young Lombard prelate could have been cardinal-nephew in Rome, but he preferred the see of Milan. There and in the ten Lombard dioceses that depended upon it, he implemented the conciliar decrees. Borromeo had a "totalitarian" view of the Church's mission, and suffered no obstacles in his path. He publicized his aims and ambitions in six provincial synods, and directed all the other bishops to follow his example. Borromeo's synods multiplied disciplinary measures, such as those imposing clerical dress and tonsure on priests. He was the font of a vast legislation curbing feasts, games, spectacles, taverns, dances, usury, and so on. He sought to end the autonomy of confraternities and change the way they operated. He supervised convent recruitment too, denying entry to girls without vocation, in defiance of their parents' projects. The saint's enemies were legion. He once cited Lombardy's chief magistrate to answer charges of obstructing his jurisdiction, and finished by excommunicating him! Only diplomatic intervention prevented him from excommunicating the governor of Milan. Borromeo turned as well to inspect rural parishes and their clergy in repeated pastoral visitations. He ended absenteeism by curates, supervised their training, gave them precise instructions for administering their parishes, and watched closely over their personal life. Borromeo wanted a parish clergy that studied pious literature, practised asceticism and refused the sociability and conviviality that other Italians took for granted. Obsessed with the reputation of priests, he tried to ban not only most of their servants, but their female close family.

This kind of intransigence forced the admiration of many who opposed him. By the time of Borromeo's death in 1584, Philip II had decided to promote church reform too, and gave instructions to his officials to further it. Borromeo's successor but one, his cousin Federico Borromeo (1595–1631), helped spread the model to other areas of the Catholic world through his correspondence. One could easily multiply examples of bishop-reformers.[31] In the middling-sized

Umbrian diocese of Perugia, all eight successive bishops after 1563 contributed in some way to Tridentine reform, although some were more consistent and energetic than others. Many were attentive to material details in their parish visitations. Not all bishops conducted visitations, but most dioceses were subject to inspections at regular intervals, and every urban altar and rural chapel, hospital, school and sanctuary was scrutinized.

Diocesan synods communicated the bishops' desires forcefully to the clergy. A synod consisted of a conference to which the bishop convoked his dependent, secular clergy to discuss the major concerns and cases of conscience. The discussions were concretized by a list of decrees and regulations published soon after. Parish priests in turn submitted their flocks to closer scrutiny, compiling a census of households in their care, and noting who received confession, communion and confirmation. The bishops instructed priests to send them the list of non-pascalizers, to tell him which married couples foundered, who were the blasphemers, the debtors, the concubines, the paupers, who indulged in vendettas, heresy or magic. Bishops could always refer obdurate sinners, like adulterers, to the secular arm; they could also procure a culprit's banishment, reclusion to a monastery, or fortress prison.

By 1650 the greatest abuses and nonchalance in the practice of religion in northern and central Italy were addressed and corrected. Confession booths stood universal, graveyards were walled round, new altarpieces raised, church roofs repaired, the host in tabernacles with appropriate baldachins. Clerics resided everywhere in their benefices and they could pass their Latin quizzes, all of which raised the clergy in public esteem. The number of secular priests surged and their education and discipline improved as well.[32] At Naples, the archbishop Innico Caracciolo (1667–85) applied stricter examinations at ordination and confirmation to a benefice, requiring testimony of good morality, adequate education, service to the Church, and proper title to the benefice.[33] The bishop's courts meted out punishment more consistently to delinquent secular clerics, and good alternative candidates were numerous. Delinquent priests were numerous enough until after 1650, but they were among the first targets of a vast campaign of moralization and disciplining.[34]

The late sixteenth century inaugurated a golden age of Catholic piety, celebrated with great pomp by teeming numbers of churchmen. At Lecce in Apulia, perhaps 12 per cent of the urban population was made up of ecclesiastics around 1625.[35] The number of religious buildings was remarkable too. Ferrara possessed 96 churches and 50 monasteries, convents and pious institutions for barely 20,000 people. With barely half the population, Noto in Sicily counted 56 churches in the town, and 14 more nearby. People attended religious events as if they were a spectacle, hung tapestries from their windows and façades, placed paintings in the streets, laid out silver reliquaries, lamps and other gifts on the altars. The translation of relics could be the scene of stupendous celebrations. In Perugia (1609) churches were decorated with tapestries and silks, the chancel painted with architectural motifs, and decked out with hundreds of candles; gold and silver decorations were placed on the main doors, statues, and triumphal arches inscribed with mottoes, epigrams and poetry. The city authorities decorated the streets with similar arches, and set up altars at strategic points. Seven hundred brothers paraded behind floats carrying "saints" and "angels".[36] One new practice was the Forty Hours devotion, sometimes called the Sacred Theatre, an elaborate presentation of the consecrated host. A succession of people relayed each other to pray or listen to sermons for forty hours. Preparations for this, especially in cathedrals or in Jesuit churches, entailed choirs and music, elaborate altar decorations, scenic lighting effects and mirrors, sumptuous cloths, canopies and monstrances.

This devout enthusiasm generated increasing pious donations. Purgatory obsessed people more than ever before. They specified more masses for their souls and elected which clergy were to officiate. Confraternity devotion flowered too, combining piety and social action. Elites expressed an authentic solidarity with their social inferiors by financing new chapels. If the members were mostly male, women derived benefits by sharing in indulgences, in joining pilgrimages to sanctuaries (often their only travel), and receiving assistance when they fell on hard times. Confraternities distributed food in hospitals, staffed shelters, orphanages and *conservatories* for deserted or abused wives, and worked to rehabilitate former prostitutes. In small towns pious institutions mobilized the business acumen and diligence of elected officials, who rented out the lands, houses and money that formed the assets, watched over the woods, the fields and the vines. They decided on the expenditures on beds, on surgeons and food supplies, under the surveillance of a governing board of local notables.[37] One form of confraternity piety was the Monte. The *Monte di Pietà* was originally aimed at combating

usury practised by Jews, and to this end friars promoted it in the fifteenth century. Its cheap capital was used actively by modest folk, but
not beggars. Ecclesiastical authorities watched closely over the rates
of interest. There were specialized institutions, like the marriage
Monte, where one could save for a dowry; or the grain Monte, which
allowed peasants to borrow seed and repay it after the harvest.[38]
Bishops kept watch that confraternity ceremonies did not supplant
parish obligations, and they tried to rein them in. Cardinal Doria
closed conventicles of aristocratic women in Palermo who met in
private houses and oratories to read books of piety, and who flayed
themselves with rods on specified days. The prelate felt there was
danger that they risked transmitting unsupervised practices to the
lower classes via the confraternities.[39]

Reform in the Mezzogiorno took longer, partly because the large
number of dioceses (130), and their small size made it difficult for
bishops to assert their power against the local *università*, the feudatory and the *chiese ricettizie*. In many districts, bishops could not reside
because of malaria, or the danger from barons and bandits, the first
threatening their lives, and the second their revenues. Over time,
the number of clergy increased substantially, but according to the
bishops, their quality was abysmal. The low social status of bishops
may have been one impediment to rapid reform. Less than a quarter
of Apulian bishops were nobles between the Council of Trent and
1650; but thereafter the proportion of noblemen rose to three-quarters and their effectiveness improved.[40]

Italian Inquisitions

The Italian Church possessed the ultimate agent of surveillance and
discipline, the Inquisition, of which there were several. We are just
beginning to understand their local impact.[41] Sicily and Sardinia
possessed the version answerable to the king of Spain. In Iberia the
institution bore down harshly on crypto-Muslims and Judaizers, in
order to transform them into good "Spaniards". In Italy this was
never an issue. Only one Judaizer was ever executed in Sicily, in
1549, and none elsewhere.[42] Jews in Italy were instead closed off in
ghettos, which were self-contained neighbourhoods. Counter-
Reformation popes like Paul IV Carafa tightened restrictions on
them, but the harshest measures were not everywhere obeyed, nor
long applied. Catholics often frequented the ghetto out of curiosity,

to observe the strange customs and rituals of both Sephardic and Ashkenazi sects.[43] Sixteenth-century elites everywhere in Europe demanded religious uniformity. A medieval inquisition, run by Dominicans and Franciscans, worked under bishops, but it no longer had a caseload. Paul III Farnese established the Holy Office of the Inquisition in 1542, and gave it precedence over every other congregation in the Roman hierarchy. Laymen vied for the privilege of becoming its informers, or "familiars", and intellectuals in universities (invariably clerics) served as consultors, drawing up the list of questions to put before the witnesses, and helping analyse the testimony. Priests instructed peasants not only to confess their own sins, but those of others too. For the first time, wives were obliged to come forward to denounce their husbands. This was new. After 1550 the Inquisition began soliciting "spontaneous" confessions and accusations concerning a wide array of crimes: sorcery, superstitions, blasphemy, forbidden sexual practices, feigned piety or sainthood, eating meat on fast days, reading prohibited books. But the machinery did not move without impulse from above. Local confessors dispatched their cases to the nuncio, then to the Holy Office in Rome, and awaited orders.[44] They rarely acted without the support of the reigning prince, although this was not always forthcoming.

Venice created its own Inquisition in 1547, with a secular judge present alongside the priests. The variety of heretical beliefs was widest in the lagoon city. In the city of St Mark some doubted Christ's divinity, many openly questioned the cult of saints, or the use of rosaries, or of votive offerings and miraculous shrines.[45] Evangelical preachers, mostly ex-Franciscans, triggered a torrent of religious debate. With the onset of religious war in France as a warning of what religious dissension could bring, the Inquisition caseload soared in the 1560s. Confraternities, now watched closely, became pillars of orthodoxy. Canon law prescribed that only the obstinate and unrepentant who refused to be "reconciled" to the Church, repeat offenders and those charged with heinous crimes, be liable to the death penalty. In Friuli, only four cases in a thousand ended with execution. The Venetian Inquisition executed 25 heretics by secret drowning. There were occasional executions throughout Italy, usually of recidivists, or people guilty of sacrilege against the consecrated host. All the Italian inquisitions put together, however, would not have executed more than three hundred people, a tiny figure beside the peacetime toll for Spain, England, France and the Spanish Netherlands. Most of the punishments involved public abjuration, or reciting endless cycles of prayers and devotions over months and years.[46] Unlike most courts, they handed down prison terms, but a "life" sentence was generally equivalent to about three years, and the conditions in Inquisition prisons were the least horrendous obtaining in Europe.[47]

In order to justify their existence, the Inquisitors began maintaining their caseloads by trying cases that had been the staple of bishops' courts. This evolution was similar to the Spanish experience after the crown expelled the Jews and Muslims. After 1580 illicit magic became the most common offence dealt with in Inquisition tribunals. In Naples where these clerics sat on the bishop's ordinary court rather than their own tribunals, Inquisitors sought to punish witches as the population expected them to. Sallmann estimates at 3,400 the number of these trials between 1570 and 1720, although only the city and its vicinity were closely supervised. Most of the magicians tried by them were male (75 per cent), usually literate and of good birth. Franciscans and Carmelites figure prominently among them, as they were very numerous and not well disciplined. Inversely, not a single Jesuit or Theatine answered to such charges. The women arrested for witchcraft were almost always illiterate, and many were prostitute specialists of love magic. Torture figured in about a third of the cases, but few people confessed to anything more. Those who submitted themselves to be "reconciled" to the Church received clement treatment, and the death penalty was never pronounced in Naples for affairs of magic. The tribunal found the accused guilty nine times out of ten, but the period of detention was generally not more than a year.[48]

Inquisition investigation of witches and magic contrasted with the trend towards greater severity occurring in tribunals in northern Europe. Pope Sixtus V Peretti outlawed judicial astrology and all other kinds of divination in 1586. Nevertheless, the prelates in the Holy Office refused to rush into zealous prosecution. They remained more vigilant against magician priests than against village women, whose magic they considered simple superstition or ignorance, judged locally and leniently without the intervention of Roman cardinals. A decision in 1588 banning procedures against people accused of attending sabbaths meant that there was no risk of a prosecution against a single person escalating into mass panic, as was sometimes the case in Germany. Few Italian witches were executed after the mid-sixteenth century, even though magic flourished.[49] In Siena, inquisitors practically dismissed cases of "diabolical" spell-casting after 1665, although they continued to investigate charges of divinatory magic well into the next century, which they treated as superstition.

By degrees the Inquisition in Rome focused on books, pamphlets and writers, and worked in tandem with the Congregation of the Index, created in 1571 by Pope Pius V Ghislieri. A general index of prohibited books appeared in 1559, independent of the Council of Trent. The Inquisition presence was felt in every diocese in Italy, and even villagers had reason to fear that their impious outbursts might be reported to the Holy Office. Concern for orthodoxy rendered devotion virtually universal and monolithic. This religion required simple conformity from the greatest number, and gave those who desired it almost unlimited possibilities of expression – on orthodox lines. But the sea-change away from anxiety and towards a lukewarm piety underpins the gradual secularization of Western society. It is difficult to track the ways this occurred, and we need to find ways to measure the depths of human conscience.

10   The Rebirth of Rome

Papal Boom Town

Mid-sixteenth-century Rome must have disappointed tourists and pilgrims encountering it, steeped as they were in ancient history and letters since childhood. The Eternal City was a shabby tangle of streets along the curve of the muddy and foul-smelling Tiber. The built area occupied less than a third of the imperial city, whose wall still marked out a vast circumference. In 1447 Rome contained barely 20,000 inhabitants, one-fiftieth of the number estimated for the ancient capital, amid the ruins of which the modern popes ruled. Renaissance Rome also included a collection of villages around the seven different basilicas visited by pilgrims, separated by scrub, vineyards and ruins of ancient monuments. Romans often used these as quarries of cut stone, if they did not neglect them altogether. Mean, low, brick and timber modern dwellings were built up against them in a jumble.

Violent faction politics of the urban nobility made Rome as turbulent as any commune in the peninsula. The Roman People was a consultative body of 500 or 600 gentlemen who elected a "senator" and several honorific "consuls".[1] The pope was represented by the Cardinal Vicar, the head of the treasury, the Camerlengo, and the Governor, who presided over the most important tribunal. The pontiff commanded reverence for the duration of his life, but this deference often vanished at the instant of his death. Romans traditionally vented their frustrations at the end of the reign, in a period of anarchy called the "vacant see", until the next pontiff emerged from the papal conclave.

In 1445 Nicholas V decided to refurbish Rome's image, commencing with a wide avenue connecting the decrepit fourth-century Saint Peter's basilica to Hadrian's tomb, which was transformed into a fortress prison, the Castello Sant' Angelo. Popes helped aristocrats and cardinals buy urban sites in the city's north-west corner, the Borgo, demolish the shabby houses on them and erect opulent palaces in their place. Sales of indulgences across Europe, various regalian rights and remittances of money from Catholic lands helped finance these projects, as did the papacy's near-monopoly of western Europe's supply of alum, a mineral substance for producing mordants that were indispensable to the woollen industry, located conveniently nearby at Tolfa. The crowning project was to replace the papal basilica with a new structure surmounted by a cupola. Work commenced in 1506, and the dream gradually materialized after the close of the Italian wars, each architect modifying the work of the previous builder. Saint Peter's was the world's largest church until very recently, and its construction cost more than 1.5 million scudi over 120 years. The popes built four palaces too, with the Vatican being the largest in the world at the time. The Lateran palace, the pope's official residence as bishop of Rome, and the Quirinal housed offices of the Curia. Lords both lay and ecclesiastic built their own palaces, notable for their size and the opulence of their decoration, conceived as they were for a large family with their numerous personnel.

The sack of the city in 1527 barely broke the stride of Roman expansion, and its population reached 100,000 by the end of the century. The pace and scale of building intensified, but it aggravated the crowding at river's edge. Much of the lower city was infested by malaria every summer, while in winter the Tiber periodically overflowed its banks. The flood of 1598 left much of medieval Rome under a thick layer of mud, rubbish and putrefying corpses, flushed out of their graves. Most of the 1,400 victims died of the typhus that broke out after the water receded. Sixtus V Peretti (1585–90) and his chief architect Domenico Fontana decided to divert urban growth away from the river and on to the plateau, tracing a network of boulevards and new streets totalling ten kilometres. Sixtus offered tax relief to those who built their houses along them, and spent much treasure building acqueducts and fountains to bring clean water to these neighbourhoods. Along the edge of the built area, there was a tendency to erect villas with lush gardens, creating a green belt. The avenues took streetscape into consideration as well.

Sixtus banned wooden extensions of buildings as a traffic hindrance, and everywhere prohibited the hanging of washing across the streets. Papal decrees enhanced the sense of order by aligning housefronts along the street, and forbidding tenants to empty their waste and their latrines on to public thoroughfares.[2]

Rome attracted social elites from Italy and beyond, beginning with the cardinals, whose number climbed from 18 in 1440 to 70 in 1590. In Rome they dispatched routine business in the congregations. Their private courts were "launching pads" (Fragnito) for young noblemen seeking careers in the Curia. If one wished to make a career in the Church or solicit any kind of temporal benefit, it was necessary to go to Rome to seek it from one of the cardinals, the "patron saints" of the papal state. Great prelates maintained hundreds of dependants in their suite. Saint Carlo Borromeo, whose personal train was very frugal, made do with 150. The Vatican palace in the 1560s had 1,500 "mouths" on the payroll, drawn from a vast area, making it Italy's largest court by far.[3] Some cardinals drew income from the kings of Spain or France, who subsidized them to turn papal policy in their favour. Many lived from pensions or taxes piled on to church benefices, particularly those under Spanish control, such as Naples and Milan.[4] Bankers migrated to Rome too, to lend money, buy offices and farm taxes, making the city one of Europe's leading financial centres.[5] As the Curial administration became more complex, the popes learned to sell offices to the sons of notables. Any litigation out of the ordinary in its importance or its complexity was heard by the great tribunal of the Rota, which employed hundreds of lawyers and magistrates, notaries and clerks. Rome also "exported" indulgences and dispensations. As much as the seat of the universal Church, Rome was a holy city containing a treasury of relics. Pilgrims converged there seeking a cure, a pardon, a blessing, or simply to satisfy their curiosity. As Counter-Reformation piety waxed stronger, the crowds converging on Rome every twenty-five years for Holy Year, or the Jubilee, swelled to prodigious numbers; there were 400,000 visitors in 1575, 500,000 in 1600, and 700,000 in 1650. They stayed on average two weeks, living sometimes on alms collected by pious Romans, and forming endless processions shuffling along the avenues. Gradually the boom town acquired enough monuments to leave a tremendous impression on them.

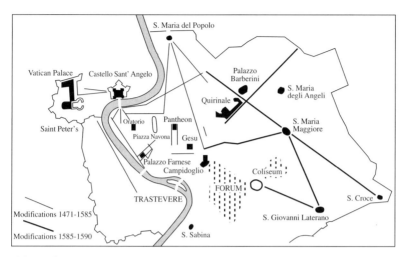

Map 16   New roads in ancient Rome

Era of Baroque Monuments

This boom lasted until around 1630, when Rome counted more than 200 churches, chapels and oratories. Attention turned from building new streets for workers and their families to beautifying the capital. Wide, straight avenues, bordered by sumptuous palaces, reflected Italian urbanistic concepts, which were preoccupied with making a *bella figura*.[6] Apart from Saint Peter's, the popes and their families commissioned a large number of monuments. Sixtus V launched more projects in his brief mandate than any other. He expanded the Vatican palace, and collected one of Europe's largest libraries there. Domenico Fontana rebuilt the Lateran palace for him too. Sixtus had no feeling for the historical or aesthetic qualities of the early Middle Ages. He demolished the ancient, sixth-century structure and replaced it with an enormous building in just four years.[7] All of this construction entailed demolishing ancient works of art, sometimes with misgivings. From 1585 to 1669 the popes displayed a remarkable continuity of purpose. They enhanced the solemnity of the liturgy and multiplied the street-pageants called *trionfi*, which displayed their power and prestige.[8] Churches multiplied along the avenues laid out by Sixtus V to resemble, in Tapié's phrase, so many altars along the path of a procession.[9] Urban VIII Barberini (1623–44) placed an emphasis on renovating, modernizing and decorating some of the ancient churches, although art historians today curse his "restorations". He also spent lavishly on military monuments at Rome, and built a great arsenal at Tivoli. Religious orders, most of which had their head office in the papal city, sponsored much building. Cardinals were bound by honour to embellish specific churches whose title they held.

Since investments in the economy were hardly worth the return, aristocrats and clergy placed their money in splendid buildings that at least brought some measure of social return. Mediterranean Catholicism rejected the evangelical model of the unadorned church. Splendour did justice to God, and heightened the sense of Divine Majesty that fixed religious precepts and religious institutions in the minds of the people.[10] Holy buildings thesaurized prodigious quantities of precious metals in the form of reliquaries, chalices and lamps, exposed on the altars in profusion on religious holidays. Church interiors were now conceived as a single space without separations or long chancels. The model was the seat of the Jesuit order in Rome, the Gesù, initiated in the 1570s. Modern church design set off the high altar where the principal mass was celebrated, elevating it like a stage, while a cupola and lantern window overhead cast light on to it.[11] The lighting, the accoustics, the open-space concept of the floor plan permitted one to see the officiants and to read liturgical texts. The church's sober two-storey exterior, surmounted by a triangular fronton or pediment, contrasted with a richly-adorned interior of altar-paintings, bas-reliefs, columns and capitals in stucco, all crowned with luxuriant ceiling frescos in trompe-l'oeil, giving the impression of limitless height reaching to the heavens. This kind of church was reproduced thousands of times in Catholic countries over the next two centuries.

Innocent X Pamphili (1644–55) reconstructed the city's central square, the Piazza Navona, with a new palace, a new church and Bernini's fountain. Building alongside the pontiffs were their relatives; the Villa Borghese, erected by the cardinal-nephew, was one of the most opulent; the nephew of Pope Gregory XV Ludovisi quickly acquired palaces in Rome and Frascati to display a marvellous collection of paintings and statues. The Barberini palace boasted a theatre capable of seating 3,000 guests. Italian princely families also needed an adequate "embassy" in Rome. Antonio Sangallo's Palazzo Farnese was the most prestigious address, becoming the French embassy after mid-century. After 1620 the Este family restored at huge expense the Villa d'Este with its gardens and fountains.

No pope devoted himself to building as single-mindedly as did the Sienese Alexander VII Chigi (1655–67), who was an art historian in his native city while still a cleric with minor orders. He rebuilt Rome with the tourist in mind, improving streets and squares where important people travelled. Roman grandeur was both practical and aesthetic, for wide, straight streets eased traffic problems created by the vogue for coaches that were now a status symbol. Rome increasingly attracted young men on a Grand Tour to learn good manners and polite conversation, improve their taste in painting, sculpture and architecture.[12] Grandiose buildings attracted tourists and employed innkeepers, domestics and provisioners, while noblemen rented out apartments in their palaces. Public building was also justified by the work it provided, as a check on chronic unemployment and begging. The supreme pontiff spurred nobles and prelates to finish the houses, *palazzi* and churches they started. In keeping with seventeenth-century concepts of propriety and dignity, empty lots were filled with decorous buildings, and the mean one-storey houses made way for taller apartment houses. Not content with completing his predecessors' buildings, Alexander VII planned his own, toying with a wooden model of Rome with movable monuments in his bedchamber.[13] New city squares imparted a theatrical effect. The Chigi pope pondered other grand architectural designs in terms of dramatic effect, and strove to transform the entire city into a giant theatre for religious pageantry. The architect he entrusted with the major projects was Gian Lorenzo Bernini, who was in addition a sculptor of genius and the pope's personal designer of coaches, medals, ecclesiastical vestments, festival apparatus and stage sets. From the 1630s Bernini was a virtual "artistic dictator" of Rome, promoting or hindering the careers of rivals.[14] Of his projects for Alexander VII, the most important was the oval-shaped colonnade before Saint Peter's. Built between 1656 and 1667, the covered colonnade like the protective arms of Mother Church could embrace 100,000 pilgrims. Another project created a ceremonial entrance to Rome on its north wall, the Piazza del Popolo, where most visitors arrived. It included a trident of streets leading into the distance, announced by identical churches opposite the gate. These dramatic streetscapes were intended to be decorated with ephemeral triumphal arches, tapestries hung from windows, symbolic figures erected in wood or painted on canvas in front of a church or palace. The most typical manifestation of baroque piety was the procession, with its floats and its machines moving along in a great cortège. The flowering of associational life, with the new religious orders and over 130 new confraternities, added to the spectacle. Ancient buildings were not always set off to good advantage; many were modified and still inhabited. Alexander took special care to restore the Pantheon, the sole remaining pagan temple, now a church. He tore away the attached buildings, and reworked the square around it to create a "panorama" effect. Chigi also commissioned work on the Roman university, the Sapienza, with its library and botanical garden. There were more parks, gardens and tree-lined avenues in Rome than anywhere in Europe, often conceived and planned by the pope in person. Alexander's successor, Clement IX Rospigliosi used his short mandate to embellish the Ponte Sant' Angelo, the bridge by which pilgrims and ambassadors approached Saint Peter's, with Bernini's ten statues of angels holding the instruments of Christ's crucifixion.

By the middle of the century the pace of Roman expansion began to wane. A number of landmark monuments would rise before the century's end, but the rapid growth was over, and money for new projects dried up. With the death of Alexander VII in 1667, the papal government paid about two-thirds of its revenues merely to service the debt. Bernini died in 1682, and the flame of great architecture passed to France, where Bernini's project for the Sun King's palace at Versailles was rejected in 1665. Foreign rulers no longer vied for Roman patronage, favours and subsidies. Before the end of the century, a series of measures to curtail papal nepotism also deprived those families of the means by which they produced monuments to their family's glory. Italy's economic crisis finally caught up with Rome.

The city fell back on its role as a cultural capital, probably Europe's third-ranking city after Paris and London. A certain cultural tourism was keenly interested in the vestiges of antiquity, and collectors eagerly sought ancient art objects. The popes and Roman collectors began to put their own antiquities into "museums" open to the public. This led to more systematic excavation of ancient sites, with little concern for archaeological knowledge.[15] The Counter-Reformation's institutions for learning were not Europe's least significant, despite the bad press occasioned by Galileo's condemnation in 1632. The Jesuit Collegio Romano acquired university status, as did the Sapienza. Clerics and bureaucrats (often the same) were clients for the eighty-nine official booksellers existing in 1622, flourishing despite the Inquisition's supervision of the titles. The Inquisition, which once kept tight watch over neighbourhoods at Easter to see that everyone took communion, left tourists alone after the 1640s unless they went out of their way to outrage Catholic tenets and customs. Protestants of good family could now be presented to the pope in person, where they prostrated themselves to kiss his toe.

Spectacle remained one domain where Rome continued to compete with European capitals. The Jesuits' pedagogical manifesto, the *Ratio Studiorum* of 1599, integrated theatre into the heart of instruction, and fostered it consistently. They banned female personages and women's clothing, but permitted music, dance, and scenography. Rome adopted opera before the middle of the century. The city's cultural life was nevertheless circumscribed by a Counter-Reformation concern for decency, depending on the pope's interpretation of it. The stern Innocent XII Pignatelli ordered the destruction in 1697 of Rome's first public theatre, built in 1671. He banned almost all of the profane spectacles, while giving unprecedented stimulus to the Oratorio form, with its *castrati* stars. Private theatre still flourished, however. The exiled queen Christina of Sweden made her Roman *palazzo* a cultural centre of European importance from the late 1650s until her death in 1689. She moved her art collection (much of it plundered from Catholic churches by Swedish soldiers in the Thirty Years War) and her library into Palazzo Riario, and received scientists and scholars among those who frequented her palace. In 1674 she founded the *Accademia Reale* as a seat of learned and eloquent discussion.[16]

Roman Society

By virtue of church patronage, Rome was the capital of contemporary art and fashions until after 1650, a world of painters, sculptors and architects, fountain-designers and hydraulics engineers, gardeners and silversmiths.[17] Rome in 1630 was also a great artisanal centre, with its 24,000 masters and journeymen, in at least 71 guilds. Elites required skilled tailors, sculptors, plasterers and stucco workers, coachmakers and gilders, and crowds of construction workers. Basilicas required musicians and choristers. These were masculine trades all. Early in the seventeenth century, there were 63,000 men to 47,000 women. The capital sucked in talent not only from Italy but a good part of Europe as well. Sixteenth-century Rome was a city of immigrants.[18] Cardinals were not their only patrons,

especially since fewer of them could afford the coaches, liveries, sil-
verware and jewels, banquets and charitable gestures that enabled
them to maintain their rank.[19] The turbulent aristocracy gradually
emerged alongside the prelates as a court nobility, prefiguring that
of Versailles. The aristocracy possessed most of the thousand-odd
coaches encumbering city streets around 1600. Along with the
expensive coaches, each requiring the purchase and upkeep of six
presentable horses, Roman aristocrats needed to uphold their rank
through ceremonies of conspicuous consumption. After the last
great building projects were undertaken under Pius VI, Rome
counted 60 great noble palaces, but 337 *palazzi* of various kinds, in
addition to the 440 villas around the city.

Along with nobles, ecclesiastics were suitably numerous. By the
eighteenth century the city counted 240 monasteries of male religious, and 73 convents of female religious. Clerics, including about
2,000 nuns, comprised about 7 per cent of the population of 140,000
in 1740. Even laymen, scholars especially, wore clerical garb in
order to acquire social standing. The papal army provided military
patronage for fewer than a hundred officers of all ranks.[20] About a
quarter of the population lived from the indolent bureaucracy,
which included 4,000 "officials" in the sole Datary, or tax office. A
new clientèle had to be satisfied with each election. Nine lay and two
ecclesiastical tribunals competed with each other for business. Their
sentences were frequently contradicted and undermined by special
exemptions. Jurisdiction was a source of honour, and so became the
object of rivalry and compromise. As the Curia defended ecclesiastical immunities and exemptions more scrupulously, the state
became increasingly paralysed.[21]

It was considered rare for native Romans to exercise a trade or
commerce. Rome was a capital for the poor as well as the rich, as
charity accounted for a healthy part of government expenditure.
The popes provided a broad range of social support services for ordinary Romans. One sign of Roman prosperity was the great number
of beggars, estimated at 10,000 in the 1660s.[22] The poor and the
chronically unemployed numbered about one person in seven or
eight. Without wishing to insinuate that easy charity created depen-
dence in early modern economies, it seems that this was indeed true
in Rome. The hospice of San Michele that Sixtus V built to intern
beggars could shelter only 200 elderly poor and 400 orphans. These
projects could not begin to staunch the flow of alms-seekers who
lived permanently in Rome. Innocent XII attempted to intern

beggars again in 1692, calling the French Jesuit Guevarre to Rome to build a "General Hospital" similar to the great building in Paris. An array of charitable institutions distributing public assistance flanked it. There were shelters for the homeless and for battered wives, and shelters for prostitutes who desired to change professions. The popes provided money to teach a trade to boys, or to dower a girl. Charity money bailed debtors out of prison, where they constituted a large portion of the inmates. Charities provided foundling hospitals for children too, which contained 2 per cent of the population in 1800. Hospitals were more freely available in Rome than elsewhere in Europe, and were well managed by the standards of the time. Alexander VII built the hospital of San Gallicano for venereal and skin diseases, where the treatment was quite advanced. Some hospitals trained physicians and surgeons in Rome by offering specialized instruction.[23] Rome also pioneered a new kind of prison, the *Carceri Nuove* (1652–5) on the model of the monastery, where delinquents did penance for their sins in small cells.

Those living an "irregular" life were more numerous than elsewhere. The imbalanced sex ratio provided prostitutes with steady employment. Popes and cardinals tried to crack down on it, and by 1600 prelates no longer frequented them openly. Various church initiatives tried to recover and convert prostitutes, or deliver their daughters from that upbringing. Much of the danger in the streets came from several hundred *sbirri*, whose ostensible task was to enforce the law. From churches to embassies, Rome was full of refuges for criminals, and harsh punishment was meted out to a small portion of them. Homicide by knife was reputedly very common.[24]

The key to public order was the provision of cheap food to the city, since the regulated market sought to shelter the population from the full impact of price variations.[25] The repetition of catastrophes marked a brutal end of the city's expansion. Famines in 1648, 1649 and 1653 were followed by a plague that killed 15,000 people in 1656 and an influenza epidemic the following year. Lethal malaria probably reflected widespread poverty more than the encroachment of the marshes. During periods of dearth, the public treasury distributed bread free. Rome consumed considerable quantities of food for the stable population. Much more was required in a Jubilee year. The *Annona* provided ever less meat, but salt cod gained popularity. Olive oil was the main fat element in the popular diet. Vegetables, legumes and citrus fruits were widely consumed and eggs were cheap. The nearby Frascati and Colli Albani vineyards provided cheap low-quality wines. The standard of living in Rome was good for the times.

Despite the relatively high standard of living for southern Europe, the economic crisis had important consequences. The city's population recovered to about 130,000 inhabitants, third in Italy after Naples and Venice, but it remained fixed there for another two centuries. The residential quarters of the medieval city had not changed much, despite the erection of great buildings on major arteries. Back streets were as mean and filthy as in other European cities, since people left their garbage there. By the eighteenth century Rome began to live on the glory of the previous two centuries. It was a large but lethargic city with no real economy outside the papal government or cultural and religious tourism. It remained locked into the model of the Counter-Reformation capital until the king of Italy's troops breached the wall in 1870. Europeans gradually forgot how modern the city had been, how urbanism and theatricality had combined to make it the universal capital that the popes had striven to create.

11   Bella Figura: the Baroque Era

The term *baroque* first appeared in the mid-eighteenth century to designate something cluttered and overblown. The connotations since have been predominantly negative, as Italians associate the style with the period of their decline. This is a pity. The baroque aesthetic sought to express grandeur, a sensibility on the wane since the seventeenth century. The modern world prefers simplicity, spontaneity, naturalism. Baroque was expansive, generous and audacious.[1] We must judge the period's achievements not by how well they accord with modern, minimalist sensibilities, but how well they conveyed the intended effect. Baroque art was "showy", but conspicuous consumption and sumptuous appearances were part of an aristocratic and religious culture that stressed façades and the importance of the *bella figura*. In an era when the adjective "pompous" bore a positive connotation Italians made a point of putting on a spectacle.

A World of Spectacle

Baroque spectacles varied little from the Renaissance ones which preceded them, but the seventeenth century witnessed an explosion of festive occasions of every kind.[2] The entire city could be the location for processions, cortèges, triumphs, and masquerades. These filed through the gates, along the main arteries where the aristocracy lived, towards the central square or another focal point, passing under ephemeral triumphal arches painted for the occasion. People in their houses and *palazzi* fixed torches above to illuminate the

147

street, and draped precious cloths or canopies from their windows to enhance the decorative effect. Floats were moving stages with changing scenery, shooting water or erupting fire. They might depict palm trees, suns, moons, flowers, allegories of fame, or victory, besides the inevitable ancient deities. Atop some floats choirs sang. On others musicians accompanied short dramatic sketches played by amateur or professional actors.

Every city celebrated carnival. Costumed and disguised revellers poked fun at social elites, such as gluttonous, lascivious friars, and bespectacled physicians wielding gigantic syringes. Popular revelry culminated on Mardi Gras, announcing forty days of Lenten austerity that began with Ash Wednesday. For ten days the elites held concerts, banquets, plays, tournaments and races. Some urban events were famous, like the marriage of Venice to the sea, in which the doge dropped a wedding ring into the lagoon. Naples celebrated the *cuccagna*, an array of live animals, birds and other foodstuffs attached to a mock fortress, on to which the crowd, brandishing knives, rushed at the drop of a cord.[3] Many cities staged horse races preceded and announced by great parades, or comical buffalo or donkey races, their cavaliers astride them thrashing each other. Princes and cardinals, accompanied by a great cortège of horsemen and local corporations or militia bands, expected elaborate entrance ceremonies.[4] Momentous events required specific celebrations. The great naval victory of Lepanto (1571) gave rise to a wave of festivities in Venice, some becoming annual fixtures.[5] Religious festivities marked the calendar year. Churches were fitted out with ephemeral decorations, or their façades were draped over to make a backdrop for elaborate spectacles or the impassioned preaching of a star orator. Funerals infinitely more lavish than our own were a good occasion to proclaim the status of the deceased and his family. Behind the bier of any of the principal inhabitants trooped whole companies of priests and religious, members of confraternities in their hoods and habits, other members of the deceased's trade or guild, crowds of beggars and the honest poor rustled up for the occasion. Even artisans and their wives joined confraternities that added pomp to these occasions.[6]

Central Italian cities still staged *mazzasscudo* games, or organized donnybrooks. The most violent, involving the use of clubs or stone-throwing, had been suppressed by 1500. Venetian artisans waged a "war of the fists" over bridges in working-class districts.[7] In Pisa gentlemen contested a bridge over the Arno, wielding a stout shield. In

Florence noblemen arrayed in battle formation played an intricate team "football" called *calcio*, driving the ball into the opposing end by assault and battery.[8] Each event was preceded by a formal challenge, processions, waving of banners, beating of drums. The battle was followed by the victor's triumph, a cavalcade of men in military array, preceding a chariot decked with allegorical figures. The medieval joust enjoyed a surprising longevity in Italian cities, reviving after 1550 as a consequence of the vogue for chivalric romances. Organizers phased out real combat in favour of a skill-testing charge in which the contestant attempted to break a hollow lance against a wooden target, with points allotted for accuracy or flourish. Many events were stage-managed by princes to glorify their policies, and were widely publicized. The prince, his leading nobles and courtiers turned out in force to enact mock battles, like the *naumachia*, in which miniature galleys simulated naval battles against the Turks. The joust was an ideal occasion for young gentlemen to show off in their native city, and most of the spectators would have been nobles too. This was a theatre for conspicuous consumption, so the descriptions dwelled primarily on the sumptuous ornamentation on the weapons and the bejewelled costumes of the participants. Tournament spectacles increasingly evolved into ballet.[9] Emblem books and mythological encyclopedias were routinely plundered during court festivals; indeed, we need these today to unravel the meaning of allusions hinted at when allegory was voluntarily obscure.[10] Emblems and devices eventually omitted the chivalric reference altogether. By 1690 street and court festivals lose all trace of references to Ariosto.[11]

Princes in Italy patronized the other arts. They bought prints, precious stones, tapestries, jewels, paintings, sculptures, ivories, bronzes, books and sumptuous furniture to ornament their palaces, and distributed them as gifts to loyal servants, court favourites and foreign dignitaries. More money was spent on theatre and music than in any other sphere. Duke Vincenzo at Mantua would not be outdone by his peers in Turin or Florence. In 1608 he built a temporary theatre seating 5,000 people for a performance of Monteverdi's opera *Ariana*. Wondrously complicated spectacle machinery underneath the stage required more than 300 men to work it. Scenographers and impresarios contrived visual wizardry to amaze the audience, aided by special effects and machinery. It was soon too complex to construct for ephemeral use, even by spendthrift princes. Ranuccio Farnese completed an innovative court theatre at Parma in 1618, the

first to use the "picture frame" stage. The population subsidized
these arts with their tax money. In other instances, wealthy aristocrats and churchmen bore the costs from their own income.
Productions of the court, the nobles, the colleges and the confraternities were all free, and academies promoted theatrical representations too. Since these spectacles were free, they enjoyed few
performances. There were also theatres for comics and comedies,
under the supervision of municipal magistrates, open to all comers
for a modest price.

Baroque Music

No art was so deeply marked by Italian baroque sensibilities as music,
where even nobles could display their '*virtù*'.[12] Churches needed
choirmasters, organists and singers to celebrate the liturgy; courts
used musicians for their ceremonies and for private entertainment.
They were always on hand for theatrical entertainments, dances and
banquets. Private individuals practised music as a pastime, with many
members of the upper classes receiving training. Even peasant
youths strummed guitars and sang *serenate* beneath the windows of
the girls they courted or scorned. The natural outgrowth of this
broadly-based musical culture was the *madrigal*, a polyphonic song
performed by amateurs for their own enjoyment. At their peak
between 1580 and 1620, Italian music printers produced as many as
80 volumes or albums of songs annually.[13] This was a genre for dilet-
tante musicians, with the lute or the guitar for instrumental accompaniment more often than the expensive keyboard. Poets wrote
madrigal verse, like the *Rime* of Giovan Battista Marino, whose lyric
poetry of contrasting metaphors and virtuoso wordplay lent itself to
musical evocations.

Musical style in the Renaissance tended to be intellectual and
declamatory. Mannerist style after 1530 favoured complexity for its
own sake; form and virtuosity became as important as content.
Religious music was quite diverse, embracing several genres, from
plainsong, through choral recitation, to polyphony with instrumental accompaniment. The Counter-Reformation intended to go
"backwards" to the simpler style, placing the emphasis on decorum
and rigid adherence to the sacred texts. Carlo Borromeo fixed
guidelines for composers of religious music, to avoid any profane or
frivolous manner in it. Like other artists, musicians were subject to

Plate 1   Luca Giordano, Un Concert *(Musée du Louvre)*

151

patronage systems. It was possible to live from music with many private patrons, such as cardinals or great nobles, or collegiate churches and confraternities. Large cities like Rome and Venice required hosts of singers and musicians to fulfil the requirements of religious celebrations. Tourists were advised in guidebooks where they might go to hear the best organists and choirs. Churches burst forth in music during the Forty Hour devotion, the triumphs, funerals, canonizations and all the anniversaries of saints and martyrs. During Lent and Advent, particularly, musical performances were frequent at the oratories. This demand led the authorities to raid hospices and *conservatories*, orphanages and convents to find the talent they needed. Venetian hospitals and orphanages had their own choirs and instruments to train their wards, using girls primarily. Elsewhere, choirmasters trained choirboys for liturgical ceremonies. Naples possessed at least four conservatories that were boarding schools given over to musical training. The boys there practised four to six hours daily, each on his own score in a deafening cacophony that trained his concentration and his ear.

Papal dislike of female singers fixing the intent desire of male spectators led to an increasing recourse to *castrati*. Singing eunuchs might have come from Islamic Spain. The first two Italian castrati were officially admitted to the Sistine chapel choir in 1599, where their success was immediate. Castrati remained part of the Roman music scene until the end of the Papal State in 1870. By castration a surgeon removed the boy's spermatic cord and testicles. In addition to losing an adam's apple and body and facial hair, the castrato gradually acquired the muscular mass of a woman. His ribcage expanded to a slightly rounder shape as a sounding box, while retaining the female pitch. Intense practice then built up the requisite muscularity in the vocal chords. The castrato voice differed from the male singing voice through its lightness and range, while differing from the female voice in its power. Roman church choirs alone employed about 200 castrati in 1780. Many castrati singers became wealthy "stars" of the international stage.

One innovation in sacred music compatible with the Jesuit *Ratio Studiorum* was the oratorio, launched in the Roman Jubilee of 1600. The oratorio was sacred theatre, designed to enhance piety. Without female personages or boys dressed as women, castrati played central roles in it. While not acted like opera, the oratorio permitted instrumental accompaniment and short dance interludes before a scenic backdrop. Promoted by colleges and confraternities, sponsored by

Jesuits in the south and Sicily, and by academies and confraternities elsewhere, these performances sometimes mobilized a cast of hundreds. The decision of Innocent XII Pignatelli to demolish Rome's first public theatre and to abolish opera and other theatrical representations in 1697 gave added impetus to the genre. Princely courts were also innovative musical forums in the late sixteenth century. Princes themselves sang, played musical instruments and cavorted with their courtiers. As virtuosity was an increasingly important feature of performing practice, a non-participant audience increasingly appreciated professional groups. Professional soloists knew how to make the appropriate facial and body expression to accompany the lyrics, for the voice was dominant over instruments until 1800. Italian and German princes competed with each other for the services of female singing stars, who were praised for "the gentle sighs, the discreet accents, moderation in trills, the skilful gestures, daring falls, soaring leaps, interruptions, onward drive, one tone of voice dying out, giving way to another which shoots up to the stars".[14]

Sixteenth-century theatre was accompanied by "intermezzi", brief dance and song interludes staged between acts. Stagecraft gradually enhanced their possibilities, as devices and machines were able to simulate fires, floods, flights from the heavens, magical effects, and appearances of monsters and gods. A trio of entertainers at the court of Florence, Jacopo Corsi, the poet Ottavio Rinuccini and the composer Giacinto Peri incorporated music, dance and scenography to the drama itself. In 1598 they produced the first "opera", *Dafne*, followed by *Euridice* in 1600, pastoral subjects that extolled the power of music. This was sumptuous court entertainment in which the number of performers and workers behind the scences might not be much inferior to the number of spectators. Florentine productions inspired Claudio Monteverdi's *Orfeo*, mounted in Mantua in 1607 by the *Accademia degli Invaghiti*. Its spectacular stage effects, mythological subject matter, allegorical figures, the use of instruments and extended choruses delighted audiences. Operas like it appeared intermittently for several decades, but they were infrequent because the genre was so expensive.

Another Monteverdi opera, *Andromeda*, staged in Venice in 1637, was a seminal event for a different reason. It was presented in a rented theatre to a paying audience. Monteverdi's collaborator, the stage-designer Giacomo Torelli, opened another theatre in Venice in 1641. With Torelli's new system of sliding wings, a handful of technicians could effect instantaneous scenery changes. Commercial opera, the sole purpose of which was entertainment, quickly became an Italian speciality. Like most commercial music, one opera soon made way for something different, but similar enough not to bewilder the audience. Public opera was "quick". There was little respect for rules of dramatic composition, rules of probability were flouted, and the sumptuous scenography, fantastical attire and happy ending compensated for the weak plot. Surprising details, like the recourse to real soldiers and cavalry horses for scenarios depicting the Trojan War, made it seem more real. Pastoral themes and deities of a mythical age still predominated, because the audience demanded "nobility" and "magnificence". The task of the librettist was to find a formula allowing for the greatest variety of showpiece tunes. The least important personage, in commercial terms, was the composer, who was sometimes not mentioned in the advertisements. Only around 1690 did several composers in the Roman academy of Queen Christina of Sweden become celebrities: Arcangelo Corelli, Bernardo Pasquino and Alessandro Scarlatti. Scarlatti composed 115 operas in all!

Commercial opera became a staple of the two-month-long carnival scene in Venice, which drew wealthy patrons from across much of northern Italy and Germany. Venetian-style operas appear at Genoa in 1644, Florence and Lucca in 1645, Bologna and Milan in 1647, Paris the same year, Germany in 1650 and England in 1656. People rented out boxes for the entire season, which protected theatre owners from a single flop. The aristocracy spent much of its time in their opera boxes, where they ate, conversed and played cards, stopping occasionally to lend an ear to a particular aria. As opera spread across Europe, it generated new subspecies, such as the French *tragédie lyrique* of Louis XIV's Italian-born composer Giambattista Lully and the Neapolitan comic opera around 1700. By the eighteenth century opera coloured even religious music and few composers wrote exclusively for the Church any more.

Visual Arts

The taste for visual splendour and grandeur that was part of the Renaissance did not diminish during the baroque age, for grandeur was in keeping both with the propensity of nobles to display their status and their taste, and with the Church's emphasis on God's majesty. Italy was the land of decorative arts: caisson ceilings, stone and wood inlay, gaily-coloured ceramics, decoration in enamelled tile, stucco work, decorative ironwork, gilt furniture, wrought silver plate and delicate crystal. Palaces and churches combined all of these to create a pompous effect. Aristocrats collected pictures that they put on view to visitors in their palazzi, where they might be jumbled one atop another, sometimes without frames. Since Catholicism used images as devotional supports, all but the poorest social groups bought paintings and statuettes.[15] The Venetian movable picture gallery gave rise to connoisseurship in painting on a new scale, whereby collectors cared more for the painter than for the subject.[16] Even minor aristocrats like the Botti of Florence could boast a collection of 200 items, including a Raphael, a Perugino and a Zuccari that attested to their concern for artistic pedigree. In contrast, Gérard Labrot and Renato Ruotolo note the slow development of aristocratic art collections in Naples, where for a long time after their appearance in 1620 they were simply a badge of wealth.

The painters and sculptors producing the images hoped to attract the attention of an influential patron whose esteem would lead to more prestigious commissions. Successful artists belonged to academies that cultivated classical traditions. Only Rome and Venice had anything like an art "market", with an abundance of antique or false antique statues for sale, or old master paintings seeking a new home. Artists displayed their wares in cloisters or squares on religious holidays to attract a clientèle. Although at first artists did not intend to sell them there, commerce soon became the focus of the exercise, and foreigners came to Italy to buy pictures.[17] By 1674 Rome counted at least a hundred art dealers selling everything from Roman antiquities to *bambocciate*, small genre scenes produced by Dutch and Flemish painters living in the city. In Naples, without a royal or papal court imposing a clear hierarchy of genres, painters responded to public fancy by producing small still lifes, landscapes and mythological scenes, decorative works alongside a plethora of devotional paintings.[18]

What exactly constitutes baroque and classical aesthetics is a point of academic debate. The closer one examines Italian art between 1550 and 1750 the less unity there seems to be. Raphael and his contemporaries sought to perfect the rules of drawing that incorporated perspective and physiognomy, shading and colour, architecture and landscape, in a corpus that students could assimilate. Perfection owed nothing to artistic individualism.[19] This art was *classical* in that

Plate 2   Federico Barocci, La Circoncision *(Musée du Louvre)*

it sought to impart an effect of reason and balance. Heinrich Wölfflin's enumeration of the five principles governing their "way of seeing" is still very useful.[20] (1) Renaissance artists conceived of objects as *delineated* forms, that is, they depicted them with lines, defining their contours and their surfaces. (2) Classical artists distributed their figures in parallel planes, generally in a frontal view. (3) The classical image has a closed configuration, that is, nothing is happening in the area just outside the edge of the frame. (4) Each part of the image can stand alone, even if solidly attached to the whole. The gaze moves from segment to segment without being drawn into a strongly emphasized central point. (5) Classical images emphasize clarity, in which shading has but a minor importance in defining forms, and colour is cosmetic.

The generation after 1530 gradually subverted these rules. Michelangelo Buonarroti idealized the creative process itself, celebrating the artist's conceptual powers in creating an image that surpassed mere skill in rendering objects. His disciples emphasized the "bizarre, capricious, fantastic inventions" that they termed *maniera*. *Mannerism* designated the artist's tendency to experiment with the rules of objectivity in order to achieve dramatic effect. Painters experimented with light and shade to achieve striking effects. They might contort the body into unlikely postures, or elongate necks, or arms and legs, or daub faces with unnatural shades of green or yellow, or compose extremely complex ensembles of personages with dogs, monkeys or birds, or anything else that they found fanciful. These preferences achieved official status when Federico Zuccari founded the first art academy, the Florentine *Accademia del Disegno* in 1566.[21] This academy was less a literary club than a "studium" open to students from everywhere. Youths began work there at an early age. In addition to sketching endlessly, they studied letters and assimilated the elegant bearing of aristocrats. Depth in letters enabled them to use art as a rhetorical tool: they "argued in paint" (Dempsey). The academy held competitions, lectures, conferences and even lessons in anatomy and mathematics. There was no notion that such rigorous training by precept killed creativity or inhibited intuition, which is a twentieth-century conceit. Such training did indeed separate these youths from mechanical artisans and village image-makers.[22] The model soon spawned imitations, first in nearby Perugia, and then in Rome where the same Zuccari established the Accademia di San Luca in 1593.

This search for originality and the taste for the bizarre (the

Milanese painter Arcimboldo constructed recognizable portraits of people out of fruits, vegetables and flowers) did not meet with unanimous praise, especially in the religious sphere. There was a demand for painters who could decorate altars, naves and vaults of churches and monasteries in a sumptuous manner. Clerical commentators and critics insisted that sacred images must be "accurate" and conform to tradition to retain their didactic value. Carlo Borromeo issued influential instructions for his clergy with regard to religious images; the artist's duty was to make his art subservient to truth. Inventions, ornaments and difficulties must not distract the ignorant. Art was a means of expressing the intangible, like the Immaculate Holiness of the Virgin Mary, the heroism of saints, the reality of transubstantiation and the legitimacy of Saint Peter's church.[23]

Baroque art rejected the fantastical aspects of mannerism. Ludovico Carracci at Bologna absorbed the works of the more sober, early mannerists. He, his brother Annibale (1560–1609), and cousin Agostino Carracci reacted consciously against mannerist excesses by creating a more realistic style. Together they enunciated a doctrine by which an artist's true path was close study and imitation of antique models, and the best of each of the modern masters. In 1583 the Carracci opened their own school in Bologna, the *Accademia dei Desiderosi*, whose members were expected to draw all things with great accuracy. They wanted to reproduce versimilitude in order to convince the spectator of truth. In 1595 Annibale Carracci took up Cardinal Odoardo Farnese's invitation to go to Rome and decorate a gallery in the sumptuous Palazzo Farnese with a mythological cycle. Agostino followed in 1597, while Ludovico remained in Bologna to train gifted painters such as Guido Reni, Domenichino and Francesco Albani, who would constitute the next generation of artists. The Palazzo Farnese cycle is one of the canonical achievements of Western art, and its completion thrust the Bolognese into international view. These Emilians would dominate Italian and European painting for the next sixty years, relaying their images through the new technique of engraved copper plates. They did so partly by organizing guilds and corporations to teach academic rules to young apprentices. Medieval corporatist structures were part of the art world until the First World War. The Bolognese and their imitators became firmly ensconced in the Roman *Accademia di San Luca*, whose members obtained the lion's share of official commissions.

Almost immediately thereafter, a new influence burst on the scene, in the form of young Michelangelo Merisi, called after his Lombard home town, Caravaggio (1573–1609). While bent on rendering objects with painstaking realism, Caravaggio never learned drawing in the academic sense, and made a virtue of painting directly from the model. Unlike the Caracci, he selected his models in defiance of the requirements of classical reference, by resorting to the common people, unremarkable in their appearance, expression and behaviour.[24] His paintings also evoked the underworld, to which he belonged, in his depictions of card-sharpers, soldiers, fortune-tellers and lute-players. His sacred painting eschewed mythology, ancient history and classical literary themes in order to focus upon the dramatic moment, to represent a scene as immediately as he could. For a brief decade, the Lombard painter shocked and impressed churchgoers with dramatic images he painted in Rome to Naples, in Messina, in Malta, always one step ahead of the law.

To return to Wölfflin's five categories, with Caravaggio we arrive at a different "way of seeing". (1) Instead of building the image from linear forms and clear outlines, the painter renders objects which blend together more smoothly. (2) Baroque painters like Caravaggio tended to adopt a perspective in depth, integrating the foreground and background into a continuous space. (3) Instead of a closed, bounded object, the baroque image leaves the spectator to imagine more happening off the edge of the canvas. (4) Baroque artists were very skilled at heightening the dramatic atmosphere of their subjects by drawing the eye to a single point that held the gaze. (5) Finally, over perfect clarity, these painters used shadow to its best effect, casting light rather on a few dramatic parts. This technique, which Caravaggio exploited more fully than anyone before, is called *chiaroscuro*. A generation of painters immediately seized upon this dramatic lighting, which became a kind of cliché for baroque painters everywhere.

Caravaggio's imprint wore off after several decades. Painters reverted to light and airy tones in the manner of Giovanni Lanfranco in Rome, and then Pietro da Cortona (1596–1669) reintroduced standard facial types from Greco-Roman sculpture and found new ways to present classical fables and mythology. A wide variety of painting styles coexisted in seventeenth-century Italy, although they usually conformed to Wölfflin's visual categories. Roman patrons gave leeway to the artist to use his own inclinations for the details, although painters often turned to poets or scholars

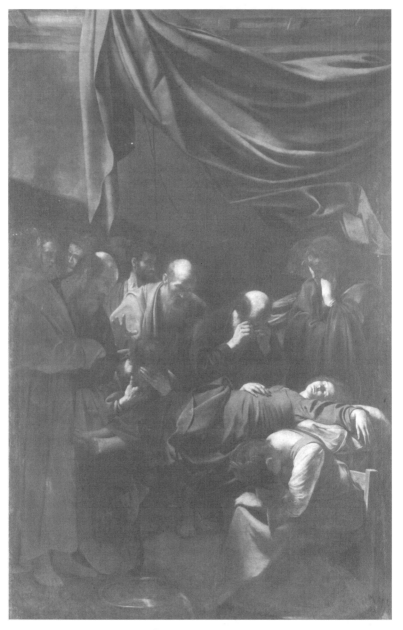

Plate 3   Caravaggio (Michelangelo Merisi), La Mort de la Vierge *(Musée du Louvre)*

for erudition on ancient lore. Artists showed new interest in surface textures, and expanded the use of solid colour on large patches of the canvas.[25] Late baroque painting indulged in illusionist techniques, or *trompe l'oeil*, such as Bernini's utilization of paint and stucco on church ceilings to give the impression of infinite space, and otherwise played with perspective to give the illusion of depth. Pietro da Cortona's ceiling frescoes for the Palazzo Barberini in 1640 were a vast expanse of swirling figures illustrating a single theme, unbroken by compartments. Painted ceilings filled the heavens with human figures perched on clouds, or gripping the edges of some fantastically high architecture. This was an art that sought to impress, to surprise, to overwhelm the spectator.

Academic painters and sculptors defined art for most of the modern era. By virtue of his magical ability to give life to stone and to infuse it with movement, Gianlorenzo Bernini (1598–1680) gave his name to the age in Rome. Bernini and other Roman sculptors then multiplied the number of bas-reliefs, which were part detached figure and part pictorial representation that blurred the lines between image and reality. Church decoration embraced stucco, which was lighter than stone or marble and could be modelled easily into audacious forms, then painted or gilt. Bernini integrated all these media in the church of Sant' Andrea al Quirinale, blending architecture and ornament, marbles, stucco, gilding and fresco.[26]

Young painters usually began in the provinces, acquiring a series of commissions in a circle of patrons, paid by the square foot. Once discovered by a prince or a cardinal, they would be lodged more like courtiers in their palace than as servants. Hence, the need for acquiring good manners, breeding, letters and a gentlemanly demeanour.[27] Painters in demand could live like lords in *palazzi* and travel by carriage, and charge hundreds of scudi for a single work. Giovanni Francesco Barbieri, known as Il Guercino (1591–1666), of very modest background conferred on himself the title of *Signore cavaliere . . . pittore eccellentissimo*. In Naples Francesco Solimena gave private lessons to barons eager to learn his secrets. Marco Antonio Franceschini, son of an Emilian blacksmith, obtained the title of noble and established his own academy.[28]

By 1700 there appeared the first signs of a new direction, influenced by the literary group around queen Christina of Sweden that took the name *Arcadia*. It consciously reacted against the extravagance and exuberance of the baroque in the arts generally. Its advocate was the librarian of Queen Christina, Giovanni Pietro Bellori,

Plate 4 Domenico Manetti (attributed), Scene Religieuse Prêché aux Portes d'une Chapelle *(Musée du Louvre)*

whose collected biographies of artists appeared in 1672. Bellori's *Lives* saw the artist as someone in search of perfect beauty, achieved by studying objects and figures in nature, selecting the best from them to combine in an ideal world, like the *capriccio* that juxtaposed snippets of ideal form in an imaginary whole. In this way, the artist surpassed mere nature, which is never perfect in itself.[29] Bellori dismissed as trivial genre painting in the Dutch style. His influence was perceptible among the French painters in Rome (Poussin in particular), and he strongly endorsed the classical doctrines of the French academy in Rome, founded in 1666. The Accademia di San Luca erected itself as the arbiter of taste by decreeing specific rules for painters to adopt, on the French model. Ceiling frescoes after 1700 tend to be airier and paler, containing smaller and fewer figures, rendered with a more delicate palette. There was increasing preference for charm, grace and decorative effect.[30] One might speak of an Arcadian style of painting that internationally took the name *rococo* – a measured, graceful, cheerful baroque appearing simultaneously in France and Catholic Germany. Italian painting remained in great demand across Europe. Foreign visitors to Venice, Florence and Rome sought out copies or imitations of old masters, and bought treasures real and fake from the increasing number of art dealers. Venice was a point of entry for foreign painting styles, especially Flemish. Italians began to collect and display more prominently genre paintings, landscapes, still lifes, and other themes outside Italian artistic traditions.[31] Painting acquired new vigour in eighteenth-century Venice, where painters such as Francesco Guardi, or Antonio da Canale, called Canaletto, daubed the equivalent of postcards for wealthy foreigners. Of the Venetians, Giambattista Tiepolo enjoyed the most brilliant career, his splendid frescoes on mythological and historical themes covered palace walls and ceilings from Friuli to Spain. This was a sensual painting that had great appeal to consumers. Even Venetian painting gradually reflected the desire for simplification.[32]

Rome remained the critical centre of Italian and even European art for the entire eighteenth century, a "free port" (Honour) of ideas. Nearly every important artist spent time there sketching the masterpieces of every age. Rome was also a Mecca for the dilettanti of Europe, a cheap city for gentlemen and painters who were steeped in classical themes. The two most influential theorists were not Italian at all: Anton Rafael Mengs in the 1760s strove for "noble simplicity and calm grandeur". He advocated a synthesis of classical sculptures and Raphael's paintings, spurred on by a Prussian writer, Johann Winckelmann, librarian to Cardinal Albani, who stressed the importance of imitating antiquity as the key to true style.[33] New excavations near the foot of Mount Vesuvius at Herculaneum (1738) and at the newly discovered Pompeii (1748) were important artistic events. They yielded a treasure trove of ancient objects and images that books of engravings made familiar to Europeans. English revival of interest in the sixteenth-century architect Andrea Palladio spread to France and Italy too. Francesco Milizia, chief of Royal Buildings in Naples after 1761, furthered this new "Greek taste" in the peninsula.[34] The reaction against the baroque aesthetic was also a moral reaction. Themes after 1750 became more high-minded, promoting not piety and mortification, nor gaety and eroticism, but an austere and stoic secular morality. The gods, fauna and satyrs of rococo, were replaced by secular figures, such as warriors, lawgivers and great philosophers. History painting was promoted as the school of virtue, rich in "role models". The simplicity acclaimed in the paintings of Pompeo Batoni was then radicalized in the sculpture of Antonio Canova, a disciple of Winckelmann. In his funeral monument to Pope Clement XIV, elaborated from 1783 to 1787 and placed in Saint Peter's basilica, Canova did away with the billowing draperies, the multicoloured marbles and rich ornaments, the illusionistic devices and symmetrical compositions that had characterized sculpture since Bernini. Baroque and rococo ways of seeing reverted to firm and unequivocal contours and bold, flat areas of paint, applied cosmetically rather than defining the image itself. Baroque diagonal composition gave way to the frontal view, and the sinuous complexities of rococo space gave way to elementary clarity. The palette faded and painters soon advocated the elimination of colour altogether in the name of purity. This was neoclassical style, no longer the official style of the Catholic religion, but rather the "way of seeing" of the French Revolution.

12   Aristocracy

Urban Nobility of Northern and Central Italy

The urban seat of Italian nobility makes it distinct from those of northern Europe. When, in the early sixteenth century, these citizens fell under the spell of social ranking, jurists and moralists defined nobility with new sharpness. Nobles exuded an excellence that was summed up in the word *virtù*. Nobility was knowledge, wealth and pedigree, valour in war and leadership over men.[1] Rank justified privilege; nobles were exempt from torture and from certain sumptuary laws; their *palazzi* were often off-limits to police searches and pursuits. Nobles celebrated their difference from roturiers through a multitude of parades enacted at the moment of elections and promotions, and during family rites of passage like weddings, funerals and conferral of university diplomas. The preoccupation with the prerogatives of nobility made it compelling to know exactly who was noble. One solution was the *serrata*, that is, the decision by governing bodies to restrict office-holding to themselves and their descendants.[2] After 1500 most cities adopted such a closed social hierarchy, based on a simple tautology: if command over subjects was a noble function, then those who wielded power were noble. Milan (1520), Genoa (1528), Lucca (1556) established their own rosters. Even in Florence, where no edict defining nobility and its privileges was ever promulgated, it was clear by 1530 which families enjoyed pre-eminence. An amalgam of merchants and bankers, bureaucrats and military nobles, all of whom owned land, made up the city patriciate and held a near-monopoly over the best religious benefices. By 1600 the city kept specific archives on its noble fami-

lies, copying or registering each of their wills, their testamentary provisions and dispositions, making it easy to establish descent or filiation. Nobles abandoned "vile" activities, restricted their marriages,
raised the levels of their dowries, inflated their titles and invested
heavily in landed estates. An explosion of works on heraldry ratified
the development, and Italians learned to decipher the dynastic
history of a house by glancing at its blazon.

Most cities retained mechanisms allowing new families access to
nobility if they fulfilled requirements of wealth, long residence and
distinction. In Tuscany the grand duke could waive the genealogical
requirements limiting access to the knights of Santo Stefano. This
effectively created a new noble family, since the "habit" ennobled its
bearer.[3] In Milan the upper bourgeoisie could imitate nobility by
buying fiefs in rural jurisdictions, often the first step towards
assuming full patrician status.[4] In many cities there was a distinction
between the older, richer families, and the more recent aggregates.
Everywhere a small number of families within the noble group held
a disproportionate number of the key positions.[5]

Karl Marx held aristocratic and chivalric ideals to be an elaborate
disguise to conceal the naked reality of class exploitation. This has
been qualified as too reductionist, but for purposes of exposition, let
us consider the urban aristocracy's multifarious ways of extracting
wealth from Italian society. Patricians combined officeholding in the
grand-ducal bureaucracy with active capitalist enterprise, drew revenues from estates growing grain or raising livestock and retained
church benefices in the family for many generations. Marx put great
emphasis on the feudal system with its many forms of tribute, service
and obligations. While tenants owed obedience to the lord as long as
he guaranteed protection and justice, formal feudal rights in central
and northern Italy were limited, despite the resurgence of granting
titles.[6] In the duchy of Milan, where there were no fewer than 1,500
feudal jurisdictions, there were virtually no "feudal" attributes of
control left, and no protests against the abuse of them.[7] Even in the
rural Marches around Jesi, fiefs were not good economic investments, if nobles drew any profit at all from them. The little research
we have on feudal justice is inconclusive. Feudal lords seemed more
likely to mitigate and pardon the sentences handed down by the
judges in their name than use fines to raise revenue.[8]

What noble families all had in common was their ownership of
land, which brought prestige, stability, resources for the family, and
the dependency of peasants. Generally speaking, the larger the city,

the more land its aristocracy possessed around it. The test for these families came from the sharp decline in agricultural prices after the plague of 1630. By 1650 we begin to see a general impoverishment, as many families were forced to sell their estates to other nobles.[9] Urban aristocrats often built their fortune on commerce and manu-facturing, functions that were not everywhere "vile", but they increas-ingly spurned the active direction of them. In Florence Litchfield speaks of a process of "involution". The patriciate never withdrew entirely from business, but such activity revolved around an ever-smaller number of large investors.[10] Those who continued to invest often did so through the *commenda* contract. In Milan an elite which had been extremely active in manufacturing in 1500, had withdrawn almost entirely from that field by 1650. One measure in 1663 excluded from nobility those who played an active role in com-merce. The crown of Spain reversed this decision in 1668, and in 1682 a royal proclamation pointedly emphasized that ownership and management of textile manufactures entailed no derogation of noble status, but this had little effect on widely held noble attitudes condemning merchant greed. Nobles with money to invest often chose to lend it to private individuals or government agencies. Even in peaceful Tuscany, the grand dukes farmed out indirect taxes to consortia of businessmen and nobles, who gained if the government did not reimburse them rapidly.[11] Nobles frequently held small IOUs on many borrowers in their clientèle, who could not always reimburse them, nor even provide good collateral.

Italian nobles enjoyed an advantage over aristocrats elsewhere in the wide range of paid activities in which they could display their *virtù* without derogating their status. No one doubted that military command was inherently noble, and princes reserved their senior positions to men of good pedigree. War was also a stepping stone to offices at court or diplomacy, but it was an expensive calling. War required costly equipment, and its participants were expected to uphold their rank despite the modest pay the state allotted them.[12] Parents destined their sons often from infancy for the crusading orders, the Knights of Malta and the Knights of Santo Stefano, which provided a modest "*commende*".[13] In lieu of sending their sons to war, parents educated them instead. Universities attracted massed contin-gents of young nobles destined for careers in medicine, on the bench and in the Church. Some professions such as law and senior positions in administration, medical licences and university profes-sorships, were given to them preferentially. Most of the canons and

senior clergymen were nobles, as were most bishops and the
plethora of officials in the Roman Curia. The timing of the invasion
of the Church by noblemen corresponds nicely to the worsening
economic situation after 1620.[14] Secular clerics required a family
patrimony that would guarantee them a basic income. Families frequently assigned (in reality, or just fictitiously) important revenues
to ecclesiastical offspring or relatives to evade state taxation. The
cleric could then transfer it back to his relatives in his will, or when
he received a benefice. The role of the Church as a fount of legal
privilege and tax exemption should not be underestimated when we
evaluate its attractiveness as a career. Many noblemen were content
to receive the minor orders and never advanced to the status of a
priest administering sacraments.

As patricians gradually became courtiers, a growing state bureaucracy opened up new avenues of employment. Prestigious offices,
like that of ambassador, were more a source of expenditure than of
revenue. Noblemen reflected the aspirations of their employer in
magnificent surroundings but produced the necessary funds from
their private fortune.[15] The prince assigned lucrative, salaried functions, which were often hereditary, to court nobles, and clothed and
fed the beneficiaries and their families even when they did not
reside at the palace.[16] A gradual increase in their salaries, the
younger age of appointment, and the practice of accumulating positions allowed many families to flourish at public expense. The prince
was also on the lookout for "poor" nobles to favour with modest
functions, deeming it unseemly for an aristocrat to live in straitened
circumstances. In order to help them maintain their rank, charitable
institutions appeared, the purpose of which was to provide dowries
and school bursaries to the daughters and sons of nobles.[17]

Discreet, even illegal, sources of revenue counted too. Both patricians and churchmen were notorious for not paying their taxes.
Their proximity to the prince allowed them to present their cases
sympathetically and obtain "adjustments".[18] What they could obtain
for themselves, they would obtain for others, for a fee. Influence-
peddling was the source of great fortunes amassed while in office,
and made access to offices worth fighting over. Brescia's religious
institutions, governed by members of aristocratic houses, served as
important lending institutions for the aristocracy, who borrowed
money at preferential rates and did not always repay it.[19] Grain-
smuggling by the leading families was also big business.

Diversification and corruption could not offset a permanent

adverse economic situation after 1620. Nobles always enjoyed different rules of inheritance from other social groups, wherein lineage considerations came before individual happiness. Different branches might make up a *consorzeria* with joint ownership of seigneurial rights and fiefs. Fathers did their best to keep the menfolk together after their death, and exhorted all their sons to respect family interests. Extended households owning property jointly could pursue different avenues of advancement simultaneously, with the aim of sharing the fruits of success. Daughters were also important, but in ways that were not explicitly recognized.[20] Their sentiments often bound them tightly to their parents and their siblings. Once married, they forged new connections and opportunities for their nephews and nieces. During the 1580s, however, more limited prospects forced fathers to favour one son, generally the eldest, and one daughter over the others. By establishing a *fedecommesso*, or an entail, fathers handed part or most of the estate to a single heir in each generation, over several generations. Heirs became merely a link in a long chain. Increasingly, only the eldest son inherited the *palazzo* and the title, by the practice of primogeniture. When the prince ratified a *fedecommesso*, he upheld the social order by looking after lineage interests. For the cadets, the most frequent destination was the Church. Some went to war, and still others entered the liberal professions. Many lived bachelor lives among rustics and small-town notables, away from the urban stage on which they could not afford to strut.

Saving the *casa* demanded celibacy from most of its offspring. New marriages became rarer, until only a third or less of each generation wed. Once parents restricted marriage to a single son, the lucky one could command a far higher dowry. This made it difficult even for wealthy families to establish more than one or two of their daughters. In Venice great families might command 200,000 ducats, a colossal sum that could beggar the father or brother who mortgaged his estates in order to pay it. In Florence aristocratic women received property on top of the dowry, the *fondo*, over which their husbands' families had no control.[21] Although women were married quite young, at 18 or 20, the median age for the men rose relentlessly. From 29 in republican Florence, it rose to 36 in 1700.[22] Such drastic measures soon led to a dramatic decline in the number of Italian nobles, because married couples could not always produce heirs. Ecclesiastics, soldiers or officials frequently went to the altar late in life to replace a deceased elder brother and procreate, if possible, with a bride twenty or thirty years younger. When that failed, houses endured by designating junior nephews on the female side to take their uncle's surname and forsake their own. New aggregations to the nobility did not reverse the decline. One might surmise that this "decline of the aristocracy" prepared a corresponding "rise of the bourgeoisie". Unfortunately for Italy, this did not occur. The poor economic circumstances after 1630 prevented "new money" from replacing older social elites.[23] Instead, the social and economic system in northern and central Italy stood immobile for a century and a half.

Feudal Nobility in the South

If urban rootedness was the experience of the northern nobility, the rural and provincial fief shaped southern society. An urban patriciate was not completely absent in the Mezzogiorno; all cities and towns contained noble houses. In L'Aquila many rose from the merchant and legal class making up the city council.[24] A few dozen families ruled each of the Apulian towns, but their number was modest compared to northern towns of similar size.[25] These houses were small fry next to the thousand or so families that owned fiefs. The fief's logic was military. The holder originally enjoyed the right to levy dues on his vassals to support his family and retainers, to maintain a military infrastructure, judicial and administrative machinery.[26] Alongside the castle, or in place of it, the lord often erected a showpiece *palazzo*. Feudatories flanked these monuments with churches and monasteries they founded or endowed. Church space was one of both piety and prestige, a meeting ground for priests, feudal lords and wealthy families of the jurisdiction. The seigneur also placed his mark on the fief by fixing his coat of arms or blazon, bearing inscriptions which proclaimed his quality, on village monuments.

There were legal limits on feudal power. Peasants were not bound to the land, as they were in Eastern Europe. Noblemen had no entitlement to claims not specifically mentioned in the statutes of the *università*. Feudatories had no property claim over common lands, and were not allowed to enclose them or plant there. Subjects could sell their crops freely, without rights of pre-emption. These were their rights. Depending upon the character of the baron and the autonomy of the *università*, they were not always observed.[27] A feudatory's power consisted of what he could get away with, the limits of his *prepotenza*. Still, in 1600 great nobles and their clients are thought to have perpetrated enormous abuses on vassals with impunity, although this impression needs extensive and close quantitative research. Noble feuding and banditry differed from northern Italy more in degree and duration than in nature. Nobles often employed hired assassins, or *bravi*, sometimes wearing their livery, who assassinated and kidnapped with relative impunity. Nobles also indulged in contraband and false coinage, and insinuated themselves into the levy of royal taxes for personal profit.[28]

The fief was a form of property that belonged to a different jurisprudence, inherited separately from non-feudal goods – real estate, public revenues, jewels or art objects – in order to prevent its breakup amongst siblings. The hold of a family over its fief was fragile because it was common for it to escheat to the crown and be sold to another beneficiary. Most fiefs could only be passed on through the direct male line; the absence or premature death of a son could often deprive a family of its jurisdiction. Taking advantage of the Spanish crown's insatiable demand for money, Neapolitan and Sicilian aristocrats gradually consolidated their hold.[29] The crown conceded them the right in 1586 to sell the fiefs to outsiders or to transmit them to lateral lineages in fictitious purchases. Overnight the aristocracy changed in composition, as debt-laden or bankrupt families were displaced by legal or financial families, the latter usually Genoese.

Then the redistribution of fiefs to new families came to an abrupt halt. The crown instead liberalized the succession rules, making it possible to transmit the fief to the third degree (1595), then to the fourth degree (1655) and finally to the fifth degree removed (1720). As barons tightened their grip on the land, so they extended their jurisdiction. In Sicily the baronage could purchase full *mero e misto imperio* after 1621. As Spanish power declined, feudal lords imposed illegal taxes of their own, and often extended their control over local government as royal administrators lacked the means to cope. The monarch sold titles too, often without fiefs attached, as a tax on snobbery. Titles inflated everywhere in Italy, even in republics like Lucca. The kings of Spain sold as many as they dared. In Sicily there were seven counts in 1500, but 21 by 1600. In the century after 1600, the monarchy sold over a hundred titles of prince in the island kingdom alone. In Naples in 1675 there were 119 princes, 156 dukes, 173 marquises and many hundreds of counts, unencumbered by any system of precedence.[30]

The eagerness for titles reflects the aristocracy's disinclination towards economic activism. Their financial caution eroded further when they abandoned their rural seats for political capitals, where other nobles pricked them into competition for status. The fief provided them with different kinds of income, which they generally farmed to a businessman; "regalian" rights accruing to their status; leasing local offices, like the notary, or the official who collected their fees, or the jailkeeper and the *portolania* who maintained the streets. They sold licences to outside vendors, for hunting and fishing. They leased mills, ovens, inns, butchers' stalls, presses or other activities. Tenants owed them a fee for taking up land, a *fida* for each grazing head of livestock, and registration fees for property transfers or successions.[31] Revenue also accrued from fines, but this gave them more power to bestow favours than it did revenue for their coffers.[32]

Baronial residence in cities entailed a fundamental shift in lifestyle. Nobles there spent huge sums on palaces and servants, horses, coaches and furnishings, in decorating chapels and convents, in processions and jousts.[33] Around 1600, half the Sicilian nobility was indebted from such excessive "liberality". Conspicuous consumption was a social problem of some magnitude, for noblemen's power also made it possible for them to avoid paying their debts. Indebtedness alone was not sufficient to force them to sell the fief, once this was possible. Creditors could demand seizure only of a part of the feudal income. Nobles rarely thought in terms of long-term economic expansion, and being satisfied with a stable rent, they confided the management details to agents.[34] The theoretical fortunes of the Neapolitan fiefholders were considerable. The median income hovered between 20,000 and 40,000 ducats; few were less than 10,000 ducats, based on a fixed capital generally twenty times as great. Debt crippled many families, and mismanagement reduced feudal revenues to a trickle. Managing the assets of the house, arranging marriages well in advance, renegotiating mortgages at better interest rates, initiating and sustaining litigation to defend or extend the family's patrimony, was a time-consuming affair, requiring expert legal and financial advice. Far-seeing marriage strategies and entails were the instrument of this struggle. The consolidation of the estate in a single heir appears around 1580, when testaments and marriage contracts stipulated conditions of inheritance with painstaking precision. Thereafter, the greater part of the patrimony passed in strict primogeniture. The length of entails was restricted to four descendants, chosen by the founder, although some property could be sold to pay legacies, debts and portions, despite prohibitions of alienation. The aristocracy divided some feudal property among different branches, and future generations passed portions back and forth between them. Spouses passed from branch to branch too. More distant branches of the same house intermarried in order to keep the estate under the same patronym, which often required a dispensation from the Church. Brides occasionally married downwards socially to strengthen patronage bonds, but *mésalliance* with merchant houses was to be avoided. Marriages often linked preferentially four families, generation after generation: parallel cousins, or crossed cousins married each other, while brother and sister married sister and brother. Dowries were the single most important cause of noble indebtedness. The bride was not so much its beneficiary as the vehicle by which it passed to her future children. When dowries went unpaid, ensuing litigation could pit lineages and families against each other for generations.[35]

These strategies to ensure the "eternity" of the noble house were preferable to multiplying the number of married couples. Supernumerary daughters were relegated to convents. Younger sons had the right to a life annuity, called the *vita e milizia*. By 1680 there was a drastic reduction of their portion as well, although prosperous uncles occasionally bequeathed their possessions to these cadets, or established dowries for their nieces. These stringent measures did not go unchallenged. They were the staple for legions of lawyers in Naples and Palermo, whose clients challenged the severity or generosity of the previous generation. In these manoeuvres, though, southern aristocrats resembled their peers elsewhere in the peninsula. Despite the difference between a city-based aristocracy and a feudal baronage, noble lifestyles varied little from one region to another.

The Noble Ethic

To quote a recent book by Richard Goldthwaite, "the ultimate definition of nobility was one of behaviour".[36] Urbanization of the nobility led to what Francesco Benigno calls a "new urbanity" around 1600. Display was central to medieval feudal culture, where in giftgiving, the objects exchanged symbolized good will and loyalty. Spanish viceroys and princes elsewhere opted for the "strategy of the court". The monopoly of important offices, the use of etiquette, and all the ritual pertaining to court and church life, contributed to the substance of noble power. The greatest families held court themselves, by attracting minor nobles to their palace as retainers. Noble festivities included jousts in the streets, banquets, music and ballet, *intermezzi*, dramas, oratorios and concerts. Sumptuous costume, a profusion of lace, gold and silver ribbons, and jewels were the rule, as was clientage of poets, musicians and artists. The expenditure paid dividends in the universal recognition of dignity and status, even at the risk of financial ruin. Even in republican Venice the model held sway.[37] Terraferma cities multiplied riding colleges and tournament societies where youngsters played at being heroes from chivalric romances.[38] This model seduced the petty nobility into living beyond its means. In Cremona conspicuous consumption drowned in debt the entire stratum of modest nobles in the later sixteenth century. Cities multiplied their sumptuary decrees to prevent the erosion of family income, to force nobles to desist from this competition, but without much success.[39] Aristocrats in church service built and decorated churches and chapels to the glory of their house. Every family celebrated the cult of particular saints, and patronized specific churches. Funerary rituals gradually became more gorgeous, with coats of arms on litters and coffins. Ostentatious burial rituals were a moment for displaying family power, its past and its continuity. Noble weddings similarly involved extravagant expenditures on jewels and costumes.[40]

No setting was so important to the family as the *palazzo*. As the feudal families moved to the capital cities, building sites multiplied to accommodate them. The *palazzo* was a large and artistically conceived building, filled with art objects and furnishings. It was not conceived as a private, but as a semi-public space where the family entertained and impressed other nobles, merchants, officials and dependants who frequented its salons. Their ornate façades greeted the entire street and great stucco coat of arms adorned their porticoes. Fountains, busts and bas-reliefs graced the courtyard, around which one found the storerooms, stables and a garage for the coach. Nobles sought the majestic, sumptuous effect of monumental staircases and frescoed ceilings.[41] The reception halls and salons on the first storey and the comfortable quarters on the floor above were especially well furnished, while a garret under the roof lodged the servants. Gradually nobles made room for libraries reflecting their cultural and spiritual interests. In Naples, aristocratic competition required ambitious men and women to renew the decor continuously, by rebuilding and redecorating in the latest taste. Northern Europeans found the places uninhabitable in the eighteenth century because of the lack of comfortable furniture, water closets, and heating in winter. By then even Italian nobles preferred to live in their country villas, near their great stables and private chapels, with their gardens so civilized that trees were pruned into geometric shapes to offer "perspectives", and clever hydraulic works played tricks with water to astonish and amuse visitors.

The new urbanity shaped behaviour to fit the model. The plethora of treatises on the nature of nobility gave way to a new concern for honour and distinction, which underpinned pedigree.[42] The campaign by moralists, clerics and magistrates to inculcate a degree of "self-control" into aristocrats began to bear fruit after 1600. The basic ethic they strove to impart was *gravitas*, a studied seriousness of gesture and conversation. Such formalism and ceremoniousness began at a very early age. Aristocratic parents confided their children to tutors or preceptors who were almost always ecclesiastics. Apart from basic literacy, girls learned the science of piety and the social graces, music and dance. There was not the intense intermingling of the sexes in Italy that was typical of the French nobility, and they would be called upon to share neither men's pastimes nor their interests. Boys and girls learned psychological distance and measure that was gentility internalized.[43] Noble children addressed their parents with the *tu* form until age eight or ten, and then adopted the polite second person, *voi*, or even the third person, *lei*, when speaking with family members. The kissing of hands, bowing and reverence they preferred were not hyperbole, but daily gestures of respect. Brothers and sisters gave each other the polite *voi* form of address too, and externalized the relationships of inequality between elders and cadets. Polished speech passed quickly to non-nobles in their wake. Servants were the conduit by which aristocratic knowledge, language and manners reached a more diffuse group. Every encounter was pregnant with the sense of rank, reflected in the specific forms of address, expressions and gestures of greeting and behavioural etiquette. Princes endowed Jesuit colleges for nobles with public money, seeing them as institutions geared to educate and train future leaders in society. Youngsters entered these institutions at about the age of seven, and then emerged at about twenty. The Jesuits did their best to keep them away from their families, in order to raise them in a closed environment. They taught *gravitas* to older boys by their example; they never joked or lost their temper, and they demanded absolute obedience. The priests demanded that children use with each other the polite forms of address, generally the third person, along with the proper title: a seven-year-old called to his playmate, "*Venga qui, Signor Conte!*" Failing this, the priests punished them. In their senior years, youths learned to write the eloquent letters of business, compliments and circumstance that the world expected of them. Students learned French, song, musical instruments, dance, drama, fencing, equestrian arts, but also etiquette and "body-language", or corporal deportment and gesture. Aristocrats codified the rules they lived by into a *scienza cavalleresca* that sought to establish the rules of proper dealing between noblemen, and determine breaches of it that called for the reparation of honour.[44] Ambitious individuals were always on the lookout for some action or word that might be interpreted as a slight or an insult, another form of competition for precedence in the theatre of the world. Fearlessly drawing one's sword in response to a challenge was part of the burden of being noble. One manual that justified this ethos was the *Duello* of Muzio. It went through 12 editions in Italian in the 35 years after it appeared in 1550, and then passed into French and Spanish translation.

More prosaically, nobles refined the art of polite sociability. Birth was generally not enough to obtain positions of wealth and power; nor was hard work and capacity. Rather, nobles in any career needed "recommendations" from well-placed patrons, whose antechambers they frequented to seek support. It helped to be charming, polite and affable. It was important for youngsters to be seen often with persons of power, pretending their presence was a sign of affable respect. They visited high-born women as well, to gather information, to learn important developments and to gain their good will, for their preferences were often important. Women visited women too, to promote their relatives and push their candidates to offices through the back door. Visiting was a delicate affair, regulated by protocol, guided by the status of who was visiting and who was visited. There were subterfuges of evasion, of "accidental" meetings, a whole ceremonial, the rules of which one learned at college and in the world.[45] These manners and values gradually lost their coherence during the eighteenth century, as a new French spirit of informality and intimacy gave ceremoniousness a new, negative connotation.

Part II

Time of Tempests, 1620–1730

Introduction to Part II

In both economic and cultural domains, the leadership role passed from Italy to northern Europe quite suddenly. The flourishing late-sixteenth-century economy was troubled only by corsair pinpricks against coastal towns and ships. The constant bleeding of resources towards North Africa induced Italian merchants to confer their cargoes on foreign carriers. Overseas trade became riskier, and Italians began to withdraw from some of their advanced outposts. Moreover, defending the coastline against the threat petrified fortunes in coastal fortresses and their garrisons, standing mostly unused, but indispensable. Regional wars in north-west and north-east Italy then undermined the long *Pax Hispanica* after 1613, as the divisions in Germany aligned Protestant states against the Habsburg emperors and emboldened Piedmont and Venice to shake the *status quo* in Italy.

The scale of war changed brusquely in 1618 with the onset of the German civil war, and the resumption soon after of hostilities between Spain and the Netherlands. France fought Spain by proxy, championing Piedmont, Venice and Mantua and inviting Italian states to shake off Madrid's tutelage. Repeat campaigns in the Po valley wrought devastation on Lombardy and Piedmont, and sucked vast resources out of the country to pay for the Habsburg cause behind which the Church and most Italians rallied. Taxes impoverished the population and punished manufactures. War weakened southern Italy as the Spanish state divested itself of its physical and political assets in exchange for short-term cash. Spanish weakness, culminating in a great revolt in Naples, helped rekindle the ambitions of Italian states that led to a short, general war between the

179

papacy and its northern neighbours. Even neutral Venice was swept
into an unequal struggle against the Ottoman Empire, and lost its
overseas Empire and its Levant trade after over a half-century of
stubborn resistance. Italian states would henceforth be disinclined to
settle their differences by force of arms, and nobles withdrew from
military careers that had become too costly for them.

The legacy of war included disease and ruin. It played havoc with
the peninsula's trade and manufactures, and accelerated the development of northern European competitors, who supplanted them
abroad and then at home. Soldiers brought disease, whose contagion hard times accelerated. The plagues of 1630 and 1656 soon
gave way to a durable era of "social epidemics" linked to the
declining standard of living of the survivors. Demographic disaster
also knocked out the supports upholding the rural economy, by
driving prices down and triggering a long rural depression. The disaster planted the first seeds of recovery in rural Lombardy, the
Veneto and Piedmont, but the Italy of urban manufactures died a
lingering death. Unlike the sixteenth century, when the country
recovered quickly from epidemics and famines, there was nothing to
fall back on.

Italy lost its cultural ascendancy in the same period, as the growing
strength of the Church bore down on unorthodox writers who
emerged from the dynamic universities and academies. After spear-
heading the transformation of the mathematization of the universe,
Italian notables formulated the first serious challenge to the
Aristotelian world view that the Church sanctioned. With the active
support of Italian princes, Rome mobilized not once (Bruno), or
twice (Galileo) against them, but durably and pervasively in the later
seventeenth century. By 1640 Europe's cultural centre of gravity
had shifted north-west from Naples–Rome–Florence–Venice, to
Paris–London–Amsterdam. Italy ceased to be a land of innovation.

13 Italy and Islam in the Mediterranean

Clash of Empires

Sixteenth-century ships teemed in the narrow seas along the Italian coasts, mostly small craft of twenty or thirty tons tramping from port to port. However, the Mediterranean was a political frontier between the Christian and Islamic worlds. The rapid spread of the Ottoman Empire in Anatolia and the Balkans hemmed in Venice's Dalmatian possessions, and Turkish *razzias* or raids spilled out of Bosnia into the Veneto plain in the 1460s. Islamic pirates based in the Albanian ports of Valona and Durres preyed on Venetian shipping that moved through the mouth of the Adriatic in proximity to the vital grain ports in Apulia. The new Ottoman navy, using Arab and Greek vessels and crews, seized Otranto in Apulia in 1480, although they relinquished it soon after. In the first half of the sixteenth century, Ottoman armies conquered Palestine, Syria and Egypt, and ejected the knights of Saint John from Rhodes. A few years later, their fleet took possession of the Barbary coast, at the behest of the Muslim corsairs already operating there. In 1534, "Turks" were using Toulon in Provence as a base from which to strike at Spain, thanks to their unholy and widely decried alliance with the king of France. Finally, in 1538, the combined Ottoman and Barbary fleets routed the Venetians and their Spanish and Imperial allies at Prevesa, off the northwest coast of Greece. Venice made a hasty peace with the

Ottoman Porte, while Muslim pirates plundered the Mezzogiorno coast and the islands.

In the western Mediterranean, Isabella of Castile and Ferdinand of Aragon finally extinguished the last Iberian Muslim state, the kingdom of Granada, in 1492. Hundreds of thousands of Jews and Muslims fled to North Africa and the Ottoman Empire over the ensuing century. To safeguard its coast and to protect its shipping, Spanish rulers embarked on a policy to seize ports along the African coast. To this day, Spain holds *presidios* in Melilla and Ceuta off Morocco. For centuries it held Oran; and briefly it occupied Peñon and Algiers in present-day Algeria, Bizerta and Tunis in Tunisia, and Tripoli in modern Libya. Virtually autonomous city republics governed by corsairs under the protection of an Ottoman garrison paid irregular tribute to Constantinople in money and ships. They were unable to defend themselves against Spanish expeditions to capture them without help from the distant sultan.

Galleys had been the classic Mediterranean warship since antiquity. In a sea subject to spells of windless calm, galleys were propelled by oarsmen, their triangular sails needed only occasionally. Their 25 or 30 benches were manned by three or four oarsmen on each side. Their shallow draught allowed them to hover close to shore and be beached to land their crews. The only artillery pointed forward on the bow. In combat the galley was designed to attach itself to its target, or glide up on to its deck from the side, and then overpower it by boarding with soldiers and seamen.[1] A galley's drawbacks were important. Great tempests sometimes sank scores of them and drowned thousands of men. Another limitation was the large number of men required to outfit each one; crowding forced it to hug the coast and stop repeatedly to take on water and food. The hull of a galley could be built cheaply and quickly, but outfitting it with rope, sails, oars, provisions and artillery was more troublesome. Most difficult of all was to find oarsmen. Many oarsmen were impressed seamen, captured pirates, and convicts brought from as far away as Bavaria. In Sicily, freemen, or *buonavoglie*, constituted only a quarter of the manpower, and the rest were chained to their benches. In lieu of corporal penalties, judges sentenced repeat offenders or serious criminals to terms on the galleys.[2] The term *galera* is still synonymous with prison in Italy. Only a few ports were capable of collecting the stores required for a whole fleet, for a hundred galleys conveyed forty thousand men or more, which was more than the grandest armies. The administrative headaches that a galley squadron necessitated periodically led Spain to rent them from private entrepreneurs, who built galleys and commanded them as an investment. For the entrepreneur, a galley *asiento* permitted him to realize hidden profits, like obtaining grain and currency export licences, or transporting valuable merchandise.[3] At Lepanto about 10 per cent of the Catholic navy consisted of galleys rented from Genoese entrepreneurs, which constituted about a quarter of the Spanish force.

The rout of the Christian galley fleet at Prevesa in 1538 marked the onset of several decades of Islamic initiatives at sea, during which corsairs continually punished the Italian coasts. Italian towns from Liguria to Sicily lived in continual fear of being stormed and sacked by scores of galleys operating with little impediment, their inhabitants carried off into slavery thousands at a time. Spain continued its policy of trying to stem the tide by capturing Barbary coast bases. Italy was the best-situated base from which to hold back the Islamic tide, and Messina, with its back to the Sicilian wheatfields and its proximity to the great workshops of Naples, was the ideal base. When historians speak of the "Spanish" fleet, they refer mostly to Italian galleys based in Naples and Sicily. The kings of Spain also subsidized the grand duke of Tuscany, the duke of Savoy, and the pope to maintain flotillas for common projects. Spanish expeditions against Muslim bases were largely Italian affairs. In 1560 a fleet of 50 galleys carrying 12,000 soldiers landed on the island of Djerba off southern Tunisia in February and proceeded to build a fort there. The Turkish galley fleet braved bad weather and crossed the eastern Mediterranean in May, earlier than the Hispano-Italians thought possible. Half the Catholic galleys and most of the troops were captured.[4] The failure at Djerba was only one of a string of reverses suffered by Spain, yet Philip II quickly reconstituted a fleet using Italian expertise and facilities.

The gravest threat to Catholic states was the Turkish and Barbary enterprise against Malta in May 1565. Malta was the base for Christian knights who preyed on Islamic shipping in the central Mediterranean corridor. The fortifications surrounding the port blunted the Ottoman onslaught, but the knights were on the verge of collapse when a Spanish and Italian relief force left Sicily. Since the Turks could not defend their ships and press the siege simultaneously, they re-embarked. Malta was thus a "defensive" victory that left the initiative in Ottoman hands. The Turkish sultan, Selim II, contemplated expanding at the expense of Venice, whose Greek pos-

sessions astride the sea lanes of the Ottoman Empire were perceived
to be an easy target. Venice had always been deaf to Spanish and
papal entreaties for an anti-Ottoman alliance, since the Levant trade
was the cornerstone of its prosperity. The Muslim revolt in Granada
and the Dutch revolt diverted Spain's attention from the Adriatic,
and allowed the Ottomans to isolate Venice strategically. Then in
1570 a strong Ottoman army landed on Cyprus and overwhelmed
Nicosia. Only half of Venice's 136 galleys could be deployed far from
home. The remainder had to reinforce the republic's Dalmatian
fortresses, which were also under pressure.[5] With the aid of the
Sicilian, Neapolitan and Genoese squadrons in Spanish service, and
more galleys from Florence and the papacy, the Catholic fleet based
in Crete stood a chance of defeating the Ottomans. The Venetian
admiral Zane decided not to risk all in a single battle, and when the
weather turned at summer's end, the fleets dispersed.

Over the winter Pope Pius V stitched together an alliance between
Spain and Venice, two traditional adversaries, with the papacy and
the Italian states as participants. The combined Catholic fleet on 7
October 1571 consisted of 207 galleys, 6 galeasses and 30 sailing
vessels bringing stores, carrying a combined 1,815 cannon, 28,000
soldiers and 13,000 seamen. The great majority of the ships and
crews were Italian. In addition, about half the soldiers and thousands
of noble adventurers hailed from the peninsula, eager to participate
in a decisive combat against the Turks. Just inside the gulf of Corinth
they encountered 222 galleys and 60 galiots of the combined
Ottoman and Barbary fleets, carrying 34,000 soldiers and 13,000
seamen, but mounting only 750 cannon. Venice's secret weapon, the
galeass, mounted artillery and firing platforms for hundreds of soldiers along the side. Almost certainly the Ottomans were unaware of
their capability.[6] After the galeasses broke the cohesion of the
Ottoman array, the two galley navies collided by the bows, and an
immense mêlée ensued. Most of the engagements were in effect
duels, where the greater number of arquebus and more body
armour gave the Catholics an advantage. Perhaps over 30,000
Turkish soldiers and seamen perished, and 200 of their ships were
captured and destroyed. About 20,000 Christian slaves were liberated. The carnage also included between 8,000 and 9,000 dead
Catholics, although only 12 galleys were lost.

Lepanto was the largest battle in European history since ancient
times, and the Christian victory was unequivocal, but Turkish sea
power was not broken.[7] By 1573 the sultan could boast 250 galleys,

13 mahones, a Turkish version of the galeass, and many smaller craft, although they carried green troops. The Holy League alliance came unstuck in 1572, as the Venetians and Spaniards disagreed on objectives. The Spanish and Italian fleet took Tunis and La Goletta in 1573, but the Ottomans recovered them only months later. Faced with a ruinous, inconclusive war, and saddled with an uncooperative ally, the Venetian Senate relinquished Cyprus to the Porte in 1574, and recovered its position as the leading commercial partner of the Ottoman Empire.

John Francis Guilmartin argues that it was virtually impossible for a fleet to achieve strategic victory in the Mediterranean, since galleys could be launched so easily, and their bases were difficult to capture and hold.[8] His thesis seems to be borne out in the Lepanto war of 1570–4, an indecisive if gigantic border conflict. Venice, Spain and Turkey could not keep up the effort for long. Much skirmishing followed, however. By combining with Malta, Savoy, Tuscany, Rome and Genoa, Spain occasionally launched great strikes, such as the 70 galleys and 10,000 troops that pounced fruitlessly on Algiers in 1601. As the king's treasury drained, the galley fleet was left to decline, and the subsidies to Italian states to maintain their flotillas were discontinued.[9] The decline in strength was no harbinger of peace, since the jihad and the crusade justified continuing the war by other means.

Corsairs and Piracy

The dispersal of the great fleets did not make the Mediterranean safer, for galleys and lighter vessels were parcelled up into penny packets and made to earn their keep by scouring the seas and coasts in search of plunder. Corsair raids on shipping and on coastal communities remained a feature of the Mediterranean world until France conquered Algiers in 1830. In the 1580s and 1590s, attacks on the Italian coast by Algerine, Tunisian and Tripolitanian corsairs reached alarming proportions. Muslim pirates operated occasionally in larger flotillas. Dragut Pasha sacked Reggio Calabria in 1585; Sinan Pasha, a Sicilian renegade, punished his native land with some 70 oared vessels in 1594, before falling upon Reggio Calabria again. Farther up the coast, tiny flotillas lurked off the islands waiting for easy targets to pass by. Oared ships based in Albania darted up the Adriatic coast, attacking grain boats and small coastal towns from

Apulia to the Marches. Since many corsairs were *renegades*, that is, Christians converted to Islam, who had scores to settle back home, targets were not often selected at random. Corsairs first scooped up as much booty as possible. Then, depending upon the existence of coastal defence forces, they lingered to sell back to the coastal communities the livestock, the elderly captives, and cumbersome objects better left behind on the return journey.[10] Coastal towns subjected periodically to such raids got to know their tormentors, and corresponded regularly with North Africa, where merchants and monks acted as intermediaries to ransom captives.

Slaves were commonplace in Mediterranean ports, although their number declined after the sixteenth century. Italians took prisoners primarily in order to use them on galleys. Groups of them could be bought in slave markets in Malta, Palermo, Naples and Livorno. Salvatore Bono estimates their total number in Italy at between 15,000 and 20,000 in the seventeenth century.[11] Spain decreed in 1597 that slavery was not hereditary, and facilitated means by which captives could recover their liberty. Gratuitous liberation was a pious duty, upon the slave's conversion to Catholicism. Most liberated slaves engaged in small commerce, selling coffee, tobacco, wine and cheese, or worked in trades. In Livorno, Genoa and Civitavecchia there were places of devotion and burial for Muslim captives.[12] On the African shore, Algiers alone counted 30,000 to 40,000 Christian slaves in 1600, of whom perhaps a third or half were Italian. Like the renegades, slaves were part of the great Algerine melting pot. It is difficult to evaluate their numbers elsewhere, as there were many slaves in Constantinople or on the benches of Ottoman galleys. In North Africa slaves were taken primarily in order to be ransomed, but their destiny depended upon their skills and social extraction, although boys were particularly prized as sex objects, and were least likely to be ransomed. Many prisoners converted to Islam and returned to sea, where they were sometimes recaptured sword in hand.

Islam seems to have held a greater attraction for captive Christians than the reverse. Bennassar estimates at about 300,000 the number of Christian captives of North African corsairs over two centuries, with Italians making up the largest segment. Living on the frontier, and crossing it easily, Sicilians, Corsicans and Calabrians often readily converted to Islam. Converts relinquished their name, their dress and their culinary traditions when they became Muslim, and submitted to the obligatory rite of circumcision that marked them for life. The ritual almost always improved their lot in Islamic society, and frequently culminated in their freedom. Many escaped back to Christendom and reconverted afterward, but renegades were a crucial asset for the Muslim world. Arabs and Turks prized European technical skills and paid handsomely for them. Converts rose to prominent positions in the Ottoman system, including the rank of grand vizier, or prime minister.[13]

Algiers counted close to 100,000 inhabitants in 1600. Its huge fleet of close to a hundred vessels employed 25 per cent of the active population. Corsair captains and their crews followed strict rules concerning the division of spoils. Two-thirds of the pirate captains were held to be renegades, and Italians made up half of those.[14] Two of the most celebrated were Euldj-Ali, from Calabria, whose galleys escaped unscathed from the disaster at Lepanto; and Sinan Pasha, alias Scipione Cicala, a Messinese patrician of Genoese origin, captured with his father, a galley entrepreneur, in the Djerba expedition of 1560. Scipione was raised as a Muslim, and eventually rose to command large fleets for the Sultan.

Italians reacted to the corsair menace by building a rampart of fortified cities and watchtowers. By 1600, the kingdom of Naples alone had erected 19 such fortresses, Sicily 8 and Sardinia 3. In addition, hundreds of watchtowers warned and protected coastal populations. They were worse than useless if without permanent garrisons. Several thousand Spanish, German and Italian infantry watched over coastal fortifications, backed by militiamen who mobilized locally whenever corsairs raided their sector. Companies of light cavalry distributed along the coast chased off corsairs who landed in order to take on water and provisions (*aiguades*). Italian galleys also patrolled the coast. Pope Sixtus V Peretti (1585–90) launched ten galleys based in Civitavecchia in 1587, but that number declined to five, which was all the popes could afford.[15] Spain's fleet consisted of three squadrons based in Sicily, Naples and Finale Liguria. Because it was impossible to ignore the constant raiding, the crown paid what it could to keep galleys operational. Any intensification of the war on corsairs by attacking their bases with infantry, such as a Sicilian expedition against Bizerta in 1600, multiplied the costs. The difficult problem of finding oarsmen justified these raids, since galley crews needed constant replenishment, and slaves once captured were too expensive to feed to leave idle.

The most effective continuous riposte to corsair attacks on the Italian coast came from a medieval institution, the crusading order of knights. The Knights Hospitallers of Saint John of Jerusalem took ecclesiastical vows of celibacy and charity, and served on the galleys of the order, before becoming full-fledged "monks", drawing income from landed estates the order possessed throughout Catholic Europe. Wielding one's sword against Muslims was an activity that brought a nobleman fortune, reputation and salvation all at once.[16] The great siege of Malta attracted a flurry of new recruits, about a third of whom were Italians. No sooner had the Turks departed than the knights laid out a new fortress city, called Valletta. By 1676, when a terrible plague struck, the island had quadrupled its population to 60,000 inhabitants, with 20,000 in Valletta alone. The flotilla's activity increased too. The knights patrolled Italian waters from Sardinia to Otranto in search of corsairs. They joined with friendly Catholic flotillas to strike at Muslim bases in North Africa, or to ward off larger enemy flotillas; and they preyed on Muslim shipping from North Africa to Syria and Greece. Like the Turkish and Barbary galleys, they hugged the coasts, or sprinted from one island to another, while warning towers announced their advance. They usually preferred to seize merchant vessels that surrendered without a fight. The knights sometimes played for larger stakes and gave battle to enemy galleys, and their coastal raids were occasionally murderous.

The success of the knights of Malta incited emulation in Italian states. Created in 1573, the Piedmontese Order of the Knights of Saints Maurizio and Lazzaro operated three galleys out of Villefranche near Nice. Much more important was the Tuscan Order of Santo Stefano, created in 1562 by the duke of Florence, Cosimo I de' Medici, after years of failed attempts to maintain an effective galley squadron. The grand duke, as grand master, recruited cadets from noble houses and established a *commenda* for them with donations from their family.[17] At the moment of greatest activity, *circa* 1600, at least a hundred knights embarked annually on the galleys based in Livorno. Others sailed on galleys belonging to the Tuscan fleet proper, and chartered corsair ships. After the 1590s and until 1612, Tuscan flotillas ranged all over the eastern Mediterranean and the Aegean seas in search of booty.[18]

Galley flotillas were always augmented by corsairs using the bases as home port. In Malta privateers were often knights who retired from compulsory service, and were now in honourable business for themselves. When a new corsair ship was launched in 1676, two friars went aboard to pray for its protection, laid their hands on every mast and other places of the vessel, and sprinkled it with holy water.[19] After 1660, 20 to 25 corsair ships flying the Maltese banner plied Ottoman waters, the larger ships cruising in the Greek archipelago where the richest prizes sailed. A ship with 10 cannon, 20 swivel pieces and a crew of 100 soldiers and seamen required an outlay of 30,000 scudi, whose owners were eager to make back their investment.[20] Most of those flying the Maltese ensign were French, but a large portion of them were Italians, as was the bulk of the seamen and "workers" in the business. In 1590 the galleys of the order themselves embarked 10 per cent of the island's active population, and perhaps 25 per cent in 1665. The landing and auction of plunder had spin-off benefits to related sectors of the economy, like ship construction, purchase of naval stores, and port services.[21] Livorno was the base for a cosmopolitan group of English, French, Dutch and Italian sea captains. Cosimo II enticed 12 English corsair captains to convert to Catholicism and exchange Algiers for Livorno in 1610. Pardoned for their past seizures, they were free to use Tuscany as a base for their attacks. The Dutch and English introduced the northern roundship, the *bertone*, into Mediterranean waters. These vessels of 100 to 300 tonnes carried a greater complement of seamen and soldiers and boasted two dozen iron cannon, while still leaving room for cargo. They could sail in most weather, and operate independently on long voyages. Barbary corsairs converted to roundships after 1610, and Catholic galleys learned not to cross their paths unless they had great advantage.[22] The viceroy Duke Osuna built a flotilla of corsair roundships and freely used regular soldiers for his private expeditions.[23] Corsairs operated continuously out of Naples, Palermo, Messina, and especially Trapani, which was close to Tunisia, and from which twenty corsair captains operated from 1675 to 1678.[24]

Privateers had a natural tendency to attack any convenient target, regardless of its banner. Genoa tried to fend off corsairs by grouping its merchant ships bound for Holland into convoys escorted by two or three warships.[25] Venice was considered fair game by Christian and Muslim privateers alike.[26] The most ferocious pirates were the Serbian *Uskoks*, lodged along the Dalmatian coast near Istria. The southern Adriatic zone opposite Albania was another zone infested with pirates, as were the waters off Crete, favourite hunting grounds for both Barbary and Christian privateers. Tuscan, Sicilian, Neapolitan and Maltese vessels lay in wait for the great Constantinople–Alexandria convoy laden with silks, spices, rice, sugar and coffee. The desperate sea-battles against those well-protected ships sometimes yielded great fortunes. There is no way to calculate the total number of ships captured. France gained ground in the Mediterranean carrying trade after 1660 because Louis XIV and his powerful new fleet of men-of-war placed French ships off-limits to privateers of any nation. Gradually the Turks, Greeks, Venetians and other vulnerable traders consigned their cargoes to French holds. In 1683, to avenge the capture of French ships by Algerine corsairs, a large French fleet bombarded Algiers for days.

The impact of corsair raiding on Italy declined after 1640, although it is difficult to determine why. For a century previously, Italian towns and cities were victim to large-scale raids. Since the Thirty Years War redeployed warships for convoy operations farther north, the fear of raids against Sicily and the Mezzogiorno persisted. In those years insurance costs for maritime transport reached close to 40 per cent of the cargo's value.[27] The danger from Muslim corsair raids against shipping and coastal communities dropped off for most of the eighteenth century, reviving after 1770. Tuscany outfitted a couple of frigates to track corsairs in their coastal lairs. Piedmont and the papacy bought similar ships from England, complete with English officers to command them.[28] Spain assembled fleets containing Maltese and Italian components to strike Algiers in 1775 and again in 1783, both times without success. In the late eighteenth century, Naples built a fleet of warships to retaliate against North African pirates. Venice bombarded Tunisian ports on several occasions with its navy. Even the fledgling American navy sent a flotilla to bombard the pirate city of Tripoli into respecting the United States' flag.

Alongside the centuries-old contest between Christian and Muslim states, the eighteenth-century Mediterranean witnessed the first large-scale forays of English ships. British privateering operations against Bourbon France and Spain patrolled the waters in a triangle between Sardinia, Sicily and North Africa. Navies sought bases in which to winter their squadrons, and Italian ports and islands became objects coveted by great powers. They all used Livorno as a supply base and a place to sell prizes.[29] The belligerents respected periods of formal peace, however, and this allowed the rapid resumption of trade with the conclusion of hostilities. The Mediterranean was gradually becoming safer, as the great powers' warships underscored their increasing predominance over the Islamic and the Italian worlds combined.

14   Fifty Years of War, 1610–59

Challenging the Spanish Imperial System, 1610–35

The *Pax Hispanica* resulting from the end of the wars of Italy was beneficial in many ways, but Spanish strength was the consequence of France's ongoing religious civil wars. Venice, the single most powerful state in the peninsula, never fitted into the framework of the Habsburg imperial system. The republic's friendly relations with both the Protestant powers and the Ottoman Porte contravened the fundamental thrust of both Spanish and papal policy, and on several occasions after 1605 armed conflict nearly broke out between the Republic and Spain. After the Venetians attacked the Uskok corsair stronghold of Senj in 1613, hostilities with Austria soon escalated into full-blown war. Both armies sparred indecisively along the Isonzo river frontier for almost three years, while the Venetians laid siege to Gradisca and Gorizia. Spain aided Austria first by blocking the Swiss passes by which Venice's German and Swiss reinforcements descended. After the viceroy of Naples, Osuna, ordered corsairs and Spanish warships to harass Venetian shipping in the Adriatic, the conflict risked spreading. In 1618 Venice broadcast the discovery of a Spanish plot to overthrow the republic, in order to put other European states on their guard. This plot probably never existed, but it justified military preparations on the republic's western border with Lombardy.[1] To distract Spain in Lombardy, Venice also subsidized Duke Charles Emanuel I of Savoy's efforts to occupy the Monferrato.

When Henri IV pacified his kingdom after 1594, he began looking
for allies to launch another great war against Habsburg hegemony.
The treaty of Lyons in 1601 amputated much of the French-speaking
part of the Savoyard state, so Charles Emanuel sought compensation
in Italy. The duke mobilized an army in 1610 in the framework of
the French alliance, but when Henri IV died by an assassin's knife
before hostilities began, his project fell apart. A new pretext arose in
1613 when the duke of Mantua died and his widow, the childless
daughter of Charles Emanuel, was sent home to Turin. The duke
demanded the Monferrato as compensation and followed up his
claim with an invasion. Spanish military intervention, supported by
contingents from allied Italian states, forced Charles Emanuel to
withdraw. Draped in the rhetoric of defending Italian liberty against
the Spanish yoke, he invaded the Monferrato again in 1615 with an
army composed largely of French and German troops. Venice under-
wrote at least a third of the cost of his campaign.[2] Spanish and
Italian confederate troops checked his advance at Asti. Chastened,
but no wiser, the duke approached England, Venice and the
German Protestant states, with the aim of establishing a vast anti-
Habsburg alliance. Expecting Venetian and French military assistance, Charles Emanuel invaded the Monferrato and Spanish
Lombardy again, until a Spanish army captured the key town of
Vercelli after a bloody siege in 1617. The ten-week Iliad mobilized
the military ardour of the Italian aristocracy – on the side of Spain!
Charles Emanuel's heady rhetoric calling for an Italy free of Spanish
power was self-serving bombast. Many non-Piedmontese Italians in
his service refused to serve against Spain, and the duke replaced
them with French and Swiss troops, including many Protestants.[3]
Only French diplomatic protection saved the duke from complete
humiliation. Charles Emanuel married his son to the sister of Louis
XIII soon after, thus lodging Piedmont in the French camp. The
Catholic duke next sought entry into the German Protestant League
so that he might be elected king of Bohemia, as the diet in Prague
cast about for alternate candidates to the Emperor Ferdinand II.[4]
Piedmont and Venice's isolation in a nation enthusiastic for the
advancement of the Catholic cause underscores how immensely powerful the Spanish monarchy was in 1620. In the absence of an aggressive French counterweight, Italians accepted the pro-Habsburg *status
quo* and offered their services to further its aims.

The most destructive conflict of early modern times began in 1618
as a German civil war. The Bohemian Diet, dominated by Protestants

intent on retaining their autonomy and their confession, overthrew the Habsburg king, the emperor Ferdinand II, and elected a German Calvinist in his place. King Philip III of Spain's decision to support his Austrian cousin with thousands of infantry raised in Naples and Flanders proved crucial, but the pope and the grand duke of Tuscany sent money and troops as well. The campaigns in Bohemia and the Rhine Palatinate in 1620 were total triumphs for the Catholic cause. Habsburg victory seemed complete. Spanish forces were then diverted by the resumption of war with the Netherlands in 1621. King Philip IV could still spare men from that theatre to help the Habsburg emperor smash the new Protestant champion, the king of Denmark, in 1624 and 1625. By 1628 Imperial armies under the Czech commander Albert, Count Wallenstein, broke up the Protestant coalition and occupied the Baltic coast. Italian officers in his army constituted perhaps as much as a fifth of the Imperial high command. Partisans of war against Protestants to complete victory, their hawkish attitude was often resented by the Germans.[5]

In 1620 the incomparably stronger branch of the Habsburgs was the Spanish one. With its strategic position improved and its finances restored, Madrid looked forward to resuming war with the Netherlands. Dutch Protestants had taken over much of the carrying trade between Spain, its Italian possessions and the overseas colonies. Philip III and his advisers may not have felt they could reconquer the rebel republic, but Spain could hope for a better peace and open Antwerp to international commerce again.[6] Ambrogio Spinola choked off Dutch commerce in Germany by seizing fortresses on the Rhine and Meuse rivers, and he unleashed Spanish warships and Flemish privateers against Dutch merchant shipping and the fishing fleet in the North Sea. Then his army gnawed at the great ring of fortresses protecting the enemy heartland. This expensive strategy was vindicated by his capture of Breda in 1625, which delivered most of the Netherlands south of the Meuse to Spanish reconquest.

These successes drove diverse states into an alliance against the Catholic monarchy in order to impede its progress, and all of them looked to France for direction. Charles Emanuel I of Savoy schemed to occupy Milan. Venice was a willing conspirator, avid to retain access to the Valtellina passes to Switzerland and beyond and to end Habsburg geopolitical hegemony. The Valtellina passage remained open to Spanish and Italian soldiers marching northward into

Germany and Flanders. The Swiss Protestant Grisons league ruled
the Catholic Italians in the valley with a heavy hand. With the con-
nivance of the governor of Milan, the Italians rose in July 1620, and
massacred several hundred Protestants in a "sacred slaughter".
Spanish troops (including many Italians) immediately occupied the
valley and fortified it to deny access to Venice. To ease international
tension, Spain allowed papal troops to garrison the valley, but this
legitimized Habsburg control in favour of the Catholic cause.

France, still convulsed by religious strife, sought to deny the
advantage to Spain without entering the war itself. For two decades
France subsidized and encouraged the Catholic monarchy's enemies
to seize any occasion in order to diminish the power of the house of
Austria. In 1624, Charles Emanuel persuaded Louis XIII and
Richelieu to support an alliance of Holland, England, Venice and
Piedmont that would strike Genoa from land and sea. This would cut
the vital axis of communication between Spain, Naples and
Lombardy, while simultaneously seizing the Spanish monarchy's
main source of loans. Late in the winter of 1625, two armies, one
French and another Piedmontese, converged on Genoa after
marching through the Mantuan Monferrato. Genoese forces virtually collapsed, and only 6,000 untrained Neapolitan and Sicilian
troops stood in the way. Although they were twice put to flight in the
Ligurian passes, they stalled the invasion's momentum. The Anglo-
Dutch force, which was supposed to strike Liguria from the sea,
landed at Cadiz in Spain instead, where the Andalusian militia
bested it. Spain and Genoa's galleys enjoyed complete control of the
Riviera coast. Then the duke of Feria in Milan called upon Spain's
allies to assemble troops in Lombardy for a counter-strike. The
emperor dispatched a force of 5,000 Imperial soldiers to bolster his
cousin's army. By the spring this army forced the French and
Piedmontese to withdraw, and Richelieu and Charles Emanuel I
were content to negotiate on the basis of the *status quo ante*.[7]

The impending extinction of the direct Gonzaga line in Mantua
was a new menace. The reigning duke Vincenzo II wished to establish the French branch, the Gonzaga-Nevers, rather than one of the
minor Italian Gonzaga branches that were Habsburg clients. The
Gonzaga-Nevers were great nobles of France, and France pursued a
policy of maintaining offensive bridgeheads in Germany and Italy.[8]
Casale Monferrato and Mantua were both powerful fortresses situated at vital crossroads on each side of Spanish Lombardy. Before
the Spanish chief minister Olivares and Duke Charles Emanuel

could act, Charles de Nevers and his son stole secretly into Mantua. They sold their substantial French estates to raise troops and pre-pared to defend their claim. As the ultimate feudal overlord, Emperor Ferdinand II decided that Mantua should surrender to him so that he might dispose of the duchy as he wished. Having crushed the Protestant forces in Germany, Imperial troops were available for an Italian campaign. Since the French king was diverted by the siege of Protestant La Rochelle, the time was ripe for the Habsburgs to reassert their authority in Italy. Spain and Piedmont invaded the Monferrato at the end of March 1628, and dug in before Casale. The siege began to stretch into months, and cost Spain enormous resources in men and money. Almost a year later, when Louis XIII came to its aid with a large French army, Casale was still holding out. The Venetian republic was emboldened to offer support to Mantua, and mobilized an army near Brescia, but when Louis abandoned his allies to quell a Protestant revolt in Languedoc, Venice lost its nerve. Philip IV appointed Ambrogio Spinola governor of Milan, with the task of capturing Casale. Simultaneously, a German Imperial army laid siege to Mantua in the summer of 1629. In December 1629 Louis XIII decided to return to Italy again, and Charles Emanuel, who was continually negotiating with both sides, dropped the Spanish alliance and joined him. When Louis returned to France a few months later, the duke of Savoy changed sides again and sent reinforcements to Spinola's army encircling Casale. Louis, now firmly behind Cardinal Richelieu's policies to block Habsburg power, returned to Italy a third time in May 1630, to break the siege of Casale.

The drama unfolding around Mantua was more decisive. Imperial troops overwhelmed the duchy in October, 1629. Mantua itself was too strongly held, so the Imperials erected a blockade around the city and wintered most of their army in the surrounding states, where they imposed heavy contributions. In the spring, they renewed the siege, aided by an outbreak of bubonic plague that killed thousands of people inside the city. The Imperial commander stormed the Venetian camp at Villabuona on 29 May and put that army to flight. Finally, on 18 July 1630, the Imperials launched their assault on the island city by crossing the lake in boats and scaling the wall almost unopposed. By military convention, a city taken by storm could be looted. The methodical looting of Mantua by 14,000 sol-diers yielded a booty purportedly worth 18 million ducats: twice the tax revenue of the kingdom of Naples! Before the siege, Mantua counted 30,000 inhabitants. At its close, only 6,000 destitute survivors remained.

Mantua's capture ended the pretext for hostilities. In the negotiated peace that followed, Duke Charles of Nevers received the investiture of Mantua, and retained Casale and most of the Monferrato, but relinquished some towns to Piedmont. It was a disappointing conclusion for Olivares, because Spain failed to eject the French invaders and because Piedmontese and Venetian plotting against its ascendancy continued. The military glory went to the Imperial army. Little of importance happened in the peninsula in succeeding years, as the war rekindled in Germany and the Low Countries. Philip IV and Olivares continued to dispatch Spanish and Italian forces northward to keep the Habsburg armies going. In 1634 the Habsburgs almost clinched complete victory again when a combined Spanish and Imperial army smashed the Swedes utterly at Nordlingen. Only direct French intervention could prevent a Habsburg triumph.[9]

The Burden of War on Italy

Richelieu prepared his intervention in Italy by beckoning to princes there to enter a new alliance. The new duke of Savoy, Victor Amadeus I, whose wife Marie-Christine was the daughter of Henri IV, was the linchpin of it. Duke Charles of Mantua entered the alliance too, but had little to offer, given the ruined condition of his duchy. Glory-seeking Odoardo Farnese, duke of Parma, levied troops on his side. Richelieu had no intention of keeping his promise to make Italy his principal campaign. Neither side fielded large armies of 30,000 men, as in Germany.[10] Only 8,000 French troops followed the marshal Créqui, who directed the allied operations in the campaign of 1635. A small French and Swiss army under the Duc de Rohan invaded Lombardy from the Alps. The Spanish and Italian defenders and the new Milanese militia proved to be more spirited and aggressive than Richelieu and his allies anticipated. The anti-Habsburg alliance, which was never strong, began to fall apart. In the space of a few months, Duke Charles of Mantua, Duke Victor Amadeus of Piedmont, and the marshal Créqui died. Duke Odoardo of Parma negotiated an exit from the alliance in 1638, and the initiative passed to Madrid.

Spain also possessed Italian allies. Despite the shattering Spanish bankruptcy of 1627, Genoa continued to furnish great sums to the Catholic king. Francesco I of Modena invaded Parma in 1636 to convince Duke Odoardo to quit the French alliance. Tuscany's ships transported Spanish troops back and forth across the Mediterranean, and Grand Duke Ferdinando II lent large sums to Spain at preferential rates of interest. Finally, Piedmont's ruling dynasty was not united in the French alliance. The duke's brother, Prince Tommaso, commanded Spanish armies in the Low Countries. When Victor Amadeus died in 1637, Prince Tommaso and his brother Maurizio raised armies to recover Piedmont from the duchess-regent. The three-year civil war was one of the most sombre periods in Piedmontese history.[11] Late in 1641, Tommaso entered negotiations with Richelieu, and in 1642 he reached an accord with the duchess-regent Marie-Christine to share power, taking over French armies in the theatre. Piedmont's forces played only a subordinate role in the war thereafter.

In 1640 the Catholic monarchy's strategic situation turned from bad to catastrophic. Olivares's forceful attempts to make Catalonia pay new taxes sparked a revolt that soon pulled it out of Madrid's orbit. That crisis triggered a separatist revolt in Portugal, Brazil and colonies in Africa and Asia. Finally, in 1643 French forces, which were becoming more proficient, destroyed the elite *tercios* of Spanish and Italian infantry at Rocroi. Skirmishing in the borderland of Piedmont and Lombardy immobilized both field armies, where the town and peasant militias in Spanish-held zones precluded further Bourbon progress.[12]

Madrid created new armies by scavenging resources in less threatened regions, such as southern Italy. The undermanned fortresses there proved irresistible for Cardinal Mazarin, the Italian chief minister of France, successor to Richelieu after 1643. Mazarin's aim was to pry apart the *status quo* supporting the Spanish hegemony in Italy. Tuscany and Modena would not move without a French military triumph in the region first. In 1646, Prince Tommaso of Savoy embarked an army on the French fleet to seize the Spanish fortresses on the Tuscan coast. Neapolitan and Sicilian galleys towing warships behind them pounced on the French fleet off Port'Ercole and killed the French admiral. Then they forced Prince Tommaso to hurriedly lift his siege of Orbetello, with heavy losses in men and equipment. In 1647 the French fleet returned and seized some of these fortresses, but Spain quickly restored its control of the Mediterranean.

Modena joined Mazarin's alliance at the end of 1646, and raised an army largely consisting of French soldiers to lay siege to Cremona. In late 1647 this army almost disbanded soon after crossing into Lombardy, for want of provisions. The next year the army advanced on Cremona again. It was still too small to capture such a large city, it being impossible to encircle the place and conduct active approaches simultaneously. In February 1649, with France in the complete political turmoil of the Fronde, Duke Francesco left the alliance and returned to the Spanish fold. So after almost fifteen years of French campaigning, its gains in Italy were negligible. Its prizes consisted of two great fortresses, Casale Monferrato and Pinerolo, both ceded by its allies.

Spanish fortunes improved in 1648 under the direction of a vigorous new governor of Milan, Don Luis de Benavides, Marquis de Caracena. No more assistance came from Sicily; Naples was in revolt and the Genoese financiers were dramatically overextended. Caracena's luck was the onset of the Fronde in Paris that sought to eject Cardinal Mazarin and end the war. The Peace of Westphalia ended Spain's war with the Netherlands, Sweden and the German Protestant states. Caracena soon restored confidence enough that Milanese patricians, hoping to attract royal favour and promotions, resumed raising *tercios* for royal service. Capturing Casale in 1652 restored confidence to the army.[13] Philip IV failed to make a satisfactory peace in the interval, however. In 1653 and later years, Caracena was constrained to fight defensively, and the Spanish system gradually imploded under the strain.

Spain's imperial system broke down from uninterrupted war since 1617. Olivares had devised a plan to establish military quotas on each of the component states of the Spanish Empire. The *Union of Arms* provided for the maintenance of an army of 130,000 men, which included 6,000 from Sicily, 8,000 from Milan and 16,000 from Naples. The soldiers were to be recruited by great nobles who would be rewarded with officer status and pay, and immunity from debt litigation. The Italian states provided the bulk of the money Olivares expected, assembled and armed troops, outfitted ships, purchased horses and provisions, cast cannon and so on. Naples purportedly raised about 50,000 men between 1630 and 1635, more than Castile, from a population only half the size, and paid a third of Lombardy's expenditures too.[14] Sicily provided few troops, but it paid half a million scudi for military operations annually after 1620. Lombardy's taxes tripled in the decades after 1618, just as the economy began to falter. Most of them were sales taxes (gabelles) placed on luxury goods first, and eventually on staples. Nobles, city-dwellers and clergy escaped the full weight of them. Another solution was to raise "extra-ordinary" revenue, by selling titles and jurisdictions. Pardons were sold for every crime but treason.[15] Spain also customarily "alienated", or sold, customs duties and monopoly rights to investors, keeping for itself a fixed sum from the revenue of each tax to provide for the army. Most of the tax machinery thus passed into private hands. Private purchasers benefited from any subsequent yield resulting from increases in consumption or price increases of taxed items. Even direct taxes levied on the *università* were alienated this way.[16]

Tax revenue was never enough to pay for military expenditures. The rest was made up by massive borrowing. The Neapolitan debt rose from 10 million ducats in 1612 to between 80 and 100 million in 1646, in a period of deflation and economic decline. This colossal debt rose sharply again to 150 million ducats at the time of the Masaniello revolt in 1647. After 1638 the crown began to renege on some of its debts, or bargained interest payments against new loans, which undermined investor confidence and drove interest rates upwards. Titles of state bonds sold for no more than 20 per cent of their nominal value. By 1647 only about a fifth of the tax money went for military expenditures, and the rest was insufficient to pay the interest on the debt. Speculative fever created colossal fortunes overnight, for those investors with good connections, but others lost heavily when the crown proved unable to reimburse them. In Sicily the king sold all his available domain revenues in the island to investors in 1634. Loans were floated for interest rates of 10 or 12 per cent, which was well above average returns of 3 to 5 per cent for commerce and agriculture. Genoese financiers placed their money at the king's disposal on the strength of the various gabelles, the acquisition of jurisdiction rights and tax capabilities of rural communes, and realized profits until the early 1640s.[17] The crown sold offices on the island at a brisk pace, often in secret transactions.[18]

The crisis came to a head first at Palermo in May 1647, when rioters protested against the high price of food. They soon directed their anger at tax officials and Spanish *malgoverno* in general. The militia companies (based on the artisans' guilds) never intended to break with the king, and entered into negotiations with the new viceroy, Cardinal Trivulzio. By September the revolt was over, having entailed only some episodes of bloody rioting, although two dozen ringleaders of it were executed in Palermo over the next several years.[19] Of much greater consequence was the revolt that broke out on 7 July 1647, in Naples, shortly after the viceroy Duke of Arcos imposed a tax on fruit. He disposed of only a few hundred soldiers in two forts, one on the heights overlooking the city and another on the waterfront. The population assembled around a charismatic fish-monger, Tommaso Aniello, called Masaniello, who levied a militia of tens of thousands within a few days. The crowd killed some nobles, their *bravi*, and others notorious for deriving their fortunes from tax offices. Rebellion then spread quickly through the countryside, where anti-feudal sentiment held sway. Large districts of the Abruzzi, Apulia and Calabria passed to the rebels.[20]

The viceroy paid assassins to dispatch Masaniello after barely a week, but the revolt widened nevertheless. When a Spanish fleet bearing Don Juan, bastard son of Philip IV, arrived in October, most of the important nobles rallied to him. For months they skirmished in the vicinity of Naples against the city militia. In November the French Duc de Guise arrived with the understanding that the insur-gents would make him king, and sever the Spanish connection. Mazarin had little confidence in the Duc de Guise as a leader, and many influential personalities began to desert the cause. As the duke's popularity declined, the strain of the war on the civilian pop-ulation turned opinion against him, especially since Spanish troops still held the fortresses around the city. Then, on 5 April 1648, the new viceroy Don Luis de Haro surged out of the waterfront citadel with five hundred soldiers and swept the rebel militia off the barri-cades. Much of the citizenry joined the soldiers as they advanced through the streets. The insurrection collapsed. A few more weeks of skirmishing in the provinces pacified the kingdom and returned it to Spanish obedience.[21]

The great rebellion forced Spain to lighten the kingdom's fiscal burden, and revenues soon plummeted. Fortunately for Spain, the Fronde in France paralysed the Bourbon regency. The marquis of Caracena, governor of Milan, finally brought Mantua back into the Spanish fold and captured Casale Monferrato with modest forces. Cardinal Mazarin was only able to break the strategic stalemate by ungrouping the smaller states that constituted the passive alliance in Spain's favour. Because Spain would not give him the prestigious post of command he sought, Duke Francesco d'Este of Modena let Mazarin talk him into a new alliance in 1654. The next year he attacked Lombardy in coordination with Prince Tommaso of Savoy, who invaded from the west with French and Piedmontese forces. The resulting siege of Pavia was a complete failure, due to the small size of their armies and the combativeness of the local militia. The duke was wounded in the operation, while Prince Tommaso contracted malaria and died. In 1656 the combined armies captured the small town of Valenza, without being able to accomplish more. In 1657 their armies failed before Alessandria. Finally, at the head of a combined French, Piedmontese and Modenese army, Duke Francesco pushed his patrols to the outskirts of Milan. He lacked the means to capture a large city, however, and he too contracted malaria and died in October 1658. His death brought the operations to a halt until the Peace of the Pyrenees put a formal end to the war in 1659.[22]

Twenty-five years of war in Italy against France and Piedmont left Spanish territories there intact. Philip IV could count on the active participation or passive assistance of several northern Italian states, while most of those passing into the French alliance were not deeply committed to it and usually abandoned it after a few years. The Spanish position was much more dire than an impression drawn from the map would indicate. Castile declared bankruptcy in 1627, 1647, 1652, 1662 and 1663, each occasion wreaking havoc in financial capitals. The monarch altered the coinage and debased the currency in an attempt to avoid paying his debts. Almost none of the silver still arriving from the Indies in 1660 finished in the crown's coffers, having been mortgaged in advance to the daring bankers who kept the finances afloat. There were similar suspensions of payments in Naples in 1632, 1645 and 1646, each one opening a long series of contentious negotiations between the crown and its creditors.[23] The 8 million ducats of revenue in 1646 fell to 5 million in 1648, and to a mere 2.3 million in 1665, a decade after the plague shattered what was left of the economy. Spanish cultural and political ascendancy had run its course by 1660. The Italian states were looking more to France as the pole of attraction.

The Castro Wars, 1642–49

The breakdown of the Spanish system meant that Madrid could no longer contain the tensions pitting Italian states against each other. In the first half of the seventeenth century, the latter had not renounced their desires to expand, to absorb the fiefs within them or around their borders, and to recover territory lost to neighbours.

Only one Italian state continued to expand and assert its authority over more territory with enhanced effect: the Papal States. Ferrara and Urbino devolved to Rome, and their bureaucracies and celebrated courts disappeared. This enlargement of the papal possessions worried other Italian states. They added this to the tally of grievances they held against Rome and the Barberini pope as a secular ruler.[24] The final straw was Urban VIII's seizure of the duchy of Castro and the town of Ronciglione from Duke Odoardo Farnese of Parma as collateral for debts he owed to the papal treasury. Castro was a grain-producing fief in northern Latium, and an ancestral seat of the Farnese. The duke refused to pay for grain export licences that Rome considered part of its domain. When Urban VIII insisted the duke pay, Odoardo responded by fortifying Castro. In October 1641, the papal army under Taddeo Barberini invaded the town and quickly captured it with 7,000 men raised especially for the task.

The *fait accompli* intensified the resentment of northern Italian states against the wilful pope. Venice was worried by papal attempts to develop Ancona and Comacchio near the Po delta into Adriatic trading ports to the detriment of its monopoly. New papal fortifications near the mouth of the great river held an implicit threat to river traffic. The Este of Modena never really assimilated the loss of Ferrara and its dependencies in Romagna. Ferdinando II of Tuscany married Vittoria della Rovere and hoped that Urbino would pass to him. Beyond these territorial disputes, these states all desired to limit the pope's jurisdiction over their respective clergies. Extensive rights of sanctuary, the invasive curiosity and rigidity of the Roman Inquisition, and the jealously guarded ecclesiastical jurisdiction transformed every minor bishop into a bulldog with regard to his prince. All these issues came to the fore with the quick siege of a village in Latium. On 31 August 1642, Tuscany, Modena, Venice and Parma signed a formal alliance.

Urban VIII was not willing to concede papal prerogative to minor powers. He was the last of the warrior-popes who lavished energy and treasure on military preparations. He built a powerful fortress on the Modenese border, as well as a huge arsenal at Tivoli, outside Rome. It may have been this preparedness that emboldened the pope to be firm with Odoardo Farnese. Not waiting for his allies to commit themselves, Odoardo Farnese marched out of Parma with 6,000 men in the fall of 1642. Papal forces hid in their fortifications, and the Parmans chased away a field force under the papal nephew, Taddeo Barberini, near Bologna. The cavalcade soon crossed the Apennines, and after marching through Tuscany, emerged into Latium at Aquapendente, near Castro, early in October. Rome was only a few days distant, and no papal force ventured to stop them. Having made his point, and unable to recover Castro by siege, Odoardo withdrew and returned to Parma a conquering hero.

The duke's military procession made the Papal States look like an easy target. Florence, Modena and Venice each raised armies formed of disparate contingents of local soldiers, French and German regiments, and militia bands they possessed in abundance. The papal forces too recalled officers from Habsburg service. Each of the allied

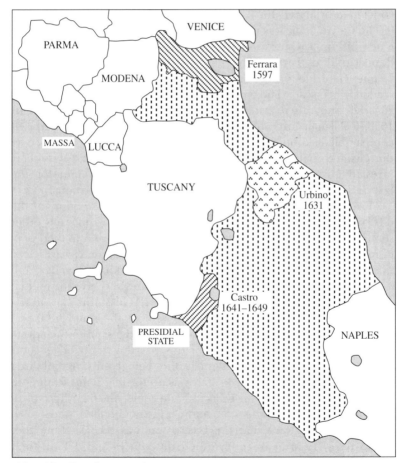

Map 17   Papal annexations

forces operated independently in a flurry of border skirmishes without a strategic result. There were a few set-piece battles involving thousands of troops per side, each of them a papal reverse. Pontifical commanders then opted for a series of diversions and raids across the Apennines and along the Tuscan border that drew off enemy forces. Skirmishes gave precious experience to the militia bands whose inclinations were to cling to earthen fortifications. As this border fighting continued, it was clear that the papal armies were far from collapse, and Urban was recruiting his largest army ever. These diversionary attacks, coupled with the failing health of the pontiff, gradually convinced the belligerents to negotiate a peace settlement, concluded by March 1644.

The Castro affair was revived in 1649, when Pope Innocent X sent a new bishop to Castro without securing the prior approval of Duke Ranuccio II of Parma. The Parman first minister, the Provençal Jacques Gaufrido, ordered assassins to ambush the bishop before he reached his seat. The pope immediately declared war on the Farnese, and raised armies in Latium and Emilia. On 18 August 1649, a Parman force of only 2,500 men met a pontifical force of comparable size outside Bologna. The Parmans broke and fled in the ensuing mêlée. The same month, a column of papal soldiers invested Castro and occupied it quickly. As punishment for the bishop's murder, papal troops razed Castro to its foundations.

This military episode still awaits a modern historian. Some of the difficulties Italian states encountered in waging war on each other stemmed from the competition with great powers for a limited pool of mercenaries and nobles who could command them. Nevertheless, none of the armies dissolved from complete lack of efficiency, and by the end of 1643 the improvised armies and the peasant militias were beginning to function more effectively. At least this war did not undermine the cohesion and development of the state, unlike in southern Italy where perennial war weakened the state to the advantage of private interests. No doubt this was the result of its short duration. Once peace was signed, the belligerents demobilized again. The Thirty Years War in Italy was no turning point leading to the advent of a standing army, as in France and Austria, where fiscal innovations rendered the state more efficient. Italian states shed their troops, unaware that the Castro war was the last time they would resort to arms to resolve their differences and defend their prerogatives. In future, European powers would ignore Italian princely dynasties and determine the destinies of their realms.

15   Economic Collapse

The pinnacle, 1590–1620

Sixteenth-century Italy's "mature" economy imported raw materials and exported finished products across the continent and beyond.[1] A century of prosperity and demographic growth made it a country with a high cost of living. Daily wages expressed in amounts of grain gradually declined in real terms over the sixteenth century.[2] There are several reasons for thinking that this low-wage period might still have held advantages for the greater part of the population. Economic buoyancy gave steady work to the entire family, and created more opportunities to divert a trickle of the great money flow into their household. Many peasants thrived on the high grain prices, and purchased luxury textiles and other finery themselves, which are revealed in their marriage contracts and household inventories.

This high-cost, high-price manufacturing economy made Italy an attractive target in a European trade war. The state, which levied taxes on the total output, upheld guild reputations and inspected the commodities artisans produced, not the firm. Around 1600, 42 per cent of the price of a bolt of Venetian fine woollen cloth was tax on the finished product.[3] In northern Europe, and England in particular, manufacturers and merchants inaugurated a marketing revolution that aimed to sell low in order to drive competition out of business. One of the weapons of this war was the fraudulent article, shoddy but attractive products that the English called "anti-

Venetian". They bore Venetian markings in order to undermine the reputation of the genuine article. They were smuggled into Venice and Venetian craftsmen and merchants often used them to gain an edge over their competition. These tactics helped England quintuple its production of the "new draperies" between 1600 and the onset of the Civil War in 1640. Inexpensive and imitative woollens such as these destroyed the Italian fine woollens industry on foreign markets. As Italian looms gathered dust, skilled Italian craftsmen left in large numbers and migrated north.

Northern Europeans were formidable competitors in maritime transport as well. English and Dutch ships first appeared in the Mediterranean in the 1570s and 1580s. Braudel qualifies their crews "proletarians from the north", whose relatively low wages and superior seafaring skills gave them a competitive advantage. Once they inserted themselves into the international circuits of commercial exchange, their high, round-hulled *bertoni* were well placed to supplant the galley fleets.[4] The Venetian merchant marine dwindled to a fraction of its former strength, as busy merchants and manufacturers resorted to foreign carriers instead. Nordic transporters penetrated the Genoese circuits simultaneously on their routes to Spain and Naples.[5] The substitution of northern European transporters for Venetian and Genoese carriers gradually reduced the investment horizons of Italian capitalists.[6]

Profits were difficult to reinvest. Agriculture held promise for a while, but by 1600 the land that could be improved at reasonable cost was all in production. As Rome borrowed to build, and Spain borrowed to fight its wars, government bonds became the most attractive investment late in the sixteenth century. The rates of interest on these bonds more than kept pace with inflation of about 4 per cent annually, and they could easily be converted into liquid assets. Most wealthy families sought security more than growth, and spread their resources across a broad range of activities, from agricultural estates, to renting city houses and shops, to investment in mercantile companies, and into bonds on different Italian and European capitals or the private *monti* issued by great noble houses.

A Disastrous Conjuncture, 1620–60

The period 1600–18 was the period of maximum mercantile and manufacturing activity in Italy, the culmination of an upward trend beginning in the fifteenth century. The onset of the Thirty Years War in Germany provoked a sudden collapse of the system, and the contest between Spain and Holland disrupted the major trading routes across the globe. (For more details, see Chapter 14.) The onset of the crisis was a disastrous three-year collapse of manufacturing demand between 1619 and 1622. Poor harvests compounded the disruption occasioned by the great war. Lucca, investigated by Rita Mazzei, serves as a good example because the merchant-republic was an active player in the economic capitals of northern Europe.[7] Some of its patrician houses, like the Buonvisi, were substantial silk-manufacturing and banking enterprises tied to other Luccan companies through a network of borrowing. The first worries emerged in 1610 when the amount of Spanish specie arriving from the Indies dropped substantially. The availability of real, metallic money was an important "lubricating" element, inspiring confidence and making trade easier. As good coin became rarer, it was more expensive to obtain and payment delays lengthened. Banking procedures became increasingly complicated and more companies went out on a limb, hoping their creditors could reimburse them before they had to make new investments. The Thirty Years War imposed sudden expenditures on Germans, who could no longer afford to purchase luxury items. German merchants, who were numerous in Lucca, disappeared overnight. Worse, their currencies plummeted in value, like that of Nuremberg, whose burghers devalued their money of account by half. This bankrupted those companies owing money to Luccans. So the military crisis simultaneously reduced the market for Italian goods, and rendered the reimbursement of Luccan loans improbable. The bankruptcy of the Buonvisi firm triggered a chain reaction through many other companies who invested money with them, through the commanditary contracts. The number of active looms in Lucca plunged, throwing many weavers out of work, and others stole raw silk to weave illegally. Hard times swelled the number of people on public assistance. Before 1620, about 4,000 out of 25,000 Luccans received some form of municipal aid. By 1630, just before the plague, that number rose to 8,000, from a much poorer community. The sudden increase in urban unemployment reduced the work opportunities for the mountain-dwellers who descended into the plain every year. These became indebted to urban merchants in order to survive.

What is true for Lucca recurs elsewhere. Customs revenue in Tuscany, based on the export of manufactured goods, fell by half between 1619 and 1630.[8] In Milan, a third of the city's 20,000 silk workers were unemployed by 1620. Crises and slumps are still part of the capitalist economic system. In the early modern period, most were provoked by a harvest failure, but the first good crop was generally enough to reignite activity. This did not happen in Italy because the onset of a disastrous wartime combination of circumstances drained the country of precious resources through higher taxes, through the devastation inflicted on large swaths of the most fertile districts, and by the massive theft of livestock and capital by marauding soldiers. Yet the industrial decline lasted for the better part of two centuries. A number of deep weaknesses in the manufacturing and commercial economy became evident now, but some aspects were simply conjunctural, the result of events that did not have their origin in the economy. All were subordinated to the great religious and political struggle in Germany.

Plague

Commercial profits provided Italian cities with the means to buy foodstuffs, even when they were dear. When unemployment spread widely through the labouring classes of Italian cities, people fell vulnerable to the periodic harvest failures that triggered lethal epidemics. The toll paid to infectious diseases like typhus steepened almost immediately, but none of them were as lethal as the bubonic plague. Late in 1629, the French and Imperial armies brought the plague into Piedmont and Lombardy. This outbreak was part of a European "pandemic" that killed millions of Europeans between 1628 and 1633, but it hit northern Italy harder than anywhere else because a decade of economic difficulty and two harvest failures had weakened the population. Across Lombardy and the Veneto, this particular plague killed about 30 per cent of the population, and provoked a stream of refugees that both spread the epidemic, and halted economic activity. In Mantua, two-thirds of the population died of the epidemic, for the besieging Imperial army prevented anyone from leaving. Plague killed above all those who had no refuge or country retreat. Urban workers and artisans, with their precious manual skills, paid a high toll. The survivors took advantage of their rarity after the epidemic to maintain their wage rates at high levels. There was another consequence: the plague alleviated population pressure, and the demand for foodstuffs declined. Noblemen who derived considerable income from supplying food to the urban markets suddenly had grain they could not sell, and its price sank. Good news for those who had to buy their food, falling food prices took money out of the economy by diminishing the value of land. Expenditures in land reclamation would not be recovered by investors.

War

War was a scourge not because of battlefield deaths, or massacre of civilians (which was rare), but rather because unpaid soldiers wrought widespread destruction and depleted the stocks of grain hoarded by rural households. Much of Piedmont, the Monferrato and eastern Lombardy suffered tremendous damage and looting as a result of the operations for the control of the Monferrato and Mantua. After 1635, full-blown hostilities strangled whatever commerce Milan and Genoa retained with France. Arms manufactures in Lombardy and Tuscany flourished, and the building trades feverishly erected fortifications. These were not "productive" investments liable to broaden the economy's base: instead, war squandered resources on a vast scale. War increased taxation, diverted precious labour to non-productive activities, and reduced expenditure on manufactured items produced by urban artisans. Even in Rome, the bellicose Urban VIII Barberini succeeded in doubling the public debt. The population paid for war with a wide assortment of higher gabelles, often on basic commodities like oil, salt, wine and cheese. Nowhere was the haemorrhage of capital to pay for the war more debilitating than in the kingdom of Naples, where gabelles tripled in the 1630s and 1640s, while reducing the economic base on which they lay.[9] Manufacturers there resorted instead to trickery to increase the weight of the fabrics, used cheaper and less durable dyes, reduced the thickness of the yarns, at the cost of the product's reputation.[10] The demand for good coin to prosecute the war made it rarer, and the coin in circulation became debased.

If countries practised trade war on each other, military victories yielded commercial dividends too. Dutch seizure of Spanish and Portuguese tropical colonies pulled the spice trade back into the Atlantic, and even Turkey purchased its spices from Amsterdam warehouses. Dutch merchants captured an ever greater portion of international specie, increasingly more expensive for Italian merchants and bankers to obtain. Dutch middlemen made Amsterdam Europe's great emporium, and skimmed off part of the profits of long-distance trade.[11] Venice missed the surge in demand for the colonial products like tobacco, coffee, tea, cocoa and sugar. The new maritime powers also filled Catholic Europe's increasing demand for salt and smoked fish, soon found in every grocer's shop.

Bankruptcy

The Spanish tax machinery was inadequate to meet the scale of the mobilization against the Dutch and their allies. Even before the Dutch intercepted the Indies treasure fleet in 1628, the crown declared bankruptcy. Genoese financiers, who were twenty or thirty families, ceded ground to Portuguese Marranos (converted Jews) in Madrid. The Genoese still dominated the finances of Naples and Sicily, and handled the *asientos* contracts to supply the Spanish armies and fleets. Nevertheless, Amsterdam became the great financial centre of Europe, while the fairs of Piacenza ceased to exist after 1628. Spanish financial posture worsened in the 1630s and financiers insisted on closer control over the running of the fiscal machine. By the 1640s, viceroys were desperate to find new loans, and attached conditions to the interest paid out. War dilapidated much of the capital which social elites had invested in the state. Public banks reduced their interest rate to 2 or 3 per cent, and often suspended interest payments altogether. Falling land and food prices pushed many rich families into debt, and forced the poor to sell their land and remain on it as tenants.

Search for Solutions

The manufacturing decline beginning in 1619 was relentless everywhere, accelerating the shift of trade circuits towards north-western Europe. The foremost economy was not politically unstable England, which would emerge in full splendour after 1715, but the Dutch republic. Amsterdam and the ports around it now became the centres for exchange of information, technology, and investment throughout the world.[12] Italy was reduced to being on the periphery of the Dutch world-economy, vulnerable through its ports, like Livorno and Naples. The loss of Italian potential was not complete:

Genoa, Venice and Florence still possessed ample capital and entre-preneurial drive, but the economic system lost its articulation. Neutral Tuscany suffered as much as anywhere. The Florentine woollen industry, which produced 30,000 pieces in 1570, only pro-duced 6,000 in the 1640s, by which time they were limited to the Italian market.[13] Silk resisted better, for the city's black silks and satins were unmatched anywhere in quality. In 1663, more than a quarter of the active population of Florence worked silk, employing women in the low-skilled preparation and spinning processes.[14] Tuscan merchants in Livorno found new outlets in Amsterdam, Cadiz (for re-export to the Spanish colonies) and even Archangelsk in Russia. But the rise in silk manufacturing did not compensate for the decline in wool, and the overall reduction in the two sectors was about 35 per cent between 1560 and 1650. Florentine investments which had once embraced most of western Europe retreated into southern Italy, before they collapsed there too after 1660. By 1670 the manufacturing economy of luxury textiles in Tuscany was much reduced. New activities replaced some of the old: coachmaking, pro-duction of musical instruments, cutlery, ceramics and glass.[15]

The powerful northern Italian urban manufactures went the same way. Woollens were everywhere more vulnerable, disappearing from Monza and Como by 1650. The Cremona cotton industry vanished similarly. Silk manufacture declined more gradually.[16] Lucca's silk looms declined from 2,000 at the beginning of the century to 500 in 1695. The Genoese industry resisted erosion by concentrating on specific products, like damasks and black velvets, but its silk looms dwindled from 4,000 in 1600 to 2,500 in 1675. In Venice the decline of fine woollen textiles was just as sudden. English and Dutch broad-cloth appealed to the republic's traditional clients in Smyrna and Aleppo, and generally substituted for the Venetian article, which it resembled superficially.[17] War against Ottoman Turkey did not drive away Venetian traders entirely, in part because Ottoman officials were paid out of the proceeds from customs duties, and they were loath to drive any Europeans away.[18] Dutch, English and French rival manufactures obliterated Venetian woollen sales after 1680. The silk industry there declined more gradually, by about 60 per cent between 1600 and 1660. Venice countered foreign competition by specializing in gold-silk cloth, the high end of the sector; but silk weaving in 1700 was only a third of the level a century previously. Non-textile sectors like printing, papermaking and glassmaking resisted better. French shippers edged out their competitors after

Louis XIV returned to a traditional policy of friendship with the sultan and launched a great Mediterranean fleet to protect French commerce. By 1699 the Venetian Levant trade was insignificant, as France took the leading position, supplying the Turks with superior textiles and glassware of their own manufacture.[19]

After Henri IV embarked on a deliberate policy to imitate Italian articles at home, France eventually prevailed over Italy in luxury silks too. Cardinal Richelieu erected high tariff walls in the 1620s, but the onset of war inhibited the growth of the luxury trades. With the return of peace in the 1660s, French manufactures were poised for heady expansion under a wider and more coherent set of regulations draughted by Louis XIV's minister, Colbert. The combination of regulations, privileges, tax concessions and channelled investment that the French state adopted from this period onwards has been labelled Colbertism, a variant of mercantilism, which was Europe's dominant economic philosophy. French manufactures created a demand for fresh motifs, patterns and styles. Lyons was soon the site of a group of artist-designers working for the silk industry that was largely responsible for the city's boom. The success of Colbert's mercantilist reforms allowed him simply to prohibit the importation of Italian silks in 1670.[20] A high technological level and a discriminating Parisian market did the rest, and by 1700 there were probably 10,000 busy looms there, many of them fed by Italian raw and spun silk thread. Lyons silks came in light textures and bright colours, in strong contrast with the dominance of heavy black and gold fabrics that left Italian looms. By the 1680s Lyons' processes outclassed all of the Italian centres in dyeing, printing and finishing. The Revocation of the Edict of Nantes in 1685 then scattered Protestant silk workers to England, Holland, Germany and Switzerland, which gave those countries the impetus to produce their own, albeit inferior, products. Italians found French fashion, like the great wigs worn at the court of the Sun King, irresistible. Turin craftsmen learned to imitate Lyons silks perfectly by copying its samples.

Why couldn't Italian manufactures recover from the catastrophe once the treaty in 1659 restored a generation of unbroken peace? The deep-rooted problems troubling the Italian economy were not just tied to a bad set of circumstances. Italian products had become too expensive to produce, and then gradually became outmoded. The technological edge the urban manufactures enjoyed before 1600 gradually diminished. Northern European states also learned to imitate Italian products, and then simply restricted their importa-

tion. Only determined changes would have saved the urban manufactures, but this adjustment was psychologically very difficult
because Italian products had dominated Europe for so long. The
urge to tighten regulations, not to loosen them, was too strong.
Understandably, guilds demanded high wages for urban craftsmen,
and defended the strict specifications imposed on each item produced. Guild organizations fought entrepreneurs straying from traditional techniques. In Genoa they attempted to stem the flow of
weavers into the villages. In Lucca the weavers' guild impeded the
hiring of foreign artisans with new techniques and defended its
monopolies. But to evoke simply the corporatist response of a group
of artisans is too simple. City and state governments reminded those
artisans willing to cut corners that traditional high-quality articles
had always sold in the past. Merchants who sold silk products reasoned conservatively, complaining that the problem of poor sales
stemmed from the poor quality and the low price of the workmanship, and urged workers to produce even more precious articles.[21]
The market picked up slightly owing to revived German demand in
1660, but by 1668 it fell off again, as French products took their
place. Under pressure to compete, the merchants in Lucca forced
the guilds to hire less-skilled, female labour, and reduced the wages
of workers in general. The standard of living of textile workers in
Lucca, as elsewhere in Italy, declined considerably.

The glassblowing industry on the Venetian island suburb of
Murano, Europe's foremost manufacturer of chandeliers and
mirrors, encountered serious French competition after 1670. Louis
XIV's ministers enticed expert craftsmen away from the lagoon and
overwhelmed them with privileges and monopolies. Fine Bohemian
glassworks, (similarly using Venetian expertise) appeared soon after
in the 1680s. At Murano the glassworkers' guilds refused to modify
regulations aiming to diversify their production and to lower their
costs. Workers were either forced to move elsewhere or turn to other
activities. The Dutch also developed comparable or superior techniques in a whole range of activities once dominated by Venice and
other Italian states: papermaking, pottery, shipbuilding, printing,
diamond-cutting, distilling.[22] Venice used subsidies to local producers and protectionist barriers to keep those foreign products out,
but the Serenissima could not prevent the Dutch from taking over
other markets.

What remained of Italian industry retreated to the countryside,
where workers were less expensive and less skilled. Already in the six-

teenth century urban merchants shifted production to villages to compress their costs. This was *proto-industry*: the production of inferior-quality manufactured goods by peasant households outside the agricultural season, for local markets primarily.[23] Villages had several advantages: fewer gabelles, cheap labour, the ability to mix manufactures with agriculture, and freedom from guild ties. It was not feasible where *mezzadria* predominated, because that system busied peasant hands with different tasks all year round. In areas of poor soils and small peasant property, on the other hand, rural manufactures were necessary for survival. Peasant weavers produced inexpensive coarse broadcloths in mountain villages in Bergamo's hinterland. The Venetian *dominante* gradually left the production of common goods, like spinning silk thread, producing woollen, linen and hemp cloth, and common ironworking, to the cities and towns of the Terraferma hinterland. Most often, it was the production and the preparation of silk thread that moved to the village. This was the low end of the industry, requiring less specialized labour. Silk reeling or throwing became an important supplementary income for peasants. Silk-spinning was practised everywhere in the North Italian plain, from Friuli to Piedmont, centred on new "Bolognese" mills with multiple spools, turned by water power. A huge foreign demand for Italian spun thread supplemented the meagre incomes of the peasantry. In Lombardy and the Venetian Terraferma, mulberry growing, silkworm breeding, silk-filament joining, weft-spinning and yarn preparation became rural activities. Italians usually exported spun yarn abroad and imported the finished goods. It was a fatal inversion of economic activities. Italy avoided complete ruin only by exporting agricultural products.

Rural manufactures producing coarse goods for the majority of the population were less influenced by fashion.[24] In Tuscany, an active woollens industry used inferior Tuscan wool. Looms and spinning wheels were common in peasant households. The textiles finished in towns like Prato were required by law to be of inferior quality, so as not to compete with the more prestigious urban productions. The goods coming off these looms were then sold in the fairs and market squares across the state, rather than in the shops of rich merchants. In Lombardy too, rural industries of this sort survived, and in some cases expanded. North of Milan, cotton weaving expanded in Busto Arsizio and Gallarate. A linen industry produced the shirts and the sheets for most of the population. Preparing the flax was a complex operation that involved extracting fibres from the stalks, combing and spinning them. Since every village possessed a few looms, linen weaving was a widespread secondary occupation for women. It is difficult to know how many northern Italian peasants laboured in this sector. They were probably many fewer than their counterparts in France, the Netherlands and England. Nevertheless, there is complete continuity in the location of this burgeoning proto-industry and the industrial and factory geography of the nineteenth century. This zone was situated across a broad band of Lombardy in the hills north of Milan, from the Val d'Aosta to Lake Garda. Other proto-industrial districts included the Riviera around Genoa, and Tuscany north of the Arno.[25] Medieval modes of production, favouring city elites and luxury markets, gave way to a cheaper and more diffuse industry, produced by semi-skilled and low-paid peasants working for mass markets.

This economic decline was not without its impact on Italian society. For one, cities soaked up the wealth of the countryside and gave little back in return. The decay of *urban* industry triggered a ruralizing process. Florence contained 10.3 per cent of Tuscany's population in 1643, but a mere 6.9 per cent in 1816. The cities retained their standard of living by enhancing their administrative control over the state and drawing higher taxes from the subject towns. An expanding pleasure industry attracted more free-spending foreigners. Most aristocrats moved out of manufacturing, or participated at a distance through the employment of straw-men who were mere fronts for capital. In Florence a handful of finance families seized control over much of the silk manufacturing sector through *commenda* contracts, and reduced the manufacturer to the status of simple manager.[26] In this process, entrepreneurs and merchants were held in lower esteem, even in the areas that had been the vanguard of European capitalism. Fewer merchants climbed into the nobility. In Venice, those new families having purchased admission to the aristocracy after 1645 were forbidden to own shops and workshops.[27]

When cities maintained their population, it was by dint of attracting finance capital and higher taxes. Commercial profits that averaged 8 or 9 per cent in Venice in 1600, declined to about 2 to 3 per cent after mid-century. In Genoa, bankers awash in capital in 1680 could only lend their money at 2 to 3 per cent. Economic lethargy made investing in state finance and bonds a more interesting placement, especially suitable for widows or persons unable or not inclined to manage business actively. Only seventeenth-century

Holland possessed credit structures as sophisticated as those obtaining in Italy.[28] With investment opportunities receding annually, those with money tended to *thesaurize* it, that is, convert it into precious objects of silver and gold. The economist Galiani estimated that the reserves of gold and silver in the kingdom of Naples in 1750 were at least four times the monetary stock in circulation. Neapolitans kept myriad silver objects stored away in boxes. All of Italy concealed or displayed these reserves of unemployed currency.[29] As Italy became an agricultural, "underdeveloped" nation, international commerce pressed the advantages of northern Europe.

16 Rural Crisis, 1630–1740

Malthusian Crisis?

Historians have long considered the famine of 1590 to 1593, which resulted from a long spell of bad weather, to be a symptom of an impending Malthusian crisis caused by overpopulation.[1] The manufacturing crisis then exacerbated the general misery and the rigidity of the system. Malthus's "positive checks" came in the triply lethal form of famine, war and bubonic plague, sweeping the northern half of the peninsula late in 1629 and lasting until 1633.[2] Southern Tuscany and Umbria escaped the plague for the most part, but the population there declined nevertheless.[3]

If this were a true Malthusian crisis, one caused by rural overpopulation, there should have been a rapid recovery for the survivors. After the pandemic, the price of cereals fell considerably, 30 or 40 per cent below the prices of the 1620s in rich Lombardy.[4] Grain prices should have risen again as the population reconstituted its losses, but the Thirty Years War and the collapse of urban manufactures deprived urban Italians of the means with which to buy food. The bad economic situation depressed agrarian income and land values at the moment when government increased its taxes to meet the war's demands.

The depression hit the revenues of the landowning class first, in the form of fewer rentals, lower incomes from gabelles and lower prices for agricultural commodities.[5] Landlords passed these losses on to their workers by compressing agricultural wages as much as they could, and by imposing harsher contractual provisions in land rental contracts. Noble or ecclesiastical landlords, producing for

217

urban markets, tailored production to maximize their own incomes. Grain cost more to produce than most other commodities, and was no longer worth producing in such quantities.[6] Landlords abandoned fields that were costly to cultivate, or converted them to grazing land. Diminished production increased the risk of new subsistence crises whenever the climate soured. It was impossible to avert famine by planting more extensively, because a glut of grain in a normal year could drive even wealthy landowners into debt. Central Italy was hit hard by a new famine in 1648–9. Frosts devastated the chestnut stands as well as the grainfields, and epidemic typhus followed in the wake of hunger. Aside from the years of poor harvests, the price for grain remained low for generations.

The chronology of the crisis for southern Italy is not identical, but the evolution was comparable. Spared the great plague in 1630, Sicily suffered at first indirectly, as grain prices gradually declined. With the fall in external demand, landlords reduced the area under cultivation. Much of the island reverted to uncultivated wasteland quickly clothed by *macchia.* In 1638 the viceroy Montalto tried to remedy the problem of shrinking grain production, which kept bread prices high while the general economy sank. In 1646 there was a real famine, hitting the smaller cities in the interior especially hard and contributing to the anti-government revolt in Palermo.[7] After the catastrophic harvest of 1671 troops had to put down disturbances in Messina and in Trapani. In rural areas, many died of hunger, and people slaughtered their draught animals for food. In the kingdom of Naples, there were signs of exhaustion well before the great plague of 1656. In Apulia the reduced demand for wool dealt the grazing industry a serious blow. After the plague of 1656 killed half the population of the capital city, commercial grain production collapsed too. At first the prices remained high, for there were not enough hands to bring the harvest in.[8] Then the price of grain dropped by about a quarter, and remained at that low level for several decades. Communities racked up debts to meet their tax impositions or pay for medical treatment during epidemics. As the economic crisis paralysed Corigliano in Calabria, both the municipal government and the Genoese feudal lord suffered drastic reductions in their income, the latter by about 40 per cent between 1621 and 1651.[9] Rural jurisdictions alienated all their communal lands to pay off debts, selling them to wealthier neighbours or to noblemen.

What was an economic crisis in the seventeenth century, if not a passing subsistence crisis? First, it was a deflation for everyone.

Unlike many economic crises, which redistribute the cards creating winners and losers, the fall in prices (deflation) sucked money out of the system and created a spiral of debts. Rents declined, and as they did, interest paid on money invested declined with them. Tax farmers could not recover their outlay and went bankrupt. Social elites scrambled to obtain church benefices and government offices. It was more difficult to raise money for dowries. Delay in the age of marriage resulted in a greater incidence of celibacy. There was retrenchment everywhere. Building ceased. Land and houses on the less productive margins were abandoned. Manufactures in the cities ceased, and in some cases the entrepreneurial skills lost could not be recovered. Population decline and falling incomes in the country-side wiped out much rural industry too.[10] The crisis of the seventeenth century created few winners.

Land Changes Hands

Low prices for agricultural products hurt peasants as well as landowners and middlemen. Rent conditions were increasingly harsh for peasants, who sought sharecropper status or even salaried work from landowners. San Secondo Parmense is an archetype of this evolution in northern and central Italy.[11] Peasants owned half the arable land in one of Emilia's lush districts in the 1560s. By 1600 their plots were generally too small to provide for their needs, but peasant landowners still numbered 483 in a community of about 500 families, and only 24 "outsiders", primarily city-dwellers, held land in the jurisdiction. By 1678 there were only 104 peasant landlords left. The fragmentation of peasant holdings into microfundia was the prelude to their expropriation during hard times. Rural debt provoked migration of peasants on a vast scale.[12] Similarly, in Tuscany periodic famine accelerated the expropriation of peasant small-holders. In Montefollonico, near Lake Trasimene, peasants sold their land in the decades after 1620, and then their dwellings during the famine of 1648–50. Almost everywhere peasants relinquished their property to their creditors, and then remained on the land as tenants. Even when they owned no land themselves, the economic crisis reduced the sharecroppers from semi-independent farmers to semi-proletarians (McArdle) tied to the land through debt.[13]

City notables, both lay and ecclesiastic, were well positioned to acquire agricultural land. At the onset of the crisis in 1635,

Venetians possessed 12 per cent of the agricultural land in the
Terraferma, but much more in the rich districts close to the lagoon.
They held 40 per cent of the land around Padua and 36 per cent of
the Polesina, much of which they reclaimed from the Po estuary
marshes.[14] The number of Roman landowners diminished relentlessly, as the papal families used their windfall status to assemble,
piece by piece, large estates. Sienese nobles owned just over half the
poderi in southern Tuscany at the end of the century, while religious
institutions run by their families owned another 20 per cent.[15] More
extensive noble ownership of land was not the outcome of a con-
scious design to expropriate peasants. Before the crisis they did not
own most of the land because they did not *need* to. There were other
ways for them to invest their money. The collapse of the manufacturing and commercial economy deprived nobles of places to invest.
Peasants were desperate for cash and food and needed to sell. And
what did greater control of the land bring to the aristocracy? The
value of their land and the rents they derived from it both declined.
The agricultural crisis hardened social stratification and crushed
many notables. At Marsico in the Basilicata, the rural crisis simplified
social structure, by reducing the number of merchants, artisans and
"farmers", and augmenting the number of labourers.[16] This concentration of land in fewer and larger holdings reinforced the absentee
nature of landowning, in which the landlord placed greater reliance
on the *fattore*, or estate agent. In conformity with classic Marxist
theory, the weakest producers disappeared to the advantage of those
with economic and political advantage.

Perhaps the greatest beneficiary was the Church. We use the singular to designate the institution, but the term hides a great multitude of autonomous benefices, commanderies of crusading orders,
colleges, hospitals, monasteries and convents.[17] They were frequently well managed by meticulous administrators, but their
purpose was not economic expansion for its own sake. The demand
for masses fuelled a massive transfer of property from lay hands to
the clergy. Property accruing to the ecclesiastical jurisdiction was
subject to *mortmain,* that is, the irreversibility of status in perpetuity.
This meant that real estate in Church hands could never in future be
relinquished to secular ownership. Churchmen escaped most taxes,
except in the Veneto, and families learned how to exploit this by
fusing their secular and religious income, making accurate tax
assessments impossible. Ecclesiastical jurisdiction also allowed clerics
opportunities for smuggling, which they seized upon with alacrity.

For lay and ecclesiastical landlords alike, the conversion of small sharecroppers' tenancies to direct management employing hired hands was the exception, confined to zones like Lombardy and the Veneto, that were close to major urban markets. In northern and central Italy, *mezzadria* and the concomitant promiscuous culture spread even further, because in a period of population decline landlords desired to fix peasants to their tenancy. Their large families cast relatively few individuals into the poorer *pigionali* status, surviving on casual labour or activities like spinning silk thread and weaving.[18] Peter Musgrave emphasizes, in his study of the rural Valpolicella outside Verona, how readily families shifted from one activity to another, or combined them in order to adapt to misfortunes or new opportunities. This makes it difficult to determine the true state of their resources. We lack studies detailed enough to determine the length of time families stayed in the same house or the same jurisdiction.[19] In the Mezzogiorno too, when grain prices fell, barons reverted to small peasant holdings with rent paid in kind, and lengthened the tenure.[20] As the population rose to pre-plague levels by 1700, peasants may have produced the same amount of food from less land.

Managing Misery

Far from liberating peasants from land hunger, the plague left urban elites more in command of the soil than before. In Lombardy, landowners and their estate managers learned to integrate arable farming and stock-raising, through a continuous rotation of cereals, industrial crops and fodder crops that maintained the fertility of the soil and eliminated fallow.[21] Elsewhere the spread of tree crops allowed peasants to feed livestock on leaves. Turin's affluent and expanding market lured peasants north from Liguria, and they introduced lemon trees and greenhouse cultures.[22]

The period witnessed the spread of two crops whose increasing acceptance banished famine outright from northern Italy. Maize appeared in the crop rotation system about 1650, displacing two medieval staples, sorghum and millet. Excellent in bread, biscuit and porridge, the rest of the plant served as animal fodder. The Veneto was the first region in Europe to grow maize widely, after its introduction in the Polesine in the 1550s.[23] Its yield (three to four times greater than wheat) quickly made it the staple food of the peasantry, allowing landlords to deliver wheat to the cities. By 1730 Venice exported 15 to 20 per cent of its wheat production, which was proportionally equal to England of the early agricultural revolution. Maize spread everywhere in the Po valley by 1700. Peasant diets there became increasingly based on maize-flour porridge, or *polenta*. Maize vanquished hunger, but the absence of other food produced a vitamin-deficiency that led to the disease known as *pellagra*.

The second boon to northern Italian agriculture was rice. Italians had been familiar with it for centuries, but despite its high yields, rice cultivation was not extensive before the eighteenth century.[24] Rice production required much more labour, capital and organization to create an intricate irrigation system.[25] Landowners consecrated important tracts of land to it in south-western Lombardy. Unlike maize, rice could not be integrated into a traditional crop-rotation system with other plants. Its adoption was tragic for the villages in its vicinity, because migrant labourers performed the operations of weeding, transplanting and harvesting. Not only did peasants spend much time barefoot in cold water, but the still water increased the incidence of malaria.

Both rice and maize required choice arable land, so it is not surprising that these innovations appeared in the Po valley. In other parts of Italy landlords converted fields to pasture, leading critics to charge that "sheep ate men". In northern Latium between 20 and 50 per cent of the land was reserved for pasture. Sheep grazed on close to half the remaining arable land that lay fallow every year, and then on the stubble in the newly harvested fields. The wool produced by these hungry and underweight mammals was not high-quality, but it sufficed for rural consumption, for stuffing and lining. For the most part, the meat and cheese ended in urban markets.

Commercial tree plantations and industrial crops were solutions that employed peasants outside traditional busy seasons. Textile plants like flax and hemp were grown in great quantity, macerated, the fibres separated and then spun in peasant dwellings. Since industrial Europe produced ever greater quantities of silk, there was a prodigious increase in the number of mulberry bushes. Silkworm-raising and silk-reeling provided the money that finished in peasant pockets and constituted dowries. Olive trees were another commercial plantation easily integrated into the promiscuous culture of the *podere*. Safron and gall nuts, both used extensively in dyes, appear locally important too. Their importance pales next to vine-growing. Until recently most Italian peasants produced a very inferior wine from vines planted in great density and receiving no fertilizer and little hoeing. The grape sugar content was much lower than in our day, resulting in a feeble alcohol level and little ageing potential. Few peasants possessed specialized winemaking equipment, such as presses, and large barrels were expensive items. Urban markets and foreign consumers clamoured for a finer product. In the Chianti hills, and around Montalcino and Montepulciano, landlords began to emphasize the quality of their wines.[26]

So there was probably space for the aristocracy to invest, but they increasingly took their leave of the mundane operations of estate management. The exodus of the nobility towards the cities might have been a cultural reason for rural economic stagnation, depriving the countryside of their vigilance and their initiative.[27] This was not everywhere true, but only extensive research on the detailed clauses of agricultural contracts and on soil use will shed more light. Tuscan landlords increased their share of the most commercially valuable products, or required the tenant to provide seed or tools, or increased the number of their livestock to maximum levels.[28] The subordination of tenant farmers and sharecroppers was never total, however harsh the contract stipulations. Peasants withheld crops, illicitly performed odd jobs, used the landlord's animals for hauling and carting on their own account. To a point, the landlord and his stewards closed their eyes.[29] The debt that bound the sharecropper to the landlord, bound the landlord to the sharecropper. Since the whole *mezzadria* system depended upon the mobility of labour, much peasant debt had to be written off through charitable clauses in wills, as peasants moved from one jurisdiction to another.[30]

The misery of the peasantry in northern Italy masks the important transformation of the rural economy that underlay the slow accumulation of rural capital. The new conjuncture forced landlords to diversify peasant activities and make them work a longer part of each year. In a way it vindicates Boserup's theory, but the transformation was too slow to be a good illustration. Promiscuous culture probably enabled peasants to produce more food and industrial crops, but there was probably no increase of *productivity*, that is, net yield from each hour of labour.[31]

With the persistent hardship of northern Italian peasants, their lot was probably enviable in comparison to the fieldworkers of the Mezzogiorno and Sicily. Outside limited portions of Campania, southern Italy never knew the more intense and varied promiscuous culture. In zones where *latifundia* predominated, ploughing, seeding and harvesting required a considerable mass of day-labourers, who worked for only three or four months, and remained underemployed for the rest of the year. Peasants did most of their work with the hoe, the spade and the sickle. Hand tools limited peasant holdings to a maximum of three hectares per family. With oxen and ploughs, they could manage 10 hectares, and achieve a productivity increase of 100 per cent. Small property-owners could not afford to keep large animals, however, and had to rent draught animals from large landowners. Greater animal power, possible in Lombardy and northern Europe where water was more abundant, liberated men for other sectors of the economy.

The agricultural depression intensified rural antagonisms. In Corigliano Calabro, the marchese tripled the number of livestock between 1650 and 1700, taking advantage of the additional scrub land where they grazed.[32] Absentee *latifundia* landlords pressed local communities for cheap labour. Calabria and Basilicata were close to collapse by 1680, and communal infrastructure like mills fell into decay. Only Apulia escaped the general marasmus, linked as it was to commercial networks in Venice, Genoa, Spain and later France. The reason for this commercial failure lay in the political confusion of late-seventeenth-century Spain, in the fiscal policies that taxed exports, the poor quality of local money and the continual manipulation of the coinage that enabled the monarchy to escape from some of its debt.[33]

Sicily's population returned to the mark of one million inhabitants by 1680, and remained there for decades. The long decline of the Florentine and Genoese silk industry depressed the raw silk exports from Messina, and fed the discontent that exploded into the revolt against Spain in 1674. The "accumulation of negatives" (Labrot), functioned in Sicily too: economic depression, the revolt of Messina and war damage to the north-eastern part of the island, the increase of banditry, the flight of peasants from their *casali* to the cities, the spread of malaria, the frequent dearths and famines, the eruption of Etna which devastated Catania, the great earthquake of eastern Sicily in 1693 – these were all scourges that added their negative effects to each other.[34]

Throughout Italy in 1700 rural living conditions were close to absolute subsistence. A Perugian chronicler noted in the 1670s that there were never so many paupers as when food was cheap.[35] When Braudel defines prosperity as "high prices and abundance", he implies that its opposite, widespread scarcity and the low cost of living, were signs of underdevelopment.[36] From 1700 onward, mortality "stabilized" but chronic malnutrition remained the norm.[37]

Governments intervened to spare populations the worst. *Annona* regulations certainly favoured the poor urban household over the wealthy landowner, who was a city-dweller too. In rural districts, local government established its own grain reserve, a *canova*, and apportioned quantities from it for the most vulnerable households. There was little effort to extinguish internal customs divisions or improve communications in order to allow foodstuffs to circulate more easily. The extraction of food from a local jurisdiction made villagers uneasy, even if they had no claim of ownership over it. Instead, villagers felt it better to establish reserves, and keep track of private hoards they could requisition in time of dearth.

In the face of poverty individuals resorted to their own coping strategies. Women's age at marriage, the contraceptive technique of traditional society, rose relentlessly over the period. In the Tuscan village of Altopascio, it climbed from about 21.5 before 1700 to 24.2 between 1700 and 1750, and 26.1 in the decades thereafter.[38] In the vicinity of Modena, the birth rate, which Cattini sees as a good indicator of the standard of living, remained low due to a greater incidence of older brides, and an almost permanent state of malnutrition. Only after 1738 did the birth rate begin to climb.[39] Another coping strategy was frugality, the fear of wanting in future. In the environs of Siena most peasants dressed in patched rags, ate bread consisting of a mixture of lesser grains, drank their wine well watered. In Lombardy the bread of the poor consisted of a mixture of maize, millet, beans and rye. Meat consumption, mostly salt pork, was very low in most areas. Supplying animals to butchers' stalls was one of the few ways peasants could raise cash to pay their taxes. Mountain-dwellers commonly ate chestnut porridge; *mangia-polenta* was long a derogatory term that applied to them. Hunger was also at the root of persistent feuding and banditry in mountain districts.[40]

Elites, craving status and security, were frugal too. Living in an economic situation without inflation and where precious metal retained or increased its value, elites *thesaurized*, that is, they transformed money into treasure and saved it in some visible form. Silver cast into tastefully worked platters, candlesticks and cutlery could one day be melted back into cash. Collections of tapestries, jewels or fine paintings expressed wealth and status; they could also be sold or pawned as the need arose to make up dowries or mortgage estates. Such treasure constituted a reservoir of wealth that flowed back into the economy after every disaster. When a tremendous earthquake struck eastern Sicily in 1693, destroying the cities of Catania, Noto, Caltagirone and most of Syracuse, nobles and ecclesiastics found huge sums with which to reconstruct churches, monasteries and municipal buildings, all finer than before.[41]

We are still far from having enough information on the "standard of living" of the popular classes in the seventeenth century.[42] Many peasants lived on the margin of a monetary economy which gives such indices their meaning. We would have to define it as the reasonable life-expectancy for the time (given the state of hygiene and medical knowledge), adequate nourishment and freedom from endemic illnesses (as opposed to epidemics to which even the best-fed were vulnerable). The relative numbers of children and of the elderly in a population are one sign of ease or penury. Despite the misgivings of our affluent society about materialism *per se*, the propensity to purchase and accumulate durable material goods must be another measure. Freedom from fear and persecution, from violence and *prepotenza*, should also be part of any such evaluation. When all of these are combined, we can be sure that such a complex "standard of living" varied widely from one region to the next, and not just along a continuous scale from north to south. As yet we know little about it.

17 Epidemics and Assistance

The Medical Context

Italian society boasted many medical professionals with advanced training.[1] Official practitioners, registered and matriculated in self-governing professional bodies, under the aegis of a College of Physicians (a governing board, not a school), required long education to earn their degree. Italian medical schools, such as Padua and Bologna, were in the European vanguard until 1650. They were the first European institutions to stress practical skills, and to create anatomical theatres and gardens of simples, or medicinal plants.[2] Most physicians also had some familiarity with anatomy and surgery.[3] Their diagnostics followed "rational" methods that emphasized textbook descriptions of the ailment. Physicians were intellectuals whose Latin education and bookish learning raised them above village surgeons. Since medicine was an intellectual pursuit, it was suitable for nobles in most of Italy.[4] Medicine was also a ladder by which talented commoners climbed socially, and it allowed Jews to mingle with the Italian establishment. Successful physicians lectured in universities, wrote books, and treated wealthy clients. City doctors competed for business. For an annual stipend, many were "on call" to noble houses, convents and monasteries. In smaller towns physicians were paid from the municipal purse, as a public service.

Surgeons belonged to the "manual trades", considered mechanical and vile. Schools for surgery opened in Florence in 1600, in Pistoia in 1650, and in Pisa in 1692. They multiplied elsewhere, but these trained only a small proportion of the practitioners, who were numerous enough to be found in every large village. Surgeons were

mostly simple "sawbones" who operated on patients with an array of
sharp tools, pincers and clamps, without anaesthetic. Small wonder
that Italians in need of urgent treatment appealed first to the miraculous intervention of the Madonna! Surgeons practised an indispensable "practical" medicine that was less ineffectual than that of
the physicians. Apothecaries were enthroned amidst their textbooks
on botany, chemistry, magic, zoology, mineralogy, astrology, arithmetic and thesaurus; their weighing scales, mortar and pestles, caul-
drons, presses to crush nuts and seeds; among pots and alembics for
distilling liquors of all sorts. To administer their vast array of remedies, they relied on their knowledge of astral movements, and on an
official pharmacopoeia, established by the medical college.[5]

Carlo Cipolla sees Italy's relative wealth as the reason why physicians, surgeons and apothecaries were so numerous, despite a wide
popular mistrust of their science. Others resorted to practitioners,
dubbed *charlatans*, who dispensed miraculous remedies and multi-
purpose ointments, talismans and good-luck charms in urban
squares, often appealing to the public from makeshift stages. They
also bled their customers and pulled teeth, lanced boils and treated
wounds. Diploma-holders were envious of their appeal and pressured authorities to rein them in, but contemporaries made use of
both types of medicine freely until the middle of the eighteenth
century.

In fairness to the medical establishment, the medical Ancien
Régime lasted until the Pasteurian bacterial revolution of the nineteenth century. Hygienic conditions depended on the density of
habitat, the quality of construction, the exposure to fresh air and the
availability of clean water. In the Mezzogiorno most rural *casali* con-
structions were primitive affairs. Calabrians and their animals often
cohabited in a single dwelling. People aggravated these conditions
everywhere by casting refuse and human waste out before their
houses. Torrential rains spread it around, the sun reduced it to dust
and the wind carried it everywhere. Clean drinking water was not
always available, and fetching it was an arduous task. Fountains and
cisterns were often kilometres distant, and women had to balance
the large, heavy jugs on their heads as they trudged back to their
houses. In summer the heat lowered the underground water tables,
water in cisterns evaporated, and thirst and malaria redoubled in
intensity.[6] In cities water carriers dispensed minute quantities of the
liquid from pails they carried on their shoulders, to individual
households. They often drew it from rivers passing through the

agglomeration, which was also where laundresses washed their clients' clothing and linen. Rivers and streams were always heavily laden with bacteria from human and animal wastes, treated only by the swiftness of the current or the intensity of the sunlight. Waste in the city was often cast into the stream-bed, but the current was often not strong enough to flush it away. People of diverse social status relieved themselves in corners and alleyways, a habit difficult to suppress. Latrines in the courtyards of houses were emptied by peasants who recovered the solid wastes for fertilizer. In poor districts, where the density of habitation was greatest, tenants neglected to empty the latrines and they soon overflowed. At the peak of a typhus epidemic in 1621, one Florentine inquest revealed that 377 latrines needed immediate emptying. In 18 cases they contaminated adjacent drinking wells. How many seventeenth-century wells of drinking water in urban courtyards would pass modern safety standards?[7]

Human wastes were not the only ones to consider. Butchers commonly cast animal waste to dogs and cats in the streets, or dumped it unceremoniously into the nearest stream. Tanners and weavers used chemicals, excrement and urines in the preparation of hides and cloths. Dyers used a wide array of chemical concoctions in their work, without a thought for urban ecology. City workers raised silkworms in their rooms and tolerated the effluents released when they boiled the cocoons. The odour of piety wafting through churches was a combination of incense, melting candle wax and putrefying corpses buried under the paved floors. These practices notwithstanding, the large proportion of brick, stone and tile dwellings made Italian cities less lethal than those elsewhere.

Fighting the Plague

Plague in Europe lingered for more than three centuries after the great pandemic of 1345–48 killed a third of the population in one cruel sweep. It was the only disease capable of multiplying the annual average of deaths by four times or more.[8] In addition to isolated epidemic outbreaks, Italy experienced three plague pandemics, in 1575–7, 1629–31 and 1656–7. The first, originating in Constantinople, penetrated Italy from both the Trentino and Sicily. With nearly 50,000 victims Venice lost a quarter of its population. The epidemic in Milan, which claimed 18,000 lives, is named after the archbishop Carlo Borromeo, who risked his life to bring succour to plague victims. He helped spread it too. In October 1576 he organized three great processions of public penance to ward off God's anger. This display of collective piety dismayed the health officers, but they did not contradict the archbishop, who unflinchingly excommunicated his adversaries.[9]

Physicians well knew how contagious the plague was. Like modern scientists, physicians allowed multi-causal explanations that embraced social conditions, moral situations and epidemiology simultaneously. They ascribed the epidemic to a combination of (a) the "composition of the air", and the position of heavenly bodies which created "general influences"; (b) a more specific "miasma" or infection stemming from decaying and poisonous matter; and (c) and "humours" in individuals which made them more or less vulnerable. Most putative plague remedies sensed that air currents bore the contagion from one person to another. Authorities countered the noxious air with strong odours and pyres releasing a purifying, pungent smoke. There was only a vague suspicion that rats and their fleas might be involved in its transmission, despite the mortality of rats that preceded the most violent outbreaks. Officials noted that the disease usually broke out in the poorest quarters, but once unleashed it killed 60 to 80 per cent of those who fell sick, after about five days' illness, regardless of the social class of the victim.

The clergy ascribed all catastrophes to divine punishment. The measures clerics proposed to combat plague inevitably widened to include operations aiming at social and moral purity, such as expelling prostitutes. The 1576 pandemic, contemporary with the witch hunts north of the Alps, gave rise to a widely held theory that magicians concocted powerful poisons from toxic plants or secretions from animals and humans which they daubed on walls and doors.[10] Venetian, Genoese and Florentine authorities were not much affected by this belief, but Turin executed at least twenty suspects in 1600–1, broke them on a wheel in the city square, then drowned, quartered and burned their remains to strike terror into such delinquents and to reassure the innocent. In Milan in 1630, these *untori* or "daubers" were arrested in their hundreds and sometimes lynched by mobs. According to rumour, they daubed doors, walls, locks, gratings, holy water and images in churches, sweets, food, money for the poor and clothes. In the countryside, peasants feared they had poisoned the wells, the sheaves of grain, loaves of bread and the fruit in the trees. During the 1656 plague in Naples, the *lazzari* similarly killed beggars and foreigners as suspected agents of mass poisoning.

Because of the uncertain aetiology of the plague, authorities pre-ferred administrative procedures to stop the contagion. The regula-tory role of the health boards originated with the plague of 1347, and these gradually became permanent bodies. Preventing conta-gion was an affair of regulations and inspections applied to a wide range of activities, such as sewage evacuation, the management of hospitals, the conduct of burials and the upkeep of cemeteries and pesthouses. Magistrates supervised the professional activity of physi-cians, surgeons and apothecaries, the activity of hostelries, and regu-lated Jews, beggars and prostitutes. Health boards combined concern for social purity with practical prophylactic measures. These boards corresponded with similar institutions elsewhere, trusting others to alert them at the first suspicious death. Magistrates also tapped merchants, diplomats and other trustworthy individuals in other cities to tip them off as early as possible.

In Turin the health board dealt with urban sanitation: slaughter-houses, street cleaning, rubbish removal, drainage, and control of carriers of infectious diseases.[11] When the plague reached Piedmont from France in 1598, the city government dusted off its regulations and multiplied the number of controllers and guards in order to block the flight of people and merchandise from infected areas. Travellers needed health certificates and passports issued by similar authorities in the towns from which they came. All activities involving contact with livestock, meat or skins was either banned or removed from the city because of the odours they created. Begging was prohibited and some beggars were sent home, while others were confined outside the city. Prostitutes came under close scrutiny for their commerce with men from out of town. Meanwhile, the city council stockpiled grain, wine and medicines, and transformed the hospital of San Lazzaro outside town into a pesthouse, erecting special quarantine huts to isolate the sick. When the plague finally penetrated the city, the ducal government withdrew to a safe area. Wealthy citizens fled from the city and barricaded themselves into country villas. City officials began to record the sick and suspect cases, registered the dead, sealed up the houses of the stricken and drew up inventories of their contents, all very expensive procedures. Suspect cases they sent to quarantine huts, or enclosed in their own houses provided they paid for their own maintenance and the guards at the door. These regulations were not enforced rigidly

everywhere; rather, they served as a bargaining framework interpreted diversely by different social groups. Nobles often escaped
inspection of their houses by the light-fingered *beccamorti*, and they
remained off-limits to urban police. Women contested the interdic-
tion to sit in their doorways, which was part of their normal domestic
space. City magistrates desperate for resources often sold exemptions from the regulations. The city had to feed thousands of people,
not only those sick and quarantined, but all of the destitute. At the
same time, commerce ground to a halt and multiplied the number
of unemployed. At the height of the epidemic these measures all
broke down. The doctors and surgeons who stayed usually sacrificed
their lives to their sense of duty, as did many of the health magistrates. In their absence, criminals, extortionate healers, and other
profiteers took over, while the healthy and sick alike were held to
ransom by the indispensable but unscrupulous *beccamorti*. Order only
gradually returned as the number of fatalities declined. Then the
disinfection began, with hundreds of people being hired to clean,
fumigate, boil and burn objects during almost two months.[12]

Much worse than the isolated outbreak in Turin was the plague
pandemic of 1630–1, after the economic depression of the 1620s
and a subsistence crisis in 1629 weakened people's immune systems.
This plague, immortalized by Manzoni's historical novel *The
Betrothed*, killed about a quarter of the population in northern Italy,
or more than one million people. Archbishop Federico Borromeo
paraded the relics of his late uncle Carlo Borromeo in a huge propi-
tiatory procession on 11 June 1630, against the advice of Milanese
health magistrates. The epidemic redoubled in intensity almost
immediately. Bypassing Genoa and Romagna, it slew half the population of Milan, or 60,000 people. Half the populations of Verona,
Mantua, Brescia, Padua and Lucca; a third of Venice and Bologna;
and a quarter of Modena's inhabitants perished in the epidemic.
Only about a tenth of Florence's 60,000 inhabitants died, and the
pandemic made little further headway in Tuscany.

We do not know why a particular outbreak inflicted apocalyptic
losses on some localities and miraculously bypassed others, although
stringent policing played a part. The epidemic reached northern
Tuscany via soldiers deserting from infected armies, and by refugees
from stricken cities moving south. In Florence the great *Abbondanza*
warehouses were filled in expectation of the worst. Healers of every
sort petitioned the young grand duke Ferdinando II to administer
their own remedies, and oral and folk traditions provided still

others. The health boards prohibited festive gatherings and closed schools, prohibited processions and religious assemblies. Ecclesiastics often resisted the transformation of their monasteries into emergency pesthouses. The Florentine pope Urban VIII Barberini excommunicated all the officers of the Florentine board at the instigation of the Tuscan clergy for violating church immunities and privileges. Merchants were as troublesome to health magistrates as was the clergy, for plague paralysed trade. The fine imported wool or expensive silk in the homes and on the looms of sick workers was considered infected, and had to be burned, or washed and fumigated, which often ruined it. Tens of thousands of unemployed workers risked death by starvation. The grand duke inaugurated a public works programme to employ some of them, and instructed merchants to stockpile their production to keep workers busy. This could not compensate for the losses, and workers backed the merchants' attempts to reverse the measures of the health magistrates by appealing over their heads.

Italians did not submit meekly to all the regulations, no matter how urgently they were framed. The onset of the plague also brusquely increased the level of interpersonal aggression, both verbal and physical. Authorities suspended normal judicial procedures for the duration, and extraordinary police and judicial measures dealt summarily with offenders.[13] Aristocrats often pressured physicians to withhold reports of the plague in their houses. Suspect houses were marked with a cross and locked for twenty-two days. If they were not evacuated to the hospitals, their inhabitants were fed from the street in baskets lowered from the windows. Healthy children followed their sick parents to the *lazaret*. Many people broke into houses closed because of contagion, although neighbourhood women were on the lookout and reported everything to the authorities. It was a criminal act to "relocate" objects from infected houses to prevent their destruction, but most people were desperately poor, and the intruders were often relatives who felt a strong claim on these things.[14] Thieves snatched goods even when there were unburied bodies present, thus placing infected objects back in circulation. When they were caught, the perpetrators were liable to summary execution, but were more commonly sentenced to serve as *beccamorti* to replace those who died.

Lazarets never completely isolated the plague victims from the healthy population. The healthy preyed on those who took their valuables to their sickbed. *Beccamorti* and hospital assistants committed thefts and sexual assaults there routinely. Given that they were predatory criminals living on borrowed time, this was not surprising.[15] Ecclesiastical institutions entrusted with furnishing supplies often dragged their feet and provoked additional want, creating a flourishing black market in foodstuffs. This gave rise to anticlerical sentiments not entirely offset by the martyrdom of friars, who served the sick in the hope of reaching Paradise quickly.

The last pandemic arrived from Seville, striking Genoa, Rome, Sardinia and the Mezzogiorno in 1656-57. In Genoa, 55,000 out of 73,000 inhabitants perished in the epidemic, probably due to the extreme overcrowding of the great port. One monk who helped supervise relief work made the connection between population density and epidemic disease. He noted that "God shaves the world when it grows too thick, and his razor is the plague". In Rome the energy of the Health Congregation limited the extent of the disaster. The cardinals in charge were seconded by the papal army, which multiplied the checkpoints and mounted continuous inspections. Public preaching was strictly prohibited. These measures seem to have helped, for only 15,000 people died out of a population of 120,000, a far lower proportion than in either Genoa or Naples. Roman urbanism was probably an asset too, for houses were lower, the streets wider and cleaner, and fresh water more widely available than elsewhere in Italy.[16]

In Naples the best efforts of the health boards could not prevent a truly massive mortality. The epidemic disembarked from Spain via Sardinia at the beginning of spring in 1656. Although the suspicious deaths multiplied at the end of April, it was only in mid-May that a health deputation was formed to combat it. By 1 June, 400 people were dying daily. By early July the system collapsed under the strain of 2,000 deaths daily. Authorities opened great trenches in the city squares and widest streets to bury the dead. By the end of the year, there were barely 100,000 survivors in the great metropolis, less than a third of the pre-plague figure. The clergy lost 80 per cent of its effectives. The Mezzogiorno, flayed for decades by economic depression and excessive taxation, lost about a million of its four million inhabitants.[17] Gradually commerce revived and survivors procreated new families to replace the ones they had lost.

Italy was the first country to be free of great pandemics. States maintained quarantine measures and health passports throughout the eighteenth century. Livi Bacci believes that the restriction of movement during times of crisis must have worked up to a point.[18]

There was always danger of plague infections arriving on ships from the Ottoman Empire, which provoked the great epidemic in nearby Marseilles in 1720, another outbreak at Messina in 1743, and one last one at Bisceglie in Apulia in 1817. The army and navy immediately responded by erecting a *cordon sanitaire*, blockading the infected zone tightly until the epidemic was over. Despite Italy's lead in epidemic prevention, the plagues wrought horrible losses that prevented recovery from the great economic collapse. It is striking how quickly the cities recovered from the great pandemic of 1575–6, which punctuated the great economic expansion after the Italian wars. But Italian city economies never recovered from the great plagues of 1630 and 1656, which carried off the urban artisans and workers whose heads and hands produced the country's fine manufactured goods. There was no longer any money to absorb the tremendous costs the epidemics occasioned, no elasticity or resiliency in the urban economy to absorb the shock. Moreover, mortality sucked the life out of the rural economy. Declining food prices ruined many landed fortunes. Contrary to Malthusian theory, times were not easier for the survivors of the plague, or for those regions which escaped it. Both rural and urban conditions worsened for a century thereafter.

The Age of Social Epidemics

The plague's competitors, typhus, smallpox and malaria, were more typically "social epidemics", closely tied to the standard of living of their victims.[19] These diseases, when they struck in epidemic form, increased the annual death toll by one-half, or doubled it. The great famine of 1590–1 inaugurated an era of social epidemics that struck intermittently until the mid-nineteenth century. Typhus was the greatest of these scourges. Known in military circles as "camp fever", it was liable to break out in soldiers' makeshift quarters whenever a siege dragged on for too long. Among civilians it appeared primarily as a consequence of crop failure. Rural workers dependent upon reaping and threshing grain found little employment. Grain prices shot upwards immediately, and the great majority of the population restricted its consumption to the barest necessities. This threw urban manufactures into a slump. Dyers, spinners and weavers lost work. Rents and wages went unpaid, and hunger soon struck the poorest segment of the population. In Italy these subsistence crises became more frequent after 1580, even though commerce and manufactures continued to expand until 1619–22. Europe seems to have experienced a cooling trend in the late sixteenth century, characterized by more frequent frosts, heavy rains, and expanding glaciers that inched down the mountain slopes. Grain yields diminished simultaneously. Italy experienced five great crises of typhus, 1590–3, 1648–9, 1671, 1764 and 1817–18, coinciding each time with a doubling of the price of grain.

Typhus was most lethal in winter. That was when people lived shut up in their rooms, washing little, and draping themselves in dirty linens and woollens.[20] The agents of contagion were body lice, that transmitted the rickettsia bacilli picked up from a human carrier. A rash appeared on the torso within four to eight days of infection, and after two weeks the patient either stabilized or died. This exanthemic typhus killed about 20 per cent of the people who fell sick with it. Europeans bathed very little, but the wealthy were generally not felled by the infection. The connection between morbidity and a low standard of living is unmistakable. If manufactures and exports remained healthy, a bad harvest or two might not lead to outbreaks of disease. In 1620, however, a poor harvest in Tuscany coincided with a massive economic downturn. By January 1621, Florence's four hospitals were swamped with more than 750 cases. Typhus patients were not transported to lazarets like plague victims, but were carried into hospitals and laid alongside ordinary patients. In Florence the magistrates finally decided to leave the stricken individuals in their own homes in order to avoid overcrowding the hospitals. They opted to deliver care and medicines to patients at home, free of charge. In the meantime, the health inspectors discovered the nightmarish living conditions obtaining in the poorest neighbourhoods of the Tuscan capital. Many of the poor slept on straw mats infested with fleas and lice.[21] The arrival of thousands of hungry, dirty and miserable peasants in the cities looking for food made this bad state of affairs much worse. The situation of Florence in 1621 repeated itself in 1629, and again in 1648. It seems clear that if bad weather triggered harvest failure, the dismal economic conjuncture of the mid-seventeenth century aggravated the demographic impact of the epidemics.

Typhus ravaged most of Italy in the 1760s, once the economy was growing again. Poor harvests after 1764 led to an outbreak of disease all over central and southern Italy. The hospitals in Florence and Siena were full of peasants seeking food, upsetting both the public and private charity networks, which were incapable of coping with crisis. In Livorno the authorities decided to "clean out" the city by driving out refugees from abandoned houses, from churches, and the various makeshift huts and shelters they erected inside the walls. With the help of physicians and priests who pointed out the dens of the miserable, civic officials herded 5,000 people into a specially equipped building. They were fed and washed there, their clothes disinfected, the sick were sent to a lazaret, and the rest were escorted from the city to their villages.[22]

In addition to epidemic crises like plague and typhus, endemic diseases such as smallpox and malaria took a high toll. The frequency of smallpox increased to one outbreak roughly every five years during the eighteenth century in Italy, France and England. It may have accounted for a third of total infant mortality in the eighteenth century, although it never sparked the panic mobilization of health authorities.[23] The English imported from Turkey the practice of individual inoculation against smallpox around 1714. The practice began in Italy at Livorno, where there was an important English merchant colony, and spread inland from there, often through the agency of unregistered practitioners, like midwives. Mass inoculation only dates from the nineteenth century, however, and constitutes the only major medical victory against epidemic diseases until modern times.

Another killer not effectively treated until the twentieth century was malaria, which advanced as people abandoned valley bottoms and coastal lowlands. Where these malarial lands were inhabited, both the human and the animal population were sparse and sickly, prematurely aged and stricken by a recurrent anaemia.[24] Malaria everywhere reduced the vitality and the productivity of its victims. In mid-twentieth-century Sardinia, where 90 per cent of the population suffered from it, officials evaluated lost work days due to the disease at 20 or 30 annually for each victim.[25] Because it lowered immunity, malnourishment was a "multiplying factor" for malaria, as it was for other infectious diseases.[26] Discovery of the role of mosquitoes as the transmitting agent of malaria dates only from the nineteenth century, but it took much longer to dissuade shepherds from maintaining shallow ponds for their animals. Doctors began treating the sick with quinine around 1650. In the Roman countryside, where it was particularly virulent, the Hospital of Santo Spirito dispensed 50,000 syrups, 10,000 doses of medicine and 25,000 "treatments" every year.

The recrudescence of infectious diseases in the seventeenth century underscores Italy's deep economic decline. They were causes as much as consequences of the malaise striking the whole of southern Europe. These demographic crises which carried off one and a half times or twice the number of dead as in a normal year, tended to become less frequent after 1660, as they did elsewhere in western Europe. Unlike northern Europe, however, life expectancies did not much improve before 1860, because infant mortality claimed 40 per cent of children before their tenth birthday.[27]

Social Prevention

Social elites sought ways to mitigate the impact of these disasters. There were multifarious attempts to deal with poverty, and large cities contained a panoply of lay and church institutions to protect people from its effects.[28] Earlier research on this theme lay in the shadow of French philosopher Michel Foucault, who emphasized the repressive intention of these institutions. Historians working from proper archives now downplay the sinister aspect. The term *ospedale* often designated a place for pilgrims to rest *en route* to a shrine, a place for hospitality, managed by confraternities of devout laymen and clergy. They took in patients too poor to afford treatment at home, but they took in foundlings and beggars as well. The late sixteenth century witnessed a wave of foundations that also gave outdoor poor relief, distributed bread to needy families, and financed a network of wetnurses.[29] At first they were financed by precarious means, forcing city elites to devise systems whereby the "deserving poor" were protected and the "lazy" or fraudulent beggars chastised.[30] Provisions to arrest unauthorized beggars were written into statutes and the poor laws, but they were not normally applied until a crisis forced authorities to act. Large cities built charity hospitals that interned troublesome cases, usually outsiders, males and vagabonds, who reduced the pool of funds available to deserving, local inhabitants, who tended to be female, elderly, or juvenile. Far from being fearsome and sinister prisons, these institutions were swamped by petitions for admission at every economic downswing. The beggars' hospital in Florence rotated inmates through it in order to aid a larger number. The guardians of the hospital defined the poor as those who had no kin to take care of them, afflicted by accident or misfortune and unable to care for themselves. The great majority of the inmates were women, and elderly women formed a big contingent of them, while others had children in tow. Very few were terrified of being shut up in the great dormitories although they would have been subject to overtly moralizing regulations while living in its confines. Children placed there by their families were usually taken back by their families when circumstances improved. Inmates were often made to work there, but more for discipline than for gain, as often happened in convents.[31]

The most complete range of institutional support existed for women and girls, whose virtue was threatened by poverty. Italian confraternities dispensed most of their alms on dowries for girls deemed most deserving. Orphans, daughters of disreputable people, wives of vicious husbands, and abandoned spouses were given priority in the hospitals, *conservatories* and convents available in cities. Around 1700 governments established more all-embracing "general hospitals" on the French model, designed to eliminate widespread begging and to provide redemption through self-discipline and punishment. But in Italy the punitive aspect never predominated.[32] Rather, social pragmatism and Catholicism as a "helping religion" converged to alleviate the worst features of structural poverty in ancien régime society.

18   Philosophy and Science, 1550–1700

A Sociable Humanism

Renaissance humanism was an intellectual predisposition that conveyed to modern men the treasure of knowledge, beauty and wisdom amassed by ancient Greece and Rome. To appreciate that treasure, humanists needed to restore the meanings of the words that had shifted sense since ancient times, and recover a universal language stripped of medieval barbarisms. In seventeenth-century Italy books published in Latin still constituted more than a third of all titles, including the great majority of scientific, medical and judicial texts.[1] Learning Latin was an arduous rite of passage. Schoolboys by the hundred thousand laboured daily on their expurgated classics. They identified and classified rhetorical figures, translated them into Italian, then worked them back again. To embellish their everyday speech, they engraved excerpts on their memories, and styled their own prose after particular classical authors.[2] Despite the increasing range of subjects taught under Jesuit guidance, all were integrated into a monolithic cultural project, within the grasp of educated gentlemen.[3]

Universities concentrated on training young adults for the professions, in the Church, at the bar and in medicine. Just after 1600, Italy boasted 25 or 26 universities, the greatest density of any country in Europe. Although student numbers were far smaller than today, they rose everywhere until the early seventeenth century.[4] In Naples registrations numbered in the thousands. Padua counted over a thousand registered students. Bologna and Pisa were important institutions with six or seven hundred each. At Bologna civic leaders

240

insisted that the university hire famous or capable instructors who would attract students there.[5] Padua attracted French, German, English, Scandinavian and Polish students, as well as Greeks and Croats, who were Venetian subjects.[6] Italian students were most numerous in the lecture-halls, but the foreigners were most intent on graduating. The distinction between attending classes to obtain knowledge and graduating with a diploma allowed Jewish students to frequent the university at Padua, above all, but also Pavia in Lombardy, and Siena and Perugia in central Italy. Protestant Germans studied at Siena, at Bologna and at Padua again, where it sufficed to refrain from mocking Catholic rituals and to attend church discreetly on feast days.

The brightest pupils never lost the taste for displaying their verve and wit to a group of peers. The academies appeared around 1540 in Padua and Florence. Italians created more than a thousand of them over the next two centuries.[7] Men of learning considered each other citizens in a literary "republic". Since humanist culture embraced every domain, academicians were able to speak on many subjects through learned quotations.[8] Literature was not a tool of social analysis; rather, it was meant to be entertaining, playful, even irreverent. Members adopted surnames, or fictional identities, sometimes with comical connotations.[9] Academies also helped unify the Italian intellectual world. It was common for them to enlist members from other cities as occasional participants or correspondents, and both the conventions and the literary language they employed – Tuscan – soon acquired a certain homogeneity. Whatever their composition, or their duration (they could disappear as easily as they formed), most academies functioned as settings for "conversations". The purpose of these literary exercises was to develop the participant's rhetorical ease, refine their vocabulary and "elevate" their minds. Academies sponsored regular debating "tournaments" staged around a question, or a *dubbio*; "whether men are more excellent than women" was a frequent topic. Neither the arguments for nor those against the proposition necessarily reflected the psychological commitment of the person making it. The purpose was in the process, the form, the dexterity of verbal fencing. Clever debating style, using evocative metaphors and learned quotations was a form of erudite sociability, an intellectual *virtù*, not exclusively masculine. Members printed a torrent of hyperbolic prose and verse, and marked every event with a confetti shower of well-turned phrases.

Some groups sponsored projects of considerable learning and

ambition. Duke Cosimo I of Florence created the Academy of Drawing in 1566 to train artists and draughtsmen according to accepted canons. The *Accademia della Crusca*, formed in 1582, promoted the study of Tuscan. It produced Europe's first great dictionary in 1612. Others sponsored civic functions, like carnival plays and pageants. Queen Christina of Sweden's *Accademia Reale* in Rome sought to dictate the elements of literary good taste, on the model of Louis XIV's classical academy in Paris. It would become the basis for the "Arcadia" movement that marked a shift in aesthetic sensibilities away from the baroque.[10]

In addition to the academies, cities possessed a variety of formal and informal settings for the exchange of ideas. Book publishers consulted the expertise of editors of texts, censors, translators and reviewers. Monasteries often possessed the largest libraries. Seminaries held classes not just for clerics but for lay students. Men discussed literature in bookstores, or sought news or tales of foreign parts in certain shops. The barber shop was joined after 1670 by the café, frequented as much for news and conversation as for its exotic beverages and ice cream. Taking all of these sites together, none was richer in novelty than the axis Venice–Padua, the intellectual fulcrum of Europe in the half-century after 1560.[11] Venice produced a flood of books: 17,500 titles in the sixteenth century, about 18 million individual books, often in cheap editions, circulating widely.

Few libraries were private in the modern sense of the word, for they were open to well-heeled scholars at fixed hours. Humanists also collected curious and beautiful objects for their own edification and the amazement of others. Collections of rare or exquisite objects were on view in churches and official buildings, open to all comers, like a tourist attraction. Late sixteenth-century Venetian *Wunderkammern* displayed rare books and manuscripts, statues, paintings, mathematical instruments, minerals, relics and occult items. The curiosity, diversity, richness, the virtuosity of execution and the very rarity of these objects motivated collectors to acquire them.[12] Only after 1650 was there a tendency for collectors to apply comparative methods and critical principles of classification. The Bolognese professor Ulisse Aldrovandi, who promoted the exact investigation of the animal and plant worlds, figures as a precursor. His pictures of imaginary animals gave credence to ancient and medieval sources in a way we would find credulous today. Yet the scale of his collection was considerable. He founded the first botanical garden at Bologna in 1568, which eventually contained 3,000 plants. In addition, his "museum" contained 18,000 specimens of animals and minerals, dried and glued plants. Aldrovandi also directed the execution of 8,000 pictures of animals, plants and minerals for his great illustrated work on natural history.[13] We are not dealing here with the modern scientific spirit, which explains ordinary phenomena in material terms, but rather with a kind of encyclopedic wonderment at the diversity of the universe.

Unorthodox Departures

In the absence of the statistical method that guides modern science, there was no clear distinction between a humanist and someone interested in supernatural phenomena. Not all humanist learning fitted the Christian mould. The science of the ancients helped explain the workings of the universe by mysterious connections between heaven and earth. According to Kearney, there were three traditions of natural inquiry.[14] One we might call organic, because it explained the natural world in terms of growth and decay. Its proponents were struck by the constant change in nature, not its predictability. This led to the view that a "final cause" accounted for regularities. Much of this tradition can be traced back to Aristotle's writings, along with Galen in medicine and Ptolemy in astronomy, although direct observation buttressed most of it. Aristotle hypothesized that the earth was the centre of the universe, that the planets and the sun revolved around it. There was complete separation of the "lunar" world from the sub-lunar; each possessed its own physics and chemistry. The lunar world was regular and predictable. In the sub-lunar world, where change was constant, matter was composed of four elements, two heavy (earth and water) and two light (fire and air), each tending to move towards its natural place. This emphasis on final causes rendered Aristotle amenable to Christianization; both Catholic and Protestant authorities supported this "scholastic" tradition.[15]

The magical tradition conferred on the Christian deity attributes thought appropriate to a magician or wonder-worker. Scholars sought Divine Meaning in the "secrets" of the universe, much as a Bible scholar seeks Truth in a close reading of Holy Scripture (a discipline called hermeneutics). Cabbalistic studies encouraged numerological investigation of scripture to find religious truths there. Mathematics was less a secular science than a mode of religious enquiry. Magic was founded on links of sympathy that united all beings in function of superior influences over inferior ones. Much of the inspiration for this came from writings attributed to an Egyptian writer, Hermes Trismegistus. A half-dozen treatises on learned magic (hermetic magic) came to Europe from Byzantium after 1453. The Neoplatonic philosopher Marsilio Ficino translated them from the Greek. The underlying premise held that God "wrote" the secrets of the cosmos in symbolic language, just as he peopled the universe with angels and demons, superhuman beings and spirits of all sorts which could be conjured as intermediaries.[16] In everything visible there was something pointing to the kernel of invisible Truth inside it. By divining analogies based on resemblance and metaphor, the magician penetrated the mystery and secrecy of Divine intention.

The third tradition rested upon a view of nature in which the analogy of the machine explained the regularity and predictability of the universe. Its development relied on the revival of Archimedean science after 1543. These natural philosophers concentrated upon aspects of the world that could be explained in mechanical and mathematical terms, without seeking to derive religious significance from it.

Catholic theology, indeed all Christianity, is based on the confusion of the natural and the supernatural: for what is the mass if not a magical ritual, revealed to humanity by God? The belief that the universe is inhabited by spirits has a long pedigree, and is not specific to Christian cultures. The ancients created two conventional sciences, alchemy and astrology, based on the hidden connections between material objects and heavenly influences. Neither was condemned by the Renaissance Church, and horoscopes were common forecasting devices. It was not far from astrology and alchemy to forbidden hermetic magic, whose secrets were not difficult to obtain.[17] Several internationally-renowned magicians hailed from Neapolitan monasteries. Giambattista della Porta's Latin work published in 1558, *Magia Naturalis*, was a great 20-volume storehouse of recipes and ideas enjoying more than 50 subsequent editions. An *Accademia dei Secreti* bankrolled his experiments, until a brush with the Inquisition in 1574 forced him to disband it.[18] Although Pope Sixtus V prohibited works on astrology and divination by the bull *Coeli et Terrae* in 1586, these "sciences" remained popular and influential.[19] Della Porta believed that living and inanimate objects all possessed sensations of attraction and repulsion, and sentiments of love and hate. He concluded that magic was entirely "natural" or "mechanical". He sought to deprive magicians and sorcerers of their monopoly of such lore by opening it up to the general public that read Latin. Magicians also consulted Ramon Lull's fourteenth-century *Ars Cabalistica* and the *Key of Solomon*, a Judaeo-Arabic hermetic text that circulated underground in manuscript form. Only a few neo-Platonic intellectuals used this lore to explain the true nature of the cosmos. Typically, baser concerns motivated its practitioners: to find hidden treasure; to learn other sciences and foreign languages; to seduce women especially. It was the masculine, bookish equivalent of the magical lore practised by women to heal and to harm, to make and break relationships. Readers of this forbidden material often made handwritten notes for themselves, seized by tribunals as evidence. These beliefs gradually dissipated among literate males in Italy during the seventeenth century.

Giordano Bruno, Giulio Cesare Vanini and Tommaso Campanella were part of the same esoteric milieu. Bruno stands out because of his unfortunate destiny. This prolific writer and forceful lecturer from Nola in Campania was a former seminarian at San Domenico Maggiore in Naples, one of the foremost Dominican institutions in Europe. Unlike his brother monks, Bruno read forbidden authors, like Erasmus and Lucretius. Called to Rome to defend himself, he fled to Geneva, where he converted to Calvinism, then to France, to England, to Germany. His work, like his genius, was multi-dimensional. One book, published in London, speculated that there was an infinite number of worlds in the universe, each revolving around its own sun. This dismissed the Christian doctrine of the Creation. Other texts penned in the 1580s were more strictly magical. He quarrelled with almost everyone, everywhere. Homesick for Italy, Venice lured him back in 1591, but after he fell out with his protector in 1592 the republic charged him with heresy and handed him over to the Roman authorities. After a lengthy trial, the Inquisition burned him in 1600. Although he figures as one of the early Copernicans, Bruno's thinking was deeply reliant on the links between the microcosm and the macrocosm, on correspondences, signatures and homologies.

Bruno was not alone, however. Italy ejected or rejected other philosophers between 1560 and 1620. Francesco Pucci of Florence was one of those executed. Like Bruno, he converted to Calvinism outside Italy, but quarrelled with everyone in his wanderings.[20] His reconversion to Catholicism was a propaganda coup for the Church, but no sooner back in Italy, Pucci beseeched the pope to denounce the errors and vices in the Church and to undertake a new reform. Giulio Cesare Vanini fled his Carmelite monastery in Naples for Paris, and then southern France, where it was believed he established an atheistic academy. In a very rare procedure for France, the Dominican Inquisition executed him in Toulouse in 1618.[21] Tommaso Campanella was an early Copernican who was preparing a millenarian uprising against the king of Spain, when he was caught and imprisoned in 1597. Spared the worst, Campanella continued to write on a wide variety of subjects during his detention in Rome, including a tract in favour of Galileo in 1616. After his release, he went to the French court, where he specialized in making horoscopes and astrological pronouncements.

This intellectual vitality endangered received tradition, both scholastic and Christian. Foreigners held Italy to be the land of atheists. They added it to the stock of (not always unfounded) negative stereotypes of Italians, which included their penchants for sodomy and poison. There probably always existed a small proportion of the male population that aggressively doubted Catholic dogma and official science. Inquisition archives document the village disbeliever who, in an unguarded moment that his neighbours remembered well, challenged the whole edifice of received wisdom by threatening to debunk it. Others resembled the Friulian miller Menocchio, made famous by Carlo Ginzburg, who cobbled together a purely materialist interpretation of the Creation from his own observations and from the varied and cheap printed literature that the literate village elite circulated to each other.[22] Educated notables scorned Aristotle's belief in four elements, and substituted a single element composed of mechanically interacting atoms, a doctrine referred to as "atomism". The more tolerant climate of the Venetian republic favoured the dissemination of such pernicious influences. Cesare Cremonini taught non-Christian Aristotelianism at Padua from 1590 to 1629, despite being investigated by the Inquisition. Some academies were breeding grounds for atheism. The Venetian *Accademia degli Incogniti*, founded in 1630 by Giovan Francesco Loredan, was especially notorious. While Loredan and his colleagues were repeatedly denounced to the Inquisition, they pursued their non-Christian studies without much hindrance for a generation. They formed part of a larger *libertine* movement which Lorenzo Bianchi defines loosely as free-thinking scholars who opposed the hegemony of the Church and its certitudes. Most were merely sceptics who were content with not knowing the origins of the Universe, and preferred to focus their curiosity on questions they thought mankind could answer. These groups were visible enough to attract attention across Europe.[23] By the 1630s and 1640s these Libertines began appearing in France too, and fed debates about the nature of Truth.

A Secular Cosmology

If the mechanistic tradition is not the sole source of modern science, it was a powerful one, boasting a solid pedigree. Machines were useful in war and in civil society. Military engineers emerged in large numbers in northern and central Italian cities. Military engineering treatises multiplied after 1560 in Italian bookstores. Between 1554 and 1600, out of 34 published works on fortification in Europe, 26 were Italian, 4 French, 2 Spanish, 1 Dutch and 1 German.[24] Engineers and artillery experts experimented with ballistics, calculated the trajectories and the impact of cannon balls on different materials.[25] This mathematization of military culture influenced surveying, cartography and topographical draughtsmanship.[26]

Although mathematicians were held well below philosophers in both esteem and pay scale, the discipline was increasingly taught in Italian universities.[27] Mathematical culture, which served both to calculate horoscopes and to express the working of physical forces, seeped into wider strata of early modern society. Principles of fortifications, arithmetic, mathematics, algebra and geometry entered the mainstream curriculum of Italian aristocrats in Jesuit colleges, who were abreast of developments until well into the eighteenth century. The practical, technical and mechanical bent in Italian culture was especially strong at Padua. While regulations dictated what could be taught, professors needing pocket money often dispensed private courses over which they wielded more control. Padua built Europe's first institutional observatory, a tower equipped with a giant telescope from which scholars could gaze at the heavens. With its rediscovery of Galen, Padua led the European medical world too. A philological reading of Galen allowed physicians a closer understanding of ancient medicine, and led to a new appreciation of Averroes and Arab science.[28] Students were taught to examine their patients in a hospital – a real innovation – with their book in hand. Andrea Vesalius, a Fleming, revolutionized anatomy by dissecting cadavers in his classes and having human organs and body parts illustrated with extreme precision in his publications. Girolamo Fabrizio d'Aquapendente, who held the chair in surgery, created the first anatomical theatre in 1594. Students and cultural "tourists" keen on novelties attended public dissections. William Harvey elaborated his theory of blood circulation as a result of his lessons and his readings at Padua. Galileo, Fabrizio and Paolo Sarpi, who worked there simultaneously, were closely connected. A friend of theirs, Santorio Santorio, fabricated medical measuring instruments, such as a weighing-scale accurate enough to demonstrate secretion of liquids through pores of the skin. Medical studies in northern Italian universities soon required courses on logic and natural philosophy, mathematics and botany, anatomy and surgery. New specialization appeared among the teaching chairs: surgery, anatomy, botany, paediatrics, geriatrics, plastic surgery.[29] While this knowledge had no effect on life expectancy, it created a climate of curiosity which would lead to an assault on received wisdom.

Aristotelian and Galenic traditions proved remarkably resilient, and many new discoveries fitted conveniently into their framework. Aristotle's writings allowed a wide diversity of opinions regarding physics. Jesuits taught the relation between mathematics and physics through Euclidian geometry. The Aristotelian theses of philosophy students, defended in Jesuit colleges like Parma, evolved subtly in the direction of mathematics and experimentation.[30] This creeping advance of new hypotheses gradually broke down the unity of Aristotle's vision and fragmented the "system" into myriad autonomous questions unrelated to each other. What the humanists lacked was the modern scientific method: that is, the elaboration of a hypothesis that could be proved or disproved by experiment. This passage from the abstract to the concrete, and then back again to theory (expressed in mathematical terms) was an investigative tool of crucial importance.[31]

In the pious seventeenth century, it was in the heavens that philosophers sought the secrets of the universe. The Copernican model that became known after the 1540s was closely linked to the Neoplatonist movement in Italy, where Copernicus studied, but only speculators like Bruno and Campanella showed much interest in him. It was Galileo Galilei, a Florentine patrician, who denatured Copernicus's thought and validated his model. Son of a Florentine musical theorist, Vincenzio Galilei, who rendered sounds in mathematical symbols, Galileo learned mathematics from a family friend, Ostilio Ricci, who taught it at the Florentine drawing academy. By

1587 he was corresponding with the most famous mathematicians of his time. The Venetian senate hired him without a degree to teach mathematics at the university of Padua in 1592. Galileo taught fortifications, then mechanics, where he invented a hydraulic device suitable for irrigation or drainage. Astronomy and cosmology were part of every mathematician's teaching duties. He knew of Copernicus's system, but set little store by it. His open conversion to it followed suddenly upon his discovery late in 1609 of the telescope, first invented in Holland. Almost immediately he developed a telescope sixteen times more powerful, which he donated to the Venetian senate, avid for inventions useful at sea. In January 1610, Galileo pointed his telescope upwards into the heavens. By March he proclaimed to the applause of the university that "the Earth is a moving star".[32] He returned to Florence with the highly paid position of "mathematician and philosopher" to Grand Duke Cosimo II. This left him with time to study. When he went to Rome in 1611, he was already a famous researcher. One cardinal he impressed was a Florentine humanist intellectual, Maffeo Barberini: one he worried was the Tuscan Jesuit Roberto Bellarmino, the head of the Holy Office of the Inquisition. Galileo pointedly advocated reinventing science through mathematics and experiment. In 1614 he established his position that religious Truth was one, and scientific Truth another. This was a heretical proposition contrary to Christian belief, and it forced the Inquisition to open a file on him. Although a discreet trial in 1616 absolved him, the Holy Office struck at him indirectly by placing Copernicus's work on the Index.

Galileo returned to Florence to continue his studies, encouraged and aided by the Roman *Accademia del Linceo* (founded in 1603) of which he was a corresponding member. His prospects improved suddenly in 1623 with the elevation of Maffeo Barberini to the papal see as Urban VIII. Galileo dedicated his new work, *The Essayer*, a polemic published in Italian, attacking traditional science and the scholastic authorities behind it, to Urban VIII. As pope, Barberini could not be as free in his judgement, so he accepted the dedication without enthusiasm. Urban multiplied his signals to Galileo that he should not goad his Jesuit and Dominican adversaries. The philosopher responded with another Italian manifesto in favour of the Copernican system, *The Dialogues*, for which he had inexplicably obtained permission to publish in 1632. As pope, the head of an enormous political entity, Urban VIII acted differently from a cardinal, and summoned Galileo to Rome. The philosopher still enjoyed the goodwill of Grand Duke Ferdinando II, but this could not spare him a condemnation. On 22 June 1633, ecclesiastical judges ordered Galileo to recant, and he complied in the great hall of the Dominican monastery. The Inquisition consigned him to residence in Tuscany, first in the palace of the archbishop of Siena, Ascanio Piccolomini, who feted him like a hero. Transferred thereafter to his own comfortable villa, Galileo went back to work, corresponding with Europe's emerging philosphers like Gassendi, Peiresc and Mersenne in France. Translations of his work appeared in France and Holland from 1634 onward, spurring him to continue his experiments. He produced what he considered to be his greatest work on physics in 1638, published in the Netherlands, and since it did not touch on astronomy, it was not condemned by the Church. He died early in 1642, at the venerable age of 78, having received many visitors in the years preceding.

Galileo's disciples multiplied at home too. Italy was long the seat of research into the workings of the heavens, because its workshops crafted the world's best glass lenses.[33] In the years 1612–18 appeared the first microscopes. Alfonso Borelli soon rejected all astrological affinities in explaining the dynamics of contagious disease, and refuted the Galenic doctrine of "humours", which was Aristotle applied to medicine.[34] To avoid the quarrels over Aristotelian orthodoxy, Francesco Redi oriented his work towards biology and parasitology. He is widely considered the founder of modern microbiology. Evangelista Torricelli carried Galileo's mechanistic approach to the study of air pressure, creating the barometer. Tuscany remained the centre of scientific research in Italy for several decades after 1630. Ferdinando II conducted experiments in his private apartments, and inherited Galileo's instruments in addition to fashioning his own. His brother, Leopoldo de'Medici, was something of a coordinator of scientific activity. His research programme consisted of experiments that Galileo had suggested, but never completed. In 1657 he founded the *Accademia del Cimento* to bring together scientists at court, although it was never a formal group with a constitution, that held regular meetings. Founded several years before the English Royal Society (1663) and the ambitious French *Académie des Sciences* (1666) launched by Colbert and Louis XIV, it was the world's first functioning scientific society. Among its members, Borelli was the most polymathic scientist, writing on mathematics, astronomy, physics, hydraulics, physiology and medicine. Carlo Rinaldini, a mathematician and former military engineer in the papal army, was a senior professor of philosophy at Pisa. He lectured on Galileo's work, notwithstanding the latter's condemnation. For a brief decade Florence was an important European centre of scientific activity. The results of these experiments were to have been published in 1661, for much information about them was circulating by letter, the traditional format for disseminating scientific information. By the time the work appeared in print in 1667, after passing through the hands of church censors, it was largely superseded. The pope made Leopold cardinal that same year. The scientists around Florence soon dispersed and joined Italian researchers looking for other employers.

Scientific work rekindled at the Collegio Romano in the 1660s under the leadership of the Jesuit Athanasius Kircher, who created a more effective microscope, and built scientific models and instruments.[35] Queen Christina of Sweden, in her desire to be held as a paragon of learned princesses, founded a royal academy that fostered and protected astrologers and alchemists as well as astronomers and chemists.[36] One of her protégés was Giovanni Ciampini, who established the *Accademia Fisico-Matematica* in Rome in 1677, dedicated to both the sacred and the natural sciences. Another such two-pronged society appeared in Bologna in 1687, sponsored by the archdeacon Marsigli, brother to Luigi Ferdinando Marsigli, a senior officer in the Imperial army and one of the founders of modern earth sciences.[37] After 1700 general Marsili launched the Bolognese *Istituto di Scienze*.[38] Marcello Malpighi, (1628–94), who was among the first to study microscopic anatomy and embryology, presided from Bologna by letter over an "invisible academy" of Italian natural philosophers. Malpighi corresponded with Henry Oldenburg, secretary of the English Royal Society and agent for Robert Boyle, whose research Italians held in great esteem. Boyle's influence permeated the Italian scientific world, disseminated by foreigners and amateurs living in Venice in the 1680s. His admirers would soon latch on to Newton.[39] Italy and the Netherlands were the only countries where Newtonian ideas were taught in universities during the philosopher's lifetime.

Naples also figured on the map of scientific activity after the middle of the century, through the *Accademia degli Investiganti*. The physician Tommaso Cornelio launched it in the aftermath of the plague of 1656. Once the group inaugurated its formal meetings in 1663, it met at the *palazzo* of the marchese di Arena each week. Up to sixty people, including nobles, physicians and prelates, attended its sessions. Descartes was first discussed there in 1666–8. The viceroy ordered it to suspend its sessions in 1670, after the guardians of pious institutions protested.[40]

The activity of natural philosophers shows that the break-up of the Accademia del Cimento did not extinguish scientific research in Italy. Scientific academies multiplied, constituting a tenth of all academies founded between 1660 and 1699.[41] As the centre of gravity of scientific thinking passed north of the Alps, Italian research increasingly took on an international outlook. A survey of mathematical publications fixes peak Italian activity in the 1660s.[42] Science became increasingly marginal after that date, and Italians came to consider association with the English Royal Society or the Académie des Sciences as the supreme mark of distinction.[43] France launched the first scientific periodical, the *Journal des Savants* in 1665. A *Giornale dei Letterati* launched in Rome three years later, helped spread ideas from abroad. Already by the 1680s, the books reviewed in Italian periodicals were mostly foreign.

Italian Culture and the Counter-Reformation

Italian natural philosophers stepped from the ranks of mathematicians to occupy a central place in the schema of early modern knowledge. Contemporaries rightly sensed that while science opened up new and cumulative advances in human potential, it also undermined an ancient Christian civilization. The old Whig tradition that Italy's promising start was broken by the Inquisition is not false. Most scholarly attention towards Inquisition pressure has been focused on the sixteenth century, culminating in the burning of Giordano Bruno. Nevertheless, it was not the zealous Church of Clement VIII or Paul V that impeded the development of modern science and philosophy in Italy, as much as the triumphant disciplinary Church of the late baroque era. The disciplinary energy that revitalized dioceses and tamed morals was applied against errant scientists too. The roots might lie in the resurgence of theology in Italian universities at the end of the sixteenth century: from one chair intermittently held in Bologna in 1550, to three in 1580, six in 1600 and nine in 1650.[44] A combination of theology, Jesuit discipline and widespread legal training fostered what Ago calls a "canonical" culture, juridical more than theological, that inculcated values of stoicism, self-discipline and marked hierarchy.[45] This outlook placed new importance on the authority of the Church. Unlike in France, where Jansenists demanded a return to a controversial sacred text to confront it with its source, in Rome doctrine came before philology and Catholics had to *submit* to it as an act of faith. The seventeenth-century Church mobilized all its authority in the defence of Tridentine certitudes.[46] The condemnation of Galileo warned Italian intellectuals to be careful, to dissimulate their true beliefs. Urban VIII Barberini dissolved the Piarist teaching order in 1643, after its founder was tried by the Holy Office for his ties to the Florentine scientist (although the order was gradually rehabilitated by later pontiffs).[47] Jesuits continued to constitute a clear majority of Italian scientists for the rest of the century, and they steered clear of controversy. Modern philosophy crept into the order in the 1680s. A few fathers used the microscope, the barometer and the vacuum; however, they were careful to separate the results of their experiments from their philosophical consequences. They always faced suspicion in their colleges.[48]

Rome began a coherent campaign against any expression of unbelief, never ceasing to investigate and prosecute natural philosophers. Galileo was left on the Index until the pontificate of Benedict XIV in the 1740s, and Catholic institutions were allowed to promote the heliocentric view of the universe only in 1822. Inquisition sentences were widely publicized, if the example of the rural Tuscan diocese of Pienza is typical. Every parish priest was obliged to copy out the complete sentence against famous writers, like Galileo and Molinos, and attach it to the church door. Physico-mathematicians aroused the greatest fears in the Curia, who held them to be *perniciossissimi* to the republic of letters and to sincere religion.[49] The doubt they inspired might motivate youths to refute the existence of God, heaven, hell and purgatory and the entire edifice of Christian teaching. The daring of young males, their sentiment of immortality and invulnerability made their education the focus of terrible scrutiny. In 1676 Rome inaugurated new inquests, first against the ex-members of the *Accademia degli Investiganti*. By the 1680s the Inquisition was looking for a pretext to discredit a whole intellectual fashion developing in Naples, among officials, lawyers, nobles and intellectuals. In 1688 Rome ordered a trial of students and others accused of "atomism" in Naples, and mobilized hundreds of monks as familiars, who threatened to arrest the members of government councils who stood in their way. The Church presented the trial as an epic battle between the Christian religion and its enemies, who were dangerous adherents of the "so-called modern philosophy". When Archbishop

Pignatelli of Naples was elected Pope Innocent XII in 1691, the trial
expanded, with new arrests. It ended in 1697 without any effective
condemnation, in a general climate of indifference. In 1690 more
trials began in Rome against members of the *Accademia dei Bianchi*,
frequented by critics of the papal government. As the battle between
the Ancients and the Moderns raged, the Inquisition and the Index
sprang to life. Some universities simply conferred their chairs of philosophy on to monks, and in Naples, the chaplain of the university, a
senior state official nominated by the viceroy, fixed the teaching
material for each professor.[50] A little army of familiars animated
each seat of the Inquisition: minor cities counted dozens of them. At
Modena in 1700, the Inquisition complement was 204 persons, of
whom 61 watched over the city, and 143 the surrounding countryside.[51]

Elsewhere the state seconded the efforts of the Curia. Ranuccio II,
duke of Parma (1646–94) personally supervised his courtiers' religious assiduousness, while his mother kept the noble ladies in line.[52]
The grand duke of Tuscany, Cosimo III (1670–1723) was the
epitome of a Counter-Reformation prince, custodian of the faith and
religious observance, entrusted by God with the spiritual welfare of
his subjects. Upon his accession to the throne, friars and Inquisitors
became fixtures at the court. Court friars underscored how grand-
ducal power formed an alliance with holiness. Cosimo was
enthroned at the apex of a clientèle system that received petitions,
arbitrated spiny disputes and dispensed privileges and protection.
There were numerous denunciations of conduct unbecoming to
Catholics. The sovereign patronized sanctuaries and convents, consulted saints at their altars and sought their intercession, promoted
religious festivals and multiplied processions. As mediator between
heaven and earth, he took it upon himself to interpret events in the
light of his austere piety.[53] Cosimo frowned on any scientific
research not directly related to medicine.[54] In 1691 he decreed that
professors at Pisa must teach only Aristotelian philosophy. As the
state took more control over the university, the student body became
more homogeneous, and organized piety and professions of orthodoxy became more important.

By 1700, Italy's role in the development of a secular cosmology
passed from the front rank to a marginal position, outside the main
currents of European science. This conclusion is somewhat premature, for it was difficult to write the intellectual history of modern
Italy as long as important parts of the Roman Inquisition archives

remained closed to historians. Now that the Vatican has opened them to scholars, historians can begin to weigh its impact more objectively.

19 Venice: Twilight of Empire

An Italian Power

As home to one Italian in six, the Venetian republic after the battle of Lepanto deserves a place apart. Venice traditionally adhered to a policy of muscular neutrality in the struggle between the Catholic and Islamic worlds.[1] Its strategic peril was twofold: that of Habsburg encirclement, to the west, north and east of the Terraferma; and danger from Ottoman expansion in the Greek archipelago and Dalmatia. Like Sweden at Europe's other extremity, Venice was a middle-ranking European power in 1600, but its strategy was defensive. The republic still entertained visions of expansion around the Adriatic rim. It would not allow the pope to develop a port near the Po estuary in competition to it. Moreover, it maintained good relations with the Protestant Swiss along its north-west border.

Military preparations occupied a conspicuous place in state accounts: 25 per cent of expenditures went to military purposes in 1602, and 42 per cent in 1641, both years of peace.[2] The republic's defences consisted of a barrier of modern fortresses in the Terraferma and throughout the Empire. In addition to the 9,000 garrison soldiers scattered around the Empire, Venice could put over 10,000 professional troops into the field at short notice, and back them up with another 20,000 men drawn from the Terraferma peasant militia. If the crisis lasted, effectives could be increased by levies raised in Italy or in northern Europe. During the war with Austria from 1615 to 1617 it deployed 23,500 in the Terraferma alone, and maintained 21,500 there still during the armed peace of 1624, numbers just slightly inferior to those available to Spain or

256

Austria in that theatre. Brescia was Italy's armaments industry capital, while the Venice Arsenal cast bronze guns and manufactured and stored gunpowder. Its magazines stocked tens of thousands of muskets, and a vast assortment of armour and blade weapons outfitting a modern army.[3] Venetian subjects in the army hailed primarily from the Terraferma cities and Friuli, but most recruits came from the Adriatic watershed, between the Po estuary and the Marches. Umbrians, Tuscans and Corsicans provided large and valued contingents as well.[4] Venice drew manpower from Dalmatia and the Greek islands, and from zones of the Ottoman Empire close to it, like the Greek Epirus and Albania, which furnished light cavalry and skirmishers.[5]

After concluding peace with the Sublime Porte in 1573, Venice reverted to its traditional posture of hostility to Spanish hegemony in the peninsula. It took umbrage when Spain negotiated an agreement with Catholic Swiss cantons in 1587, fearing hostile intentions.[6] Those became manifest after 1600 when Count Fuentes governed in Milan. His alliance with the Grisons in 1600 touched off decades of competition with the republic over the control of the Valtellina. By interdicting the passes, Spain blocked the mercenaries descending from the Alps to serve Venice in 1606, 1615 and again in 1643.

Venetian relations with Rome, its other Italian neighbour, were also occasionally strained. The underlying problem was the republic's determination to prevent any "foreign" influence over its policies. Patricians criticized the opulent courts of cardinals and the power of papal nephews. The republic's refusal to admit the Roman Inquisition, and its overt recruitment of Protestant students to the university of Padua rankled with the popes. Venice became the first power to recognize the Protestant Henri IV as king of France. Then the senate refused to publish the Roman Index without first obtaining a concordat giving it power over the Church in Venetian territory. Instead of mollifying the pope, the senate dispatched anticlerical ambassadors to the Holy See. In March 1605 the senate forbade any new religious foundations without its prior permission. Simultaneously, it arrested and imprisoned two ecclesiastics for common misdemeanours. Paul V Borghese responded in 1605 with an *Interdict* on the entire republic, absolving Venetian subjects of their obligation to obey their rulers. The doge, Leonardo Donà, the senator Niccolò Contarini and the Servite monk Paolo Sarpi led the riposte, rallying both regular and secular clergy in the state to their defence. The senate pressured Rome further by expelling the Jesuits and imprisoning clerics who sided with the papacy. By April 1606, diplomatic relations between Rome and Venice were broken, and both sides began to hire troops. An angry pamphlet dialogue between Sarpi and the Tuscan cardinal Roberto Bellarmino, the Church's most influential theologian, enounced the respective principles. Sarpi advocated limiting papal power to the spiritual sphere only. His attack on the benefice system in its entirety argued for the existence of autonomous "national" churches. This was not far from Henry VIII's Anglican Catholic church, a solution many Venetian patricians thought was ideal. Spain supported the papacy morally, but could spare no resources from its Netherlands war. French mediation defused the crisis and averted war, but neither side conceded any points of principle.[7]

Venice adhered loosely to French strategy objectives in subsequent years, and was likely to side with the kingdom in any general struggle against the Habsburgs. Its own griefs with the house of Austria focused on the pirate activity of the Uskoks of Senj, who harassed Venetian shipping in the Dalmatian archipelago, and on the corsairs based in Sicily and the Mezzogiorno, who seized the republic's vessels with the viceroy's active encouragement.[8] Venice's strike against Senj in 1614 touched off a border war with Austria that escalated into general mobilization. Skirmishes and raids ravaged a large arc of territory across Friuli and Istria. To prevent Spain from aiding its Austrian cousins, Venice subsidized Piedmont to the tune of almost a million ducats a year. Its strategy was to provoke a war over the Monferrato and tie down Habsburg forces there. After over two years of inconclusive skirmishing, this conflict almost escalated into a general anti-Habsburg war. The viceroy of Naples, Osuna, unleashed his ships against Venetian commerce, and the two war fleets confronted each other off the Dalmatian coast. The republic's brinkmanship worked, for King Philip III forbade Osuna to embroil Spain in direct hostilities. Venice prevailed against Austria in the Treaty of Madrid in September 1617, and succeeded in having the Uskoks expelled from their bases.

The Valtellina became even more important once Ferdinand II of Austria provoked civil war in 1618. A Catholic uprising against the Swiss Protestant overlords deprived Venice of access to the valley in 1620. France and Piedmont promised to support the republic if it entered open conflict against Spain, but the cautious senators did not trust French promises and preferred to fight by proxy. When the Mantuan succession crisis deepened between 1627 and 1630, Venice approached the brink of general war. After the Imperials routed the Venetian army deployed behind its earthworks at Villabuona in 1630, the republic mobilized in earnest, appointing the French Huguenot leader the Duc de Rohan commander-in-chief.[9] Nevertheless, the senate would not do the irreparable and unleash an offensive war on Austria and Spain. The irruption of Gustavus Adolphus of Sweden into Germany in 1631, coupled with France's direct entry into the war 1635 reduced the Habsburg threat in Italy so that Venice could pursue its interests elsewhere.

Its last foray into Italian power politics came in 1642, when the republic sided with Parma, Tuscany and Modena in an anti-papal league. Venetian troops fared indifferently against the Pontificals in the fighting of 1643 and early 1644. The papal forces were not as amateurish as was anticipated, and they devastated parts of the Polesine. The expenditures were not worth the political return that a hypothetical victory would bring. More important, by 1644 Venetian relations with the Porte were collapsing, and new dangers were appearing outside Italy.

Clinging to Empire, 1645–1718

Venetian efforts to remain on friendly terms with the Ottoman Porte broke down under the strain of incessant corsair raiding. In 1638 sixteen Barbary galeots plundered Calabria and the Adriatic coast almost as far as Ancona, before sheltering in the Albanian port of Valona under the protection of the Turkish guns. The Venetian admiral Cappello forced entry to the port with his galleys and destroyed the entire flotilla at anchor. Christian corsair raids by the knights of Malta and Santo Stefano in the Aegean irritated the Ottomans too. The knights of Malta provided the *casus belli* in 1644 by seizing part of the Alexandria convoy, and capturing a concubine and a son of the sultan himself. Maltese galleys then repaired their damage on Crete before leaving the Aegean. In Ottoman eyes, this made Venice an accomplice of the knights. Turkish desire for renewed expansion may have been the principal motive for declaring war.[10] Venice looked like an easy target, and Crete lay in the heart of the Ottoman zone of influence, far from Corfu, the nearest friendly base. In August 1645 the Turkish fleet landed an army at La Canea, and captured the town in only eight weeks. The first Venetian campaigns in Crete were disappointing. When

Rethimnon fell in 1646, the Ottomans massacred its garrison to instil terror elsewhere. Soon Candia itself was under siege, although Venetian ships kept the sea lanes open and stopped Turkish progress. Simultaneously, the Turks launched an invasion of Dalmatia from Bosnia to divert precious resources away from the island.

Venice's mobilization revealed its residual muscle. To pay for the war, the senators resolved to sell entry to the nobility for 100,000 ducats apiece.[11] Feverish activity in the capital and Corfu outfitted warships and converted merchantmen for war. The senate hired English and Dutch ships, with their native officers and crews. Soon the Serenissima boasted stable effectives of 30,000 to 35,000 soldiers and large numbers of militiamen. In addition to the defensive Cretan campaign, Venice waged a very bitter skirmish war in Bosnia.[12] Venetian and Croat officers led Croatian irregulars against nearby towns, made off with whatever booty they could seize, and planted ambushes for the Ottoman troops and Bosnian Muslims dispatched to repel them. The Venetian command recognized the band leaders as officers and gave them considerable autonomy in exchange for 10 per cent of their booty.[13]

Venice played its naval card for all it was worth. Its sailing vessels blockaded the Dardanelles from 1646 onwards, while galleys scoured the Aegean to intercept Turkish ships. After 1650 large sea battles pitted the Venetian fleet against the Ottomans almost every year. The Venetians usually emerged victorious. In 1655 a Venetian fleet of almost sixty units, half sailing vessels and half galleys and galeasses, virtually destroyed the Ottoman fleet in the narrows, provoking panic in Constantinople. These successes staunched the flow of Turkish reinforcements and slowed the Cretan war to a stalemate. Unlike other sieges of that age, which lasted a month or two, Candia's was prolonged. Annual contingents from Venice and its allies reinforced Candia by sea and kept the Turks at bay. The end of the Thirty Years War in Europe made hiring mercenaries easier, so German veterans joined the Italians, Greeks and Croats on the ramparts.

The Ottoman Empire underwent a dramatic series of reforms and purges to raise money for the war. By 1667 the Porte was ready to renew its efforts against Candia.[14] Venice was unable to match the effort. Exclusive of fleet expenditures, the defence of Crete cost over 4 million ducats in 1668.[15] The Candia war devoured men as well as munitions. Typhus and other infection claimed more lives than

Turkish projectiles, as the city crumbled under the impact of explosions. Pope Clement IX Rospigliosi tried to create a new anti-Turkish league to offset the Porte's new energy, and papal money, men and ships committed to the struggle were considerable. Even Louis XIV reversed France's traditional pro-Turkish policy, and sent sizable contingents in 1667 and 1669. They were wasted in spectacular general sorties. The last phase of the siege was a contest of tunnelling, mining and localized sorties; of outworks seized and then recaptured. Wounds and disease claimed tens of thousands of lives on each side, including 280 Venetian patricians, equivalent to a quarter of the Maggiore Consiglio. A Venetian renegade taught the Turks the method of digging parallel siege trenches, instructed them how to use the superior Venetian guns to best effect, and convinced them to focus their approaches on the seaward bastions protecting access to the port. The withdrawal of the French contingent in the summer of 1669 meant that further resistance was hopeless. When Francesco Morosini finally capitulated in September 1669, both Venice and the Ottoman Empire needed peace badly.

The epic siege of Candia and the consistent victories at sea upheld Venice's martial honour. The impression of the young Colbert de Seignelay on his visit to the Arsenal in 1673 confirms this reputation.[16] The son of the famous minister, whose father was a fervent advocate of French sea power, was favourably struck by the institution. Its huge forge, its three foundries and its fifteen furnaces; its cranes; a ropeworks; storerooms stocked with armour and a thicket of thousands of muskets; pyramids of cannon balls; stocks of masts, and rows of galleys kept in storage made a strong impression on him. In the Palace of San Marco, another storeroom held thousands of weapons for the patricians, with the necessary munitions, all clean and well kept. Brescian forges and armourers filled an order that year for 24,000 firearms to outfit the army of Spanish Naples.[17] The republic possessed more galleys than the other Italian states combined, and not many fewer than the forty available to France. In the late 1660s it began to launch specialized warships, as in England, Holland and France, carrying up to sixty or seventy cannon, as well as soldiers.

The Ottoman failure before Vienna in 1683 convinced the senators that the hour of retaliation was at hand. They struck an alliance with Austria and Poland in March 1684 that committed them to wage an amphibious war in the Aegean. As in the past, Tuscany, Rome and Malta sent auxiliary contingents. Regiments hired from

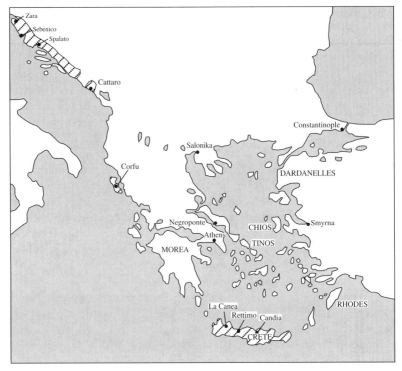

Map 18   Venetian seaborne empire

German princes made up a third or half of the ground forces dispatched year after year to the Morea (Peloponnese) under the
global direction of Francesco Morosini, the hero of Candia. This
force captured most of the peninsula by 1687, and briefly occupied
Athens. In addition to the war of sieges, the Venetian forces and
their Greek guerrilla allies raided much of mainland Greece. A
second theatre developed along the eastern Adriatic shore, where
Venetian forces and Italian auxiliary allies picked off the
Montenegrin, Albanian and Greek pirate lairs. Venice experienced a
string of successes until 1688, when Morosini undertook the siege of
the port of Negroponte (Khalkis) on Euboea island, just off the
mainland. His polyglot army of over 16,000 men was the largest
single force Venice had fielded since Lepanto. Here, too, an Italian
deserter directed the Turks to build earthwork redoubts and to site
batteries to hamper the siege. The outbreak of plague compounded

the difficulties and with a much diminished force, Morosini withdrew.

Venetian success ended abruptly in 1689 when France invaded the Holy Roman Empire and forced Austria to divert its troops from the Danube to the Rhine. Venetian initiatives thereafter were failures. Occupying Chios split the Venetian army into two forces, the other being based on Corinth on the isthmus between Attica and the Peloponnese. The Turks were able to build up their forces on the Anatolian mainland, and two bloody naval battles in February 1695 forced the Venetians to abandon their conquest.[18]

The general peace of Karlowitz in 1699 made the Morea, along with all the Ionian islands, a Venetian colony. They increased the population of the republic by over 10 per cent. Venice prepared to stay in Greece by building great fortresses at Corinth and Nauplia. The 300,000 Greeks there tolerated the republic's rule, although Venice's policy of raising the Roman Catholic minority over Greek Orthodox subjects irked the great majority. In 1710–11 the republic encouraged the Montenegrins to revolt while the Turks were embroiled in a war with Russia. The Turks unexpectedly won their war in 1713, and the next year began to collect ships for an expedition against the republic.

In 1715 a great Ottoman fleet and an army of 40,000 men moved on the Morea and captured the fortresses in a scant three months, in part because the Greeks refused to aid the Venetians. Corfu was the target of the 1716 campaign. A dispirited collection of Germans, Italians, Slavs and Greeks under the Saxon general von Schulemburg manned its massive fortifications. While the general kept the Turks at bay, Spain, Portugal, Malta, Tuscany and the Papal States sent naval contingents to join the Venetians. The Turkish army withdrew when Austria decided to join the war. In 1717 the fleet fought a series of bloody battles off the Dardanelles and in the Aegean, with no decisive result. The army was just beginning to make progress against Ottoman bases on the Montenegrin coast when Austria decided to make peace in 1718. The treaty of Passarowitz marked the end of the republic's Greek Empire that had once included Cyprus and Crete. Venice remained at peace with the Ottoman Empire until the end of the republic itself in 1797.

Serene Splendour

Basking in the glow of its recent victories in the Aegean, Venice
looked appealing to both sides in the War of the Spanish Succession,
which mobilized larger armies than any in European history. In that
War, and in the war of the Polish Succession (1733–35), the armies
of both sides levied "contributions" and devastated districts around
Verona and Brescia that separated Austrian Tyrol from Lombardy.
Without a desire to conquer more Italian territory, there was
nothing for the republic to gain, but it kept its defences up just in
case. After the disastrous Corfu war, Marshal Schulemburg completed the Venetian army reforms along lines common in Germany,
and established the force at just about 20,000 men. Venetian patricians withdrew almost entirely from the forces, except for the navy,
which retained a reasonable level of proficiency. In 1775, Venice
possessed a navy of twenty-three ships of the line (Britain and France
counted about a hundred each), fifteen frigates and about thirty
smaller vessels.[19] In the 1780s admiral Angelo Emo instilled new discipline and vigour into the navy to restore its efficiency. He used it to
clear the Adriatic of Russian corsairs operating out of Trieste, and
then bombarded Tunisian ports to curb pirate raids on its shipping.
The Arsenal launched the occasional warship, but the activity there
was only a shadow of previous centuries, and it became something of
a tourist attraction.[20]

Like Sweden, Venice ceased to count as a second-line power after
1718, but it remained a dynamic regional economic hub. In 1700,
despite the loss of its Turkish markets, it was still the most active port
in the Mediterranean. Venice was only overtaken by Marseilles later
in the century. It had no competition in the Adriatic until Trieste
and Ancona were promoted by their respective masters in the 1720s
and 1730s. There were few profitable outlets for capital accumulated
in previous centuries, so Venetians tended to invest their money in
prestige building. From 1670 to 1796 the city witnessed the construction of forty *palazzi*, forty churches, a dozen theatres, six hospitals, a
dozen *scuole*, or guild headquarters, and almost six hundred villas on
the adjacent Terraferma.[21] The city's sheer monumentality helped
launch a new industry – tourism. The city was a magnet for pleasure-
seeking gentlemen and aristocratic youths completing their education. By the middle of the century, an estimated 30,000 of the city's
140,000 inhabitants were foreigners, including a large number of
Englishmen. They rented aristocratic apartments or entire houses

and made the city a centre of international culture. Many thousands more flocked to the city because the freedom (or licentiousness) in Venice stood in stark contrast to the staid Terraferma, where the Inquisition was active and monks were held in higher esteem.

Stability marked the government as well as the economy. Wits noted that in Venice people were free to do anything except participate in politics. There was little pressure from the Terraferma cities for a greater voice in government. The governments of those cities were still "family compacts", tied to each other by centuries of intermarriage. The social climate improved considerably as an increasing measure of social and religious discipline finally eliminated traditions of vendetta from the aristocracy. In place of turbulence there emerged a long stability.[22] Nowhere was the family compact more in evidence than in Venice itself. If two hundred families enjoyed complete political franchise, only forty-two decided general policy, co-opting each other on to the principal committees.[23] The patriciate declined relentlessly after the Candian hecatombe of the 1660s. Between 1646 and 1718, the senate sold nobility to 132 families for 100,000 ducats each. The aggregation of new families was never more than a fiscal expedient and their admission did little to prevent the decline in numbers. In 1714 there were still 1,731 nobles eligible to sit in the Maggiore Consiglio, but only 754 at the end of the republic. In 1766 the 3,500 noble individuals of both sexes and all ages constituted 2.5 per cent of the city's population, compared to 4.3 per cent in 1586.[24] The economic weight of the aristocracy declined too, since it remained rooted in agricultural pursuits and virtually abandoned trade.

Nobles continued to fill most of the more than 700 government positions reserved for them. There was a festering constitutional crisis between 1744 and 1797 as patrician reformers and conservatives quarrelled over access to the levers of power. Part of the nobility was inclined to expand the Maggiore Consiglio's power, without extending political privileges to other categories of the population. Given the patriciate's numerical weakness, more power devolved to the officials of the citizen class, who staffed the tribunals and ensured that the state remained efficiently run. Even those offices had become practically hereditary among a narrow caste of administrative families.[25] As compensation for being deprived of power, Terraferma cities paid very modest taxes. Venice itself shouldered the greatest fiscal burden.[26]

The Serenissima was not a spent force in 1796, when young

Napoleon Bonaparte brought the army of a young republic into the Po valley. The contrast between the French regime, resting as it did on a very narrow social base and continually improvising its constitution to maintain a military clique in power, with its medieval counterpart in Venice, ruled by aged civilian aristocrats who scrupulously adhered to the constitutional order, could not have been more striking. A century previously, Venice was still able to consider war an option. In 1796, despite all its assets, there was no longer a military lexicon in the political vocabulary of the Venetian government. It capitulated to France without a struggle and vanished from the European scene.

Part III

A Slow Thaw, 1730–1800

Introduction to Part III

The breakdown of the political, social, cultural and economic "old regime" began well before the onset of the French Revolution, but noticeably later than it did north of the Alps. The future was sketched most clearly in that part of Italy nearest to France. The French model of kingship had been applied consistently in the domains of the House of Savoy since the sixteenth century. The absolutist "revolution" wrought by the dynasty was motivated largely by the need to find money to fight wars. After 1650 the mobilization of the prince's subjects and their money had no parallel in Italy, except briefly and intermittently in Venice. Successive princes annexed a greater part of public activity to their own jurisdiction, until by 1730, when the process slowed, the king wielded more authority than any of his peers in Italy. He gambled resolutely for high stakes in the great power politics of the eighteenth century, as the rest of Italy watched over his shoulder, unable to influence the outcome. Spain's decline to its nadir around 1700 inaugurated a new Austrian era of Italian history. After 1700 most of the old princely dynasties disappeared, as the Viennese Habsburgs and then the Bourbons split the peninsula between them, eager to use Italian resources for their own ends. After being shaken and bruised in the 1730s and 1740s, the Habsburgs adopted the absolutist model themselves, determined to abolish the last vestiges of the city-state order.

The old court aristocracies were obliged to make room for a new aristocracy of talent, pliable to foreign direction. Absolutism's need for its own obedient cadres underlines the changing contours of social influence. Bled white by decades of economic decline and stagnation, nobles were too few in number to retain their leadership.

269

A new "civil" society, embracing well-to-do commoners schooled in law, medicine and administration, dissolved the laws and the world-view of aristocratic lineage. In the Mezzogiorno and Sicily, monarchs and their ministers trimmed endlessly the extent of feudal jurisdictions without taking the final step to abolish them entirely. Open to secularizing and levelling trends from north of the Alps, Italy's elites let themselves be seduced by dreams incompatible with Tridentine doctrines and papal supremacy. By 1750 this ferment placed the Church on the defensive. Some of the changes, particularly relating to the curtailing of traditional Catholicism, were more radically utilitarian than most Italians desired. There was no massive dechristianization in the late eighteenth century, no "cultural revolution" in behaviour, no rush to mass instruction as one finds in France, or Britain or Germany. Italy was now close to the rear of the European pack.

Italy lagged behind northern Europe economically too. After the crash of the 1630s, the Italian economy recovered later and grew more slowly in the eighteenth century than did its neighbours. The country continued to lose the remnants of its urban manufactures. It ruralized gradually, importing finished goods and exporting food and raw materials to feed northern European manufactures. Its commerce and shipping passed for the most part into foreign hands. For a time, the rural world prospered again. Governments experimented with more laissez-faire approaches to the economy in order to stimulate trade and manufactures, without ever achieving the successes they hoped for. As a creeping polarization heightened rural and urban poverty, Italian society acquired a new complexity. Perhaps a small majority of Italians benefited from the quickened pace of economic life in the eighteenth century. Those who did adopted new models of consumption, enjoying both domestic and imported commodities in greater amounts.

So Italy's "ancien régime" did not tumble before invading French armies with their Jacobins in tow. Rather it was rendered almost unrecognizable by foreign monarchs and their cosmopolitan ministers who imposed their reforms with only passing concern for Italian traditions and sensitivity.

20 The Piedmontese Absolutist State

Absolutist Antecedents

Outside the network of medieval communes and their civic nobili-
ties, Piedmont's peripheral location, next to France, conditioned its
singular evolution. The duke of Savoy's limited power almost proved
his undoing during the Italian wars, when France virtually annexed
both Piedmont and Savoy. Duke Emanuel Philibert's career in
Habsburg service permitted him to recover his birthright in 1559,
save for Geneva, which embraced the Protestant Reformation and
broke away to join the Swiss Cantons. That duke's innovations –
strict control over feudal investiture; a permanent direct tax, the
taille; and the formation of a peasant militia – led to Piedmont's
rapid recovery to a potent second-rank power, compliant to Spanish
policy.

France's prolonged religious wars tempted Emanuel Philibert to
seek territorial expansion there.[1] Duke Charles Emanuel I
(1580–1630) dreamed of conquering the lands all around his states,
and raising his house to royal rank. Spanish court protocol introduced to Turin emphasized the sacrality of his person. Like Counter-
Reformation theology, which exalted an omnipotent God, Spanish
etiquette elevated the prince to heroic proportions and reduced
once-mighty feudal lords to mere ornaments or loyal lieutenants.[2]
Royal marriages likewise broadcast the duke's ambitions. Charles
Emanuel's marriage to the Infanta Caterina of Spain in 1584, and
Prince Victor Amadeus's marriage to Princess Christine of France in

1619 introduced scores of Spanish and French courtiers to Turin. French, Spanish and Imperial diplomats considered such posturing extravagant, but the duke gave the impression that Piedmont was a state to contend with.

The prince distributed fiefs and revenues in exchange for unstinting loyalty.[3] Courtly culture under a strong-willed prince transformed feudal seigneurs into a kind of service nobility, whose social privilege entailed obedience to the duke. Courtiers served his household for an obligatory three months a year. By this means, he created four times as many functionaries as if he had awarded a permanent position to a single beneficiary. Some of the most influential courtiers were Italian "foreigners", from the Este territories, from Milan, Brescia, Parma and Rome. They overshadowed the native Piedmontese and Savoyards at first, who spurned the court city in favour of their rural estates.[4] Nobles who basked in the duke's reflection were required to follow him into battle, and disburse their own money on campaign. Between 1588 and 1659 repeated wars imposed taxes of money and blood on the aristocracy.

Court culture gradually transformed Turin too. In 1571 it counted only 14,000 people, but Charles Emanuel's entourage turned the city into the only Italian capital besides Rome to experience demographic growth.[5] By 1614 its 24,000 inhabitants pressed against the limits of the old walls. By 1700, its 45,000 inhabitants placed it ahead of Mantua, Parma and Modena, and not too far behind Florence and Genoa as a capital city. The military culture of the court permeated the aesthetic choices of the new Turin, the dynasty's showcase.

Charles Emanuel's expansion in the face of Habsburg opposition forced him to mobilize his subjects as never before. His army swelled and contracted with each mobilization and crisis, and foreign levies played a more prominent role than local militias.[6] From his subjects the duke mainly demanded money. Taxes in Piedmont and Savoy tripled in the eighty years after 1560, account taken of inflation.[7] War also prompted the dukes to create manufactures to generate tax revenues. Victor Amadeus I was, like his predecessor, a soldier-king in pursuit of dynastic glory and territorial expansion. By the Treaty of Cherasco in 1631, he consigned the stronghold of Pinerolo to France in exchange for its alliance. The offensive treaty of Rivoli in 1635 committed the duchy to aid a French offensive in Italy in exchange for Casale Monferrato, Milan and the royal title. The duke's nominal command over French armies was meagre compensation for the secondary role that Richelieu assigned to the Italian theatre. Both the duke's brothers, princes Tommaso and Maurizio, passed into the Spanish camp. On Victor Amadeus's death in 1637, Richelieu attempted to bring the regent Christine under his close control by placing French garrisons in the principal fortresses, and tried to annex Savoy simultaneously. This plunged Piedmont into civil war. In 1642 the princes' adhesion to the French alliance was not enough to restore autonomy to the duchy.

Piedmont remained a French satellite for another generation, its options limited by policies decided in Paris. Duke Charles Emanuel II (1637–75) established a small permanent army in 1664, but it was only employed in operations given French blessing.[8] The duke's invasion of the Genoese republic in 1672 was a complete fiasco, made possible only because the French king invaded the Netherlands that year. He hoped to conquer Genoa with the aid of a plot hatched by the patrician Raffaele della Torre. Genoese senators uncovered the plot in time, and intense combats in the mountain passes resulted in the partial destruction of the Piedmontese army. The Genoese rallied, armed new regiments, and halted the invasion before concluding a peace in November 1672. Deprived of an opportunity to expand in Italy, the duke's alternative was to complete great defensive projects throughout the duchy, of which the refortification of Turin was the most important. The capital was easily the largest and strongest fortress in Italy. Only a great army could encircle it and press the siege simultaneously. The possession of these strongholds, and a proper army to garrison them, made the duke an asset or a threat to the great powers on his borders.

Victor Amadeus II and the Absolutist Revolution

The death of Charles Emanuel II in 1675 placed the state in the hands of a French princess-dowager closely supervised from Versailles, while Victor Amadeus II grew to maturity. Madame Royale attempted to dispatch the prince to Lisbon through a royal marriage, but he rebelled at the last moment and scuttled her plans. In 1684 the 18-year-old took power in a coup against his mother, with the tacit support of Louis XIV.[9] Despite the latitude he gave to competent ministers, the duke was jealous of his power for the rest of his life.

The young duke's policies were mirror images of those applied in

France, and in continuity with his own predecessors. Eliminating privileges enjoyed by particular districts or social groups would fill tax coffers and permit new recruitment for the army. The introduction of the French-model *taille* in 1560, levied on each parish, was the first step towards permanent direct taxation. Mountainous regions near the Riviera, which could smuggle contraband from the coast, usually escaped the full force of gabelles. The duchess-regent's attempt to increase the salt gabelle at Mondovì and Ceva in 1680 met with a simple refusal. Notables in the towns felt that the unilateral imposition of taxes was a violation of their liberties. Her insistence led to a "salt war", where 3,000 troops had to force their way into the hills around Mondovì in July 1681. Like absolutist rulers elsewhere, the duke viewed this contractual concept of monarchy as an anachronism.[10] By absolutism, historians designate not "totalitarian" control over every aspect of government and society. Absolutism signified, rather, that the power of decision over policy resided in the prince alone, after taking counsel from wise advisers of his choosing. Charles Emanuel I established the *referendari* in 1624, whose task was to supervise the collection of taxes in the hands of local bodies and speed up their delivery. These gradually took the French name for the same type of official, the *Intendant*.[11] They differed from their French namesake only in that the territory they administered was more compact, making it easier for them to transmit orders. Officials like these were often low-born, but hard-working and intelligent administrators. Intendants revised the tax registers, held corruption and vested interests in check, reduced privileges and immunities, maintained public order and repressed banditry, provided the markets with grain and directed public works. This was "police" in the ancien régime sense of the term. The Intendants prevented kin groups from monopolizing local offices or from transferring their property into church benefices to remove it from taxation. They controlled membership of parish councils, appointed notaries, judges and tax officers, and marginalized those who resisted the pull of the capital.[12] A virtuous circle of centralizing efficiency developed, which one observes simultaneously in Louis XIV's France. The only limit was an armed refusal of the population to pay. In 1699, when the Mondovì district rose against the salt gabelle again, the army fought a vicious guerrilla war to disarm and punish the disobedient villages. The effort resulted in a thousand dead, and the deportation of three thousand rebels to the malarial rice-growing plain around Vercelli.[13]

Another French-inspired policy forced the Calvinist Vaudois to convert. Charles Emanuel I seconded Saint François de Sales's policy of using a *douce violence* to bring them to their senses. That worked in Savoy where small Calvinist enclaves were quickly assimilated, but the effect was negligible in the close-knit valleys of the high Alps. In 1685 and 1686, Louis XIV and the pope urged the duke to imitate the French king, whose soldiers forced virtually the whole Protestant population to convert. With intimate knowledge of difficult alpine terrain, the Vaudois proved to be excellent guerrilla fighters. Since several thousand Piedmontese soldiers were insufficient to the task, French troops lent a hand, shooting resisters out of hand and burning their villages.[14] The persecution of the Vaudois resulted in 2,000 dead, between 4,000 and 6,000 forced conversions, and 2,000 to 3,000 more individuals deported into the rice paddies. Hundreds of children were dispersed in orphanages, and a few thousand survivors fled to Switzerland and Germany. In 1689 the duke allowed them to return in exchange for British and Dutch subsidies in the impending war against Louis XIV.

Victor Amadeus's moment to assert his independence came when king William III of England, Stadthouder of the Netherlands, invited him to join the League of Augsburg. Foreign subsidies enabled the duke to multiply the number of his soldiers. The French punished the duchy with a scorched earth strategy, but such harsh measures rallied the inhabitants around their prince, and Vaudois guerrillas tormented their columns. With his Spanish and Imperial allies, Victor Amadeus twice confronted the French marshal Catinat at Staffarda (1690) and La Marsaglia (1693) only to be thrashed both times. In 1695 Victor Amadeus began negotiations in earnest with Louis XIV, and he recovered Pinerolo, the alpine fortress. Casale Monferrato, its fortifications demolished, returned to the duke of Mantua by the same treaty. This delivered Piedmont of any French presence east of the Alps for the first time since 1631. Meanwhile, the duke enticed back to his allegiance many aristocrats who had fought the war on the French side. Like their prince, many noble families entrusted their survival to a duplicitous policy of committing themselves actively to both sides.[15] The end of the war of the League of Augsburg gave Victor Amadeus a respite which he put to good use. In 1696 he extended the Intendants to cover virtually the entire state. Their exertions, and the duke's repeat tax hikes, increased state revenues by about a third between 1689 and 1700.[16]

In 1700 Louis XIV pressured him to join the alliance to defend the Bourbon inheritance against the Austrian Habsburg pretender, and his English and Dutch allies. While preparing for a rupture with Versailles, Victor Amadeus revived Piedmont's contorted and duplicitous foreign policy.[17] When Louis disarmed his best troops in 1703, Victor Amadeus plunged into the anti-Bourbon alliance, encircled by enemies. As an ally of Britain and the Empire, he bought enough German, Swiss and Piedmontese soldiers to maintain an army of over 26,000 men, exclusive of militia. In 1706, the year of greatest peril, foreign subsidies represented 40 per cent of all state revenue.[18] It was almost insufficient. After conquering Nice and Savoy, the French occupied much of Piedmont and settled into a lethargic siege of Turin itself during the summer of 1706. The duke's small field army was unable to break the outer ring of earthworks to relieve his capital. Prince Eugene of Savoy, the duke's cousin, conducted an epic march of hundreds of kilometres to his aid, and the battle outside the walls of the city on 7 September changed the course of Italian history.

By the Treaty of Utrecht in 1713, the House of Savoy made the first significant acquisition of territory since the Middle Ages, annexing the cities of Alessandria, Valenza and Casale, the Langhe fiefs around Acqui, the Val Sesia north of Biella. It also established the frontier east of Turin along the alpine watershed. The duke acquired the kingdom of Sicily with its coveted royal title as part of the spoils of the Spanish Empire. Victor Amadeus's large peacetime army of 23,000 men required the reorganization of the administrative machine to make it more efficient. In 1717 he created new departments for internal affairs, foreign affairs, and war. The prince diminished, without eradicating, the traditional exemptions and immunities of the nobles and the clergy. Victor Amadeus confronted the pope by challenging Rome's prerogatives on the matter of ecclesiastical patronage; for instance, he insisted that all holders of benefices in his states be his subjects. The duke sought the right to name his own candidates to abbeys and bishoprics, and demanded regalian rights (bishops' revenues during the interval that their see was vacant) similar to those acquired by Louis XIV. He exceeded the French king by curtailing religious legacies, which removed property from the state's taxable base.[19]

Another vector of this fiscal policy diminished the regional variation in taxation. The alpine Val d'Aosta was too small to matter. Its Estates still met every five years to vote taxes. In Nice and Savoy, the Intendants took over the Senate and the *Chambre des Comptes* after

1713. Ducal functionaries examined municipal accounts to judge which of their debts would have to be paid. They overturned local decisions on the use of common lands, to prevent the powerful from taking them out of the taxable base. The greatest innovation of all was the *perequazione*, or cadaster, which required the surveying of agricultural land, establishing of ownership and customary access, and estimating of revenues from it.[20] Surveyors established a parcel map, numbered each parcel, listed the nature of the crops grown there, the quality of the soil and the yields recovered. Then they converted all the production estimates into monetary equivalents. Intendants centralized and stored this information, updating it whenever new crops were introduced, or when a parcel changed ownership. Even though it was only completed in 1731, this cadaster was a monument to administrative efficiency and bureaucratic integrity. The *perequazione* was also the pretext for obliging nobles to present proper feudal titles to land they possessed. The duke took back into his domain many fiefs on the pretext that they had been usurped. He also suppressed the *Chambre des Comptes* of Savoy in 1720, in order to centralize tax assessment in Turin.

Finally, Victor Amadeus used the regulatory power of the state to stimulate the manufacturing economy. To that end he introduced a series of mercantilist measures designed to generate taxable revenues. Savoy's forges produced army material after 1630.[21] Charles Emanuel II launched a silk-spinning industry at Chambéry, and forced the inmates of charitable institutions to work in it after 1656. In 1668 he introduced Bolognese mechanical spinning frames. Manufactures in Savoy dyed and wove silk stockings under state supervision. Simultaneously, silk manufacturing ventures multiplied in Piedmont, in Turin, Fossano and Racconigi. The value of this manufacturing output quadrupled in the half-century after 1700.[22]

The "absolutist revolution" entails other developments besides the twin concerns for money and soldiers, but military motives were always the prime consideration. Compared with other bureaucracies, the Piedmontese machine was lean and active, and churned out an enormous quantity of business under the duke's firm hand. Victor Amadeus saw his senior officials every day and like his martinet contemporary, King Friedrich Wilhelm of Prussia, he expected high standards of application and integrity. Mack Smith's description of the prince on inspection in Sicily brings to mind his Prussian counterpart.[23] In a coat of undyed wool, large boots and a casual travelling wig, he strolled about on official visits with a rough walking stick, before retiring to private quarters in order to work. The meagre salary accorded to Intendants did not permit them much ostentation. In Piedmont, unlike France, few offices were venal. French officials bought their post, and perceived a salary as a kind of return on their investment, with the ability to sell the position in future to a qualified candidate, subject to the prince's veto. Offices in Piedmont were transmissible for only a single generation. This enhanced the tendency for Piedmontese families to keep their career options open. They blended service in the army with careers in government and the Church, both of which further entrenched the service nobility ethic.

Unlike his monkish contemporary Cosimo III of Tuscany, Victor Amadeus saw religion as an instrument of power; it was to be used to inculcate morality and obedience into subjects. This more "utilitarian" approach to religion, typical of the eighteenth century, justified royal interference in domains that were previously the Church's realm. By the Concordate of 1727, he excluded non-subjects from church benefices, and subordinated the Inquisition to his supervision. He also intervened in education, which in Europe was almost everywhere the Church's exclusive domain. He founded a new university in Turin in 1720 to train servants of the state. Strict examinations selected candidates for public service as well as the priesthood. Students could now select courses in view of a specific career, such as engineering, surveying, architecture and surgery. All of these professions entered the university curriculum for the first time. The university of Turin grew from almost nothing to enrol 2,000 students by 1730: Padua had fewer than 1,000 students, Bologna 400, and Pavia only 150. In 1729 the sovereign set up a special residential college with 174 places reserved for youths from poor families to study free of charge. This was part of a policy promoting non-noble "bourgeois" candidates to positions of authority.

King of Sicily in 1713, Victor Amadeus undertook to reform it on Piedmontese lines, as his descendants would do after 1861, using Piedmontese officials in the island's key posts. Paid less than their Sicilian counterparts, they were more efficient and reliable, imposing taxes with more rigour and fewer exemptions. Victor Amadeus objected to the Spanish practice of selling offices, for the purchasers sought to recover their investment, and venal office brought with it tax exemptions and honorific rights. Piedmontese officials axed redundant posts, and attempted to inject efficiency and curb corruption in the offices remaining.[24] Sicilians were not

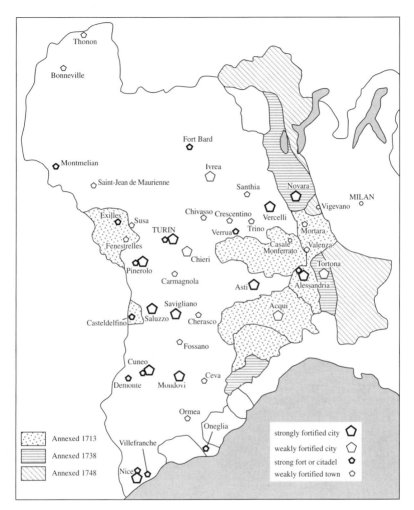

Map 19   Piedmontese expansion

grateful. When a Spanish army invaded the island that year, the regime collapsed. In 1719 Victor Amadeus received the island of Sardinia in compensation, which also had a royal title, but little else.

In 1730 the old king chose to retire from ruling in favour of his son. He continued to follow government business from a distance, and within months tried to grasp the sceptre back. Charles Emanuel III banished his father to an isolated residence, where he died in

October 1732. An early imitator of Louis XIV, Victor Amadeus never swerved from the ancestral policies of his house. His single reign restored Piedmont-Savoy to the status of a principality that counted in the concert of European states.

Eighteenth-century Continuity

The great reforms were complete by 1730 when Victor Amadeus II retired. Only after 1762 did his son take another step, by abolishing the most archaic forms of serfdom in Savoy. In 1771 Charles Emanuel III decreed the abolition of seigneurial dues in that region. This was not a revolutionary measure, because peasant communities were expected to reimburse their lord the value of these dues. For the rest, the kings of Sardinia (as the dukes were now called) were content to follow the policies of their ancestors.

    Charles Emanuel III (1730–73) and Victor Amadeus III spent the fruits of reform on a large standing army. With a Bourbon to the west and a Habsburg to the east, Charles Emanuel III weighed his options during the succession crisis to the throne of Poland in 1733. Piedmont deployed 40,000 soldiers, of whom a third were foreign mercenaries. Charles Emanuel sided with France and Spain (the Gallispans, as they were called), in exchange for additional territory carved from the duchy of Milan. The French and Spanish did most of the fighting, ejecting the Habsburgs from the kingdom of Naples. Easy success led Charles Emanuel to anticipate the next war with eagerness. The war of the Austrian Succession exploded in 1740 when Maria Theresia mounted her father's throne, and European powers sought to despoil her of her inheritance. For two years the king listened to offers both from the empress and from the Bourbons. This time he sided with Austria, on condition that it transfer immediately to his rule the rich districts of Lombardy west of the Ticino river, including Novara. A Spanish army marching through France occupied Savoy almost without resistance in 1742, for the Savoyards realized that their prince would gladly exchange them for territory in Italy. The king tried to offset Savoy's apathy by appealing to the martial leanings of Italians outside his states, for the House of Savoy sometimes draped itself in the rhetoric of Italian independence.[25] In addition to the regular army and the provincial militia regiments, irregular bands of peasants levied during wartime harassed enemy communications, descended on their convoys and supply depots, and picked off stragglers. Charles Emanuel kept the Spanish and French armies at bay in the campaigns of 1743 and 1744, fighting a pitched but inconclusive set-piece battle near Cuneo. When the Genoese learned of the Austrian and Piedmontese plan to dismember the republic, they threw themselves into the Bourbon camp. In 1745 a great French, Spanish and Neapolitan force based on Genoa marched northward, and routed the Piedmontese army along the Tanaro river line. Incompatible strategic aims of France and Spain enabled the Austrians and Piedmontese to encircle the Bourbon army near Piacenza, which extricated itself only with great difficulty. When Spain secretly withdrew from hostilities at the end of 1746, Piedmont was saved. Austrian and Piedmontese troops advanced into Provence, supported by the English fleet. The revolt of Genoa against its Austrian occupants diverted the allies' attention. A French army invaded Piedmont from the west in 1747, along the direct road to Turin. At Fenestrelles, on a mountain-top, the Piedmontese army butchered an impetuous French assault. It was the Savoy dynasty's greatest military success.[26]

As the state expanded, the army grew to over 50,000 men in 1744 and 70,000 in 1796. Meanwhile, it incorporated more specialized units that reflected the increasingly complex art of war. German mercenaries constituted about a third of the whole, but Piedmontese volunteers supplied almost all the remainder. The officer corps became progressively more Piedmontese just as Italians in other regions withdrew from the military profession. Military salaries proved attractive to an aristocracy whose revenues from land, trade or finance, could not compare with those of Milan, Genoa, Naples or Palermo.[27] Under the pressure of war, the dukes of Savoy and their descendant kings of Sardinia consciously sought to increase the number of nobles in their service.[28] From 1722 to 1796, the royal domain sold 819 letters of nobility to aspiring candidates. Since the majority of officers were nobles, and the army was universally considered a career worthy of their standing, the army attracted wealthy commoners seeking to enhance the status of their house. Authentic *roturiers* (plebeians) constituted about a third of the Piedmontese officers, although few of them rose very high in the hierarchy.

Military innovations were the ferment for other transformations. The artillery school created in the 1740s spurred numerous technical vocations. The crown encouraged this interest in military science and subsidized the foundries and chemical works related to it. Modern science and philosophy found a home in Piedmont for the first time, among aristocrats with close connections to the army and the court. Their influence spread from arms industries to mining, porcelain works and metallurgy, putting Piedmont on the industrial map of Italy. Then, in the 1780s a multitude of academies, intellectual and political societies sprang up. They were animated by courtiers and army officers who lobbied Victor Amadeus III to rationalize the kingdom on Prussian, not French lines.[29]

Alone of Italian states, then, Piedmont coalesced around an army. Although one could not compare it to the kind of "army state" that the kings of Prussia fashioned during the same period, the German militaristic model gradually supplanted the French one. War for Piedmont brought power to the state and wealth to its inhabitants.[30] On several occasions its territory was subjected to deliberate destruction, but the damage inflicted was almost exclusively limited to agriculture. Enrico Stumpo estimates the damage between 1703 and 1713 as amounting to the agricultural revenue of a single year; while the plague of 1630 killed eight times as many Piedmontese as all the wars combined! While the rest of Italy was locked into a prolonged agricultural recession, the value of land in this region increased by over 60 per cent, precisely in the period of greatest conflict, between 1680 and 1717. Both the state and local communities found the means to make important productive investments in the economy and its infrastructure. By 1800 it possessed the most powerful and diversified manufacturing economy in northern Italy.[31] The fiscal reforms, unlike any others in Italy in that period, may have had beneficial effects on the economy too. The dukes borrowed large sums to fight their wars, but instead of reimbursing the capital, the dukes distributed noble titles, fiefs and jurisdictions, knighthoods and offices. One reason for this relative prosperity was that Piedmont's allies traditionally paid much of the bill. England and Holland paid for almost half the military expenditures incurred by the War of the Spanish Succession. Much of this money was then redistributed throughout the Piedmontese economy. It is an excellent example of a state where war accelerated economic and political *progress*.

21 Italy as a Great Power Pawn, 1660–1760

Spanish Decline

Until the Peace of the Pyrenees ended the Franco-Spanish war in 1659, the smaller Italian states were sometimes participants in the grand politics of kings and battles, bit-players in the European tragedy unfolding during the war. Individually, they were not able to change the outcome. They might have had some influence had they united against a single belligerent, but most of them vacillated between the king of Spain and his enemies, according to the interest of the moment. That they left the Spanish alliance at all is indicative of the profound decline of the Catholic monarchy. Under the strain of never-ending war, rebellion and a catastrophic economic situation, the tremendous resources of the monarchy slipped out of the hands of King Philip IV. Madrid declared partial or complete bankruptcy in 1627, 1647, 1652, 1657 and 1665.[1] The monarchy's decline made it harder to cultivate friends and attract allies. The aristocrats whose blood and treasure coursed through the veins of the Imperial system, decided to cut their losses, plead poverty and cultivate their gardens. Philip IV hoped that by making peace with Cardinal Mazarin he would be able to concentrate his resources on subduing Portugal. It proved impossible to reconquer the rebel kingdom, despite scouring Flanders and Italy for experienced veterans. Spanish military strength ebbed with each passing year. The 77,000 soldiers employed in 1660 proved insufficient to shore up all the critical points and produce a credible field army in Portugal. The

Portuguese, helped by small but effective contingents from France and England, defeated the Spanish forces repeatedly, until Madrid finally consented to make peace in 1668.[2]

Thus, the great duel between France and Spain ended to the clear advantage of the former, even before Louis XIV acceded to personal rule in 1661. He would devote the rest of his long reign promoting his house at Habsburg expense. The short War of Devolution (1667–8) in the Low Countries saw Louis's armies take what they wanted with little opposition. Spanish military power now consisted in its ability to mobilize foreign soldiery and the resources of its allies. At the onset of the Dutch War in 1672, Spain signed twelve defensive treaties with different European states to ensure the defence of its own territory. The Treaty of Nijmegen in 1678 confirmed Spanish weakness by ratifying France's conquest of Franche-Comté.[3] Italian noble participation was not negligible, but it could not offset the withdrawal of Spaniards from military vocations. Spanish service no longer attracted Italian peasants and artisans, and the notables who led them served mainly to attract the viceroys' favour.[4]

Spanish dominions in Italy were largely left to their own resources. The viceroy in Sardinia gradually reinforced royal power at the expense of municipal institutions by overseeing their functions and by intervening in the king's interest. In Naples successive viceroys applied a policy of *tranquilidad y buen goberno*, in order to curtail noble impunity and repress rural banditry.[5] In the aftermath of the revolt of 1647, Spain built great fortifications around the capital, but troops never filled the cavernous new barracks. Of the 4,000 foot paid out of the kingdom's resources in 1696, half were stationed in the presides along the Tuscan coast, leaving less than 2,000 infantry and about a thousand cavalry to protect the kingdom. The garrison companies in Naples were at only 40 per cent effective strength.[6] During the Dutch War, the kingdom provided 17,000 men for the Spanish war effort, but few of the units were up to strength, and the enormous proportion of officers to ranks underscored recruitment difficulties. The militia units were all paper forces. The kingdom came to life again in the great coalition war against France (1689–97). It sent 11,000 troops to Lombardy and Catalonia, and the supply services filled out new orders for cannon, galleys and uniforms. After 1700, Neapolitan regiments fought for Spain in Lombardy, Iberia and the Low Countries.

Sicily paid next to nothing for the defence of the rest of the

Spanish Empire. Some anti-Spanish sentiment among the nobility forced the viceroys to rule cautiously. The Mediterranean collapse of manufactures and population decline thrust the economy into the doldrums, and revenues tumbled simultaneously.[7] The 1671 famine created widespread unrest throughout the island, which in the space of several decades went from being a major grain exporter to suffering periodic dearth. Rioting broke out in several cities, at Catania and especially Trapani, where officials hanged about twenty leaders of a popular uprising. Nevertheless, the revolt in Messina that exploded spontaneously on 7 July 1674 was primarily local in its inspiration, and reflected urban grievances. The Messinese called on France to expel the Spaniards from the kingdom and promote Messina to the rank of capital.[8] Spain's weak response to the revolt is the best illustration of its incapacity to defend its Empire at the nadir of its decline. Even reducing its other garrisons to skeleton effectives, it was still only able to concentrate less than a thousand regular soldiers in the weeks following the revolt. This motley force could only establish a loose blockade, but Spain soon began to shift troops to the island. From 1675 onward, Sicily became the main focus of the Spanish war effort, surpassing Catalonia and the Low Countries. The force was weakened by the presence of the French fleet, which tied it down to coastal defence everywhere and made concentration difficult. Louis XIV envisaged the revolt as a useful diversion of enemy forces, and the contingents he sent there never exploited their advantage. A few northern Italian aristocrats stepped forward to offer their swords to the French king, but Louis XIV avoided using Italians in the theatre. In 1676 the French navy battered the combined Spanish and Dutch fleets in repeated encounters, and gained the initiative completely at sea. The commander Vivonne would have seized the kingdom of Naples easily, were he capable of daring initiative, for the capital contained only a thousand soldiers, and the other fortresses had such small garrisons as to render them defenceless. Instead, the French regiments skirmished aimlessly around Messina. Early in 1678, when diplomats were nearing the conclusion of a general peace, the French withdrew to their ships along with the families most compromised by the rebellion, and sailed away. Madrid deprived Messina of its economic and political privileges as a punishment. It was the onset of a long decline, to the benefit of nearby Catania.

Spanish weakness meant that defensive alliances between Spain and its client states were no longer credible, and they were ready to pass into the French camp. Although these states had no permanent armies of their own, they often possessed fortresses and arsenals of great potential. Garrisons in these places were usually meagre, sometimes inferior to the number of cannon on the ramparts.[9] Sentries functioned more like security guards responsible for the upkeep and maintenance of the place, for street patrol and sentry duty. The absence of permanent field forces did not make these states harmless, since most European powers hired regiments on an international market. Italian princes and republics were still capable of entering into alliances and bartering their resources to their own advantage. In 1677 Grand Duke Cosimo III tried to recover the Tuscan presidial territories from Spain by diplomacy, on the pretext that he could better protect them from French seizure. Despite their pitiful condition and skeleton garrisons, Spain realized their strategic importance and refused to cede them.

As Spain's decline became more manifest, Louis XIV's promotion of French ascendancy in Europe irked and alarmed Italians.[10] Italy never became a primary focus for the French king, who was content for Italian states to be neutral, and he rarely solicited their alliance.[11] In August 1662 some Corsican guards in Rome rioted against the French embassy after the ambassador's soldiers insulted and knocked one of them down. Louis XIV inflated the incident into an international affair, and used the occasion to occupy the papal enclave of Avignon in Provence. In 1663 the cardinal nuncio made a spectacular apology in Paris, and after Rome hanged a few of the Corsicans involved the papacy erected a special monument to commemorate its own humiliation. Such bullying was part of a wider programme of asserting the king's *gloire*, popular at home but worrisome for France's neighbours. Louis and his ministers created new occasions to raise France and lower Spain and the Empire simultaneously. Duke Ferdinando Carlo of Mantua went over the French clientèle in 1678, when he concluded a secret treaty with Louis XIV to sell Casale to France. Even after recovering Casale in 1697, the duke remained in the French camp, and offered Mantua and Casale as forward bases for Bourbon troops in the war of the Spanish Succession. Modena withdrew from the Spanish alliance after 1678, when the duke's daughter married James, duke of York, the future James II of England and solid French client. Parma remained only formally part of the Spanish alliance, until it withdrew in 1691. As for Tuscany, Cosimo III's wedding to a French princess was disastrous for his house, and failed after a few stormy years, but the grand duke eyed Paris more anxiously than he did Madrid.

No ally was so close to Spain as the republic of Genoa. Louis XIV resented the republic's loans to the Spanish crown, and the disposal of its shipyards and drydocks for Spanish warships. The city was also a competitor to Marseilles in the scramble for Mediterranean commercial supremacy. Louis disliked these *Hollandais d'Italie* as much as the Protestant burghers of the northern republic. From 1679 he decided to "mortify" them, and in May 1684, the French fleet appeared off the city to demand that it turn over four galleys the republic was building for Spain. On the senate's refusal, the fleet bombarded Genoa for ten days, until its ammunition was exhausted. A thousand Spanish troops came to Genoa's defense to keep order in the city and to shoot looters. Genoese support for hapless Spain in its war against France in 1684 was unswerving. However, Louis XIV and his advisers achieved their objective: Genoa stayed out of the League of Augsburg, formed in 1686 to stop French expansionism. By 1690, the Habsburgs complained of excessive Genoese benevolence towards France.[12] The French ministers who advocated an aggressive line towards Italy, Colbert de Seignelay and the marquis de Louvois, imposed their views until their deaths in 1690 and 1691 respectively. French power over Italian princes had clearly replaced that of Spain, but that power was not perceived as benign or indeed preferable to the Habsburg tradition.

Austrian Ascendancy in Italy

If the Austrian branch of the Habsburgs was the weaker one in 1554, a century later Spanish exhaustion inverted the roles. Germans never forgot that northern Italy was part of their Empire, and jurists there reminded the emperor of his rights over it. The papacy declared most of its territory and adjacent Tuscany to be free of Imperial suzerainty, and Venice refused Imperial claims over the Terraferma, but these unilateral declarations were never recognized by Vienna.[13] In 1656 Emperor Ferdinand III dispatched several regiments to Milan to help Spain against France, but part of their mission was to recover all the fiefs occupied by Madrid.[14] Most northern Italian states saw in the Imperial crown an ultimate arbitrator in their quarrels. Tuscany, Piedmont and Mantua periodically dispatched aid to the emperor in his struggles against Protestants and Turks, all the while claiming that such help was not due to the sovereign by any right. Leopold I (1656–1706) planned to restore the Empire to its early grandeur by imposing his authority over these states. His goal was to recover the Dalmatian coast from Venice along with the Terraferma and to reunite the Austrian branch of the Habsburg dynasty with Spain.

From Piedmont to Naples, nobles had long served the emperor in a personal capacity. As Spanish service attracted fewer of them, the Imperial cause took its place.[15] Italians served in Vienna in a broad range of activities, from music and court entertainment, through religion and Counter-Reformation reform, to war and diplomacy. Leopold I was an Italophile who preferred Italian to German in official correspondence.[16] Foremost among the Italians in his service was the Modenese general Raimondo Montecuccoli, the creator of the Imperial standing army in the 1650s, who remained president of the war council until his death in 1680. There were hundreds of other Italian officers in the Imperial army, although the troops they led were almost always Germans or Slavs.[17] Most were keen partisans of Austria's eastern policy of expansion against the Turks, while Germans urged the emperor to resist the French king's encroachment on their homeland. The place of Italians in Imperial service was striking around 1670, but their numbers declined afterwards as a German lobby contested their pre-eminence.[18]

The Imperial army did not really stabilize until after 1680, for financing a large force was difficult for a relatively poor and disjointed state totalling barely five million inhabitants. The invasion of the Empire by a resurgent Ottoman power in 1683 called for exceptional measures. German states, such as Saxony and Bavaria, mobilized large contingents to aid the emperor, and with decisive Polish aid under King Jan Sobieski, they routed the Turks outside the Imperial capital. With the Ottoman army in disarray, Germans, Poles and Venetians concluded that the hour was at hand to repel the Turks from central Europe. Hungary was plundered continually by Imperial commanders intent on feeding their soldiers. Italians were no gentler than Germans towards the emperor's Hungarian subjects.

In 1689 Louis XIV invaded Germany and devastated the Rhine Palatinate. Unwilling to make peace with the Turks now that he was winning, Leopold was nevertheless forced to send an army west to block France. The commitment of important Imperial forces to the Po valley marked the beginning of an "Austrian" era in Italian history that would continue to the conclusion of Italian unification in 1866. Italian elites often welcomed Imperial aid, for the French king upset European peace repeatedly. French invasion of Spanish territories in 1683, when the Empire was preoccupied with the Turkish siege of Vienna was a stab in the back of the Christian cause. No one forgot the bombardment of Genoa in 1684. Louis occupied papal Avignon in 1688 to pressure Rome into conceding church revenues to him. The brutal dismantling of the Rhine Palatinate just when the Empire was engaged in a decisive struggle against the Turks proved to Italians that Louis XIV was the objective ally of the Turkish sultan. Even Piedmont embraced the anti-French cause in 1690 and mobilized troops to join a great alliance. Its defection ruined French influence in Italy.

What dismayed Italian princes was the force with which the emperor Leopold asserted his Caesarean rights over Italian states, in a much more peremptory way than the king of Spain ever did.[19] After the middle of the century, most of them cultivated the trappings and titles of royalty, that reflected the greater independence they enjoyed, as German princes were wont to do in the aftermath of the Peace of Westphalia. The number of courtiers and the greater articulation of their functions expressed the prince's desire to imitate Europe's great monarchs, at least within the limits of their modest resources. The revival of Imperial ambitions in the peninsula was a rude awakening for them. Italian states paid "contributions" as far as they were in the path of hungry troops.[20] It made no difference to the Imperial plenipotentiary Antonio Carafa that these states proclaimed their neutrality. Vienna now referred to Italian states as its "vassals". Instead of forging alliances with them, as the king of Spain had done, Vienna now summoned them to find money and provisions. Faced with Carafa's inflexibility, his reputation for brutality, and his army of hungry soldiers, Italian princes complied. Italian states paid over a million scudi to the Imperial treasury in 1690, and three million between 1707 and 1713. This helped Austria *decuple* its revenues and transform itself into a European power.[21] Only Piedmont refused to contribute anything, since its standing army gave it a position of strength. Peace accords in 1696 were favourable to the allies in Italy. France abandoned its dangerous bases in the Po valley, ceding Pinerolo to Piedmont and Casale to neutral Mantua.

The end of the century was dominated by a new diplomatic crisis which the old French king originally tried to defuse. The death of King Charles II of Spain posed the problem of the balance of power with new urgency. There were two well-placed lines of succession. One was the Habsburg dynasty of Vienna. Leopold's eldest son Joseph would inherit the Danubian Empire, while his cadet the arch-duke Charles would mount the throne in Madrid. The other possible heir was one of Louis XIV's grandsons, Philippe d'Orleans, since Louis's queen, Marie-Thérèse was daughter of Philip IV of Spain, and Louis's own mother was King Philip's sister. Bourbon diplomacy had worked towards the Spanish succession since the 1650s. Simultaneously, Paris and Vienna explored compromise solutions that awarded advantages to each. This was reckoning without the Spaniards themselves, who had no wish to partition their Empire to satisfy other powers. Charles II chose the Bourbon candidate as the one most likely to guarantee imperial integrity. The potential union of France, Europe's strongest power, with Spain and its colonies around the world, would create a political and economic colossus of global proportions. The Castilian nobility quickly rallied to Philip, who descended on Madrid with a great retinue of French officers and administrators intent on recasting the Spanish Empire on more efficient French lines. For years their real master would be Louis XIV at Versailles.[22] Louis also marched French troops into the Spanish Netherlands to occupy the great fortresses there. A new coalition of the emperor, German princes, the Netherlands and Great Britain united to contest these developments. By 1701 an Imperial army came down the Adige to expel the French and Spanish (known as Gallispans) from Italy.

Prince Eugene of Savoy became Imperial commander-in-chief of Italy at the outbreak of the war.[23] Austrian forces made little headway, despite the defection of Piedmont to the coalition in 1703. While one French army held the Germans at bay in the central Po valley, another overpowered Piedmontese fortresses. The siege of Turin in the summer of 1706 was clearly a decisive operation. Prince Eugene's relief army skilfully manoeuvred across Lombardy to deploy behind the French siege lines. His stunning victory at Turin clinched Austria's hold over the peninsula. The next year an Austrian army occupied the kingdom of Naples without much resis-tance, passing through the Papal States, despite Rome's protests. An Anglo-Dutch fleet captured Sardinia without resistance in 1708, and handed it over to the archduke Charles.

The emperor made the "recovery" of his rights over Italy the prin-cipal axis of the war effort, even after he had conquered Milan, Naples, Sicily and Sardinia from the Bourbons.[24] In 1706, the new emperor Joseph I declared unilaterally that Parma, Ferrara and Comacchio were Imperial, rather than papal fiefs, and proceeded to quarter troops on them. When Clement XI Albani finally excommunicated Prince Eugene in 1707, Imperial troops occupied larger districts and submitted them to contributions also. In 1708, exasperated by Austria's attitude, the pope declared war on the emperor, and raised troops to reconquer the Romagna. An Imperial army under Marshal Daun marched leisurely towards Rome, with the papal militia bands wisely keeping out of their way. The pope capitulated in January 1709, and Austria continued its levies undisturbed.

The war ended in triumph for the Austrian Empire in central Europe and Italy. The Peace of Utrecht and Rastadt in 1713 and 1714 left Spain and its Indies Empire in Bourbon hands. The Low Countries, Milan, the kingdom of Naples and Sardinia passed to the former archduke, who succeeded his brother to the Imperial throne in 1711 as Charles VI. The emperor deposed the Gonzaga duke Ferdinando Carlo who chose the wrong side, and annexed Mantua to Imperial possessions. About a third of the German emperor's subjects were now Italians. The disparity of forces between the emperor and the princes was much greater than in the time of the Spanish kings. Vienna's huge standing army of 144,000 men stood in striking contrast to the Italian principalities' garrison forces. Italian aristocrats also ceased to serve European armies in sizable numbers. Apart from Piedmont and Venice, Italian states were henceforth incapable of participating in great power rivalries, or choosing sides.

The decades after 1713 largely confirmed Austria's predominance in Italian politics. Under Charles VI, the Imperial territories were still only loosely stitched together. The governor of Milan and the viceroy in Naples continued to rule, as under Spain.[25] Italian states sometimes turned to the emperor to resolve their disputes, as they had done with Spain a century previously. Austrian power did not rely upon the cooperation of regional elites. As a result, the Empire was something of a colossus with feet of clay; it impressed by its size, but not its solidity. The new Habsburg order in Italy had been imposed by force of arms. This meant that the fate of Italian territories hung in the balance of military power.

Spain plotted a return in force to the peninsula under the direction of its wilful new queen, Elisabeth Farnese, once Philip V descended into prolonged depression. While the succession to the Spanish domains fell to Philip's son, Ferdinand, by his first wife, Elisabeth insisted that her two sons, Charles and Philip, should each

have an Italian throne. Her Italian prime minister, the low-born cardinal Alberoni, quickly raised Spain's military profile by launching a
new fleet. Spain's army, recast on the French model and tempered
during the Spanish war of succession, reached a level of proficiency
not seen for many decades.[26] In 1717, while Austria was rolling back
the Ottomans in the Balkans, this Spanish fleet landed 8,000 men in
Sardinia, quickly overwhelming its feeble garrison. A year later,
30,000 troops disembarked in Sicily, and stole it from Piedmont.
Only the rapid intervention of British, French and Austrian forces,
and the destruction of the fleet by the British admiral Byng in
August 1718 off Cape Passaro, forced Spain to relinquish its conquest and dismiss Alberoni. Spanish diplomats forged new alliances
for the next round. At the extinction of the Farnese dynasty in 1731,
Austrian troops occupied and annexed Parma to the Empire. The
impending extinction of the Medici dynasty focused European
powers on the need to find compromise solutions agreeable to all
the great powers.

A new European war on the pretext of the succession of Poland in
1733 pitted the Bourbons against the Habsburgs, and gave Spain its
opportunity to overturn the Treaty of Utrecht. Three Gallispan campaigns from 1733 to 1735 expelled the Austrians from almost all
their Italian territories. In 1734 a Spanish fleet landed another army
under the adolescent prince Charles at La Spezia, which invaded the
kingdom of Naples from the north. The Habsburg regime there collapsed after a decisive battle at Bitonto in Apulia. Sicily, too, welcomed the return of the Spanish regime. Naples and Sicily were
fused together into an independent kingdom, but Charles's instructions arrived in the mail packets from his mother, who selected his
counsellors and monitored him closely.

Bourbon military superiority checked Austrian designs on Italy.
After the Turks humiliated Imperial arms at Belgrade in 1739,
Italian states virtually ignored Vienna's summons to send help.
Nevertheless, Austria remained the most important power in Italy.[27]
By the peace of 1737, Vienna consolidated its hold on Milan and
Parma, while Duke Francis of Lorraine, husband of the emperor's
heir Maria Theresia, received Tuscany in compensation for con-
ceding Lorraine to France. This Austrian ascendancy threatened col-
lapse when the death of Emperor Charles VI opened the crisis of the
Austrian succession. During his lifetime, Charles persuaded one
European power after another to consent to the smooth succession
of his daughter to the hereditary lands, and to her election to the

Imperial throne alongside her husband Francis of Lorraine, by a *Pragmatic Sanction*. This diplomatic solution appeared to succeed at the time of the emperor's death in 1740, but within months the new Prussian king, Frederick II, tore up the agreement and invaded Silesia. As Austrian forces reeled in defeat, France, Bavaria and Saxony mobilized to seize their share. Spain marched an army through southern France intent on reclaiming Milan, but Piedmont's alignment on the Habsburg side blocked that advance. A Spanish seaborne army with reinforcements from Naples marched into Emilia from the south to aid Modena, which joined the Bourbon alliance. Austrian and Piedmontese forces overran Modena before help arrived. The war widened further in 1744 when Britain joined Austria in a formal alliance, and France committed itself fully against both. With naval bases in Minorca and Gibraltar, the British fleet contested Bourbon seapower in the Mediterranean.[28] In 1744 a reinforced Austrian army attempted to reconquer Naples from King Charles. The Spanish and Neapolitan army defeated it at Velletri, near Rome, in a decisive gamble. The following year, a great Gallispan army with Neapolitan and Genoese contingents marched north from Genoa, swept the Austrians from Milan and Parma, and threatened to overrun Piedmont from the east. An Austrian counter-offensive in 1746 almost destroyed that invasion force around Piacenza, and the Gallispans left Genoa to Austrian occupation in their retreat. Maria Theresia intended to punish the republic for its "treason" and considered annexing it to the Empire, after imposing huge financial penalties on it. Spain's new monarch, Ferdinand VI, quietly ordered his generals to cease fighting, without informing his French ally. Only Genoa's uprising against Austrian forces at the end of 1746 prevented Imperial and Piedmontese victory in the theatre. When peace was signed at Aix-la-Chapelle in 1748, the belligerents reached an Italian stalemate. Almost everywhere else, the French were successful, and the treaty awarded Parma to Elisabeth Farnese's son, Philip, as part of the spoils.

Italian states were by now pawns in the great conflict between Bourbons and Habsburgs. There was no chance they could contest any great power solutions to their destiny. The remarkable *renversement des alliances* in 1756, uniting those two dynasties, removed Italy from great power rivalry until the French Revolution. Modena and Piedmont, although intent upon expansion, now lacked allies in the region. Austria consolidated its ascendancy in Italy by occupying the Este duchy after 1763, ruled by one of Maria Theresia's sons. The

empress's daughter Maria Carolina then wed King Ferdinand of
Naples in 1768 and opened the Mezzogiorno to Austrian influence,
as she concentrated power in her hands. France's only gain was the
purchase of rebel Corsica from Genoa in 1768. The inability of
Corsicans to unite their factions and their clans around their charismatic leader, Pasquale Paoli, meant that no European state considered Corsican independence a viable option. France claimed its
prize at the price of a vicious counter-insurgency campaign.

  In the half-century after the battle of Turin in 1706, almost all the
familiar Italian dynasties disappeared. Gone were the Gonzaga in
Mantua, the Farnese in Parma, the Medici in Florence and the Este
in Modena. Italy, more completely under foreign domination than

Map 20   Political boundaries, c. 1770

ever before, was now divided between the Bourbons of Spain in Parma, Naples and Sicily; and the Habsburgs in Milan, Mantua, Florence and Modena. The Papal state was, in terms of great power politics, a mere phantom. Venice resolutely avoided becoming embroiled in dynastic rivalry. Italian principalities were thus to be passed from one power to another in diplomatic summits. One immediate result was that the peninsula enjoyed another long era of peace after 1748.

22 Justice, Order and Social Control

Judicial Autarky

Most people lived in small communities of villages and hamlets where they knew the people they interacted with. Face-to-face relations were not always harmonious whenever amoral familism and agonistic competition held sway. Much early modern conflict derived from relations of proximity. Pasturing livestock on a neighbour's land might be interpreted as accidental, but records of the damage they inflicted (called *danno dato*) imply intentional slights against the victim.[1] Families were on their guard just before the harvests, sleeping outdoors in their fields, or patrolling with loaded muskets to ward off intruders. Preferring confrontation to litigation, Italians managed their conflicts locally. Urban tribunals operated not on the basis of local considerations, but according to general principles laid out by Latin codes, dispensed by judges who were paid for each procedural step.

Italian society was not strong in coercive institutions to which all were answerable. So people developed their own moral and political safeguards. A keen sense of justice based on reciprocity is probably universal. Italian culture added a rigorous separation of women and men to a keen sense of public honour. Sanctity of the family cell and the blood line took precedence over all other affiliations. Family members were bound by honour and interest to help each other. Bastards, who were fairly numerous before the mid-seventeenth century, could mobilize the solidarity of their half-siblings.[2] Informal "justice" was inseparable from private vengeance. Even, society's weakest elements, widows and orphaned girls, could get revenge by turning to witches and their spells.[3]

The most common form of alliance was the faction, which coagulated around the most influential family heads of the village. They jockeyed for access to common lands, to establish the tax rolls, to distribute charitab'e relief from the confraternities, to award positions of chaplain and schoolmaster. When important interests were involved, clashes between factions could be bloody and durable. Villagers labelled their factions: blacks or whites, Guelphs or Ghibellines, Spaniards or French. Villagers united, however, to defend their common patrimony against neighbouring communities. Boundary disputes often took the form of punitive raids, seizing livestock and burning crops in the field.[4]

The most agonistic society was undoubtedly Corsica, where the state played a very minor role in local affairs until after the French conquest of 1768. Families competed over "interests" that might be based on property and grazing rights. Powerful men extended protection over all their adherents, their blood kin and even their "spiritual", baptismal kin. People without relations took on the names and the quarrels of the dominant families, and expanded the strength of the latter. These groupings were meant to contain feuding with the threat of retaliation. It was "a system of primitive law and restitutive justice" (Wilson).[5] If so, this system was remarkably inefficient, resulting in rates of violence unknown in the world today. In the absence of state institutions they could trust to act as arbiters or punishers, Corsicans applied their own code of vengeance, or *vendetta*, following set rules everyone recognized.

Feuding and vendetta were vestiges of ancient practices once widespread throughout Italy. One source attributes to the island *circa* 1700 one of the highest homicide rates (750 per hundred thousand annually) in recorded history, compared to a modern southern European average of about 2 per hundred thousand.[6] Disputes over damage to plants and crops by goats, over rights to passageways through fields, over access to common land for one's sheep, over access to positions of local power, led to cycles of aggression and vendetta retaliation. Corsicans planted villages in easily defended sites, and designed buildings to withstand sieges until the 1860s. Since individuals perceived themselves more as kinsmen than as "egos", they knew the role society expected of them in a *feud*. In theory, all the male relatives of the family head were implicated, up

to the third degree of consanguinity. Family councils carefully calibrated their actions, deciding when to escalate hostilities and when
to appease the other side. Once they warned the enemy of what was
to come, the designated avengers left the house for their *macchia*
hideouts. The womenfolk shared this culture, with their laments for
family victims, which were a folk art form of vengeance poetry.
Reluctance to avenge a death could bring the accusation of *rimbecco*,
or cowardice, that discredited the individual in the eyes of everyone
who knew him. These feuds, or *faide*, could last for several generations, and continue until the extermination of the clan's menfolk.

Sixteenth-century authorities functioned as arbiters and peace-
makers. Genoese officials tramped around Liguria with their escorts
of Corsican soldiers, a notary and a scribe, to restore tranquillity to
these forbidding hamlets. A few judges might deal severely with families pursuing feuds, but the universality of attitudes that fed them
inclined most magistrates to adopt a conciliatory role.[7] Judges who
punished individuals harshly would themselves be the object of
vendetta, with the assent of the population. Because they lacked
coercive force, governments preferred pacification to trials and
public retribution. Criminal statutes, like those imposed on Corsica
in 1571, often followed the principle of collective responsibility of
kin. Relatives usually *were* partially responsible for the rash actions of
one of the family members. Outlaws were never far away, and often
crept home at night. Villages were fearful of outside intervention,
and resented paying for any kind of outside police force, even when
it proved effective.[8] Peace was best concluded by the families themselves, in a public treaty signed by both sides (to several degrees of
kinship). These treaties were followed by a ritual meal where former
enemies ate from the same platter. One pacification treaty among
twelve different factions, concluded in 1579, "reconciled" no fewer
than 195 heads of households. Some feuds were settled by
exchanging brides, uniting former enemies into kin relations.

City factions in both north and south Italy employed the same language and identical tactics as villagers. In Cremona (Lombardy) the
state intervened only when retaliatory killings upset the public
peace. Murderers almost always fled across a nearby border, and
were sentenced to death or banishment *in absentia*. The outlaw eventually addressed a petition to the king requesting pardon or mitiga-
tion of his sentence. If the relatives of the victim agreed to this, the
pardon was usually forthcoming. No doubt the authorities exhorted
and threatened the victim's family into making peace. For horren-

dous crimes such as counterfeiting, repeat killings, raping reputable women, or sexual intercourse with nuns, highway robbery, poison, killing officials or other activities impeding justice, pardons were reserved for royal assent only.[9] Nearby, Brescia's aristocrats frequently divided into factions employing armed retainers, vagrants, gypsies, or army deserters, as their *bravi*, or hired assassins. Faction politics became eternalized in cities like Ravenna and Faenza in the Romagna, or Perugia and Assisi in Umbria, and Ascoli and Fermo in the Marches. Factions seizing power avenged themselves on their adversaries, whose members withdrew to rural castles where they could make their spite felt.[10] Over time, central government imposed limits on this kind of behaviour, and political marriages cementing warring families together into kin relations took the sharpest edge off factional infighting by the early seventeenth century.

Not all these conflicts were solved by judicial action. There was a bewildering variety of jurisdictions, and the fact that one's henchmen belonged to a specific corporation or came from a particular town entailed long delays. Jurisdictional imbroglio was then compounded by the tendency of Italians to use the courts as a weapon by which to smite their enemies, bribing judges and perjuring themselves. The Inquisition in Sicily handed out ten times as many condemnations for perjury as any equivalent Spanish tribunal.[11] Only the naive could trust Sicilian courts to render justice, and Spanish officials often preferred to catch and execute suspects summarily. When unable to collar the culprits, the viceroys sometimes made secret agreements with them to curtail their crimes.[12] Judges were reluctant to intervene when barons or members of powerful institutions were involved.[13] More typical of Sicilian crime was organized extortion by noblemen, who carved up the territory over which they ruled. The crown tried to repress lawlessness by establishing district "captains", who were paid from property confiscated from bandits, but these officials soon escaped central control. Occasionally a strong viceroy took exceptional and illegal measures. Osuna overturned acquittals, searched the archives for excessively light sentences in order to reopen trials, banished aristocrats, clapped vagabonds in jail and encouraged local authorities to dispatch bandits expeditiously. These methods helped, but they were short-lived.

The system of vendetta manufactured bandits on a large scale. The bandit was someone who by legal decree no longer enjoyed the protection of the law. His enemies could kill him with impunity, and the state confiscated his goods and laid a price upon his head. Bandits were a structural feature of early modern Mediterranean Europe. Village factions sometimes employed them as hired guns. In Liguria they levied tolls over the mountain passes on the merchants and transporters bearing grain or salt. Youths enjoyed this free life. These aggressive vagabonds wore coloured shirts, sported silk hand-kerchiefs around their necks and planted feathers in their caps like soldiers.[14] Normally they operated in tight little bands of ten to fifteen men. Mezzogiorno bandits in baronial service occasionally murdered bishops or their vicars-general, or chased them from their dioceses.[15] Certainly they enjoyed feudal liberties to escape the heavy hand of urban law. Even when they did not employ bandits themselves, nobles cared little what these men did outside the fief. They were especially numerous in border regions, which allowed them to dodge pursuit. Bands of desperadoes were difficult to corner. They could break up into small clusters and mingle with the shepherds descending to the coast with their flocks. They prowled the countryside, levying tolls on messengers and on merchants not travelling in well-armed convoys. They extorted money from wealthy landowners, both lay and clerical, and burned the grain stores of those who refused. Some daring gangs prowled around the cities, where they melted into the crowd. Many of the police were ex-bandits, ex-soldiers, and ex-galley slaves, whose mischief the popula-tion feared as much as the outlaws.[16]

Bandits were useful friends. A few, largely mythical Robin Hoods took from the rich to give to the poor; like the Calabrian Nino Martino, who dowried poor girls during his heyday in the mid-1570s.[17] Bandits enjoyed protection and complicity at all levels of rural society, whether this was based on loyalty or fear. A notorious, but typical bandit was the outlaw from Latium called Catena, who confessed to 54 homicides in addition to extortions and thefts over a period of twelve years. He boasted that he killed his victims "hon-ourably", for they were all his personal enemies or their relatives, and not "innocent" people. He survived because Cesare Caetani, a young Roman noble, hid him in his fiefs.[18] Roman authorities exe-cuted both Catena and his noble protector in 1580.

The phenomenon of rural banditry gradually worsened after 1560, when peace released turbulent noblemen and their retainers from army employment. It grew from endemic to epidemic after 1575. Rosario Villari calls it a general insurrection of the countryside against the city.[19] This is no doubt excessive, for peasants cooperated with bandits out of fear, not admiration. The papal confiscation of fiefs transformed many nobles into deliquents who dreamed of getting even. Alfonso Piccolomini, turbulent scion of the prominent Sienese house, operated throughout Tuscany, Latium and the Marches. In 1581 his band seized and sacked the town of Ascoli Piceno and killed the papal governor. The Abruzzi noble Marco Sciarra combined various bands in central Italy, totalling over a thousand men in 1585–6. They wrought vendetta on the pope across a vast territory from Campania to Romagna. Operations against bandits like these were conducted in a military fashion, with the papacy, the king of Spain and the grand dukes of Tuscany hiring mounted units to track them in the mountains. Feudatories and villagers caught in the crossfire practised the law of silence. They refused to send sentries to guard the passes, or neglected to ring the alarm bell to warn of bandit presence. They might shut the town gates when the soldiers arrived, allowing the bandits they were hiding to escape. But these larger operations were sometimes successful.[20] The bandit's personal enemies, hungry for booty and revenge, joined the soldiers and spurred them into action. From the time of Paul IV Carafa (1555–9), laws toughened against outlaws, as jurists defined just who was a bandit with greater precision, and then legalized summary procedures against them. As a result, their numbers multiplied. Sixtus V estimated at 27,000 the number of bandits operating in the Papal States, five or six times the number of soldiers in all the papal garrisons combined.[21] Tribunals worked tirelessly, using torture to extract the names and the hiding places of accomplices. Public executions, the exposure of bandit heads on public monuments, the exemplary execution of aristocrats, gave the impression the government was winning.

Then the famine of 1590 swelled up the bandit gangs with hungry and desperate peasant refugees. The greater number of effectives made the bands more fragile, vulnerable to treachery, and more preoccupied with foraging for food from hungry peasants. Alfonso Piccolomini's 400 men ravaged a large district of Tuscany, Umbria and the Romagna. The papacy closed its eyes when a Tuscan force seized him in papal territory. The outlaw duke was hanged from the window of the city hall in Florence in January 1591. In 1592 Marco Sciarra and 500 outlaws sacked the town of Lucera in Apulia during the great fair, killing the bishop, and reportedly carrying off two million scudi in money and merchandise – equivalent to half the tax revenue of the kingdom of Naples! His band scaled the walls of Recanati in the Marches near Ancona, and then prowled around Loreto with its fabulous treasure of *ex votos*.[22] The viceroy of Naples mobilized 4,000 infantry to eject the bandits from their Abruzzi castles. Then a papal army pressed the bandits from the west. Sciarra retreated to the coast with several hundred followers and embarked on Venetian warships to serve the republic in Dalmatia. After six months, he deserted and returned to the Papal States. While crossing into the Abruzzo, his lieutenant Battistello murdered him in exchange for gold and a pardon for him and a dozen followers.

The most effective method of fighting bandit gangs was to bribe outlaws to sell the heads of their companions. Governments pardoned anyone, provided they killed a bandit who had committed a more serious offence. Since almost everyone in the countryside knew bandits or were related to them, this commerce in severed heads led to a grisly rendering of accounts. A few good harvests allowed more peasants to return to their villages, and papal armies recruiting for war in Hungary absorbed many more. Banditry then returned to its endemic form, allowing governments new opportunities to impose their justice.[23]

State Justice

Despite the prevalent private conception of violence, Italian communities did not lack tribunals or judges. Medieval Italian cities pioneered the modern court and the inquisitorial procedure, dispensed by professional magistrates, who had neither kin nor property in their jurisdiction. Village judges were often notaries or lawyers holding the position for a year or two, with the aid of a textbook. Alongside the judge was the sinister *sbirro*, or constable and jail-guard, often a bully with a murky past. They had a reputation (amply corroborated by judicial archives) of being abject thugs who chose police life in order to browbeat honest subjects. Employees of the various tax farms came from their ranks too.[24] Many jurisdictions in northern Italy, and most in the south belonged to feudal lords. Giorgio Doria, whose work is based on a single, poor hill village, condemns feudal courts out of hand, but his conclusion seems excessive.[25] As the state gradually imposed its presence, feudal lords took care not to alienate their subjects.[26] Vassals did not hesitate to address petitions to their lord in the city if they had a problem.

While mountain communities like Doria's Montaldeo were exceedingly violent, high levels of violence and faction feuding were not everywhere in evidence.[27]

Local magistrates pushed litigants to make peace with each other, but the state gradually confiscated more of the judicial process to itself. Princes saw justice as the cornerstone of public tranquillity, and their concern is apparent in their legislative work. Cosimo I de'Medici issued endless orders and regulations dealing with public order. Their preambles proclaimed the prince's desire for greater personal moral rectitude and social discipline in his subjects. This sensibility flows from the same wellspring that nourished religious reform.[28] Orders and regulations were not always full legislative texts; still less were they integrated into coherent legal codes, which date from the eighteenth century.

A wide variety of courts dispensing justice against criminals is characteristic of Ancien Régime Europe. Most large cities possessed a kind of supreme court, modelled on the Roman "Rota", which exercised appeals jurisdiction over outlying courts. But there were dozens of sectorial tribunals, and a serious confusion over their jurisdictions and attributions, as judges competed to maintain their caseloads. Nothing opposed multiple or contradictory sentences from different tribunals for the same case. This tended to eternalize trials unless one of the parties obtained a decision from the prince. In Piedmont guilds handled most offences except when the crime was serious, like homicide. Hospitals and poorhouses punished their own inmates; the army's system of martial law tended to be more lenient; even Jews managed their own affairs, under the sovereign's distant supervision.[29] Delinquents cheerfully took advantage of the system. They had a mental map of the special jurisdictions and knew which solutions, like joining the army, would resign authorities to drop the charges.

No organization enjoyed sweeping jurisdiction more than the Church, which judged its own delinquent members. Not only did it have exclusive jurisdiction over ecclesiastics, but it could also try crimes like sacrilege, adultery, witchcraft and concubinage that involved violation of sacraments or profaning sacred institutions. The procedures it followed resembled those of lay courts, and both lawyers and priests were trained in both secular and canon law. Diocesan courts, run by a vicar-general, could torture suspects just as any secular court could.[30] The Church safeguarded its jurisdictional rights with great vigour. The use of religious buildings as sanctuary was one of its privileges. The *sbirri* tried to coax criminals out by ruses, but bishops frowned on the practice. Many local magistrates simply damned the consequences, and wilful bishops excommunicated them to underscore their authority. Rome established a special Congregation for Immunity to judge the innumerable disputes with secular authorities.[31]

Just as there were many different tribunals, so there were different prisons, which served as holding pens for people awaiting trial, or places to intern debtors to force their families to repay their debts. Jailers used and abused their power to extract money from their prisoners, who paid for their own incarceration. In Sicily these jails were more lethal than the executioner, for not only did prisoners without connections die of hunger, but typhus and other diseases swept through them unchecked. Despite the ill will of prison personnel, confraternities often brought comfort and food to prisoners, and many brotherhoods substituted tax farmers in their management. Solemn events, great victories, papal elections and important religious festivals often witnessed mass pardons and amnesties, when all but the most dangerous returned to the streets.[32]

Italians often took their causes to tribunals, even if they waged war on their enemies simultaneously by other means. Claudio Povolo affirms that humble village people in the Veneto had recourse to the tribunal only if conflicts in the community could not be resolved informally. In Montefollonico and San Secondo Parmense, local government empowered a minor official to denounce any quarrel to the judge, who then proceeded to instruct the case according to the norms of the nearby city.[33] There the judicial machine deliberately sought to circumvent the traditional law of silence. The sovereign or his representative could intervene in any case, at any time, and they vetted all the serious sentences.[34]

In many regions of Italy, the first reaction of the magistrate in any dispute was to force family members to swear to a peace, and to fine those who refused. Magistrates assumed that individuals would lie to harm their enemy, and only the threat of torture was likely to draw the truth. Although it was infrequent, even witnesses could be tortured to extract information. Most cases involved assault and battery, insults and other attacks against persons, rather than property crime, although money, land and women were often underlying motives. Tribunals preferred to compose these conflicts, because the judge saw himself the arbiter responsible for public order. Consensual sodomy was not everywhere prosecuted, and there was a wide gulf between judicial practices in Tuscany, where such cases appear rarely, and Sicily, where at least a hundred sodomites were strangled and their bodies burned in Palermo alone in the century after 1540: after which that act was no longer punished by execution. In Siena, the rape of boys was not treated differently from sexual crimes against women and girls.[35] Women were frequently called to account for verbal violence and minor theft. Crimes against property were assuredly more frequent than the judicial archives indicate. Many villages had separate mechanisms for composing conflicts arising over *danno dato*. Judges were also lenient when poor people stole food, but punished them severely when they feared that impunity would result in a wave of similar offences.[36] Over time crimes against authority became more common as well.

Trials gradually became more complex. Judges could collect proofs on their own initiative, issue summonses and hear testimony, before carrying the case to final judgement, if they did not drop it for lack of evidence. Magistrates convoked the witnesses alone, in secret, where the scribe transcribed the questions and answers virtually verbatim.[37] Magistrates did their utmost to obtain confessions, and used torture to procure them, if other evidence linked the suspect to a serious crime. The standard practice was to bind the prisoner's arms behind his back and to hoist him on a pulley, dropping him from time to time to inflict greater pain. Meanwhile the magistrate interrogated the suspect and the notary scribbled the dialogue, pained cries and all. However, only a minority of tortured suspects ever confessed, and any confession obtained under torture had to be ratified and confirmed from other evidence. Judges were rarely gratuitously cruel, and did not prolong torture for more than an hour. They reluctantly freed vicious career criminals robust enough to resist their best efforts, and against whom other evidence was not sufficient to gain a conviction. Torture's frequency diminished after the mid-seventeenth century and gradually fell out of use, as judges placed the emphasis on evidence.[38]

Once the judge considered the evidence weighty enough to find the suspect guilty, he had great leeway in sentencing.[39] The crime had many "qualities", such as age and status of the parties, the intention to do evil, and the context. For an equivalent offense, women were almost always more lightly sentenced than men. From the different opinions found in legal reference books, the judges picked the sentence that best fitted the case at hand. The lash was common. Exile from the state, or to an isolated corner of it was another option, for with any luck the culprit might die of malaria. Serious crimes like nocturnal theft, rape or unintentional homicide were often punished with time on the galleys. Although judges frequently handed down harsh sentences, the number of actual executions is much smaller due to the routine granting of pardons by the prince.[40] Usually, the accused was in hiding and had never been apprehended. In other instances, a condemned criminal called upon his family's patrons and protectors to use their influence to soften the sentence. When they occurred, executions tended to be public events of reparation, held in a market square. Public confession, communion and tearful apology by the victim for his misdeeds were an important part of the ritual, but people remembered defiant gestures too.

Judges were assisted in their task of maintaining public order by soldiers and militiamen who had orders to impose law and order everywhere. Nowhere was this more striking than in the kingdom of Naples. Difficult economic conditions, and sheer distance from the capital meant that bandit activity enjoyed a resurgence, protected by the complicity or the neglect of barons. In the 1670s great bandit gangs controlled much of the Abruzzi. United bands, totalling 1,200 men controlled the zone around Teramo and Chieti, and imposed their own taxes. The Spanish viceroy, Del Carpio, dispatched 2,000 troops, threw half a dozen dukes and princes in prison, and exiled others from their estates. Expeditious judicial procedures and an assortment of rewards and incentives for bandits to hand over their companions began to yield results. In 1684 the papal governor of the southern Marches pressed the mountain border from the other side, forcing the large bands to split up. Many outlaws left their refuges to join the Venetian army fighting in Greece and nearby Montenegro. By 1685 the Abruzzi and Apulian shepherds offered their congratulations for having crushed rural outlaws and for rendering the sheepwalks safe once more.[41]

A More Disciplined Society

Anxious concern for salvation wore off as the wave of mysticism ebbed. However, after 1650 a "second wind" of religious zeal invigorated Italian bishops, who expressed more concern for moral and social reform than for individual salvation. The late seventeenth century seems to mark a change in the behaviour of Italians, as violent crime began to fall. This trend is not specifically Italian, but has parallels in western Europe.[42] We lack a detailed chronology and geography of the process, but Oscar Di Simplicio's studies based on Sienese ecclesiastical and judicial sources constitute a model. The origin of the trend lies in the Counter-Reformation's heightened awareness of sin. A wave of monastic handbooks for confessors marks a clear point of departure. Clergy consciously used confession and exclusion from communion as a way to bring their wards into line, for people who harboured hate in their hearts against an enemy committed sacrilege if they took communion. Parish priests passed on to the bishop the names of those who avoided the sacrament.[43] Although they were not more perverse than laymen, the parish priests' behaviour left much to be desired.[44] In the diocese of Siena, clerical delinquency collapsed after 1630, as a new *gravitas* emerged in their behaviour. The improved priesthood raised expectations in their flock too whose heightened sense of impropriety held their pastors more accountable, and introduced a "virtuous circle" (Di Simplicio). At the same time, the Council of Trent's campaign to "moralize" society pushed Italians into the conjugal straight and narrow, as bastardy became rarer, and prostitutes became the object of ever more restrictive decrees.[45] Bishops were certainly a catalyst for reform, multiplying their inspections and their visits. Missionaries were another agent of behavioural change in rural populations. In central Italy the missions of Jesuits and Capuchins which multiplied after 1660 terrorized people with the consequences of sin.[46] Italian princes backed the priests' exertions for their own salvation. Bishops petitioned secular officials to imprison or banish delinquents, and judges found it difficult to ignore them on these matters. Clerical behaviour improved even in the kingdom of Naples.[47]

The popes were also champions of a vast moralizing campaign aimed at uprooting traditional laxity. This had never been absent from Catholic reform, and the most exemplary legislation was Borromeo's in Milan. By the late seventeenth century moral rigour was the spirit of the times. Innocent XI Odescalchi, who lived austerely in his apartment, waged a battle against luxury and ostentation in Rome. His successor after 1691 was the 76-year-old archbishop of Naples, Antonio Pignatelli, Innocent XII, who saw that all carnival transgressions went punished, regardless of the offender's status. Clement XI Albani (1700–21) likewise hardened the rules across the board. He did what he could to stamp out prostitution in Rome, and transformed prisons into reformatories. He reduced papal pomp to

a minimum, toning down the revelry and noise of religious processions. All these popes saw catechism instruction and close surveillance as the key to moral reform. Clement XI decreed that no one
could receive the sacrament of confirmation or contract marriage
without a testimonial from his parish priest attesting to his diligence
at catechism.

Secular rulers supported this campaign as never before. Cosimo
III in Tuscany, who spent hours each day in prayer, tried to uproot
carnival and May Day, increased the number of religious holidays,
multiplied parades and religious processions in which he took a conspicuous part. He decreed sumptuary laws to uphold public decency,
imposing black as the colour of dress in public for laymen. His office
of Public Decency tried to hamper and suppress prostitution, and
worked to moralize society. After Cosimo's reign the state strengthened its hold over society by extending its jurisdiction at the
Church's expense. Beginning with Venice, in 1701, governments
decided to ignore the rules governing sanctuary of criminals in religious buildings. The concordat with Naples in 1741 confirmed the
trend, and the popes gradually stopped fussing over it.

If there was a growth in any field of crime, it was no doubt smuggling of goods such as salt and tobacco, on which governments
imposed increasing taxes. Everyone smuggled, everywhere. Laws
against smuggling provided for harsh punishments, and the *sbirri*
were sometimes pitiless with the persons they caught, but the punishments were not systematic, nor were they applied equally to all categories of the population. People generally bought the minimum
legal amount of salt at the official price, but for the rest, smugglers
fed a vast market. Monasteries opened their doors to smugglers and
served as depots for contraband salt. Religious dressed smugglers
in their habits, and dispatched real monks to escort disguised
smugglers in order to trick the guards.[48] Because it could be grown
anywhere, tobacco was an ideal product to smuggle. People collaborated with smugglers wholeheartedly along the borders. In Venetian
Friuli, armed bands of smugglers operating across the border could
count on the sympathy and assistance of the population.[49] Whatever
mobile troops the states possessed were employed scouring the
border regions to intercept these mule trains of contraband goods.
In the Papal States, smugglers joined the cavalry militia, which gave
them the legal right to patrol the borderlands with their weapons.[50]
Clashes with armed smugglers replaced banditry as the chief
headache of governments in the countryside.

The replacement of violence by crimes of theft or deceit mirrors a trend that Pierre Chaunu first indicated in France after subjecting judicial archives to quantitative scrutiny. Close investigation of criminal procedures at various levels of the judicial hierarchy has shown that judges never dealt with more than a fraction of actual crimes, but after a generation of research interest, Chaunu's intuition probably applies to Italy too.[51] Perhaps the extension of sharecropping, which separated dangerous neighbours every few years, contributed to defuse feuding and vendetta in the countryside. We need some careful quantitative local studies of homicide before we can determine this. As private violence declined, public punishment was phased out. Rome was a pioneer in the use of prisons as punishment, beginning with the Carceri Nuove (1655) and then the correctional house of San Michele (1703). Elsewhere, incarceration began to appear late in the eighteenth century as a form of punishment for criminals, alongside debtors. Debates over crime, punishment and social perfectibility would soon constitute Italy's great contribution to the European Enlightenment.

23   The Italian Enlightenment

A Cultural Revolution

Counter-Reformation devotion reached its peak intensity around 1700. The papacy trumpeted its certitudes, its traditions and its juris-dictions to ward off encroachment by princes north of the Alps. The Church sponsored innovative scholarship, primarily in the domain of religious history, but more generally in philology, classical history and literary criticism, generically labelled "erudition". The French Benedictine *abbés* of Saint-Maur, Bernard de Montfaucon and Jean Mabillon from 1650 onwards subjected ecclesiastical texts and tradi-tions to critical scrutiny. In their hands this research had more in common with the new scientific disciplines than with edification. Mabillon's "reasonable certitude" was Cartesian doubt applied to religious history. Armed with the new tools of chronology and diplo-matics (the formal analysis of ancient documents), scholars forged revolutionary results comparable to Galileo with his telescope.[1] The Saint-Maur "school" of church history developed rapidly in Italy even before the monk travelled there in 1685. He left behind a circle of admirers and imitators. Fellow Benedictine Benedetto Bacchini emulated his French mentors in rejecting authority in sacred history as an arbiter of truth. Scholars like him returned instead to primary sources and sacred history to illuminate the study of theology. Clement XI Albani (1700–21) gave new impetus to the revision of church history. He surrounded the papal throne with a number of erudite polymaths, with the intention of buttressing papal claims in jurisdictional battles with European states.[2] Nostalgic in intent, this research sparked a new appreciation for the Middle Ages, the history

310

of which entered the Jesuit curriculum. An academy for the critical study of religious tradition appeared in Rome in 1708, and another, formed under the patronage of Cardinal Gualtieri in 1714, were the first to restore the dialogue with the sciences, although Rome never became a major centre of scientific research.

Two intellectuals emerged after 1700 to define the lines of force of the new era. The Veronese patrician, Scipione Maffei, and the Modenese ecclesiastic, Lodovico Muratori, were both disciples of Bacchini. Maffei formulated the first coherent critique of the noble honour ethic, in a book entitled *La scienza cavalleresca* (1710).[3] It marked him as a rationalist innovator advocating a "policed" society obeying more utilitarian norms. He then launched the important monthly *Giornale de' letterati d'Italia* to bring to public attention significant books published in Italy and abroad.[4] It played an important role between 1714 and 1717, when 1,500 to 2,000 people subscribed to it all over Italy. Maffei also proposed to establish a great institution for the furtherance of new knowledge at Padua. Since the Venetian senate showed no interest, he devised a plan instead to reform and modernize the university of Turin.

The archivist and librarian, Lodovico Antonio Muratori (1672–1750), achieved even greater renown. Ordained priest in 1695, he began his career at the Catholic Ambrogiana library in Milan. He then held the position of court librarian at Modena for fifty years. These libraries and the archives nearby were repositories of ancient manuscripts, over which he pored indefatigably. His long labour produced three important works: a 28-volume collection of medieval Italian sources, the *Rerum Italicorum Scriptores*; the *Annali d'Italia*, a survey of Italian history from the years 500 to 1500, later continued to 1749; and the *Dissertazione sopra le antichità italiane*, in which he attempted to describe every aspect of Italian medieval life.[5] He wholeheartedly believed in the efficacy of scientific reason as an instrument to realize the progress of European civilization. Like Maffei, Muratori's interests spanned a wide arc of intellectual activity, including economics and politics. His most revolutionary books dealt with religion. Published in 1747, *On a Well-ordered Devotion* announced a vast reform programme to uproot "superstition" in the common people. Muratori also contributed tirelessly to various journals and reviews, and corresponded with a vast European network of librarians, archivists and scholars.

None of the historical works could avoid the thorny problem of the Church's place in politics and society, which is called variously, *jurisdictionalism* or *curialism*. Fra Paolo Sarpi's polemics, calling for the abolition of the pope's temporal powers, were still controversial over a hundred years after their publication. The Neapolitan historian Pietro Giannone's anticurial *Civil History of the Kingdom of Naples*, published in 1723, denounced Rome's pretensions over the kingdom. Papal displeasure soon forced Giannone to flee to Venice, a haven for Italian *esprits forts*, where there was an ongoing tradition of writing hostile to Jesuits.[6]

A crack in the fortress of monolithic Tridentine devotion appeared at the end of the seventeenth century in the form of Quietism, sometimes called Molinism after its founder, the Aragonese monk, Miguel de Molinos. In Lombardy in the 1560s, lay preachers taught that interior prayer was more important than the sacraments in salvation. The Inquisition soon suppressed this "heresy of Saint Pelagia", but a strain of it resurfaced a century later. From 1650 onwards, numerous publications promoted contemplative, passive approaches to prayer, written by authors of impeccable orthodoxy. Molinos taught in his *Spiritual Guide* that God did not wish our cooperation in his work on our soul, and that external penance and the veneration of the saints was futile. His intense "spiritual" prayer spread throughout the Oratory, and appealed to many educated people in Rome, including Pope Innocent XI, Queen Christina of Sweden and several cardinals. The anxious, ascetic spirit that rejected ceremonies and showy prayers as superfluous vanities soon spread to nuns seeking mystical paths to heaven. The Jesuits gradually mobilized against Quietism after 1680, for the piety they promoted was much more visible, ritualistic and accessible. The Roman Inquisition tried Molinos and condemned him to abjure before a large crowd in 1687, after which it imprisoned him. The Inquisition moved against priests, confessors and nuns who forsook their ritual devotions.[7]

The Jansenist controversy made its appearance in Italy not long after. Jansenism was predominantly a French form of Catholic rigorism which claimed that God restricted salvation to a few elite souls who approached divine communion with trepidation and mental preparation. Inspired by the writings of Saint Augustine, Jansenists regarded salvation as the outcome of the cultivation of one's interior life. They scorned the Jesuit tolerance for a traditional religion of easy outward "devotions" for popular consumption. In France, Louis XIV persistently tried to uproot Jansenism, but it seeped into much of the French lower clergy and some religious orders. Since it admitted the divine presence in the host, the seven sacraments and papal supremacy, it was never clearly beyond the bounds of orthodox Catholicism. No pope condemned the movement as irrevocably as Clement XI did in his bull *Unigenitus* in 1713, but the current proved impossible to suppress, and diehard partisans of it henceforth made the papacy a target of their criticism. Eighteenth-century Jansenism advocated a slimmed-down hierarchy, a Church in the hands of parish priests to be treated as brothers by the pope. Their bishops would rule the Church by means of a "sovereign" council on which their delegates sat. Once Rome condemned them outright, Jansenists sympathized with those who advocated *anticurialist* or *regalist* doctrines proposing tighter state control over the Church, like the French Gallican tradition. Although these doctrines influenced an increasing number of bishops, placed in their sees by princes, its popular resonance in Italy was never very great, unlike in France.

The sensibility from which Jansenism sprang nevertheless spread through the eighteenth-century Church. Never before had the lower clergy, as a group, been so well educated and disciplined.[8] Priests often swam with the intellectual currents of their time. Benedict XIV Lambertini (1740–58), sometimes called the "Enlightenment pope", gave some ground to the reformers. He tried to reduce the number of feast days, stripped legends from the Breviary, lightened the Church's ineffectual ban on usury, defended the Copernican system of astronomy (although he did not allow churchmen to promote it), and brought the Index up to date. Ecclesiastical censorship was weakening. No longer did a panel of secretaries pore over new releases, sniffing out passages that might be heretical.[9] Censors generally left books by Protestant authors alone. The Index of 1758 that resulted from this reform was the most painstaking ever promulgated by Rome. At that date, the Church's censorship was perhaps milder than most secular jurisdictions. In the process, the Church rehabilitated the vernacular Bible, but there was no effort to place it in the hands of the faithful.

Benedetto Croce once argued that the term "liberal pope" was an oxymoron. Even Benedict XIV was distraught at what he considered the march of atheism, materialism and irreligion. Rome moved against the new currents occasionally. They were too widely established in Italy's universities to be uprooted by a new wave of Inquisition trials, but the era of prosecutions was not quite over. The Holy Office denounced the Newtonian monk Galiani in 1733, after decades of allowing him to teach in public institutions. Under papal pressure, princes sometimes withdrew their protection of writers denounced by Rome. Victor Amadeus III imprisoned Pietro Giannone in Piedmont until the writer's death in 1740, to curry favour with the pope. In 1734 the Congregation of the Index banned the writings of John Locke (author of a treatise on religious tolerance), and in 1738 Rome proscribed Freemasonry too.

Princes noticed the shifting cultural sands. Armed with a more secular sense of history, they were emboldened to seek new terms of coexistence with the Church through the concordat. Following trends in France, princes ceased to consider religion as a matter of salvation, but as a matter of morality, the cement that held society together. The shift in emphasis has dramatic implications for the history of both church and state. Bureaucrats thought increasingly of religion in *utilitarian* terms. This secular way of thinking prompted all of the princes to take over prerogatives previously held by the Church. On Cosimo III's death in 1723, his libertine son and heir, Gian Gastone de' Medici abolished pious committees, dismissed ecclesiastics from state employ, abrogated restrictions on Jews, and soon welcomed foreign Freemasons to his capital.[10] Victor Amadeus II wished to end the virtual teaching monopoly held by religious orders.[11] After 1720 he established a network of 24 colleges for his entire kingdom, for which he determined the curriculum. The trade-off with Rome, sanctioned by a concordat in 1729, placed a heavy burden of outward devotion on students. Secular priests, who accepted meagre salaries in addition to their benefices were still the great majority of teachers. At the university of Turin, intellectuals inspired by Muratori, like the Sicilian Francesco d'Aguirre, had to fit the clerical mould. The new Bourbon king Charles, in Naples, similarly introduced secular reforms to the university in the capital.

Eighteenth-century popes were gradually obliged to come to terms with the new secularism. In 1715 Clement XI declared an end to the medieval concession whereby King Victor Amadeus II exercised legatine powers in Sicily. When the Piedmontese prince imprisoned hundreds of priests for obeying the papal order, the pontiff cast an interdict on him. The measure undermined the king's authority over his new subjects, but the prince retaliated by expelling clerics loyal to the pope and replacing them with his own appointees. Popes avoided employing the interdict thereafter, and conceded their prerogatives to princes little by little. Princes sought to prevent further church growth in both its numbers and its wealth. Ecclesiastics constituted an astonishingly high proportion of the population. In Naples (1734) the secular and regular clergy numbered 112,000, that is, about 4 per cent of the kingdom's population, and the figure climbed to 150,000 around 1750.[12] Their cultural weight was out of proportion to their numbers. They would have constituted about 8 per cent of all adults, and perhaps close to half of the literate individuals. The concordats signed in the middle of the century aimed chiefly at reducing these numbers. By 1786 the total clerical population of 72,600 constituted about 1.5 per cent of the kingdom's five million inhabitants. In Tuscany, the Lorraine regency council cut back the possibility of bequeathing money to the Church, and forbade property legacies outright. Laws against mortmain in Tuscany (1751) were echoed in Genoa (1762), Lucca and Parma (1764), Venice and Lombardy (1767), Naples (1769), and Sicily (1771).

The new "intellectual" class came to see the monks, seminarians and professors as their enemies.[13] Traditional guardians of orthodoxy, like the Dominicans and Franciscans, were explicit targets. After the Holy Office in Florence arrested and tortured a Freemason poet, Duke Francesco Stefano shut down its operations for over a decade. Secular writers advocated that the state seize control of censorship. At issue was not whether ecclesiastics should be censoring books; rather governments insisted on appointing their own churchmen alongside secular censors.[14] Tuscany was the first to demand it, followed by Venice (which had never allowed the Church to have full control over censorship) in 1754, Parma in 1767 and Milan in 1768. Learned culture gradually veered to an anticlerical stance after 1750, as Italian states confronted the papacy over jurisdictional issues. The Jesuit controversy was the crucial test for the Enlightenment. Critics of the order identified it with the Inquisition, with papal supremacy and Aristotelian philosophy. It was in defence of royal jurisdiction that the Portuguese prime minister, Pombal, decided to expel them from the dominions of that crown in 1759. The Jansenist-leaning Parlement of Paris forced Louis XV to expel them from France in 1764, and Charles III of Spain followed suit in 1767. Naples and Parma promulgated identical decrees in a display of dynastic solidarity. The combined pressure of the Bourbons in France, Spain and Italy then forced Pope Clement XIV to dissolve the order outright in 1774.

While broad, these new intellectual currents were not deep. Some regions of Italy, like Sicily, were scarcely affected by them.[15] The

scholarly debate surrounding the reality of magic and witches, which
had been resolved in France before 1700, raged in the 1750s. Even
in the female convents, mysticism continued to be the dominant
form of spontaneous devotion. The efforts of bishops and confessors
to temper the nuns' ardour only reduced the number of vocations,
as more daughters of notables went to the altar with a groom in flesh
and blood.[16] In the district of Padua, erstwhile capital of Italian libertines and free thinkers, non-pascalizers around 1750 were 1 in
1,000 in the countryside, and a mere 1 in 200 in the city, values
much smaller than in the sixteenth century. Modena was relatively
more secular with fully 2 per cent of parishioners avoiding Easter
communion.[17] Still, an active Inquisition investigated cases of
feigned holiness and diabolical possession, the latter manufactured
by zealous exorcists. Further south, baroque sensibility was largely
intact in the lower classes, even in the cities. Images of the Virgin
Mary figured everywhere, tended by pious neighbours. In Naples,
Muratori's *moderata devozione* never made much impact even on the
elites. Indeed, the Dominican friar Gregorio Rocco (1700–82), who
had a huge following amongst the *lazzaroni*, served as a precious intermediary between the anticlerical government and the populace.[18]
The eighteenth century was the golden age of the Redemptorist missionaries in the rural Mezzogiorno, alongside the Jesuits and the
Capuchins. The Basilicata diocese of Muro Lucano witnessed the
first durable efforts of missionaries to uproot "superstition" in the
1720s, about a half century after central and northern Italy.[19]
Missionaries viewed themselves as teachers, and the most famous of
them, Saint Alfonso de' Liguori, recommended toning down the traditional macabre rhetoric in villages and towns they visited.[20]
Preaching missions in Tuscany were placed under strict supervision
by the state in order to prevent manifestations of "fanaticism".

   Much of the stripping away of baroque pomp from funerals was a
result of government meddling in the religious sphere. Some secular
clerics wished to "simplify" and "purify" the faith and reconcile it
with modern utilitarian thought. In Modena, state officials and ecclesiastical reformers wished to curtail bequests for post-mortem
masses. Muratori challenged bequests on theological grounds, but
even he left money for 400 masses in his own will. When the state
began to suppress monasteries and chapels it created havoc with
these pious legacies, and the remaining monks and chaplains were
too few to handle so many foundations. People continued until the
end of the century to prefer post-mortem masses to charitable dona-

tions to the poor.[21] In Siena, also, purgatory lost its grip when the state channelled pious donations away from traditional religious outlets.[22] The wills of northern Italians ceased to beseech the intercession of traditional saints. Testators neglected to regulate their burial cortège. Social elites were given to austerity and simplicity in their religious practices, and felt the separation between the living and the dead more keenly. Nevertheless, the demand for religious services remained very high everywhere. Priests without benefices served as domestic chaplains and tutors in many houses; they also taught catechism, preached, assisted the dying, administered sacraments, attended funerals, and prayed in the choir. There was no noisy dechristianization in Italy, as there was in neighbouring France, where unsettling public quarrels between Jansenists and traditionalists rent the Church's unity.

Intellectuals and Power

The "intellectuals" emerged from a broad segment of the social elite we have recently begun calling "civil society". The previous consensus held that only nobles could be "civil", and that members of that group possessed a natural aptitude to govern.[23] Around 1690 noble academies multiplied in order to teach urbane social skills to young gentlemen, saturated in the ethos of France's court nobility. French courtesy and manners, French institutions such as the royal academy, the Louvre and the Bibliothèque Royale held great appeal among the upper classes.[24] For much of the eighteenth century, Italy's academic community continued to be dominated by traditional elites. Alongside them, and sharing broadly the same vision of the world, emerged magistrates and lawyers, medical doctors and engineers. Their entry into academic institutions gave provincial academies new vigour and relayed trends in the capitals to remote corners of Italy.[25] Their increasingly secular outlook undermined the effectiveness of the guardians of orthodoxy. After 1750 social elites no longer volunteered their services to the Inquisition. In Emilia, active doubt and irreligion appeared first in the 1740s at the Este court. By the 1770s it was fashionable in polite society, among teachers, lawyers and physicians, to affect a condescending attitude towards traditional religion.[26]

Libraries grew in number and size during the century, and literary and scientific academies bought books as a matter of course.[27] The place of religion on the whole declined only gradually. The reading public grew relentlessly, so it became easier to import and sell books. Another sign of increasing readership was the shrinking size and cost of the books being published. Venice was still Italy's most important publishing centre, although it lost its preponderance. Producing 50 or 60 titles annually circa 1700, Venetian presses printed more than 500 titles in 1790. Literature made up 60 per cent of that. Women's publications began appearing also.[28]

In contrast to the absolute decline in religious and theological output, the number of scientific publications surged, parallel to trends in Paris. The anticlerical tone of much of the production, which also echoed French thought, passed government censors unchallenged after 1750. Censors were often cultivated intellectuals, who read critically and widely.[29] Many authors received "tacit" permission to publish; that is, their works could still appear without the official *imprimatur* provided they were not specifically prohibited. Italian states competed against each other to produce books that would have been banned by other governments. There were innumerable pirate editions too. It was common for books to be published with false place names, to trick censors or customs agents. The result was that forbidden books were common in the libraries of notables, especially those with a taste for French literature. One official, conservative estimate after 1750 stated that one book in six appearing in Venice was written in French.[30] French was also the original language of publication of three- quarters of the translated works in Italy.

The journals and periodicals that had such an important impact on spreading new ideas were intended for a more select audience.[31] The earliest example was the *Giornale Veneto de' Letterati* in 1671, and two more appeared before 1700. Maffei's *Giornale de' Letterati d'Italia* was perhaps the most successful, with as many as 2,000 monthly copies distributed throughout Italy. The journalists who contributed to it lived in many regions of Italy, and reviewed books coming from local presses. More typical was the Florentine *Novelle Letterarie*, published by the ecclesiastic Giovanni Lami, which maintained a subscription list of several hundred in the decades after 1740.[32] Enlightenment Italy was a rarefied elite living primarily in Lombardy, Emilia-Romagna, the Veneto, Tuscany and the Marches; Rome and Naples were isolated southern outposts. Similar journals appeared almost everywhere in northern Italy, including the Trentino.[33]

Theatre was also an important vehicle for the Enlightenment, whose demand for plays and libretti was insatiable. Venice possessed seven public theatres in the eighteenth century, in addition to private ones, that churned out new plays running a week or two.[34] The most famous, and most "philosophical" dramatist besides Voltaire was Carlo Goldoni, who wrote more than 200 plays. The baroque theatre was a place of sociability and distraction. With its own gaming and drawing rooms, customers could pay and receive visits. They went to "see" the plays and operas more than to listen to them. The mood changed after mid-century, when the sensuous and carefree rococo aesthetic was transformed into high-minded and earnest sermonizing which promoted an austere and stoical morality.

Elite Italian culture was usually generated or amplified in France. Visiting foreigners like the *abbé* Mabillon had a powerful influence on it. During the War of the Spanish Succession, the governor of Milan for the Bourbons, the Walloon prince de Vaudemont introduced the Parisian-style salon, in which ladies and gentlemen were present at the same *conversazioni*. Foreign influences grew steadily stronger, as the number of language courses taught in Italian colleges multiplied after 1680. German Protestant officers in the Piedmontese army mingled freely with the local elites, and dared them to break religious precepts.[35] Army officers prided themselves on their independence of judgement, and so were among the first to possess forbidden books. The army also spread scientific knowledge and technology across a wide segment of social elites. Foreign visitors on the Grand Tour attended sessions of the academies. Under the aegis of the famous philospher Condillac, a French-style court appeared at Parma early in the 1760s. French had always been spoken in Turin, and in Florence the plenipotentiaries of the regency council were francophone Lorrainers.

While the new philosophy spoke with a French accent, the originators were often English. One current originating in England, but spreading quickly on the continent, was the new interest in agriculture, or agromania. The English established the first Italian Freemasons lodge at Florence in 1731, but Italians soon entered it, as they did the Neapolitan lodge formed a few months later.[36] Freemasonry was a philanthropical and philosophical movement whose members formed a club, not unlike an academy, where they discussed questions of common interest. Masons considered themselves brothers and equals inside the lodges, and admitted candidates of modest social background to the officers' functions. The principles of the society were these: reciprocal aid to brothers; political and religious tolerance; equality of members; a cosmopolitan spirit; promotion of universal causes; and secrecy concerning the discussions. In Rome the Inquisition arrested and tried minor personalities and punished them with prison or exile. Italian Freemasons were more clandestine and anticlerical. They frequently attracted libertines and non conformists, where French and English lodges were much closer to the mainstream. As elsewhere in Europe, Freemasonry became increasingly fashionable among the upper classes in the 1770s and 1780s.[37] In Naples the Freemasons (who counted numerous army officers) cultivated the occult tradition and multiplied the esoteric initiation rituals. The chief minister Bernardo Tanucci tried to suppress the movement, but the Habsburg queen Maria Carolina saw in the society an instrument by which to lessen Spanish influence, and protected its members. By 1770 there were five lodges in Naples, and its aristocratic members eventually acceded to the most powerful charges of the state. Although magistrates, merchants and priests all joined the lodges, nobles enjoyed the highest profiles in the organization.[38]

Nowhere did the utilitarian trend lead to a secular vision of society as much as it did in Milan. Its leading spokesman, the patrician Pietro Verri, a soldier, journalist, historian, jurist and economist, founded the *Accademia dei Pugni* (fists) in his *palazzo* in 1762. One of the members was a patrician jurist from Pavia, Cesare Beccaria. In fact, he considered jurisprudence only a sideline. Beccaria, like Verri, was a polymath, compiling memoranda on trade, manufacturing, mining, agriculture and forestry, business organization and taxation, weights and measures, public health, popular diet, schools and workhouses, and population statistics.[39] The group subsumed all of these interests under the heading of economics, which they considered a science for the betterment of humanity. Through their English-style periodical, *Il Caffè*, the published proceedings of the group between 1761 and 1766 attracted attention throughout much of Italy. Their reform proposals to Vienna addressed the problems of ignorance, discussed the utilitarian basis of happiness, the promotion of equality, the noxious influence of privilege, the inhumanity of torture, the necessity of a rational legal code, the advantages of internal free trade, and the need to have wealth circulate to benefit the greatest number. From this movement came Beccaria's *Essay on Crimes and Punishments* (1764), which guided judicial and penal reforms around the world. The proximity of the members of the *Pugni* to positions of power in the Habsburg system was unusual. The new criminal codes of Modena and Tuscany, both from 1786, incorporated many of Beccaria's proposals, separating the notion of crime from that of sin, abolishing debtors' prisons and capital punishment. Other projects came from Vienna itself, such as the reform of the university of Pavia to produce the scientific, legal and ecclesiastical cadres that the empire needed.

Elsewhere the advocates of the Enlightenment farther removed from the corridors of power could afford to be less cautious. Voices appeared advocating freedom of the press, free speech and religious toleration, and a few even criticized the new liberal economic doctrines as being at the origins of widespread pauperism. In the 1780s and 1790s there developed a more subversive Jacobin current in Naples, composed of people who began as Freemasons, especially university professors, students, lawyers and renegade priests who had numerous contacts with the large, politicized French community in the capital. The wintering of the French fleet in the capital in 1792 gave birth to revolutionary clubs. They would soon learn how isolated they were.

The Coefficients

Pierre Chaunu's idea that the Enlightenment is important primarily in the way social developments magnified its extension, helps us understand how the Italian context differs from England, Germany and France. Just how much influence did the Enlightenment have on Italian society? The islands experienced little change. In Sicily, Spanish dress, language and customs, including bullfights, lingered long after 1750. The Italian language and cultural influences from Naples made inroads there without transforming baroque traditions.[40] The echo of the French Enlightenment was muted in Palermo and Catania, and almost inaudible elsewhere.

Sicilian cultural lag underscored how deep-seated the transformations were on the mainland. One trend that constituted a veritable social revolution was the envelopment of the nobility by a broader "civil society". When the economic circumstances improved after 1740, aristocrats benefited, but their numbers were too small to maintain a commanding position. Lucca's 224 noble families of 1628 were only 88 in 1787, making it necessary to amend the republic's constitution to allow them to govern uninterruptedly.[41] In Genoa patricians ceased adhering to caste traditions of marrying other aristocrats.[42] Almost everywhere the ideal nobility acquired the same utilitarian emphasis that applied to the clergy. As military colleges multiplied in the peninsula (Turin, Venice, Modena, Naples), officer candidates were inculcated with a similar professionalism, and acquired ever more specialized technical knowledge. Noblemen competed for entry into technical schools.[43] Principalities suppressed the rotation of untrained patricians through elective magistracies and appointed permanent, professional judges in their stead. After 1770, non-nobles dominated every sector of the administration, and reduced the nobles to an honorific elite. This evolution paralleled French absolutist legislation that gradually marginalized the traditional nobility, and habituated people to identify a "nobility of talents" alongside that of pedigree. In both Bourbon and Habsburg territories, men honoured by their communities and elevated by their contributions to the state henceforth enjoyed the perquisites of true aristocrats. Even in Venice the patriciate lost its sense of self-importance and began to open up to other groups around the middle of the century. In Tuscany Grand Duke Pietro Leopoldo banished ostentatious clothing from his court, as well as genuflecting and handkissing. The Prince and his ministers, like the nobles, played at being citizens of a republic. If they were not entirely equal before the law, then princes and senior officials became disproportionately responsible for public happiness.

The "democratization" of Italian elites also subverted the aristocracy's rigid family structures. The tight self-discipline began to break down in the more permissive eighteenth century. Legislators began to strike down fedecommesso provisions, which loosened up inheritance laws considerably.[44] Families began to revert to egalitarian inheritance, and many intellectuals advocated abolishing the fedecommesso laws altogether. Women circulated everywhere more freely, although not to the same extent as in France. Early in the century memorialists mention the appearance of maidens at public comedies in papal cities like Perugia, to the keen displeasure of the ecclesiastic rulers. This was followed by the emergence of what Barbagli calls the intimate conjugal family that replaced the patriarchal one. The extreme formalism of the late-seventeenth-century marriage led to the institution of the *cicisbei*, a male "retainer" of the wife's rank who showered attention (in theory platonic) on her. As the social distance between husband and wife diminished, relations based on open affection blossomed between parents and their children, and among siblings. The *cicisbei* disappear entirely after 1780. Italian families also ceased interning their daughters in convents: 75 per cent of Milanese noblewomen born in the first half of the seventeenth century were still unmarried at the age of 50; that rate dropped to only 7.5 per cent after 1800.[45] These shifts, which appear first in England and France, became more apparent in central and northern Italian cities. No doubt a clutch of good studies on *mésalliance* would teach us much about these trends. The more widespread adoption of *coitus interruptus* in the Italian aristocracy supposes a marked change in the relations within the couple. Even at more humble levels, couples formed with less community input than before, and young women and their families lost the benefit of communal sanctions against wayward suitors.[46]

While these trends show that Italy was open to the same influences that transformed northern Europe, we should not lose sight of the fact that Enlightenment multipliers operated from a weak coefficient. They were more limited to social elites than in England, France, Holland or Germany. Daniel Roche has pointed to the crucial role that domestic servants played in relaying the values and the tastes of elites to the rest of the population. These cultural mediators were proportionally fewer in Italy, especially in the Mezzogiorno. There was not the rotation of youths through middle- and upper-class households with anything like the frequency common north of Naples.

A heavy burden on Italy was the stagnant rate of literacy. Sallmann suggests that the lack of a Protestant threat made the Church complacent.[47] The progress in that direction lost its impetus after 1600, and so Italy lost its lead. Schools teaching the rudiments of reading, writing and numeracy certainly existed, such as those run by the Scuole Pie. The order was suppressed for having shown too much interest in the new science, but there was a need for schools to teach the sons of prosperous commoners, and it was revived. In 1784 they possessed 218 houses in Italy. In the countryside, literacy was the privilege of the happy few, usually dispensed by a priest who needed the money. Increasingly numerous, especially in the Mezzogiorno, were lay congregations of pious women who worked as schoolmistresses for girls, but they seemed to have little effect on feminine literacy rates.[48]

The late eighteenth century was nevertheless a turning point in northern Italy, especially after governments suppressed the Jesuit colleges, and recast the educational system on more secular lines. Numerous petty officials, like police officials or customs officers, needed to read and write in order to carry out their duties. Writing figured in the parish registers, the censuses and statistics, cadasters, street names, civic numerations, tax rolls. The administration issued all kinds of affidavits, licences and permits. People produced their own documents, through a notary or public scribe, to use communal property, to submit petitions or requests. Prussian experiments in mass schooling caught the interest of Maria Theresia and Joseph II, who were tempted to imitate them in their own states. The Italian precursor was the francophone Parman chief minister Guillaume du Tillot, who inaugurated civic schools in the duchy's two cities in the late 1760s. Writers saw in the schools the instrument by which to combat rural ignorance and superstition. In 1774 the Habsburg monarchs decided to create "normal schools" in each province, to train schoolteachers and to diffuse more effective pedagogical methods. In Tuscany Pietro Leopoldo created a few public primary schools in the 1780s that were run by the Scolopians, but he never attempted to create a system of mass instruction.

It took two years of continuous attendance at school to learn how to read, but it took five years to acquire the dexterity to write, which placed it beyond the reach of many parents, even when the instruction was free. In the Po valley capitals like Parma, Piacenza, Bologna and Modena only 45 per cent of grooms and 25 per cent of brides knew how to sign the marriage register in 1800, which was equivalent to small towns in backward areas of France on the eve of the Revolution.[49] In rural Savoy literacy rates for men in 1750 hovered around 50 per cent, several times higher than in neighbouring Piedmont, the most literate part of Italy.[50] In rural hinterlands, barely more than 10 per cent of the men and less than 5 per cent of the women could sign their names. Literacy was common to people who changed their station, and schools also flourished in zones where peasants managed their own land. Even in the Mezzogiorno, literacy rates could be considerable wherever artisans sold their own products. Servants were unusually literate. In seventeenth-century Lecce about a third of male servants could sign their names, and even chambermaids in cardinals' households in Rome were frequently literate. The army was another institution promoting literacy in Naples, inspired as it was by the Prussian model. Elsewhere in the Mezzogiorno, literacy rates were very low, especially in rural zones close to the city, where day-labourers or *braccianti* tilled the fields.[51]

There was a widespread semi-literacy, much harder to measure, that was based on the ability to read, but not to write, that concerned women more often than men. Elite women's education was less specialized and socially differentiated than was the case for men.

In 1860, when the new unitary state commissioned the first nation-wide censuses, Italy was still near the rear of the European pack, although there were wide regional variations. In Piedmont, Lombardy and Liguria, roughly one adult in three, or one male adult in two could read and write. In central Italy, including the Abruzzo, that proportion was only one adult in five or six, a proportion far lower than in northern Europe, where most of the population was literate. In southern Italy, the rate was everywhere (save for Naples and Palermo) less than one in ten, and less than one in twenty for women. The north also showed clear signs of quickening progress, as rural and female literacy began to close the gap with urban males. Thus, while the same trends towards secularism and individualism operated there as in countries north of the Alps, Italy was to England and France what Calabria was to Piedmont. The brilliant intellectual developments of the eighteenth century did little to close the gap.

24   An Equivocal Recovery

Agricultural Challenge

The tragic seventeenth century was followed by a long spell of warmer weather, whose good harvests fed an ever-increasing population. Italy's increase from about 13 million in 1700 to 18 million inhabitants in 1800 was one of the most gradual in Europe. Unlike the rest of Europe, where the weight of cities gradually increased proportional to the whole, this population ruralized as it expanded. In the Venetian republic, the total population of cities over 10,000 inhabitants constituted 14 per cent, down from 21 per cent in 1548. Tuscany and the kingdom of Naples ruralized too.[1] This growth may be the consequence of an increased life expectancy.[2] Venice's crude rate of mortality also declined through the century: from 33 per thousand inhabitants in 1600, to 31 per thousand in 1700 and 28 per thousand in 1790. However, infant mortality rose from 26/00 in 1700 to 41/00 in 1797. Such figures imply that although waves of mortality diminished in frequency and intensity, much of the population lived in straitened conditions. Social epidemics continued to ravage town and country, especially in periods of dearth. A surge in the incidence of smallpox killed countless children.[3] As elsewhere in western Europe, Italians delayed marriage.

Population recovery hit the traditional double-barrier of limited land and stable or declining productivity per worker. Umbria provides a good illustration of the limitations of Italian agriculture.[4] Peasants hacked out a bit of extra land from the forest, sowed grain on it until they exhausted the soil, and then let it revert to bush. Slopes soon lost their topsoil, and erosion uncovered the roots of productive trees, whose yields soon declined. Flocks of sheep inflicted grievous damage on the vegetation too. Defences against the deterioration of the landscape under the pressure of overpopulation existed, but they were expensive. The intensification of promiscuous culture and terracing limited erosion, for vines and olive trees helped keep the soil in place.

Population growth spurred the peasantry to work harder to provide extra food. There were no dramatic improvements in yields per hectare before 1850. Most of the increase resulted from more persistent effort, but as a result, Italy became a net exporter of foodstuffs. Increasing reliance on maize and rice took the pressure off more marginal land. Triennial rotation spread gradually too, although Lombardy remained exceptional with its two annual harvests. Landlords resumed the land *bonification* they interrupted after 1620. Cultivating the rich valley bottoms required considerable labour to raise the river bed, dyke its course and plant trees on it. In the Veneto, near Padua, the lower Po and the Polesine district, bonification involved reclaiming land from the marshes. A *consorzio*, sometimes financed from taxes, dug irrigation canals, kept up the dykes, ditches and roads, equalized the surface of the fields, transformed the hillsides into terraces.[5] In the most crowded regions, the process began as early as the 1730s. In Piedmont a network of irrigation canals improved the fertile plain.[6] In most regions, the depressed agricultural situation bottomed out between 1720 and 1740. Higher prices for grain triggered a new desire among landowners to earn more from their estates. Many confided their estates to "farmers", who paid their leases in cash and in kind, and then hired day labourers to produce the food. This was still short of an agricultural revolution, but profits from the soil were often several times higher than average returns in commerce or manufacturing.

Landlords expressed their agromania in an impressive rural cartography that helped them deploy their resources better.[7] Agriculture became a respectable topic of conversation in salons and academies. In 1753 a group of Florentine notables formed Italy's first agricultural academy, the *Accademia dei Georgofili*.[8] This inspired similar associations, some with specialized journals and publications. Italy's first university chair in agriculture appeared at Padua in 1765, and divulged to an elite audience the latest research.[9] Noblemen were not about to imitate their English counterparts who had their portraits painted alongside prize-winning cows, but patricians and their estate agents studied harvest statistics more closely. They gave orders to multiply the ploughings and the hoeing, to rotate the crops in a more systematic manner, to experiment with fodder crops, to select strains, to breed animals in new ways. Even in the Mezzogiorno, where barons avoided upsetting traditional usages, they introduced more careful land management and better accounting practices.[10] They were always seeking to utilize peasant labour in more economical ways.

More intensive and efficient cultivation was often introduced by the capitalist estate agent, who goes by different names. In the vicinity of Rome, the *mercanti di campagna* leased large estates from noble and ecclesiastical landlords, and recruited workers to feed the great urban market. There were only about 70 of these in 1700, which gives some idea of their large scale.[11] In Sicily the agents of transformation were known as *gabellotti*. The *gabellotto* paid the price of his lease at the outset, in cash. They, and the landlords they leased from, often unilaterally suppressed the long-term emphiteusis contracts by which peasants held their tenures, and transformed tenants into day labourers. An ambitious *gabellotto* was a busy man: supervising all the personnel; making out all the contracts; verifying the expenditures on salaries, products and other affairs; noting all the movement of seed and other assistance given to tenants on a great roster; touring the estate repeatedly; filling out all the permits to weigh grain and to harvest grapes. Above all he corresponded regularly with the landlord, the *università* and local government bodies, each concerned with their own revenues. He oversaw the lord's judicial administration too, and managed the multiple lawsuits.[12]

Renewed activity everywhere resulted in a greater complexity of rural society. Increased rents profited landlords first, but the benefits trickled down to rural merchants who commercialized the harvests, and rural administrators who shared with the landlords the fees, taxes and jurisdictional rights they collected from tenants. Buoyant markets gave birth to a host of small entrepreneurs who moved around, renting ovens, mills, butcher's stalls and taverns with the capital they had accumulated. Their children filled the ranks of rural notables, the medical doctors and surgeons, the priests and notaries who drew their incomes from small communities.[13] Wherever *mezzadria* predominated, a class of richer sharecroppers created a strong demand for consumer goods.

Districts already densely settled and cultivated could become more so. The spread of artificial pastures around Vicenza soon doubled the grain yields there, making them equal to the best in Europe. Near Turin great agricultural units, called *cassine* multiplied during the eighteenth century, using large numbers of casual labourers and the greater part of the region's oxen.[14] The steady increase of agricultural production was accomplished by greater input of peasant labour, rather than by improving methods. Few peasants could afford to keep large livestock. In Piedmont the number of head dropped by almost half between 1734 and 1809, thanks to the elimination of pastures, woods and fallow land, which shrank from a quarter of the arable to only a sixth in the same period. Uninterrupted population growth in mountain villages reduced peasant holdings with every generation, and pushed youths into permanent or seasonal migration.

Unlike in central Italy, where promiscuous culture provided the peasant household with a wide array of tasks, southern peasants spent much of the year with little to do. Extensive cereal cultivation, pasture on fallow and cropped fields remained characteristic of at least three-quarters of the kingdom of Naples. As the largest landowner, the baron was usually able to set local prices, and export whatever he wished. This power was offset only by his propensity to contribute charity to the poorest families.[15] The population climbed more quickly than that of northern Italy, from three million inhabitants in 1734, to four million in 1765 and five million in 1790. Land-hungry peasants sometimes seized the margins of uncultivated districts, such as the wild Sila plateau in Calabria, where they burned off the *macchia* cover and planted precarious crops. Some districts knew gradual economic progress. Landlords and merchants in Campania financed fruit and vegetable production to supply the huge capital city; Apulia supplied grain and olive oil for cooking and for textile finishing or soap-making; and Calabrian raw silk invigorated the local economy.[16] Prosperous districts remained the exception, and it is not certain that agricultural productivity – that is, the amount produced by a single peasant – increased in any substantial way. Moreover, this kind of commercialized agriculture benefited most the merchants (many of them foreigners, or based in Naples), who provided the money for the seed, cash to pay hired hands and for the renewal of farm plant. Merchants and capitalists thus reaped the profits from commercial agriculture more than in central Italy, where the sharecropper retained half the harvest for himself.

The shortcomings of Italian agriculture were brutally underscored by the disastrous harvest of 1763. Cities were spared the worst because authorities did their utmost to keep them supplied. The typhus epidemic in the famine's wake killed 20,000 to 30,000 people in Naples, often among the rural beggars seeking aid, and killed 200,000 people across the kingdom, about 5 per cent of the total population. The great famine was hard on Sicily too, where Mack Smith estimates that there were at least 30,000 fatalities.[17] The famine of 1764 was a watershed year in Italian economic history. Everywhere it gave momentum to critics of traditional ways of thinking about the land, the consistency of agricultural contracts, the inconveniences of excessive concentration of land, and the weight of annonary regulations that protected urban consumers at the expense of rural producers. These writers were all themselves landowners, belonging to a nebulous group of early liberal economists, the most famous of whom was the Frenchman François Quesnay, who advocated a theory called *physiocracy*. Its premise held that the "wealth of nations", including manufactures and commerce, derived in some way from agriculture. (This was not absurd in the eighteenth century.) To increase society's total wealth, economists argued, it was necessary to encourage agriculture, not manufactures, as Colbertist bureaucrats were accustomed to do. The theory held that the free movement of grain would permit a rational distribution of food according to the law of supply and demand. High prices would tempt landlords to increase production. Any interventionist meaures that "artificially" held prices down, like the annonary regulations, should be suppressed outright. Instead, the state should provide an infrastructure of roads, bridges, canals, stable currency and system of credit to foster economic exchange and intensify movement. It should suppress the multitude of internal customs duties that added considerably to the cost of merchandise. Other critics focused their attacks on a fiscal system that weighed more heavily on the countryside than on the city. Intellectuals in Naples and Rome found it scandalous that so much land was abandoned to sheep, because the state levied taxes on hides and meat, when the shortage of arable land caused widespread hunger. The Sienese Sallustio Bandini, author of a famous treatise in 1737, argued for the landlord's liberty to sell his harvest to the highest bidder, political boundaries notwithstanding. Landlords should enjoy stable individual possession of their property, free from gleaning and grazing by villagers; and be free to produce whatever they wished, without community constraints. Farmers and tenants would profit from improvements through longer leases.[18] Bandini's treatise received a wide audience, but it took the famine of 1764 to spur government action. The enthusiasm for innovation that agricultural academies promoted soon crept into government departments. With the warm endorsement of the Habsburg court, the Milanese *Società Patriotica* encouraged experiment as a civic duty. Grand Duke Pietro Leopoldo (1765–90), younger brother of the emperor Joseph II, put Tuscany into a pilot role by enacting a number of liberal measures.[19] He removed most of the restrictions on the movement of grain in 1767, and he suppressed the Florentine annonary agencies, the *Abbondanza* and the *Grascia,* in 1768. After 1781 landlords could ship their "surplus" wherever they wanted, and grain ships from Livorno were soon docking in Marseilles. Partly to increase the amount of arable land, partly to provide work for the poor, and partly to combat malaria, Pietro Leopoldo inaugurated bonification projects on an unprecedented scale, drawing workers from famished mountain villages. His belief in the virtues of private property and individual initiative led him to enact legislation to curb latifundia and landlord absenteeism. The lands of Jesuits and suppressed religious orders were distributed to smallholders in order to foster a rural bourgeoisie; emphyteusis contracts were established for very extended periods. The freedom granted to the commercialization of foodstuffs, was extended by Pietro Leopoldo to other crops, like silk.

Tuscan measures became the benchmarks for reforms in other regions, but the results did not live up to the expectations. As the number of landless *braccianti* multiplied, these strains became more apparent. Grain riots multiplied, as peasants plundered private granaries and stopped the conveyance of foodstuffs from their communities. In the kingdom of Naples, the economists Antonio Genovesi and Ferdinando Galiani proposed reforms similar to those of Tuscany as part of a grand scheme to transform the economic culture of the Mezzogiorno. Genovesi advocated the abolition of the Neapolitan *annones* after the famine of 1764. He and other prominent aristocratic thinkers, like Palmieri and Grimaldi, also advocated mass schooling to spread agrarian innovation and modern methods among the peasantry.[20] They urged the crown to abolish the Dogana of Foggia that entrenched graziers' interests over grain production in the fertile expanses of the Apulian Tavoliere.[21] The royal government, under the cautious Bernardo Tanucci, only fitfully liberalized the movement of cereals. Tanucci's plan was to redistribute lands confiscated from the Church to propertyless peasants on long leases (called *livelli*), in the hope that they would create a countervailing economic force to the barons in the countryside. In Sicily about 30,000 hectares were distributed to smallholders in this way. Like many "social engineering" schemes, this one produced exactly the opposite result to that which was intended, for peasants without access to capital like oxen and ploughs and the means to maintain them, soon fell into debt and sold their land to richer neighbours. If barons lost ground in the rural economy, it was to wealthy commoners who were poised to take advantage of improved conditions.

Grain prices rose relentlessly from the 1760s onward. In Lombardy the landless rural population was reduced to the rank of a Marxian proletariat.[22] In Tuscany there was substantial opposition to free trade not only from urban dwellers, but also from many peasants who were forced to buy food. Peasants living on larger *poderi* benefited, joining producers across Europe who experienced a measured prosperity. Most peasants wore proper shoes and dressed in finer clothes. With food prices up and industrial prices down, rustics acquired more goods. Observers commented, sometimes acerbically, on the new consumption habits of a good portion of the peasantry.[23] On the other hand, the number of landless labourers also increased, reflecting trends across western Europe. Agricultural academies helped find technical solutions to the problem of feeding more mouths, but they would not be widely applied until the next century. When grain riots broke out in Livorno in 1790, the grand duke intervened to dismantle his own liberal legislation.

Liberal economic theory is built on the premise that the law of supply and demand creates a natural harmony ensuring the well-being of the entire population. On this point, the jury is still out. Rising grain prices certainly enhanced the well-being of landowners and large producers, but made life more difficult for peasants with insufficient land, or for town-dwellers with no fixed livelihood. Since the supply of labour rose as quickly as, or more quickly than the total agricultural production, the Malthusian ceiling remained perilously close. Hunger and low wages increased the incidence of vagabondage in the late eighteenth century.[24]

Economic individualism did not work at all in mountain communities, where villagers vied for access to tracts of common lands for their flocks.[25] Population growth created a tremendous demand for wood for construction and for fuel. Pietro Leopoldo was astute enough to realize the disastrous consequences of breaking up common lands and selling them to individual landlords. So he established a *Comunità della Montagna* administration to prevent massive deforestation, dispensing subsidies and tax exemptions to mountain villages. The process of agricultural adaptation to population growth accentuated the contrasts between one region and another, and between the rich and the poor. This would be apparent in other economic sectors too.

Commercial Revival

Italian ports fairly bustled with energy and activity, as the rising population quickened economic exchange. The dynamic international situation gave a boost to all western economies, including peripheral ones like Italy. The gravitation of large-scale trade towards the Atlantic seaboard led to an explosion in transatlantic volume. Ports along the Atlantic seaboard doubled and tripled in size. The quays of Cadiz, Bordeaux, Rotterdam, London, Dublin, Hamburg, Copenhagen, Stockholm and Riga were jammed with ships as never before. English and French shipping penetrated every corner of the Mediterranean, seeking outlets for their manufactures and re-exporting colonial products like sugar and coffee, indigo and cod. The principal Italian ports still held their own. The profits of Genoese investors in 1785 were still equal to half the total income of the city.[26] Livorno's population climbed to more than 50,000 in 1790, when it was one of the Mediterranean's great ports, receiving 6,000 ships annually.[27] Tuscany's merchant capital acquired cafés, taverns, a theatre, a Turkish bath in the Oriental style, and a great central square that served as a stock exchange, but it could not rank with Marseilles or Cadiz.[28] Southern Europe remained one of the principal outlets for British commerce and industry. After 1700 Italian peasants began to buy printed cottons, *indiani*, unloaded from English vessels. Italian merchants used English ships to convey their goods, and insured them with London firms, generating invisible profits. English merchants collected Spanish silver in Livorno, Cadiz and Naples that paid for their purchases in China, in a new world-economy based on London.[29]

In 1719 the Austrian emperor attempted to promote Fiume (modern Rijeka in Croatia) by building a road to it from Vienna. The pope decreed Ancona a free port in 1732, and tried to launch Civitavecchia similarly in the 1740s. Ships from Naples were permitted to trade freely in the Adriatic after 1734. None enjoyed such

expansion as Trieste in the Austrian Empire, the closest port to
Vienna, Bohemia and the Danube corridor. The value of its commerce tripled between 1762 and 1782, to a level equal to 70 per cent
of the traffic of nearby Venice.[30] Despite the new competition,
Venetian seaborne commerce tripled in the decades after 1735. Its
400 ships in 1780 constituted only about 2 per cent of the European
total, and Levantine commerce was only a shadow of its past glory,
although Venetian companies trading with the Ottoman Empire
were situated in third place, after French and English ones.
Agricultural exports from Venice surpassed the manufactured ones
in value in the eighteenth century.

What dynamic Italian ports all had in common was the colonial
nature of their trade, exporting foodstuffs and semi-finished raw
materials, and importing manufactured goods. Naples imported textiles, leather and metal goods, and exported olive oil, wheat, wool
and raw silk. Shipments of Neapolitan wool went primarily to the
booming textile manufactures of southern France. Naples imported
twice as many silks as it exported; four times as much cotton, and
fifteen times as much linen.[31] These figures must be considered
minima, for legitimate commerce was a screen for smuggling on a
vast scale. Sicilians smuggled out products in order to avoid the
export taxes, while smuggling silks and tobacco into the kingdom
from vessels hovering offshore. All the large merchants indulged in
it; they could operate under false flags, or make false declarations of
tonnage. They could bribe, or use brute force to chase away the
customs agents. Society sympathized and collaborated with smugglers, and the government usually turned a blind eye for fear of
antagonizing the population. The royal administration proved so
inefficient that *philosophes* considered smuggling a necessary evil. It is
impossible to know either exact trade quantities or even who benefited most.[32]

Italian manufacturing in 1720 was only a shadow of its splendour
of a century earlier. After 1650 Italians preferred luxury textiles
"made in France", or else imitations of them. Silk manufactures
faced serious competition from France, and, increasingly from the
Dutch and the English. Conventional solutions were generally mercantilistic, that is, they followed the belief that government should
regulate the production and distribution of commodities or manufactures in order to avoid wasteful competition. The prince's tools of
intervention were many: he could confer monopolies for an entire
country, or for a city or region, permanently or for a fixed term;

raise customs duties; bestow patents; decree fixed prices; grant tax relief; make loan guarantees or outright gifts to defray start-up costs; dispense with guild regulations, or favour merchants and artisans with speedy and inexpensive justice.[33] French, English and Dutch success in their state-sponsored or protected ventures made mercantilism the accepted economic orthodoxy everywhere, and the promotion of the economy became one of the responsibilities of a conscientious prince.

The Austrian emperor promoted such policies in the areas that came under his sway after 1708, in a variant of mercantilism known as *cameralism*.[34] The state itself was a consumer with a prodigious appetite for military commodities.[35] The manufacturing activity benefited the Imperial heartland of Vienna and Prague essentially, while little returned to Milan or Naples or Brussels, which were regional capitals. Nevertheless, the Austrians undertook mercantilist initiatives of their own. Charles VI made plans to create new industries for Sicily, establishing Messina as a free port in 1720. The city would become with state support a "pole of development" which would give new scope to existing industries, such as cloth and silk, and create new ones producing paper, soap and glass. This approach is markedly similar to the strategy adopted to industrialize the Mezzogiorno in the 1960s. Vienna backed the textile manufactures that the Swiss entrepreneur Teuffen established in Lombardy in 1704, and encouraged the Germans Kramer and Schmitz to establish new ones at Milan and Monza. Austrian cameralists also encouraged a silk textile industry in the Adige river valley south of Trento, whose products were sold in the Imperial heartland. It granted silk entrepreneurs privileges and charters, handed out subsidies and provided trained help, making Rovereto one of the most important silk-producing areas in Italy.[36]

The Bourbons retained Colbertist traditions in Parma and Naples, where princes founded manufactures by decree. The court in Naples and Caserta was a major source of consumption. Charles III created an assortment of prestige industries on the example of his great-grandfather, Louis XIV, like a tapestry factory similar to the Gobelins manufacture in Paris. His Saxon queen nurtured a porcelain factory on the model of Meissen, which produced exquisite items for the court. Charles established a royal academy of design in 1752, and then an academy of architecture in 1762, all projects which had an impact on the amount and the quality of building in the city. Ferdinand IV created manufactures of silk, leather goods, porcelain, cotton and shipbuilding, but without the capital and prestige acquisitions of the royal court, these enterprises were uneconomical and could not survive.[37] In the 1780s the court favourite, John Acton, launched a significant fleet of warships and built a constellation of military establishments around the bay. He transformed Castellammare into the largest naval yard in Italy, and built a weapons factory nearby at Torre Annunziata.

State-protected industry further depressed surviving private manufactures. Silk-weaving declined almost everywhere in the eighteenth century. The number of workers it employed could still be locally considerable. Of the 25,000 textile workers in Florence in 1765, a third worked silk, but Italian products aimed generally for the low end of the market. Piedmontese skilled artisans often came from Lyons, the centre with the most advanced production techniques. The manufacture of silk textiles in Europe exploded in the late seventeenth century, first at Lyons, then at Spitalfields near London, Krefeld in Germany and Zurich in Switzerland. It was established by French Calvinist refugees. Circa 1770 European looms produced 11 million pounds worth, two-thirds of it using Italian raw materials. The production of raw silk and silk thread, dried in great furnaces, and then spun in water-driven mills using a little peasant labour, became the principal Italian "industry" of the eighteenth century.[38] The *mezzadria* system made it difficult for vast numbers of peasants to spend time working at looms, as in England or France, but it did enable landlords to introduce new "industrial" crops alongside the traditional ones. A staggering increase in the amount of land consecrated to mulberry trees tried to meet the international demand for raw silk.[39] Villagers, especially the landless *pigionali*, intensified the rough stages of the silk-making process: mulberry-growing, silkworm-breeding, silk-filament joining, weft-spinning and yarn preparation.[40] Technology varied considerably from one region to another. Calabrian and Sicilian thread was the most rudimentary. In Tuscan centres like Pescia, water turned the mills for threading and twisting. Piedmont's factory mills in Turin and Racconigi produced the finest grades.[41] Italian states attempted to reap the benefits of this huge production of raw materials by forbidding its export, but subjects flouted these laws everywhere. It was not enough to have the best raw material on hand to sustain a vigorous silk-weaving industry, like in the past. French products were superior and competitively priced. Italian producers not only used archaic technology, but their market was fragmented into small jurisdictions.

Woollens declined too. They were completely outclassed by imports from England, France and Holland. Italian products employed poor thread, poorly dyed and badly woven in comparison with foreign goods. A new phase in Italian industry commenced at Schio, near Vicenza in 1738, when Niccolo Tron introduced the flying shuttle of John Kay, complete with English machinists, in a proper factory operated by water power. Other Schio looms produced French-style woollens to compete on the Italian, German and Turkish markets, but they enjoyed only mixed success. Cotton manufactures appeared here and there in northern Italy, at Chieri, in Milan, and in the villages of the Brianza, where parish priests instructed women and girls how to weave it. The first cotton mill using the mule jenny was introduced by Kramer at Monza in 1795. Linens, cottons and woollens, often with a mixture of hemp thread, left hand looms in increasing numbers. This was the production of rural towns, like Biella in Piedmont, Busto Arsizio in Lombardy, Prato in Tuscany, Schio and Thiene in the Veneto. Only occasionally does one find the concentration of hundreds of workers, like the Milan cotton works of the brothers Rho, who produced cheap articles for the lower classes. Italian manufactures lagged far behind their north European rivals.

Most other industries lost their impetus as well. In Milan the arms and metallurgy industries moved to mountain valleys and simplified their processes. The Milanese and the Brescian industry began hiring Germans to run the mines and the foundries, both as owner-managers and as paid workmen. There was no revival of urban manufactures. In the republic of Venice, all the master artisans of the state combined amounted to less than 20 per cent of the peasant families. Venetian exports that had held up during the previous century – paper, glass and gold-leaf silk – gradually declined. Glassware suffered from French competition, and then from Bohemian crystal. Instead, rural-based manufactures produced cheap articles for popular consumption. Their operation made recruitment of rural women and children a necessity for simple products, like draperies. Only rarely did such work pay workers living wages, but they were complementary to agricultural earnings. Merchants gave out work as well to convents, hospitals and conservatories, where the inmates laboured to achieve redemption. Proto-industry was necessary for peasant survival, and it flourished only because wages were amongst the lowest in Europe. It was not everywhere viable.

How did guilds adapt to these transformations? A regulated economy usually pursues goals other than simple material abundance. The rules of the trades were deeply imbued with principles of moral economy: the just price, the common good and distributive justice. They fostered prudence, equilibrium, cooperation and order. Eighteenth-century corporations were more intransigent than ever over questions of priority and competition. They still acted as tribunals to limit market "opportunism" that threatened to upset the urban manufacturing economy. To the protestations emanating from master craftsmen, urban authorities either reissued the old regulations or turned a blind eye to their infraction. Venice moved towards opening its corporations in 1719. In Tuscany the reforms of 1770 emptied them of their force. In papal Bologna the cardinal legate undermined the guild system by giving out permits and licences indiscriminately. Governments hesitated to take the radical step of dissolving guilds altogether and opening trade and manufacture to free enterprise, but the traditional institutions lost their monopolies nevertheless.[42]

Governments did what they could to reverse industrial decline, by allocating resources to infrastructure like roads. There were few good roads for wheeled vehicles in Italy, outside Piedmont and Lombardy. In 1766 Pietro Leopoldo of Tuscany diverted much tax revenue to building an infrastructure of roads, bridges and canals, alongside expenditures on social welfare such as hospitals, schools and mineral baths. The Bourbons of Naples began work on a modern road network too. Army engineers repaired harbour facilities and highways in the wake of earthquakes. As in France and Spain, the system was designed to make it easier to reach the capital, rather than to improve access from the interior to the nearest port. While the agrotowns of Apulia and the lush districts of Campania were well served, it remained difficult to travel from one province to another by road, and this accentuated regional disparities rather than reduced them.[43]

The eighteenth century gives the impression of prosperity when compared with the bleak depression of the century after 1630. No initiative brought Italy back from the rear of the European pack in terms of economic development. Hard times in the 1770s and 1780s swelled the number of families living on relief and soured the traditional benevolent attitude towards urban workers and the poor.[44] If, in relative terms, Italy dropped even further behind northern European countries, the malaise was not everywhere visible. There were more shops than ever before, selling on credit. Cafés, delicatessens, dry-goods shops appeared even in small towns.[45] Minor centres producing low-quality goods for the inhabitants of the countryside profited from the increasing food prices. Alongside the nobles and clergy appeared more modest rural and town elites with money to spend.

One compensation for the negative balance of payments must have been the development of sightseeing, for young gentlemen on the Grand Tour with money to burn.[46] Eighteenth-century Italy was cheap for a northern European. Tourists flocked to aristocratic palaces to view the art accumulated there over centuries. They ventured to the excavation sites of Herculaneum, unearthed in 1738, and Pompeii after 1748, to view ancient civilization first-hand. Venice continued to be the capital of hedonism. Rome was also more interested in attracting tourists than pilgrims, for their purchasing power was incomparably greater. Antiquarianism became a burgeoning activity. Guides presented themselves to gawking tourists and worked with "agents" selling fake masterpieces to avid amateurs. Painters portrayed the local sights, such as the canal scenes of Canaletto or Francesco Guardi in Venice, or the Roman vistas of Pannini, elaborate postcards or mementoes. Hanns Gross calls the art market the true *Datary* (revenue office) in eighteenth-century Rome. Entrepreneurs undertook the excavation of archaeological sites like open-cast mines, and sold the treasures to buyers across Europe.

However, economic history still focuses on the concept of "development", the long process of capital accumulation. The eighteenth-century innovations did not prepare Italy for the industrial revolution after 1880 in any meaningful way. Large-scale manufacturing further declined for most of the nineteenth century, after the Napoleonic conquest disrupted whatever existed.[47] We know little about the other important dimension, that is, the standard of living of the population that extensive work on post-mortem inventories will elucidate in tandem with more studies on infant mortality.[48] The framework of material life became more diverse after 1750. There were new objects, of better quality, produced more cheaply than ever before. People were a bit better educated, living a bit longer. A large minority, or perhaps a small majority of Italians were living better than before, and innovative policies of Enlightenment regimes might have aided this development.

25 Absolutist Reforms in Bourbon Italy

The Bourbons and Naples

Prince Charles's conquest of his Neapolitan and Sicilian thrones in 1734 turned out to be a military promenade, cheered by Neapolitans nostalgic for the low taxation and the light-handed rule that characterized the late seventeenth century. Now Naples would be a proper kingdom, with its own monarch and a host of institutions proper to it: a court, an army and a fiscal administration. The adolescent Charles's reference monarch was his great-grandfather, Louis XIV, but beyond that influence, the Bourbons in both Madrid and Naples were more anti-feudal, anti-papal, more centralizing and more systematically mercantilistic than the Spanish Habsburgs had ever been.[1] Charles also consciously imitated his royal great-grandfather by pursuing a policy of *gloire*, expressed through a panoply of new artistic institutions. Charles needed monuments of royal dimension, which were almost entirely lacking. Palaces rose near his favourite hunting grounds: at Portici, the Capodimonte, and finally Caserta, which would be a great ministerial palace within easy reach of the capital, just like Versailles.[2] Another instrument of royal *gloire* was the army. Philip V gave his son a veteran nucleus to a larger force he would establish on the French model. Madrid's plan was to build an indigenous army, in order to help Spain restore its Italian hegemony. To lure the nobles into it, Charles founded a chivalric order in 1738 to inspire dynastic devotion in Neapolitan nobles, but to little avail. The appeal of an honourable career in the king's service was not enough to rally the aristocracy to the army.[3]

Neapolitan nobles could see that Charles, for all the Bourbon trappings, was not an autonomous monarch. His chief minister, the Count of Santo Stefano took orders from Charles's mother. The next chief minister was another Spaniard, the Marquis de Montealegre, who for eight years referred all important matters to Madrid. Charles was only "emancipated" in 1746 when his father died. The Spanish-appointed personnel nevertheless laboured to reform the kingdom in a spurt of initiatives between 1736 and 1742. Bourbon policy with its Gallican roots sought to curtail ecclesiastical jurisdiction and asylum almost immediately, and pondered ways to overturn ecclesiastical mortmain.[4] Critics claimed the Church immobilized almost one million hectares of land in the kingdom, about 15 per cent of the total surface.[5] Royal pressure on the Neapolitan Church bore fruit with the conclusion of the concordat with Rome in 1741. This accord subjected ecclesiastics to significant royal taxation for the first time and also established a royal presence on church courts.

Another series of policies aimed to enhance the effectiveness of the sprawling judicial system, which was mostly in feudal hands. The monarchy would willingly have extinguished feudal jurisdictions, but it lacked the money to pay for magistrates and police.[6] Madrid placed judicial affairs in the hands of a Tuscan law professor from the University of Pisa, Bernardo Tanucci. The reform he launched in 1736 forced feudal magistrates to submit their conclusions on homicide cases to the upper-level royal tribunals of the *Real Udienze* (in the provinces) and the *Vicaria* (in Naples). Moreover, to prevent the routine sale of pardons, judges were to report all of the compositions following homicides. A more ambitious measure created the *Supremo Magistrato del Commercio* at the end of 1739. Because delay caused irreparable harm to merchants, specialized courts dealing exclusively with trade aimed to disentangle litigation quickly. The Neapolitan version introduced Italian as the procedural language; charged only a third or a quarter of the usual court costs; admitted experts in business to present arguments alongside lawyers; and placed judges and scribes on a fixed stipend to dissuade them from multiplying the decisions in each case. Magistrates saw this as the annexation of much of their business by the Crown, and placed obstacles in the way of its implementation. It was symptomatic of the disappointment Neapolitan elites felt before more forceful rulers.

Charles's involvement in the War of the Austrian Succession in 1741 made his minority status painfully obvious. The royal parents commanded their son to dispatch an army to the Po valley. War brought the period of sweeping reforms to a halt, and obliged the young king to negotiate new taxes with the *seggi* of the capital city and with the Church. Arbitrary tax hikes, coupled with reforms that struck at ecclesiastical and judicial autonomy, caused widespread dissatisfaction. Charles and his justice minister Tanucci came down heavily on noble plotting by arresting 800 people in 1742 and 1743. The Crown tried them before a special jurisdiction, the *Giunta d'Inconfidenza*. Charles subjected his fate to the outcome of a single battle, at Velletri, on 11 August 1744. Spanish regular troops and Neapolitan levies repulsed the Austrian attack on their entrenchments, although king Charles narrowly missed being captured. The victory saved the regime and resigned the plotters to the perenniality of the dynasty. Most of the previous reforms had to be jettisoned in 1746, however, in exchange for precious *donativi* to continue the war.

Charles's most difficult task was to ally the aristocracy to his regime. The Naples *seggi* nobility retained considerable power over urban matters and the annones administration by which the city was fed. They served as a sounding board for royal policies, and did not hesitate to oppose projects that threatened their interests. Nobles were exempt from most taxes, and were allowed to declare their own revenues to tax officers, which they habitually underestimated. The army was supposed to be another integrative institution that simultaneously rewarded nobles and shaped them professionally. The creation of a dozen "national" regiments tried to reverse the demilitarization affecting the Italian aristocracy as a whole. Another way to professionalize nobles was to create technical institutions for them, like the naval academy founded in 1735, artillery academy in 1744, and an engineer school in 1754. The encouragement of the "service nobility" ethic reflected an official desire to open up the aristocracy to families possessing money, talent, or a record of public service. A special cadet corps reserved for the sons of noblemen also admitted sons of provincial magistrates and of important merchants. Notables living in provincial towns gradually pushed their way to influential positions. This undermined the traditional network of patronage and power accruing to the great families of Naples.[7] If nobles retained the monopoly of prestige positions at court, the crown offered power in the state and the Church to people it considered faithful servants, as in France.

Crown policy over time sought to reincorporate feudal jurisdictions to the royal domain. By 1789 at least 20 per cent of the kingdom was in the royal jurisdiction, and feudal prerogatives had by then been reduced to a shell. Barons had few reasons to be grateful to the new regime. From the outset, Tanucci intended to prune the extensive feudal privileges in the Mezzogiorno, even though barons were less likely to be *prepotente* criminals in the more "policed" eighteenth century. If seigneurial violence was more the exception than the rule, barons still perpetrated a number of customary jurisdictional "abuses" against municipal governments.[8] They usurped communal lands and expected vassals to pay a fee for each animal grazing there. They often shifted their own fiscal burden on to the *università*, like the tax imposed on feudal lords in lieu of military service. They expected their vassals to subsidize family events, like weddings and baptisms, and made the community pay for baronial employees. They often expected their vassals to provide unpaid service, called *angarie*, carting and hauling, repairing and restoring, providing firewood. They undermined communal monopolies by setting up butcher's stalls, ovens and taverns that competed with those of the community (whose licence fees provided revenue for the town). Barons often forced the community to award generous contracts to their clients, insisted on the right to veto the community's elected officials, or else expected the *università* to approve the slate of clients they presented to them. Court challenges to these abuses often lasted decades, and constituted a serious drain on local treasuries.

Although Charles III considered himself an absolute monarch, Bernardo Tanucci emerged as the leading personality in the 1740s. By the 1750s he was drawing intelligent Neapolitan collaborators into the administration to replace foreigners. Charles appointed him head of the royal household and minister of foreign affairs. One commission he launched in 1742 drew up a compendium of laws to lessen judicial confusion and create a legal consciousness in civil society.[9] Tanucci also supervised the completion of a cadastral register in 1742 that laid the groundwork for further improvement in calculating direct taxes. The energetic Tuscan bureaucrat also set out to redeem royal rights over customs duties and excises that had been alienated to creditors of the regime. By simplifying procedures, he almost doubled state revenue by the time of Charles's departure for Spain in 1759, and yet the per-capita tax weight on subjects diminished. However, since a broad cross-section of the kingdom held stock in state debt, the crown hesitated to assume complete ownership and collection of taxes.[10]

Tanucci stimulated the economy with Colbertian mercantilist measures. His reorganization of the University of Naples created a new
chair in political economy for Antonio Genovesi in 1754. Genovesi
preached radical economic reform, and the loosening of the corset
of monopolies and regulations governing the agricultural economy.
Since he did not share the philosopher's faith that free markets
would benefit most subjects, Tanucci was usually deaf to Genovesi's
entreaties. Instead, he tightened regulations on the annones, which
profited speculators and purveyors of foodstuffs to the capital.[11]
After the dire famine of 1764, he assented to some liberalization,
and followed Genovesi's ideas about land reform more closely. The
economist wanted to force landlords to concede long-term rents to
peasant tenants who would cultivate land better and reap the benefits. Tanucci obliged him by redistributing land confiscated from the
Jesuits in 1767 in small parcels to peasants.

Tanucci left a deep mark on southern Italy through his suspicion
of priests and friars, and of the Roman Curia most of all. Elite public
opinion was alarmed by the vast number of priests, monks and nuns,
their jurisdiction over families and communities, their wealth and
their immunity to taxation. The Concordat of 1741 between
Benedict XIV and Naples addressed some of these complaints. The
clergy lost its immunities to customs duties, ecclesiastical lands paid
half the taxes paid by secular owners, and lay judges sat by ecclesiastical judges in diocesan courts. Tanucci's anti-curial attitudes hardened over the years, and Charles left him much leeway. Pious
organizations were forbidden to acquire new land by sale or donation. The royal government established its own poorhouse in Naples
in 1751, an enormous hospice under the supervision of the
Dominican, Gregorio Rocco, the *lazzaroni* missionary. Tanucci and
the minister De Carlo supported and protected Jansenists, often in
defiance of Rome.

In 1759 Charles III succeeded to the Spanish throne following the
death of his stepbrother Ferdinand VI. When he departed for
Madrid he left his adolescent third son Ferdinando king in his stead.
Tanucci now had no counterweight in the regency council. First he
claimed the revenues of vacant benefices that traditionally belonged
to the pope, called the *regale*. Then he tried to detach Neapolitan
religious orders from the tutelage of their Roman headquarters.
Following the initiative of other states, he forbade testators to leave
legacies for masses in their wills. He quickly and enthusiastically followed Madrid's initiative in expelling the Jesuits in 1768, on the spe-

cious grounds that the order was worldly and corrupt. In subsequent years Tanucci passed a series of anti-clerical laws, suppressing convents and tithes, forbidding mortmain, and exacting royal permission for allowing the publication of ecclesiastical decrees, which was known as the *exequatur.* Tanucci set an example to the Habsburg monarchs, who followed with similar legislation soon after. He ordered other monasteries to set up free schools for the poor from their own resources. When relations with the new pope Pius VI Braschi soured, Tanucci suspended payment of the *chinea,* the symbolic annual tribute that recognized the Pope's suzerainty over the kingdom. His successors issued decrees in a similar spirit. In 1782 the crown appointed one of Italy's most vociferous Jansenists, Giovanni Andrea Serrao, bishop of Potenza. He used his position and his authority to spread the ideas of "liberty" among his clergy and the population, while trying to uproot the popular miraculist and dolorist religion of his flock. A decree from Naples prohibited the recruitment of new friars without royal permission, and in the 1780s the viceroy of Sicily closed down all the Capuchin noviciates in the island. The effect of these measures on monastic recruitment paled next to the great Calabrian earthquake in 1783. The crown awarded itself relief funds in a *Cassa Sacra,* suppressing monasteries and seizing their properties, on the false pretext of giving the proceeds to the victims.[12] All of these measures went against the grain of the evangelization of the rural masses by missionaries. The reforms only deepened the cultural chasm between the Enlightenment elite and the rural population.

After practically forty years of uninterrupted power, Bernardo Tanucci eventually wearied the court circles in Naples. Ferdinando had become king at the age of 16, but remained long after an ignorant and uncouth boy who frolicked with lackeys, earning the nickname of the *lazzaroni* king. In 1768 his father married him to Maria Carolina, daughter of the Habsburg Empress Maria Theresia, in one of a spate of Bourbon–Habsburg marriages that cemented the alliance between the dynasties after 1756. The queen was eager to play a political role and to supplant the Madrid influence that Tanucci incarnated with a Viennese one. Bourbon tradition only admitted her to the royal council after she had given birth to an heir, seven years later. She then engineered the downfall of Tanucci, who was gracefully retired in 1776.

His replacement, the marquis of Sambuca, and other ministers were students of Antonio Genovesi and Ferdinando Galiani. They placed economic reform before the struggle against Rome, expecting that other benefits would flow from it. They identified the power of the Church and feudalism over the countryside as social evils. Naples in the 1770s was opening to influences from France, Germany and England as never before. Intellectuals and even on occasion ministers advocated a liberalized grain trade, but the government preferred to retain the annones, which assured the well-being of the capital. The crown, like many *Ancien Régime* governments, viewed the economy primarily as something from which to draw revenue. Like France, the complexity of the fiscal system defied description. There was no single reference for weights and measures in the kingdom. Some royal dues were still ceded to private individuals or to feudatories. The customs administration was clumsy, complicated and time-wasting, but its suppression would have entailed a serious short-term loss of revenue. In the silk sector, poorly-paid officials regulating production and collecting the duties (or *tratte*) helped organize the contraband themselves. Only tolerated illegality saved the sector from collapse.

In 1778 the royal couple sent for a dashing Franco-Irish Jacobite who had served in the French and Tuscan navies, named John Acton. Queen Maria Carolina found him the perfect collaborator. She awarded him the war ministry in 1780, the finance and commerce ministries in 1782, and then the position of chief minister in 1789. Acton, who referred most political decisions directly to the queen, laid out a series of ambitious economic reforms after 1782. He revived a Supreme Council of Finances that served as a ministry of economics, similar to the one functioning in Habsburg Milan. Acton virtually dismantled the grain provisioning system, and began undermining guild jurisdictions and monopolies. He reduced high protectionist duties, signing a series of commercial treaties with Tripoli, Piedmont-Sardinia and Russia (1785–7), and restored the free port at Messina. In 1787 the Supreme Finance Council proposed sweeping measures to encourage the cultivation of fallow land, which justified further interference in local jurisdictions at the expense of feudal lords. In the 1780s the anti-feudal polemic began in earnest, as the monarchy decided it could dispense with the system. The Neapolitan *philosophe* Gaetano Filangieri called for the crown to abolish feudal jurisdictions outright. This might not have been a good thing, owing to the confusion and the corruption of the royal bureaucracy, but the crown was listening. In 1791 the Supreme Finance Council decided that fiefs that devolved to the crown should be broken up and distributed to smallholders, free of any feudal charges, in order to encourage full property rights and agricultural individualism. In 1792 Filangieri approved the decision to privatize communal lands and abolish traditional grazing rights. The onset of the French Revolution then completed the rapid disarticulation of the feudal system that had weighed for centuries on the Mezzogiorno. Only with the French occupation in 1806 did the state suppress all monastic orders, sweep away all the fiefs, and confiscate all state revenues in private hands.[13]

By the 1780s Naples was firmly in the Habsburg sphere of influence. Joseph II visited the kingdom in 1783 to consolidate the policies promoted by his sister and her Jacobite minister. Naples ceased to pay the *chinea* to Rome. This was tantamount to declaring independence. Acton launched the Neapolitan navy from virtually nothing to a sizeable force within a decade, and a weapons factory at Torre Annunziata diminished the dependency on France. He also repaired and strengthened fortresses, and his army engineers rebuilt harbours and highways in peacetime after earthquakes. Acton sought to rebuild the army, by importing foreign officers and cadres, primarily French, to increase its efficiency. He had no more success than his predecessors. Many of the French officers and non-commissioned officers he relied on went home during the Revolution, and Germans took their places. The soldiery resented the severe discipline of Prussian-style drill and tended to desert in droves. The performance of the units sent to hold Toulon against the Republican army left much to be desired. These war-clouds on the horizon stalled the momentum of the anti-feudal reforms that had marked the previous half-century.

The Bourbon Regime in Sicily

Charles united both Naples and Sicily in 1734 in an entity called the kingdom of the Two Sicilies. Nevertheless, he ruled Sicily as an autonomous dependency of the crown. Establishing a French-style absolutist monarchy in Sicily was more daunting than in Naples. Sicily's social immobilism, its vendetta tradition, administrative corruption, its inextinguishable banditry scandalized Victor Amadeus of Piedmont in the five-year Piedmontese experiment (1713–18), just as it stymied Charles VI in Vienna. The Austrian interregnum was forced to come to terms with the inherent pro-Spanish sentiment of the population. Sicilians welcomed the Spanish again in 1734, and while they resented being reduced to an appendage of Naples, they cherished the Iberian connection. The island's noble-dominated parliament made a vigorous defence of the kingdom's traditions and of its own interests.[14] After the first failure of a Supreme Magistracy of Trade, Charles tried to avoid requesting *donativi* from the island's Parliament. Local nobles still enjoyed uncontrolled discretion to allocate local taxes, while government censuses and property registers on which taxes were assessed were decades out of date. The numerous excise barriers were also obstacles to trade, for they restricted consumption. These limitations of the king's power were compounded by widespread administrative corruption, itself practically "structural". Inspections of the Palermo customs office under the Piedmontese, Austrians and the Bourbons revealed a perennial system of kickbacks, whereby privileged landowners who could export grain without a licence extended this benefit to their relations and clients. Consumers, however, preferred a system of controls on their grain supplies.

The proliferation of separate courts, with their overlapping civil and criminal jurisdiction and privileges, proved to be an even greater impediment to good government.[15] Competing procedures were a daunting hindrance to trade. They gave merchants freedom from seizures while appeals were pending, and transformed every commercial complication into an entrepreneur's nightmare. Such a situation made any kind of economic reform difficult. The inadequate system of road transport for wheeled vehicles to connect the ports with the interior only compounded the evils of legal imbroglio and official corruption. The viceroys were rarely forceful enough to impose Naples's decisions on the island's elites. Even in smaller royal jurisdictions, relatives of a baron would exempt themselves from taxes, place their wards in comfortable public orphanages, commandeer civic charities and divert municipal revenues for their private benefit. Elsewhere the baron and his *gabellotho* hired private "guards" to compel peasants to obedience. Over time the feudatories lost ground to their own *gabellotti*, who increasingly took the economic initiative. When a series of grain riots in Palermo shook the Bourbon regime in 1773, King Ferdinando decided to treat Sicily more sternly. Viceroys were instructed to send nobles to prison for their misdemeanours. Naples also began to lift the much-abused market regulations on the Sicilian economy, to the applause of the more dynamic merchant community of Catania. No measure had more impact than the dispatch of the Neapolitan *philosophe*, Domenico Caracciolo, to the island as viceroy in 1781. Having resided in Paris for some years, he had only contempt for the traditional religiosity of the great mass of Sicilians, and felt that a strong hand would work wonders. Caracciolo was a moderate anti-clerical who intended to suppress ecclesiastical tax immunities, curtail the jurisdiction of church courts and end the practice of seeking asylum in churches. When he suppressed the Spanish Inquisition in 1782, it held only three witches in its prisons. Caracciolo erred, however, in truncating the five-day festival of Santa Rosalia in Palermo, which almost provoked an uprising. The king and queen, who normally stood behind him, countermanded the order. Caracciolo worked also to prune back the number of officials, in an attempt to increase government efficiency. Collectors of taxes, superintendents of public works, civic officials were instructed to have their accounts ready for audit. He also restricted the carrying of weapons in the streets, banned indecent masks and festivities in Carnival, restricted gambling, and tried to stop bull-fighting and nocturnal celebrations, all customs he considered too "Spanish".

Caracciolo's main concern was the dominant place the baronage occupied in Sicilian society. First, he required documentary proof of their jurisdiction, and he verified it. No longer could feudatories arrest their vassals without stated reason. Furthermore, Caracciolo encouraged vassals to buy back their rights to the royal demesne. Feudal towns began to appeal against baronial requests for money to the crown. The Crown arrested nobles for protecting delinquents, for browbeating local authorities, or for suborning witnesses. These measures helped undermine traditional deference, and creditors began to pressure aristocrats to pay their debts. The levelling trend led to a project aimed at subjecting nobles to direct taxes in proportion to their wealth. This measure required a new census, and with it a proper evaluation of property free from parliamentary interference. Another egalitarian measure from Naples sought to encourage the development of small farms with the spoils of the Jesuit order. Despite the ambition of these reforms, Caracciolo had no team of enthusiastic supporters to help him transform the kingdom. Sicilians objected to his Parisian manners and openness to talents that were hallmarks of French Enlightenment aristocracy. Notables felt that he was undermining the traditional constitution, which was true, and pressed for his recall.

The king replaced him with another Neapolitan Freemason, the prince of Caramanico, who pressed on with reforms after 1786. He persuaded Parliament to accept the land survey, to restrict feudal privileges, and to tighten laws of inheritance, all of which penalized the aristocracy. In 1788 the king also decreed that barons should henceforth hold their fiefs in exchange for service. Royal confirmation and a special payment were exacted before any fief could be inherited, and fiefs would revert to the crown upon interrupted succession. Another edict in 1789 abolished the last traces of personal servitude, or serfdom properly speaking.

The French Revolutionary period saw the emergence of a meagre number of Jacobins in Naples itself, consisting of young aristocrats, students and seamen. As elsewhere in Europe, the Revolution assassinated the Enlightenment, and brought to an abrupt halt the most ambitious reform programmes. The queen, who was distraught at the fate of her brother-in-law, Louis XVI, and then of her sister, Marie-Antoinette, established a new *Giunta d'Inconfidenza* to arrest and try plotters against the monarchical regime. In 1798, with Napoleon Bonaparte stranded in Egypt, Lord Nelson convinced Acton and Maria Carolina that it was time to expel the French republican armies from Italy. But the units dissolved on contact with French troops. Ferdinando and Maria Carolina salvaged a few ships and made for Sicily, where the British fleet protected them from pursuit. In 1799 the monarchy was restored by a rising of peasant guerrillas following monks, under the global direction of Cardinal Ruffo. They swept from power the Jansenists and republicans who emerged in the brief French-supported republic. Peasant insurgents butchered in his bed the leader of the Jansenist clergy, Bishop Serrao, and paraded his head around Potenza on a pike, as French revolutionaries were wont to do with aristocrats. For the Mezzogiorno, the most innovative period before the mid-twentieth century was over.

The Bourbons of Parma

The Bourbon family compact prevailed at the peace of Aix-la-Chapelle in 1748, as their arms tended to prevail on the battlefield. Philip, the second of Elisabeth Farnese's sons, ascended the throne in his mother's Parman birthplace, where Austria had ruled since the extinction of the dynasty's direct line in 1731. Philip in Parma and Charles in Naples still depended upon their half-brother

Ferdinand in Madrid for their soldiers, their diplomats and their finances. The Bourbon alliance with Austria in 1756 secured the regime from danger of reconquest.

The Bourbon regime in Parma was long dominated by a single powerful minister, Guillaume du Tillot, who arrived in Parma in 1749 as the ducal secretary. The son of a minor French functionary who followed Philip V to Spain at the turn of the century, he personified the Bourbon officials administering both France and Spain. Du Tillot emerged as the leading minister in Parma in the late 1750s, ironically as an agent of Bourbon absolutism. He remodelled the court on French lines. Theatre, the fine arts and literary salons all followed French fashion, and the ducal library accumulated an impressive number of French books. Du Tillot employed French specialists even at the subalternate levels of artists, bankers, soldiers, gardeners and cooks. Native Parmans resented their preponderance. His policy measures were in keeping with Bourbon traditions. He limited feudal jurisdiction from the outset. Not particularly devout, du Tillot participated in religious ceremonies only on feast days. His economic measures were Colbertist in inspiration. Foreign skilled labour and special privileges helped launch new textile and soap manufactures. Du Tillot also encouraged the silk industry by planting mulberry trees. He retained protectionist customs barriers, leaving the guilds undisturbed outside the official manufactures. There was no initiative to lift the controls on the grain trade, but he promoted agriculture, sponsored new crops and products, and helped transform Parman patricians into agronomists.[16]

The peril in Parma came from the papacy's claim to the duchy, since it had been originally created for the Farnese family out of the Papal States, and had never been returned. In 1764 du Tillot issued a decree prohibiting mortmain, after negotiations with Rome on the issue had fallen through. Parma seemed a small, easy target for Rome to recover ground lost to princes elsewhere, so the Curia retaliated with a decree denouncing the ducal edict. Du Tillot was thus pushed to create a Royal Junta of Jurisdiction. The Junta limited the authority of ecclesiastical courts, imposed a royal *exequatur*, disciplined the regular clergy, and suppressed a few convents. The duke of Parma banned all appeals by clergy to Rome without ducal assent; forbade clergy from applying to Rome for pensions and benefices; and made it illegal to confer a benefice on anyone not a ducal subject. All papal briefs and bulls were invalid unless they carried the duke's signature. Parma also followed Madrid's lead in 1767 by expelling the Jesuits. Pope Clement XIII replied with a brief proclaiming the edict to be null. In April 1768 the ambassadors of Spain, France and Naples demanded that Rome retract the brief. When the pope refused, the Bourbons occupied the enclaves of Avignon in France and Benevento in the kingdom of Naples, and then appended a demand that the pope suppress the Jesuit order outright. In 1769 du Tillot suppressed the Inquisition, and transferred its duties to the bishops, who were assisted by secular authorities. The reform of public charity the same year transferred those services to the state. On du Tillot's dismissal in 1771, Parma receded from the limelight.

The Bourbons brought their own Gallican traditions and absolutist reflexes to Italy and deeply transformed the areas they ruled. These reforms, on the whole, were intended to lift these states to the level of Louis XV's France, to pull Italy into the eighteenth century of the administrative monarchies and enlightened despotism. Where their reforms failed, it was not for the lack of resolve of the monarch or his ministers, but for social resistance from conservative Italians.

26 The Habsburg Revolution

Fragile colossus

The historian of Austrian pretensions in Italy, Salvatore Pugliese, underlined the paradox that the Turks kept Italy free for two centuries, by tying the hands of the emperor, who had never renounced his claim of suzerainty over half of Italy.[1] As soon as Austrian arms cleared Hungary of the Ottomans, Leopold dispatched an army to Italy and presented his claims more forcefully. Charles VI gradually escalated his claims to include all the territories that once figured in Charlemagne's realms. Italians constituted a third of the emperor's subjects in 1720. They were governed under an umbrella Council of Italy sitting in Vienna, as it had in Spain. Austria differed from Spain in one important respect. Its peacetime army of over 100,000 men had to be supported. This was a German army; Italian troops represented no more than 5 per cent of the establishment.[2] Large garrisons held the conquered territories still while Vienna proceeded to administer its version of Louis XIV's absolutism. Efficient administration and military power went together in the minds of political scientists. The Sun King's reinforcement of central authority constituted the model for Enlightenment monarchies. Vienna's absolutism rested on an efficient bureaucracy, imposing order and levying taxes with fairness and firmness. The targets for reform were corruption, inefficiency and *prepotenza*. These ailments of the public body were held to be characteristic of Italian states ruled by threadbare patrician families and their weak princes.

Charles VI set much store on the kingdoms of Naples and Sicily, which were both densely populated and strategically located.

Sicilians did not overtly defy the Habsburgs, but their sullen obedience proclaimed an enduring affinity with Spain.[3] It was necessary to
rely on pro-Spanish notables, if they were competent and respected,
simply because the emperor had so few partisans. The viceroy
Portocarrero (1722–8) tried to inaugurate administrative reforms
through a judiciary composed of able and honest ministers, often
"new men". The Sicilian parliament duly voted the viceroy a large
donativo, but due to irregular and confused accounting practices, the
sums voted bore no relation to the amounts actually collected.[4]
Vienna attempted repeatedly to make the tax system fairer and less
damaging to the economy, by means of information-gathering
inquests and by auditing accounts in its own offices. A proper census
would have given the regime a useful instrument in this regard, but
the barons exempted most of their feudal property from the tally.
Grain export licence fees yielded modest revenues, because widespread smuggling benefited those with good connections. Vienna
established some manufactures in the port cities, but they lan-
guished, as better-quality manufactured goods arrived from Genoa
or France.

Similarly in Naples, the Austrian regime never attracted the adhesion of the elites. The attempt to stimulate economic growth by multiplying the number of free ports failed. The planned census
encountered hostility from both the aristocracy and the Church,
who were suspicious of its fiscal aims.[5] Viceroys also sought to
expand Vienna's power over the kingdom by curtailing the
autonomy of feudal courts. Precariously-paid judges extracted stiff
fees from litigants or fought each other for cases, as in neighbouring
Sicily (and indeed in most of Europe). Vienna was still searching for
ways to "professionalize" the judiciary and extend royal guarantees of
fair justice, when the regime fell.[6] So the Austrian regime in
southern Italy was an interlude, rather than a period marked by fundamental changes in direction.

Theresian Reform and Josephine Revolution, 1740–90

Two quick campaigns by Gallispan armies ejected the emperor from
both southern kingdoms, and from Milan too. Austria's defeat at the
hands of the Turks in 1737–9 rubbed salt into the wounds. It
demonstrated the ramshackle nature of the Empire with its weak
centre and its unwieldy periphery. When Maria Theresia mounted

the throne in 1740, the Empire was at a critical juncture. Proving its resiliency, Austria fought a see-saw war with British support to a general peace in 1748. The experience proved that Austria's fate depended upon the ability of its administration to find money to buy soldiers.

The motivation for these reforms was predominantly military. Maria Theresia was determined to tie Milan and Mantua more tightly to Vienna. No central committee relayed Vienna's orders in Milan; no system articulated the different organs, as in the Spanish period, when the governor shared power with the patrician senate. Government consisted of a series of independent magistracies, operating by judicial forms. Patricians had found ways to take over tax collection, and monopolized the highest levels of the Church. Nobles understood their interest to be the *status quo*, and their inertia meant that change would have to come from outside.[7]

In 1749 Maria Theresia unleashed a short-lived purge that constituted the only political persecution of the century. Vienna intended to create an administration that bypassed the traditional magistracies, recruiting its agents without regard for birth or rank. Bureaucratic ideology exalted competence and specialized training, and condemned nepotism as a system of promotion. Vienna intended that its agents should replace traditional local elites and homogenize the various institutions. Regional government would relay decrees from Vienna and supervise their execution.[8] In Milan the result was the *Magistrato Camerale*. This body reduced the management corps by more than half, and introduced merit as the primary qualification for employment, although patricians held ample place within it. The governor and chief public servant in Milan, the Genoese-born count Gian Luca Pallavicino, recommended consolidating indirect taxes into a state bank, leased to a single general tax farm. The greater revenues it generated would then finance an exact cadaster from which to create a land tax. Eventually the crown would be able to buy back all the revenues it had alienated, and substitute its own functionaries for tax farmers who represented private interests.

The reforms began with the peace in 1749, with the creation of a royal fiscal body, the *Tribunale del Censo* under the direction of the Tuscan Pompeo Neri. He was part of a new class of cosmopolitan functionaries, like Pallavicino, and the francophone Lorrainers in Tuscany, Emmanuel de Richecourt and Marc de Craon, whose administrative skill and legal knowledge served princes against the vested interests of administered groups. Neri wished to refashion the administration along simple pyramidal lines, suppressing offices and levying taxes more equally.[9] New communal assemblies, composed of village and town notables, discussed local issues and ways to enhance their own efficiency. In 1756 Vienna imposed uniform structures on district governments. This gave country elites far more power with respect to city nobles. These innovations virtually destroyed the traditional directive role of the *dominante* city over the *contado* around it. The new institutions were all the more subversive of traditional power structures in that the empress preferred to rely on non-Lombards to run them, although Italians always predominated. A bureaucratic chain of command now led from the village to the plenipotentiary in Milan, and from there to the Council of Italy in Vienna.[10] A Bergamasque tax farmer, Antonio Greppi, combined separate gabelles into a streamlined General Tax Farm. Next, Neri resumed work on a Lombard land register (cadaster) inaugurated in 1718, but sabotaged by privileged groups and then suspended in 1733. The cadaster was completed by 1757, and taxes based on its information were levied from 1760 onwards. It was a decisive step towards making individuals, not communities, liable for taxes. Instead of trusting landowners to declare accurate assessments, surveyors and assessors measured the properties, listed the types of cultivation and estimated the yields. Once it was properly categorized, each parcel of land was subjected to a fixed tax; any future improvements in productivity on it would benefit the owner before the government.[11]

In 1753 Vienna appointed another Genoese, Beltrame Cristiani, to the status of Minister Plenipotentiary to assist the governor, as the conduit through which to reform provincial and communal administrations. Cristiani, who was the architect of the Concordat of 1757 with Rome, had no intention of completely overturning patrician rule in Milan, and his underlings granted abusive exemptions. Patricians also appealed to Vienna to obstruct the completion of the cadaster or to appeal their own assessment. By March 1760, there were no fewer than 7,000 appeals pending in Vienna, and their number grew until the empress decided to back her officials decisively.[12] Meanwhile, the financial reforms proceeded. The *Monte di Santa Teresa*, the new state bank chartered in 1753 to redeem a multitude of public debts, extinguished them entirely by the 1770s.

Improved revenues enabled Maria Theresia to fight a long and bitter war against Prussia to recover Silesia (1756–63). The disappointing outcome of the Seven Years War redoubled Vienna's zeal to tighten its control over its taxation machinery.[13] In 1757 Vienna abolished the Council of Italy, and replaced it with an "Italian department" that was part of the state chancery. Carlo Firmian, a Trentino noble who replaced Cristiani as plenipotentiary in 1759, wished to lift the provincial administration out of Milanese hands entirely. Maria Theresia and her leading minister, Count Kaunitz, were ready to renew and quicken the process of reform.[14] Kaunitz saw Lombardy as a kind of laboratory for Habsburg administration. Although he preferred German as the language of everyday government, he considered himself to be a member of Pietro Verri's *Accademia de' Pugni*, and appointed its members to senior positions in Milan. Affairs were proposed in written reports compiled by Italian secretaries in Vienna. Each report then proceeded to Kaunitz, who signed it, and laid it before the empress, who placed her seal upon it and returned it to the department. The secretaries then wrote up a dispatch and gave it to the empress to sign. Kaunitz added his "vidit", and off it went to Milan.[15] Lombard and Tuscan *philosophes* largely approved the direction the regime was taking. Intellectuals beheld a radiant future being realized by conscientious monarchs, who were misnamed "despots" by the next generation.

With the death of the emperor François-Etienne in 1765, his eldest son Joseph mounted the throne beside his mother. The same year Vienna created the Supreme Economic Council, to which Pietro Verri was appointed. The Council served as a final appeals court for financial matters. It rapidly became the most important organ of government, with a mandate to administer and improve almost everything.[16] Matters of taxation, commerce, manufacturing, monetary regulation, local government, and even book censorship, piled up on the tables of its officials. These administrators were also gradually won over to physiocratic theory. They sought to unify the domestic market by removing hindrances to the movement of goods. Verri's group also attacked guilds, which were seen to hamper production with "useless" regulations. There was a growing belief in Cameralist circles that free trade and free exports, resulting in higher commodity prices, would stimulate production. Verri and the Supreme Economic Council fixed most of their attention on manufacturing and the export market: what economists generally considered the "noble" part of the economy. Verri and Beccaria abolished many of the guilds between 1769 and 1774, before Joseph II accelerated the process in 1781. The changes were gradual, however, since

Vienna did not adopt all the measures that the experts proposed. Like other regimes, the government viewed economic reform as a means to the end of acquiring more soldiers. It was hesitant to relinquish secure sources of revenue in the present, in the hope of reaping theoretical benefits in the future. Transit dues were only abolished in 1781; customs duties were unified only in 1787. The state still tried to protect specific industries with privileges, subsidies and tariffs. Nevertheless, Pietro Verri successfully abolished the Lombard tax farm in 1770, and assigned tax collection entirely to government officials. Despite these successes, the Supreme Economic Council had to refer all its decisions to the Italian Department in Vienna before implementing anything. In 1770, the Milanese institutions were replaced by a Royal Cameral Court for administration, with a single Treasury supervised by a Court of Accounts and a Senate whose power was limited to judicial matters. Apart from Beccaria and Verri, who were pro-Vienna patricians from the region, most of the senior personnel consisted of foreigners (non-Lombards) or outsiders of modest origins. The Imperial government almost systematically excluded conservative aristocrats from important posts in the administration.

Joseph II was a much more "systematic" or doctrinaire thinker, who intended to reorder his states on a rational, uniform basis, for the benefit of the peoples he ruled. Diminishing local autonomies in favour of central control, he went much further than Italian intellectuals like Verri intended. The city-based administrative units of Lombardy were jealous of their past autonomy. Joseph abolished them all in 1786, and replaced them with eight uniform circumscriptions, each under an Intendant. He abolished almost all the existing jurisdictions in favour of a simple hierarchy of local courts, appeal courts and a supreme tribunal. They were part and parcel of a new, central administration, the *Consiglio di Governo*. This was much more radical than any Bourbon reform, which tended to conserve and render ancient institutions more efficient. Maria Theresia and Joseph simultaneously eliminated religious orders and charitable institutions that noble families dominated and drew revenue from.[17] Many notables resented the complete loss of regional autonomy, and adversaries of government complained of "ministerial despotism", a term employed by French parlementarians calling for an end to absolutism in France. Joseph acted similarly in neigbouring Italian Tyrol, whose cultural institutions and intellectual elites were closely in touch with Milanese developments.[18] There he extended conscription, already applied to the Danubian heartland, in 1784. His decree that German be the sole language of administration there created new tensions and gave rise to national feeling and hints of separatism.

No sweeping fiscal reform could leave the Church untouched. The Concordat of 1757 in Lombardy provided for a Junta of Stewardship to advise the Crown on church–state relations. In 1762 the empress unilaterally decreed that herewith, papal letters and decrees would require a royal placet, the *exequatur*, before they could be operative in her states. At this stage Vienna intended primarily to tap church revenues. In 1768 Maria Theresia and Kaunitz inaugurated a long train of secularizing reforms. The state, following a radical reform programme proposed by Carlo Pilati, decided to suppress most monastic orders, create state-run seminaries, and reduce the number of secular clergy. For Maria Theresia and Kaunitz, the purpose of higher education was to encourage prosperity and train honest and efficient bureaucrats. A restructured university of Pavia introduced modern, "useful" subjects under government supervision. Traditional religion, and the host of ecclesiastical privileges and exemptions that maintained it, gradually came to be a target of regalist reformists in the Church and state. Under Maria Theresia, who was a conservative Catholic at heart, the Church was relatively safe, for she bridled the idealism of her son and co-ruler. This changed upon her death in 1780.

Joseph attempted to suppress traditional Catholicism outright in a way that anticipated all but the most virulent anti-Catholic measures of the French Revolution. He began in 1781 by denouncing the concordat and proclaiming simultaneously an Edict of Toleration for all the Christians of the Empire. He replaced the Junta of Stewardship with an Ecclesiastical Commission to control every aspect of ecclesiastical life. The pontiff would no longer be allowed to correspond with the clergy, to dispatch legates or proclaim legal measures without Imperial consent. Pope Pius VI Braschi was desperate enough to travel to Vienna in 1782 in a vain attempt to dissuade Joseph from implementing these measures.[19] Six state-run seminaries in the entire Empire, including one in Pavia, graduated priests, and bishops lost their prerogative to nominate or confirm them in their benefices. The Jansenist catechism promulgated at the university aimed at uprooting peasant superstitions in the name of social utility. The emperor then regulated the number of masses and their length; he also specified the furniture for churches and chapels. There would be no processions unless approved by the authorities, no pilgrimages tolerated, a reduction in the number of side-altars to specific saints, no clothing the statues of Mary. Holy pictures could not be touched; rosaries could not be fingered; relics could not be kissed. There was to be no kneeling in the streets when the host passed (but hats were to be doffed) and no talk of religion permitted in taverns. Corpses could no longer be buried in churches or in family tombs, but in cemeteries without lights over the graves. Coffins were outlawed in favour of sacks. Joseph ordered the suppression of most of the monasteries, both male and female, in 1784. The proceeds of their confiscated properties went towards a state-administered Religion Fund, to establish parishes, to support retired or sick priests and schoolteachers. Joseph's hand-picked bishops welcomed these changes for this was Jansenism with a vengeance. But the measures were deeply unpopular and revolt simmered just beneath the surface. In 1790, on the death of the revolutionary emperor, his brother and successor Leopold II decided to suspend their application.

Habsburg reforms in Milan were closely watched elsewhere in northern Italy. Modena was Vienna's closest ally: Duke Francesco III strayed briefly from the fold in 1741 to join the Gallispan assault, and paid for it with the occupation of his duchy. He expected to renew this expansion at the first opportunity, but the alliance between Bourbons and Habsburgs in 1756 placed Italy outside the theatre of international conflict, and confirmed Austrian hegemony. Ulterior marriages between the Este and the Habsburgs, such as that between his granddaughter Beatrice to Maria Theresia's son Ferdinand in 1771, returned Modena to Vienna's orbit. Francesco imported to his capital some of the reforms under way in Milan, such as the creation of a great magistracy for Trade and Agriculture in 1762, entrusted with economic improvement. He attempted to increase central control with another magistracy governing local communities, although they could not bypass local interests in a duchy where 111 out of 136 districts were feudal jurisdictions, admittedly with modest prerogatives.[20]

Ercole III joined the assault on religious jurisdictions and suppressed the Holy Office in 1785. His chief minister, Lodovico Ricci, was the epitome of an eighteenth-century reformer. His major reforms were agricultural: planning irrigation canals, financing land reclamation, extending rice cultivation, building new roads and bridges, abolishing the grain provisioning system. Ricci drew up a cadastral register in 1788–91 and calculated taxation rates from them. As elsewhere in Italy, such measures did not spark a universal improvement of rural living conditions. Ricci's church reforms also followed Austrian precedents. He persuaded Rome twice to reduce the weight of obit masses so that the state might direct the legacies toward institutions of public assistance run by the state. By the 1780s, intervention in the Church's jurisdiction was designed to buttress state power at the expense of the Church.[21]

The Habsburg Impact on Tuscany

Tuscany passed to the Habsburg dynasty in 1737 to compensate the husband of Maria Theresia, François-Etienne for the eventual annexation of Lorraine by France. The couple visited Florence only once, just before ascending the Imperial throne in 1740. Francesco Stefano, as his subjects called him, and his francophone advisers believed the Muratorian doctrine by which the prince must bring "public happiness" to the maximum number of subjects. They shared a low opinion of the efficiency and honesty of Italian administrators. The new duke intended to make the patrician class dependent upon him. In itself, this was not new. The Medici administration similarly had subordinated magistrates' committees to grand-ducal secretaries.[22] Nevertheless, the multitude of separate taxes, each with its own bureau, allowed patricians easy access to state resources. Each tax was levied in a particular manner. There were some exemptions for ecclesiastics, but the Tuscan clergy paid more taxes to the state than most others in Italy.[23] Contentious cases came before elected noble magistrates who judged the matter.

The debilitating effects of aristocratic government were compounded by the continuing implosion of noble houses. The quality of the candidates for government offices declined along with the quantity, as was revealed in a spate of corruption cases and mismanagement by noblemen unfit for administration. Waquet labels this a continual process of the confiscation of the state by the aristocracy in homeopathic, repeat doses. Cosimo III (1670–1723) rarely punished his nobles (or indeed, anybody) to the full extent of the law, and tolerated a measure of prevarication and influence-peddling by his subjects. The Lorrainers' contempt for lax government in Tuscany was thus not unfounded.[24] Like elsewhere in Italy, these nobles also held the purse-strings on the public debt, which earned them a modest but stable 3.5 per cent interest, which was comparable to other long-term investments available before the economic resurgence after 1740. Tuscany's almost unbroken neutrality and its marginal role in great power politics allowed the system to continue without disruption. Most Italian territories paid only a fraction of the taxes levied in northern Europe.[25]

Francesco Stefano intended to transform that situation and instil a new sense of rigour and propriety. He preferred Lorrainers, Frenchmen and even Piedmontese to Tuscans in key positions.[26] He reduced the government to three councils: a Council of State under Marc de Craon; a Council of Finance under Emmanuel de Richecourt; and a Council of War under Carlo Rinuccini. All of them answered to a Council of Tuscany in Vienna. Marc de Craon immediately denounced the "rapine" by urban magistrates of the duchy's finances, and reduced the number of treasuries.[27] Richecourt pushed many officers and soldiers to quit simply by ending their pensions, or making them personally liable to serve. Rinuccini was instructed to replace the grand-ducal garrisons with a small but effective army of 5,000 men, many of whom were Germans.[28] Between 1740 and 1765, Florence spent an unprecedented sum of 6.77 million scudi to subsidize Vienna's war effort. Tuscany maintained a regiment in the Seven Years War, but even the rumour of conscription for it led to a flight of young men into the Papal States.

Measures to improve efficiency and reduce privilege included combining the multiple gabelles into a single tax farm in 1740. In 1745 the Regency council invited Pompeo Neri to meld all the Tuscan legal codes into a single, coherent text. A few years later, he proposed to define nobility as part of this project. He saw usefulness as an essential component of the aristocrat's social purpose, and proposed a category of service nobility to vie for honorific posts alongside the titled aristocracy.[29] Vienna saw the Church as a source of money from the beginning. The granducal minister, Giulio Rucellai, attacked the Church's immunities in 1745, ended ecclesiastical sanctuary, virtually shut down the Papal Inquisition in Florence in 1754, and protected Freemasons into the bargain. In 1751 the government prohibited further gifts in land to religious institutions in mortmain.

With the death of Francesco Stefano in 1765, the duchy passed to his second son, Leopold, known to Italians as Pietro Leopoldo, who quickly moved to Florence and dispensed with regency-style government. A wide and avid reader, Leopold advocated what he called the "scientific method" of governing; that is, he chose to gather information from many sources so that he would not have to rely on the observations of single individuals.[30] His approach to government was essentially utilitarian, designed to increase the public happiness. The cessation of war contributions to Vienna after 1765 allowed him to reduce the public debt by half. In addition to large outlays for debt reduction, Pietro Leopoldo made money available for public buildings, roads, bridges, canals, drainage, hospitals, mineral baths, leper houses and schools. Abolishing the Tax Farm in 1768 made tax collection the exclusive responsibility of government officials. The measure unified the multitude of excise taxes and eliminated the exemptions of privileged groups and communities. A cadaster was contemplated, but was not undertaken until after the Napoleonic era. Pietro Leopoldo went out of his way to eliminate nobles from government, and after 1770 non-nobles predominated in every sector of the bureaucracy, while provincials were preferred over Florentines. This definitively ended the system of the *dominante* characteristic of Italian states. By suppressing all the elective and rotating magistracies in Florence and Siena in 1784, he decreased the size of the bureaucracy by 30 per cent. Tribunals he made uniform, and restricted them to judicial functions. Administrative fees disappeared, pensions were regularized, pluralism in office ended, and trained judges with fixed tenures replaced patrician rotating magistrates. The grand duke also established the ministry of the *Buon Governo*, with regulatory powers over hygiene, spectacles, prisons, and family squabbles. A great deal of legislation proposed to tighten morals and outlaw prostitution and gambling.[31]

In the 1770s the most influential adviser to the prince was Francesco Maria Gianni, who favoured giving landowners administrative responsibilities alongside the nobility, in local assemblies, as in Lombardy. In the 1780s the grand duke established uniform municipal governments, supervised by appointed communal chancellors. The prince and his ministers also overhauled the justice system, along lines inspired by Beccaria. It calibrated the punishment to fit the social gravity of the crime and suppressed afflictive corporal penalites. After 1782 debtors were no longer imprisoned; and in the new legal code of 1786, torture and the death penalty were abolished. Public order survived the more lenient treatment of lawbreakers. In the 1780s, Pietro Leopoldo disbanded the army, and replaced it with a small body of landholding militiamen, much like the National Guard that would appear in revolutionary France at the decade's end.

Leopold's peaceful reign was perturbed only by the harvest failures between 1764 and 1767. They prompted the government to rethink the usefulness of regulations governing the grain trade, as everywhere the mainstay of the economy. Leopold was aware of the new physiocratic theories, and decreed the complete freedom of the grain trade in 1775. Physiocratic deregulation accompanied rising production on large estates, which was fed by the growing foreign demand for grain. Leopold believed that it was desirable to create a dynamic rural bourgeoisie of middling farmers to diminish the chasm between great landowners and landless labourers.[32] At one point, he decreed that common grazing lands should be divided and sold to private individuals. Corvées, obligatory work details imposed on peasants for bonification schemes, he suppressed as an unnecessary burden on rural populations.

Pietro Leopoldo's most original innovation was his decision to endow Tuscany with a written constitution, inspired partly by those of Pennsylvania and Virginia. Francesco Maria Gianni, supervised at every step by the sovereign himself, completed drafting the document in 1782.[33] The grand duke, sensitive to the *philosophes'* strident criticism of ministerial "despotism", proved sympathetic to individual rights over bureaucratic efficiency. The "people" did not include peasants, for electors were to be members of municipal councils. Still, the assembly would review accounts of financial administration and salaries of officials, and advise the grand duke on on the drafting of new legislation. Subjects enjoyed wide civil liberties, private property and the pursuit of their legitimate needs as natural rights. The grand duke was to retain control of the armed forces, appoint public officials, nominate bishops, grant titles of nobility and fulfil the functions of justice and grace. If it had been applied, this constitution would have been the most liberal in Europe, and probably in the world at the time, surpassed only by the French constitution of 1791. It never became operational because Joseph II in Vienna advised strongly against it.

Pietro Leopoldo followed his brother Joseph's religious initiatives closely. While outwardly pious, the grand duke disliked holy beggars and hermits, whom he tried to suppress in 1776 in spite of the popular support they enjoyed. Discussions on the radical reform of Catholic tradition began in 1769, with the further restriction of mortmain. Other measures included the *exequatur*, the restriction of rights of refuge and of ecclesiastical courts, as well as the suppression of monasteries in 1773. The grand duke considered himself an "external bishop", who could prescribe books to the clergy, nominate clerics to benefices and suppress monasteries. Like his brother, he banned burials inside churches and removed graves beyond the walls of towns, which was disturbing to both clergy and their flock. The *philosophe*'s concern for hygiene contrasted sharply with the age-old reminders of death that constituted a pillar of Catholic religiosity. In 1785 he decreed the dissolution of most of the confraternities, which traditionally provided the lion's share of social assistance to the poor.

The grand duke's instrument in applying these changes was Scipione de' Ricci, appointed bishop of Pistoia and Prato in 1780. Ricci argued that religious life should focus on the parish and its ceremonies. This meant banishing the competing liturgies of the regular orders, and eliminating the multitude of private chapels, shrines and oratories that were a hallmark of Tridentine devotion. Every parish would have its boundaries fixed at a reasonable size, and dispose of enough priests to administer the sacraments conveniently to the laity. Parish service was to be simplified, focusing on the high altar and not a sacred picture or a venerated statue. All the liturgy should be chanted in vernacular Italian rather than in Latin. The people would receive vernacular translations of the gospel, permitting them to follow what was being said. Purgatory offices for departed souls would be abolished. Pictures and statues that promoted "superstition" would be removed, and the silver ornaments and fine clothing that adorned the statues stripped away. Cults to doubtful saints, indulgence tables, and even music should be curtailed. As for the monks, they would no longer be exempt from the bishop's jurisdiction. The diverse religious orders would be blended into a single order, with only one house per city. Permanent vows for men and women were to be abolished, allowing monks and nuns to quit religious life and, it was hoped, marry and produce useful subjects.

Despite the openly hostile reaction of much of the clergy and many bishops, Pietro Leopoldo encouraged de' Ricci to apply these reforms in his own diocese while awaiting the convening of a "national" synod, which would decree their application for all of Tuscany. Preliminary consultations took place in the ducal palace in April and May of 1787, and the synod of Pistoia was convened soon after. While discussions were going on, riots broke out at Prato over the rumour that the altar consecrated to the Madonna's girdle was about to be demolished. The crowd burned the bishop's throne in the town square, sacked his palace and invaded the seminary. Anti-Jansenist bishops at the synod of Pistoia rallied to the popular sentiment and the great majority denounced the proposed reforms. Leopold concluded by closing the papal nuncio's tribunal and separating religious orders from their foreign superiors (1788). However, the simmering resentment at this assault on Catholicism generally halted new initiatives. When Leopold left in 1790 to succeed his brother in Vienna, the great reform was cancelled.

The reforms of the 1780s swept the Habsburgs' Italian subjects off their feet and ushered in new resentments, and perhaps the first feelings of what would become nineteenth-century nationalism. Italians gradually lost their cultural ascendancy in Germany, as a new generation of poets, philosphers and musicians emerged there after the Seven Years War. Italian aristocrats retreated from the military posts they occupied, and invested their talents in civilian offices at home. Administrative modernization brought northern Italy to the level of the most efficient regions of Europe and served as a suitable base on which Napoleon would build his military regime. Jacobin and Napoleonic revolutionary decrees were not introduced into a conservative land, locked into traditional institutions. Rather, wave after wave of Habsburg decrees, relayed by professional bureaucrats, disfigured the *ancien régime* and rendered it unrecognizable.

Conclusion

The Bourbon and Habsburg reforms of the eighteenth century gave the illusion that Italy had finally recovered its place in the concert of European nations. Such an impression would be misleading. The economic improvement after 1730 probably exacerbated the sharp division between north and south. But this fundamental division in Italy is not one of two nations experiencing different processes, but rather of one zone lagging behind the other. For the south was not immobile. The south's eternal maledictions, inscribed into geography, bore heavily on it still: the prevalence of malaria, the incidence of earthquakes, the lack of water for long periods. Drought prevented peasants from raising more cattle and horses, whose energy could multiply that of men and increase their standard of living. And yet progress there was. The gradual increase in population in the south attests to it, as does the increasing number of merchant ships in the kingdom's ports.

Eighteenth-century administrations also undermined the political and social hold the barons exercised, both in northern and southern Italy. Chroniclers everywhere noted how society, and above all the elites, were more "policed" and less inclined to resolve their quarrels by force. We lack a history of *prepotenza* for Italy as a whole, and it is urgent that we should have one. Aristocratic *prepotenza* may have lasted longer in the Mezzogiorno, but a closer examination of homicide would reveal a more complex cartography of the phenomenon than the simple contrast of north and south.

The south lagged behind, but followed the north in its cultural development too. But the slow pace of change that characterized the kingdom of Naples was not the case in Sicily, where the institutional recovery of the Church was more rapid. The long coexistence and interpenetration of a theological culture and a magical universe was characteristic of Brescia and Modena as it was of the Mezzogiorno, although southern magical traditions may have been more widely shared and survived longer. There is no mistaking that the adoption of clerical discipline in the kingdom of Naples began by the 1690s, and the process accelerated again after the 1720s.

Intellectual Italy was urban; its epicentre remained in the centre and north. But Naples was always an important intellectual capital in Italy, Messina and Palermo being minor ones. Scientific academies were not limited to the north and the centre. The eighteenth century finally saw the spread of Tuscan as the hegemonic language even in Sicily after 1750. No part of Italy experienced widespread dechristianization, even during the period when French troops encouraged irreligion. The anticlericalism of revolutionary officers and ranks scandalized most Italians, who nourished a deep resentment not entirely due to French indiscipline. Italian Jacobins who came out of the closet from Turin to Naples never constituted more than an infinitesimally small minority of the population, destined to fall whenever French soldiers moved away.

In short, the Mezzogiorno and the islands in 1750 were the museum of cultural and social norms that had held sway everywhere two centuries previously. The processes at work there were mirror images of those evolving elsewhere in Europe, but the chronology lag made the southern realms occasionally seem foreign. Italy as a whole appeared increasingly archaic to northern Europeans who discovered the peninsula in increasing numbers.

There was indeed an age of decadence in Italian history; not merely a crisis, for that term implies an agitated interlude before a new stasis. The crisis that struck Italy between the onset of the Thirty Years War and its end towards 1660 was not characterized by a recovery in any domain. Economic decline struck every sector, durably. The seventeenth-century decline was not as disastrous as we imagined. Nevertheless, it was an absolute impoverishment, that transformed an urban civilization into an *ancien régime* society. The north and centre lost their technological edge by 1640 and could not recover it. Italy continued to fall behind in the eighteenth century too, in relative terms at least, and probably did not begin to improve until the second half of the nineteenth century. If Italians numbered more than one European in seven in 1600, two centuries later they were no more than one in ten, with a lower standard of living than most. Italy's economic and cultural lag with respect to France, England, Germany and the Netherlands never appeared greater than during the Risorgimento. The spread of *mezzadria* and intensive agriculture demonstrated the adaptive capacity of the country once, by providing enough food for a rising population until the 1620s. The growing rural crisis in the seventeenth century demonstrated a lack of innovation, a retrenchment outside a relatively small district of the Po valley. No rural or urban bourgeoisie displaced a dwindling aristocracy. Innovation and social and economic dynamism seemed to go together.

The connection between economic innovation and cultural enterprise and activity is more a philosophical question not readily amenable to empirical demonstration. The concordance of the economic decline with Italy's fall from cultural ascendancy is nevertheless striking. Northern Italy's technological precociousness extended even into the military sphere. Italy's high urban literacy rate, compared with other parts of Europe, made it a fulcrum for innovations, particularly at the universities where Italian manners and letters, culture and science attracted foreign students and professors and helped radiate Italian culture abroad. Academies spread this learned culture to a vast audience of wealthy and educated men, whose predilection for erudite sociability did not impede real accomplishments. The peninsula's artists and musicians defined the concepts and practices followed elsewhere on the continent until 1640.

The inversion of the trend was brusque and unmistakable. Northern European engineers had begun to displace their Italian forebears by the Thirty Years War, and outclassed them completely by 1650. The age of Roman baroque ceased after 1660, due to a new spirit of austerity and retrenchment. Italian universities began to lose their cachet around 1640, and soon lagged behind Holland, France and England in accomplishments as in prestige. Italy's literacy rate, even in the cities, began to fall behind northern Europe despite the pious initiatives, probably because the Church did not feel threatened enough to wish to inoculate the population against heresy through reading. The philosophical developments that planted deep roots in England and France could not have involved many people in Italy, and Italian *philosophes* were soon looking towards France for their cues.

Italian history, then, took a cyclical turn for the worse. However, one might conclude here that "progress" consists at least in part of people living in ever larger and more articulated "communities" beyond the family, the hamlet and the village. The modern state, Counter-Reformation religion, the civilization of morals pushed Italians out of their village factions and into larger political and social entities. The Risorgimento and Unification were further steps down that road, as is European unification and the adherence to a global economy in the new millennium. Italian decadence, lasting two full centuries, did not impede *that* civilizing process.

Notes

Notes to the Introduction

1. Romolo Quazza, *Storia politica d'Italia: preponderanza spagnola (1559–1700)* (Milan, 1938), p. 1; Benedetto Croce, *Storia dell'età barocca in Italia* (Bari, 1967), pp. 44–7.

2. Camillo Manfroni, *La marina militare del granducato mediceo*; Romolo Quazza, *Storia politica d'Italia: Mantova e Monferrato nella politica europea alla vigilia della guerra per la successione (1624–1627)* (Mantua, 1922) and his *La guerra per la successione di Mantova e del Monferrato (1628–1631)* (Mantua, 1926); Luigi Simeoni, *Francesco I d'Este e la politica italiana del Mazarino* (Bologna, 1922); Franco Valsecchi, *L'Italia nel seicento e nel settecento: società e costume* (Turin, 1967); Emile Laloy, *La Révolte de Messine, l'expédition de Sicile, et la politique française en Italie (1674–1678)*, 3 vols (Paris, 1929); Ludwig von Pastor, *History of the Popes*, 40 vols (London, 1950).

3. Jean Boutier and Brigitte Marin, "Regards sur l'historiographie récente de l'Italie moderne", *Revue d'Histoire Moderne et Contemporaine*, 45 (1998), 7–14.

4. *Storia d'Italia*, 5 vols, vol. 2 (Turin, 1973).

5. *Storia d'Italia*, ed. Giuseppe Galasso, 25 vols (Turin, from 1978).

6. Jean Delumeau, *L'Italie de Botticelli à Bonaparte* (Paris, 1978).

7. Stuart Woolf, *A History of Italy, 1700–1860: The Social Constraints of Political Change* (London, 1979).

8. Dino Carpanetto and Giuseppe Ricuperati, *Italy in the Age of Reason, 1685–1789* (New York, 1987); Eric Cochrane, *Italy, 1530–1630* (New York, 1988); Domenico Sella, *Italy in the Seventeenth Century* (New York, 1997).

Notes to Chapter 1: Italy *circa* 1700

1. Pierre George, *Géographie de l'Italie* (Paris, 1964), p. 15.

2. Domenico Sella, *Crisis and Continuity: The Economy of Spanish Lombardy in the Seventeenth Century* (Cambridge, Mass., 1979), pp. 3–7.

371

3. Population figures, unless otherwise specified, come from K. J. von Beloch, *Bevolkerungsgeschichte Italiens* (Berlin, 1936–61), 3 vols.
4. Salvatore Ciriacono, "Venise et la Hollande, pays de l'eau (XVe–XVIIIe siècles)", *Revue Historique*, 578 (1991), 295–320.
5. Monica and Robert Beckinsale, *Southern Europe: The Mediterranean and Alpine Lands* (London, 1975), p. 53.
6. Henri Desplanques, *Campagnes ombriennes: Contribution à l'étude des paysages ruraux en Italie centrale* (Paris, 1969).
7. Raffaele Molinelli, *Città e contado nella Marca pontificia in età moderna* (Urbino, 1984), p. 16.
8. Jean Delumeau, *Vie économique et sociale de Rome dans la seconde moitié du seizième siècle* (Paris, 1957–9), 2 vols; M. R. Caroselli, "Aspects of the economic history of the Roman 'Campagna' in the modern and contemporary world", *Journal of European Economic History*, 13 (1984), 591–8.
9. Aurelio Lepre, *Storia del Mezzogiorno d'Italia*, 2 vols (Naples, 1986), vol. 1, ch. 1.
10. John A. Marino, *Pastoral Economics in the Kingdom of Naples* (Baltimore, 1988).
11. Raul Merzario, *Signori e contadini di Calabria: Corigliano Calabro dal XVI al XIX secolo* (Milan, 1975), p. 3.
12. Domenico Ligresti, "Introduzione", in *Il governo della città: Patriziati e politica nella Sicilia moderna* (Catania, 1990), pp. 5–16.
13. Quentin Hughes, *Fortress: Architecture and Military History in Malta* (London, 1969); Michel Fontenay, "La place de la course dans l'économie portuaire: l'exemple de Malte et des ports barbaresques", *Annales: Economies, Sociétés, Civilisations* (1988), 1321–47.
14. Maurice Le Lannou, *Pâtres et paysans de la Sardaigne* (Tours, 1941).
15. Paul Arrighi (ed.), *Histoire de la Corse* (Toulouse, 1971), p. 255.
16. M.-R. Marin-Muracciola, *L'Honneur des femmes en Corse, du XIIIe siècle à nos jours* (Paris, 1964), p. 4.

Notes to Chapter 2: Family and Sociability

1. Renata Ago, *Carriere e clientele nella Roma barocca* (Bari, 1990), p. 177.
2. Raul Merzario, "Land, kinship and consanguineous marriage in Italy from the seventeenth to the nineteenth centuries", *Journal of Family History*, 15 (1990), 529–46.
3. Giovanni Levi, *Inheriting Power: The Story of an Exorcist* (Chicago, 1988), p. 55; and "Family and kin in Italy – a few thoughts", *Journal of Family History*, 15 (1990), 57–67.
4. Gérard Delille, *Famille et propriété dans le royaume de Naples, XVe–XIXe siècles* (Rome, 1985).
5. Francesco Benigno, "The Southern Italian family in the early modern period", *Continuity and Change*, 4 (1989), 165–94; Anthony Galt, "Marital property in an Apulian town during the eighteenth and early nineteenth centuries", in *The Family in Italy from Antiquity to the Present*, ed. D. Kertzer and R. Saller (New Haven, 1991), pp. 304–20.
6. Levi, "Family and kin – a few thoughts".

7. Marzio Barbagli, *Sotto lo stesso tetto: mutamenti della famiglia in Italia dal XV al XX secolo* (Bologna, 1984), pp. 152–8.

8. David Herlihy and Cristiane Klapisch-Zuber, *Tuscans and their Families: A Study of the Florentine Catasto of 1427* (New Haven, 1985); Marco della Pina, "Famiglia mezzadrile e celibato: le campagne di Prato nei secoli XVII e XVIII", in *Popolazione, società e ambiente: Temi di demografia storica italiana, secc. XVII–XIX* (Bologna, 1990), pp. 125–40; Emmanuel Todd, "Mobilité géographique et cycle de vie en Artois et en Toscane au XVIIIᵉ siècle", *Annales: Economies, Sociétés, Civilisations*, 30 (1975), 726–45; Vito Caiati, "The peasant household under Tuscan mezzadria: a socioeconomic analysis of some Sienese mezzadri households, 1591–1640", *Journal of Family History* (1984), 111–26.

9. Madeleine-Rose Marin-Muracciole, *L'Honneur des femmes en Corse, du XIIIᵉ siècle à nos jours* (Paris, 1964); Osvaldo Raggio, *Faide e parentele: lo stato genovese visto dalla Fontanabuona* (Turin, 1990), pp. 80–123.

10. Raul Merzario, "Land, kinship and consanguineous marriage in Italy".

11. Lucia Ferrante, "Il matrimonio disciplinato: processi matrimoniali a Bologna nel Cinquecento", in *Disciplina dell' anima, disciplina del corpo, disciplina della società tra medioevo ed età moderna* (Bologna, 1994), pp. 901–27.

12. Sandra Cavallo and Simona Cerutti, "Onore femminile e controllo sociale della riproduzione in Piemonte, tra '600 e '700", *Quaderni Storici*, 15 (1980), 346–83.

13. David D. Gilmore, "Performative excellence: circum-Mediterranean", in *Manhood in the Making: Cultural Concepts of Masculinity* (New Haven, 1990), pp. 30–55.

14. Giulia Calvi, *Il contratto morale: Madri e figli nella Toscana moderna* (Bari, 1994).

15. Marzio Barbagli, "Three household formation systems in eighteenth- and nineteenth-century Italy", in *The Family in Italy, from Antiquity to the Present*, ed. D. Kertzer and R. Saller (New Haven, 1991), pp. 250–70.

16. Giovanna Da Molin, "Family forms and domestic service in Southern Italy from the seventeenth to the nineteenth centuries", *Journal of Family History*, 15 (1990), 503–27.

17. Thomas V. Cohen and Elizabeth S. Cohen, *Words and Deeds in Renaissance Rome: Trials before the Papal Magistrates* (Toronto, 1993), pp. 3–33.

18. Madeleine-Rose Marin-Muracciole, *L'Honneur des femmes en Corse, du XIIIᵉ siècle à nos jours* (Paris, 1964), pp. 85–97.

19. David D. Gilmore, "Performative excellence", in *Manhood in the Making*, pp. 30–55.

20. Edward C. Banfield, *The Moral Basis of a Backward Society* (New York, 1958).

21. J. du Boulay and R. Williams, "Amoral familism and the image of limited good: a critique from a European perspective", *Anthropological Quarterly*, 60 (1987), 13–25.

22. Michèle Benaiteau, "Una nobiltà di lunga durata: strategie e comportamenti dei Tocco di Montemiletto", in *Signori, patrizi, cavalieri in Italia centro-meridionale nell' età moderna*, ed. M. A. Visceglia (Bari, 1992),

pp. 193–213; Sydel Silverman, "Rituals of inequality: stratification and symbol in central Italy", in *Social Inequality: Comparative and Developmental Approaches* (New York, 1981), pp. 163–80.

23. Laurie Nussdorfer, *Civic Politics in the Rome of Urban VIII* (Princeton, 1992), p. 166.

Notes to Chapter 3: The Renaissance Origins of Modern Italy

1. Notker Hammerstein, "Relations with Authority", in *A History of the University in Europe*: vol. 2, *Universities in Early Modern Europe, 1500–1800*, ed. Hilde de Ridder-Symoens (Cambridge, 1996), p. 115.

2. Jean-Claude Margolin, *L'Humanisme en Europe au temps de la Renaissance* (Paris, 1981).

3. Jean Delumeau, *L'Italie de la Renaissance à la fin du XVIIIe siècle* (Paris, 1991), pp. 121–4.

4. Christian Bec, *Les Livres des Florentins (1413–1608)* (Florence, 1984).

5. N. S. Davidson, "Unbelief and atheism in Italy, 1500–1700", in *Atheism from the Reformation to the Enlightenment* (Oxford, 1992), pp. 55–86.

6. Hans Baron, *The Crisis of the Early Italian Renaissance* (Princeton, 1966).

7. Wilhelm Schmidt-Biggemann, "New structures of knowledge", in *A History of the University in Europe*: vol. 2, *Universities in Early Modern Europe, 1500–1800*, ed. Hilde de Ridder-Symoens (ed.) (Cambridge, 1996), p. 497.

8. Delumeau, *L'Italie de la Renaissance*, pp. 62–7.

9. Lauro Martines, *Power and Imagination: City-states in Renaissance Italy* (New York, 1979), p. 209.

10. Peter Burke, *The Italian Renaissance: Culture and Society in Italy* (Princeton, 1986), ch. 3, pp. 43–87.

11. Peter Burke, *The Italian Renaissance: Culture and Society in Italy*, pp. 62–73; Eric Cochrane, *Italy, 1530–1630* (New York, 1988), pp. 19–26.

12. Armando Petrucci, "Per una strategia della mediazione grafica nel Cinquecento italiano", *Archivio Storico Italiano* (1986), 97–112.

13. Paul Grendler, *Schooling in Renaissance Italy: Literacy and Learning, 1300–1600* (Baltimore, 1989); Jean-Michel Sallmann, "Alphabétisation et hierarchie sociale à Naples à la fin du XVIe siècle et au début du XVIIe siècle', *Sulle vie della scrittura: Alfabetizzazione, cultura scritta e istituzioni in età moderna*, ed. Maria Rosaria Pelizzari (Naples, 1989), pp. 79–98.

14. Delumeau, *L'Italie de la Renaissance*, p. 75.

15. Hugh Kearney, *Science and Change, 1500–1700* (New York, 1971), pp. 91–140.

16. Giorgio Simoncini, *Città e società nel Rinascimento* (Turin, 1974), 2 vols.

17. Jean Delumeau, *Rome au XVIe siècle* (Paris, 1975).

18. Christopher Duffy, *Siege Warfare: The Fortress in the Early Modern World, 1494–1660* (London, 1979), pp. 8–23; Simon Pepper and Nicholas Adams, *Firearms and Fortifications: Military Architecture and Siege Warfare in Sixteenth-century Siena* (Chicago, 1986); Michael Mallett and John R. Hale, *The Military Organization of a Renaissance State: Venice, 1400–1617*

(Cambridge, 1984), p. 398; Giorgio Spini, "Introduzione", in *Architettura e politica da Cosimo I a Ferdinando I* (Florence, 1976), pp. 9–77; Hélène Vérin, *La Gloire des ingénieurs: L'intelligence technique du XVIᵉ au XVIIIᵉ siècle* (Paris, 1993); Luigi Maggiorotti, *L'opera del genio italiano all' estero*, 3 vols (Rome, 1933–9); Christian Bec, *Les Livres des Florentins (1413–1608)* (Florence, 1984), p. 72.

19. Fernand Braudel, *Civilization and Capitalism, 15th–18th Centuries:* vol.1, *The Structures of Everyday Life* (London, 1981), pp. 470–8.

20. Richard Goldthwaite, *Wealth and the Demand for Art in Italy, 1300–1600* (Baltimore, 1993), pp. 153–7.

21. Claudio Donati, "L'evoluzione della coscienza nobiliare", in *Patriziati e aristocrazie nobiliari: Ceti dominanti e organizzazione del potere nell' Italia centro-settentrionale dal XVI al XVIII secolo: Seminario di Trento, 1977*, ed. C. Mozzarelli and P. Schiera (Trent, 1978), pp. 13–36.

22. Paul Grendler, "Chivalric romances in the Italian Renaissance", *Studies in Medieval and Renaissance History* (1988), 57–102.

23. Mario Praz, *Studies in Seventeenth-century Imagery*, 2nd edn (Rome, 1964).

24. Richard Barber and Juliet Barker, *Tournaments: Jousts, Chivalry and Pageants in the Middle Ages* (New York, 1989), p. 209; Roy Strong, *Art and Power: Renaissance Festivals, 1450–1650* (Woodbridge, Suffolk, 1984), pp. 50–2.

25. Richard Goldthwaite, *Wealth and the Demand for Art in Italy, 1300–1600* (Baltimore, 1993).

26. Claudio Donati, "L'evoluzione della coscienza nobiliare", in *Patriziati e aristocrazie nobiliari: Ceti dominanti e organizzazione del potere nell' Italia centro-settentrionale dal XVI al XVIII secolo*, ed. C. Mozzarelli and P. Schiera (Trent, 1978), p. 17; Giovanni Muto, "'I segni d'honore': Rappresentazioni delle dinamiche nobiliari a Napoli in età moderna", in *Signori, patrizi, cavalieri in Italia centro-meridionale nell' età moderna*, ed. Maria Antonietta Visceglia (Bari, 1992), pp. 171–92.

27. Francesco Benigno, "Aristocrazia e stato in Sicilia nell' epoca di Filippo III", in *Signori, patrizi, cavalieri in Italia centro-meridionale nell' età moderna*, ed. Maria-Antonietta Visceglia (Bari, 1992), pp. 76–93.

Notes to Chapter 4: From Communes to Principalities

1. Karl Otmar von Aretin, "L'ordinamento feudale in Italia nel XVI e XVII secolo e le sue ripercussioni sulla politica europea: un contributo alla storia del tardo feudalismo in Europa", *Annali dell' Istituto storico Italo-Germanico in Trento*, 4 (1978), 51–94.

2. Marco Cattini, "Congiunture sociali e dinamiche politiche nei consigli municipali di Parma e Piacenza in età moderna", in *Persistenze feudali e autonomie comunitative in stati padani fra Cinque e Settecento*, ed. G. Tocci (Bologna, 1988), pp. 47–76.

3. Lauro Martines, *Power and Imagination: City-states in Renaissance Italy* (New York, 1979), pp. 45–70.

4. James Cushman Davis, *The Decline of the Venetian Nobility as a Ruling*

Class (Baltimore, 1962); see also Alexander Cowan, *The Urban Patriciate: Lubeck and Venice, 1580–1700* (Cologne, 1986).

5. Paul Grendler, 'The leaders of the Venetian state, 1540–1609: a prosopographical analysis", *Studi Veneziani* (1990), 35–61.
6. Cowan, *The Urban Patriciate*, p. 97.
7. Dorit Raines, "Pouvoir ou privilèges nobiliaires: le dilemme du patriciat vénitien face aux agrégations du XVIIe siècle", *Annales: Economies, Sociétés, Civilisations* (1991), 827–48.
8. John Hale, "From peacetime establishment to fighting machine: the Venetian army and the war of Cyprus and Lepanto", in *Il Mediterraneo nella seconda metà del '500 alla luce di Lepanto*, ed. G. Benzoni (Florence, 1974), pp. 163–84.
9. Amelio Tagliaferri, "Ordinamento amministrativo dello Stato di Terraferma", in *Atti del Convegno: Venezia e la Terraferma, attraverso le relazioni dei rettori; Trieste, ottobre 1980* (Milan, 1981), pp. 15–43.
10. Yves Durand, *Les Républiques au temps des monarchies* (Paris, 1973), p. 98; Andrea Zannini, "Un ceto di funzionari amministrativi: i cittadini originari veneziani, 1569–1730", *Studi Veneziani*, 23 (1992), 1312–45.
11. Luciano Pezzolo, "Aspetti della struttura militare veneziana in Levante fra Cinque e Seicento", in *Venezia e la difesa del Levante, da Lepanto a Candia, 1570–1670* (Venice, 1986), pp. 86–96.
12. Jan Morris, *The Venetian Empire: A Sea Voyage* (London, 1980).
13. Wayne S. Vucinich, "Prince-Bishop Danilo and his place in Montenegro's history", in *East-Central European Society and War in the Pre-revolutionary Eighteenth Century*, ed. G. Rothenberg, B. Kiràly and P. Sugar (Boulder, Col., 1982), pp. 271–99.
14. Giovanni Treccani degli Alfieri (ed.), *Storia di Brescia*: vol. 3, *La dominazione veneta (1576–1797)* (Brescia, 1964), pp. 5–20. See also Joanne Ferraro, *Family and Public Life in Brescia, 1580–1650: The Foundation of Power in the Venetian State* (New York, 1993).
15. Jean Georgelin, *Venise au siècle des Lumières* (Paris, 1978), p. 201.
16. Edoardo Grendi, *La repubblica aristocratica dei genovesi: Politica, carità e commercio fra Cinque e Seicento* (Bologna, 1987); Carlo Bitossi, *Il governo dei Magnifici: Patriziato e politica a Genova fra Cinque e Seicento* (Genoa, 1990).
17. Bitossi, *Il governo dei Magnifici*, p. 44.
18. René Emmanuelli, *Gênes et l'Espagne dans la guerre de Corse (1559–69)* (Paris, 1963), p. 72.
19. Pierre Clément (ed.), *L'Italie en 1671: Relation d'un voyage du marquis de Seignelay* (Paris, 1867), p. 287.
20. Marino Berengo, *Nobili e mercanti nella Lucca del Cinquecento* (Turin, 1965); Rita Mazzei, "La questione dell' interdetto a Lucca nel secolo XVII", *Rivista Storica Italiana* (1973), 167–85; Antonio Mazzarosa, *Storia di Lucca, dalla sua origine fino al MDCCCXIV* (Lucca, 1833), vol. 2.
21. Judith Hook, "Siena and the Renaissance state", *Bollettino Senese di Storia Patria* (1980), 107–22; Ann Katherine Chiancone Isaacs, "Popolo e monti nella Siena del primo Cinquecento", *Rivista Storica Italiana* (1970), 32–80; Simon Pepper and Nicholas Adams, *Firearms and Fortifications: Military Architecture and Siege Warfare in Sixteenth-century Siena* (Chicago, 1986).

22. Furio Diaz, *Il Granducato di Toscana: I Medici* (Turin, 1987).

23. Giorgio Spini, "Introduzione", in *Architettura e politica, da Cosimo I a Ferdinando I* (Florence, 1976), pp. 9–77.

24. Luca Mannori, *Il sovrano tutore: pluralismo istituzionale e accentramento amministrativo nel principato dei Medici* (Milan, 1994).

25. Raymond Burr Litchfield, *Emergence of a Bureaucracy: The Florentine Patricians, 1530–1790* (Princeton, 1986).

26. Roberto Cantagalli, "Mario Bandini, un uomo della oligarchia senese negli ultimi tempi della Repubblica", *Bollettino Senese di Storia Patria* (1964), 51–77; see also Claudio Donati, *L'idea di nobiltà in Italia (secoli XIV–XVIII)* (Bari, 1988), pp. 215–19; Danilo Marrara, *Riseduti e nobiltà: profilo storico-istituzionale di un' oligarchia toscana nei secoli XVI–XVIII* (Pisa, 1976).

27. Irene Polverini Fosi, "Un programma di politica economica: le infeudazioni nel Senese durante il principato mediceo", *Critica Storica* (1976), 660–72; Serena Burgalassi, "I feudi nello stato senese", in *I Medici e lo stato senese, 1555–1609: storia e territorio*, ed. L. Rombai (Rome, 1980), pp. 63–74.

28. Marco Cattini, "Dall' economia della guerra, alla guerra 'in economia': prime indagini sull' organizzazione militare estense nei secoli XV e XVI", in *Guerre, stati e città: Mantova e l'Italia padana del secolo XIII al XIX* (Mantua, 1988), pp. 31–40; Romolo Quazza, *Storia politica d'Italia: Preponderanza spagnola (1559–1700)* (Milan, 1950), pp. 110–14.

29. Janet Southorn, *Power and Display in the Seventeenth Century: The Arts and their Patrons in Modena and Ferrara* (New York, 1988).

30. Giuseppe Coniglio, *I Gonzaga* (Mantua, 1967), pp. 477ff; Marzio Romani, "Les réformes institutionnelles de Guillaume III Gonzague", in *Pouvoir et institutions en Europe au XVIᵉ siècle*, ed. A. Stegmann (Paris, 1987), pp. 57–64; Cesare Mozzarelli, *Mantova e i Gonzaga dal 1382 al 1707* (Turin, 1987), p. 62.

31. Bellonci, *A Prince of Mantua* (New York, 1956); Selwyn Brinton, *The Gonzaga: Lords of Mantua* (New York, 1928).

32. James Dennistoun, *Memoirs of the Dukes of Urbino (1440–1630)*, 3 vols (London, 1851), vol. 3.

33. Bandino Giacomo Zenobi, *Tarda feudalità e reclutamento delle elites nello stato pontificio* (Urbino, 1983).

34. Giuseppe Papagno & Marzio Romani, "Una cittadella e una città (il Castello Nuovo farnesiano di Parma, 1589–1597): tensioni sociali e strategie politiche attorno alla costruzione di una fortezza urbana", *Annali dell' Istituto Storico Italo-germanico di Trento*, 8 (1982), 141–209.

35. Marzio Romani, "Finanza pubblica e potere politico: il caso dei Farnese (1545–1593)", in *Le corti farnesiane di Parma e Piacenza (1545–1622)*, 2 vols, ed. Marzio Romani (Rome, 1978), p. 36.

36. Giovanna Solari, *The House of Farnese* (New York, 1968), p. 141; Gian Luca Podestà, "Dal delitto politico alla politica del delitto (Parma 1545–1611)", ed. Y.-M. Bercé and E. Fasano Guarini, *Complots et conjurations dans l'Europe moderne* (Rome, 1996) pp. 679–720.

37. Cristina Stango, "La corte di Emanuele Filiberto: organizzazione e gruppi sociali", *Bollettino Storico-bibliografico Subalpino*, 85 (1987), 445–502.

38. Walter Barberis, *Le armi del Principe: la tradizione militare sabauda* (Turin, 1988), pp. 7–29.
39. Pierpaolo Merlin, *Tra guerre e tornei: la corte sabauda nell' età di Carlo Emanuele I* (Turin, 1991).
40. Roland Mousnier, *La Renaissance en Italie au XVIe siècle* (Paris, 1964), pp. 1–3; Ludwig von Pastor, *The History of the Popes*, vol. 25 (London, 1937), pp. 87–8.
41. Jean Delumeau, "Le progrès de la centralisation dans l'Etat pontifical au XVIe siècle", *Revue Historique* (1961), 399–410.
42. Wolfgang Reinhard, "Finanza pontificia e stato della Chiesa nel 16 e 17 secolo", in *Finanze e ragioni di Stato in Italia e in Germania nella prima età moderna* (Bologna, 1984), pp. 353–87.
43. Cesarina Casanova, "Da 'parziale' a 'buono ecclesiastico': Continuità o rottura?", in *Persistenze feudali e autonomie comunitative in stati padani fra Cinque e Settecento*, ed. G. Tocci (Bologna, 1988), pp. 247–61.
44. Gigliola Fragnito, "Cardinals' courts in sixteenth-century Rome", *Journal of Modern History* (1993), 26–56.
45. Janet Southorn, *Power and Display in the Seventeenth Century: The Arts and their Patrons in Modena and Ferrara* (New York, 1988), p. 125.
46. Wolfgang Reinhard, "Papal power and family strategy in the sixteenth and seventeenth century", in *Princes, Patronage and the Nobility: The Court at the Beginning of the Modern Age, ca. 1450–1650*, ed. Ronald G. Asch and Adolf M. Birke (Oxford, 1991), pp. 329–56; Madeleine Laurain-Portemer, "Absolutisme et népotisme: la surintendance de l'état ecclésiastique", *Bibliothèque de l'Ecole des Chartes*, 132 (1973), 487–568.
47. Renata Ago, *Carriere e clientele nella Roma barocca* (Bari, 1990).
48. Paolo Prodi, *The Papal Prince: One Body and Two Souls. The Papal Monarchy in Early Modern Europe* (Cambridge, 1987).

Notes to Chapter 5: Spanish Regimes in Italy

1. Alan Ryder, *The Kingdom of Naples under Alfonso the Magnanimous: The Making of a Modern State* (Oxford, 1976).
2. H. G. Koenigsberger, "The statecraft of Philip II", *European Studies Review* (1971), 1–21; *The Government of Sicily under Philip II of Spain* (London, 1951).
3. Francesco Benigno, *L'ombra del rey: la lotta politica nella Spagna dei Validos (1598–1643)* (Palermo, 1990).
4. Mireille Peytavin, "Le calendrier de l'administrateur. Périodisation de la domination espagnole en Italie suivant les Visites générales", *Mélanges de l'Ecole Française de Rome: Italie et Mediterranée*, 1 (1994), 263–332; Antonello Mattone, Bruno Anatra and Raimondo Turtas, *Storia dei Sardi e della Sardegna*: vol. 3, *L'età moderna: dagli Aragonesi alla fine del dominio spagnolo* (Milan, 1989); Giancarlo Sorgia, "Progetti per una flotta sardo-genovese nel Seicento", *Miscellanea di Storia Ligure*, 4 (1966), 177–93.
5. Dennis Mack Smith, *A History of Sicily*: vol. 1, *Medieval Sicily, 800–1713*

(London, 1968), pp. 115–18 and p. 141; Pietro Castiglione, *Storia di un declino: il Seicento siciliano* (Syracusa, 1987).

6. Mack Smith, *A History of Sicily*, vol. 1, p. 122.

7. Koenigsberger, *The Government of Sicily*, p. 47.

8. Giuseppe Giarrizzo and Vincenzo d'Alessandro, *La Sicilia dal Vespro all' Unità d'Italia* (Turin, 1989), p. 264; and E. William Monter, *Frontiers of Heresy: The Spanish Inquisition from the Basque Lands to Sicily* (New York, 1990), pp. 165ff.

9. Koenigsberger, *The Government of Sicily*, p. 135.

10. Castiglione, *Storia di un declino*, p. 99.

11. Francesco Benigno, "Aristocrazia e stato in Sicilia nell' epoca di Filippo III", in *Signori, patrizi e cavalieri in Italia centro-meridionale nell' età moderna*, ed. M. A. Visceglia (Bari, 1992), pp. 76–93.

12. Koenigsberger, *The Government of Sicily*, p. 46.

13. Ryder, *The Kingdom of Naples*.

14. Giuseppe Galasso, "La feudalità napoletana nel secolo XVI", in *Potere e società negli stati regionali italiani fra '500 e '600*, ed. E. Fasano Guarini (Bologna, 1978), pp. 241–57.

15. Giuseppe Galasso, *Napoli spagnola dopo Masaniello: Politica, cultura, società* (Florence, 1982), pp. 122ff.

16. Giuseppe Galasso, "Trends and problems in Neapolitan history in the age of Charles V", in *Good Government in Spanish Naples*, ed. A. Calabria and J. A. Marino (New York, 1990), pp. 13–78.

17. Enrico Stumpo, "Un mito da sfatare? Immunità ed esenzioni fiscali della proprietà ecclesiastica negli stati italiani fra '500 e '600", in *Studi in onore di Gino Barbieri: Problemi e metodi di storia ed economia*, vol. 3 (Milan, 1983), pp. 1419–66.

18. Benedetto Croce, "Scene della vita dei soldati spagnuoli a Napoli", in *Uomini e cose della vecchia Italia* (Bari, 1927), pp. 109–32.

19. Maria Antonietta Visceglia, "Dislocazione territoriale e dimensione del possesso feudale nel Regno di Napoli a metà del Cinquecento", in *Signori, patrizi, cavalieri*, pp. 31–75.

20. Gérard Labrot, *Quand l'histoire murmure: Villages et campagnes du royaume de Naples, XVIe – XVIIIe siècle* (Rome, 1995).

21. Aurelio Lepre, *Storia del Mezzogiorno d'Italia*, 2 vols (Naples, 1986), vol. 1, p. 49.

22. Giovanni Muto, "'I segni d'honore': rappresentazioni delle dinamiche nobiliari a Napoli in età moderna", in *Signori, patrizi, cavalieri*, pp. 171–92; Gérard Labrot, "Le comportement collectif de l'aristo-cratie de Naples à l'époque moderne", *Revue Historique* (1977), 45–71.

23. Benigno, *L'ombra del rey*, p. 70.

24. Gérard Delille, *Famille et propriété dans le Royaume de Naples, XVe–XIXe siècles* (Paris, 1985); Maria-Antonietta Visceglia, *Il bisogno di eternità: i comportamenti aristocratici a Napoli in età moderna* (Naples, 1988).

25. Rosario Villari, *La rivolta antispagnola a Napoli: le origini (1585–1647)* (Bari, 1976); Giuseppe Galasso, "Trends and problems", in *Good Government in Spanish Naples*, pp. 13–78, 74.

26. Giovanni Muto, "The form and content of poor relief in early modern Naples", in *Good Government in Spanish Naples*, pp. 205–36.

27. Tommaso Astarita, *The Continuity of Feudal Power: The Caracciolo di Brienza in Spanish Naples* (New York, 1992), p. 21.
28. Antonio Calabria, *The Cost of Empire: The Finances of the Kingdom of Naples in the Time of Spanish Rule* (New York, 1991); Francesco Caracciolo, *Sud, debiti e gabelle: Gravami, potere e società nel Mezzogiorno in età moderna* (Naples, 1983).
29. Astarita, *The Continuity of Feudal Power*, pp. 110ff.
30. John A. Marino, *Pastoral Economics in the Kingdom of Naples* (Baltimore, 1988), p. 158.
31. Giovanni Muto, "Come leggere il Mezzogiorno spagnolo. Fonti e problemi storiografici in studi recenti", *L'Italia degli Austrias: Cheiron*, 9 (1993), 55–80.
32. Domenico Sella, *Lo stato di Milano in età spagnola* (Turin, 1987).
33. Sella, *Lo stato di Milano*, p. 24.
34. Romano Canosa, *Milano nel Seicento: Grandezza e miseria nell' Italia spagnola* (Milan, 1993), pp. 39, 200.
35. Stumpo, "Un mito da sfatare?", in *Studi in onore di Gino Barbieri*, vol. 3, pp. 1459–65.
36. Domenico Sella, *Crisis and Continuity: The Economy of Spanish Lombardy in the Seventeenth Century* (Cambridge, Mass., 1979), pp. 151ff.
37. Canosa, *Milano nel Seicento*, p. 272.
38. Giorgio Politi, *Aristocrazia e potere politico nella Cremona di Filippo II* (Milan, 1976).
39. Mario Rizzo, "Militari e civili nello Stato di Milano durante la seconda metà del Cinquecento. In tema di alloggiamenti militari", *Clio* (1987), 563–96.
40. Yves-Marie Bercé, "Les guerres dans l'Italie du XVIIe siècle", in *Le XVIIe siècle en Italie* (Paris, 1989), p. 314.
41. Geoffrey Parker, *The Army of Flanders and the Spanish Road, 1567–1659: The Logistics of Spanish Victory and Defeat in the Low Countries' Wars* (Cambridge, 1972).
42. Manuel Rivero Rodriguez, "Felipe II y los 'Potentados de Italia'", in *La dimensione europea dei Farnese: Bulletin de l'Institut historique belge de Rome*, 63 (1993), 337–70.
43. Thomas Dandelet, "Spanish conquest and colonization at the Center of the Old World: the Spanish Nation in Rome, 1555–1625", *Journal of Modern History*, 69 (1997), 479–511.
44. Martine Lambert-Gorges, "Le roi, les ordres et le péril barbaresque: un exemple d'utilisation des ordres militaires castillans par le pouvoir royal dans l'Espagne du XVIe siècle", forthcoming in *Potere e ordini militari-cavallereschi nell' Europa mediterranea dell' età moderna* (Brussels: in press). I wish to thank Mme Lambert-Gorges for graciously sending me the typescript of her article.
45. James Westfall Thompson, *The Wars of Religion in France* (New York, 1910); Felix Rocquain, *La France et Rome pendant les guerres de religion* (Paris, 1924); James B. Wood, "The Royal Army during the early wars of religion", in *Society and Institutions in Early Modern France*, ed. Mack Holt (Athens, Ga., 1991), pp. 9–33.

Notes to Chapter 6: The Great City-Economies to 1620

1. Immanuel Wallerstein, *The Modern World-system*: vol. 1, *Capitalist Agriculture and the Origins of the European World-economy in the Sixteenth Century* (San Diego, 1974), p. 102.
2. Raul Merzario, *Signori e contadini di Calabria: Corigliano Calabro dal XVI al XIX secolo* (Milan, 1975), p. 7.
3. Jean Delumeau, *Vie économique et sociale de Rome dans la seconde moitié du XVIe siècle* (Paris, 1957), vol. 1, p. 81.
4. Fernand Braudel, *Civilization and Capitalism, 15th–18th Century*: vol. 2 *The Wheels of Commerce* (New York, 1982), p. 171.
5. Michel Carmona, "Aspects du capitalisme toscan aux XVIe et XVIIe siècles: les sociétés en commandite à Florence et à Lucques", *Revue d'Histoire Moderne et Contemporaine* (1964), 81–108.
6. Fernand Braudel, *The Mediterranean and the Mediterranean World in the Age of Philip II* (New York, 1976; first pub. 1949), p. 309.
7. Braudel, *Civilization and Capitalism, 15th–18th century*: vol. 3, *The Perspective of the World* (London, 1982).
8. Léon van der Essen, *Les Italiens en Flandre au XVIe et au XVIIe siècle* (Brussels, 1926), p. 5.
9. Suraiya Faroquhi, "The Venetian presence in the Ottoman Empire (1600–1630)", *Journal of European Economic History*, 15 (1986), 345–84.
10. Ugo Tucci, "The psychology of the merchant in the sixteenth century", in *Renaissance Venice*, ed. J. R. Hale (Totowa, N.J., 1973), pp. 346–78.
11. Donatella Calabi, "Les quartiers juifs en Italie entre XVe et XVIIe siècles: quelques hypothèses de travail", *Annales: Histoire, Sciences Sociales*, 52 (1997), 777–97.
12. Alberto Tenenti, *Piracy and the Decline of Venice, 1580–1615* (Berkeley, 1967); Gigliola Pagano de Divitiis, "Il Mediterraneo nel XVII secolo: l'espansione commerciale inglese e l'Italia", *Studi Storici*, 27 (1986), 109–48.
13. Ruth Pike, *Enterprise and Adventure: The Genoese in Seville and the Opening of the New World* (Ithaca, 1966).
14. Braudel, *Civilization and Capitalism*, vol. 2, pp. 396ff.
15. Carmona, "Aspects du capitalisme toscan".
16. Lucia Frattarelli Fischer, "Città fondata e sviluppo demografico: Livorno dal 1427 al 1750", in *Vita, morte e miracoli di gente comune: Appunti per una storia della popolazione della Toscana fra XIV e XX secolo* (Florence, 1988), pp. 118–33.
17. Carlo Cipolla, "The decline of Italy: the case of a fully-matured economy", *Economic History Review* (1952), 178–87.
18. Bruno Caizzi, *Storia dell' industria italiana, dal XVIII secolo ai nostri giorni* (Turin, 1965), p. 9.
19. Carlo Poni, "Norms and disputes: the shoemakers' guild in eighteenth century Bologna", *Past and Present*, 123 (1989), 80–108; and "Local market rules and practices: three guilds in the same line of production in early modern Bologna", in *Domestic Strategies: Work and Family in France and Italy, 1600–1800*, ed. Stuart Woolf (Cambridge, 1991), pp. 69–102.
20. Richard Mackenney, *Tradesmen and Traders: The World of the Guilds in Venice and Europe, c.1250–c.1650* (Totowa, N.J., 1987), p. 94.

21. Richard Mackenney, "In place of strife: the guilds and the law in Renaissance Venice", *History Today* (May 1984), 17–22.
22. Braudel, *The Mediterranean*, p. 430.
23. Carlo Poni, "Innovazione tecnologica e rivoluzione dei prezzi: il caso della seta", in *Studi in onore di Gino Barbieri: Problemi e metodi di storia ed economia*, vol. 3 (Milan, 1983), pp. 1261–8.
24. Robert C. Davis, "Arsenal and 'Arsenalotti': workplace and community in seventeenth-century Venice", in *The Workplace before the Factory: Artisans and Proletarians, 1500–1800*, ed. T. M. Safley and L. N. Rosenband (Ithaca, N.Y., 1993), pp. 180–203.
25. Domenico Sella, *Crisis and Continuity: The Economy of Spanish Lombardy in the Seventeenth Century* (Cambridge, Mass., 1979), pp. 19–22.
26. Braudel, *Civilization and Capitalism*, vol. 1, p. 380.
27. Luciano Allegra, *La città verticale: Usurai, mercanti e tessitori nella Chieri del Cinquecento* (Milan, 1987), pp. 108ff.
28. Carlo Marco Belfanti, "Dalla città alla campagna: industrie tessili a Mantova tra carestie ed epidemie (1550–1630)", *Critica Storica* (1988), 429–56.
29. R. Morelli, "Men of iron: masters of the iron industry in sixteenth-century Tuscany", in *The Workplace before the Factory: Artisans and Proletarians, 1500–1800*, ed. T. M. Safley and L. N. Rosenband (Ithaca, N.Y., 1993), pp. 146–64.
30. Rita Mazzei, *La società lucchese del Seicento* (Lucca, 1977), p. 19.
31. Allegra, *La città verticale*, pp. 143–50.
32. Giovanni Vigo, "Real wages of the working class in Italy: building workers' wages (14th to 18th century)", *Journal of European Economic History*, 3 (1974), 378–99.
33. Delumeau, *Vie économique et sociale de Rome*, vol. 2, p. 676.
34. Allegra, *La città verticale*.
35. Luciano Pezzolo, "Elogio della rendita. Sul debito pubblico degli stati italiani nel Cinque e Seicento", *Rivista di Storia Economica*, 12 (1995), 283–328.
36. Aldo De Maddalena, *Moneta e mercato nel '500: la rivoluzione dei prezzi* (Florence, 1973).
37. Pike, *Enterprise and Adventure*, p. 167.
38. John Francis Guilmartin, *Gunpowder and Galleys: Changing Technology and Mediterranean Warfare at Sea in the 16th Century* (Cambridge, 1974), pp. 30ff.
39. Braudel, *The Mediterranean*, p. 507.
40. Ibid., pp. 501–7.

Notes to Chapter 7: Feeding the Cities

1. Emilio Sereni, *History of the Italian Agricultural Landscape*, ed. R. Burr Litchfield (Princeton, 1997; first pub. 1961).
2. Jacques Revel, "Les privilèges d'une capitale: l'approvisionnement de Rome à l'époque moderne", *Annales: Economies, Sociétés, Civilisations* (1975), 563–74.

3. Osvaldo Raggio, *Faide e parentele: lo stato genovese visto dalla Fontanabuona* (Turin, 1990), p. 70; Danilo Barsanti, *Allevamento transumanza in Toscana: bestiami e pascali nei secoli XV–XIX* (Florence, 1987), p. 63; Gabriele Metelli, "L'alimentazione del ceto nobile e delle classi meno abbienti a Foligno, tra Cinque e Seicento", in *Alimentazione e nutrizione, secc. XIII–XVIII: Atti delle Settimane di Studi*, vol. 28, Istituto di Storia Economica Francesco Datini di Prato, ed. Simonetta Cavaciocchi (Florence, 1997), pp. 867–76.

4. Fernand Braudel, *Civilization and Capitalism, 15th–18th Centuries*, vol. 2: *The Wheels of Commerce* (New York, 1982), p. 289.

5. Giorgio Doria, *Uomini e terre di un borgo collinare, dal XVI al XVIII secolo* (Milan, 1968).

6. Raggio, *Faide e parentele*, p. 80; Aurelio Lepre, *Storia del Mezzogiorno d'Italia* (Naples, 1986), p. 52.

7. Baldassare Licata, "Il problema del grano e delle carestie al tempo di Ferdinando I de' Medici", in *Architettura e politica, da Cosimo I a Ferdinando I* (Florence, 1976), pp. 335–419.

8. Ester Boserup, "Population and technology in preindustrial Europe", *Population and Development Review*, 13 (1987), 691–701.

9. Marco Cattini, *I contadini di San Felice: Metamorfosi di un mondo rurale nell'Emilia dell'età moderna* (Turin, 1984).

10. Paolo Malanima, *Il Lusso dei contadini: Consumi e industrie nelle campagne toscane del Sei e Settecento* (Bologna, 1990), p. 105.

11. Piero Camporesi, "Les routes du fromage", in *Les effleuves du temps jadis* (Paris, 1995), pp. 59–80.

12. Henri Desplanques, *Campagnes ombriennes: Contribution à l'étude des paysages ruraux en Italie centrale* (Paris, 1969).

13. Giuliana Biagioli, "The spread of mezzadria in central Italy: a model of demographic and economic development", in *Evolution agraire et croissance démographique*, ed. A. Fauve-Chamoux (Liège, 1987), pp. 139–54.

14. Vito Caiati, "The peasant household under Tuscan mezzadria: a socio-economic analysis of some Sienese mezzadri households, 1591–1640", *Journal of Family History* (1984), 111–26.

15. Emmanuel Todd, "Mobilité géographique et cycle de vie en Artois et en Toscane au XVIIIe siècle", *Annales: Economies, Sociétés, Civilisations* (1975), 726–44.

16. Giovanni Vigo, "Real wages of the working class in Italy: building workers' wages (14th to 18th century)", *Journal of European Economic History*, 3 (1974), 378–99.

17. Domenico Sella, *Crisis and Continuity: The Economy of Spanish Lombardy in the Seventeenth Century* (New York, 1979).

18. Aurelio Lepre, *Storia del Mezzogiorno d'Italia* (Naples. 1986), pp. 78ff.

19. Gérard Delille, "Agricultural systems and demographic structures in the kingdom of Naples", in *Good Government in Spanish Naples*, ed. A. Calabria and J. A. Marino (New York, 1990), pp. 81–126.

20. Timothy B. Davies, "Village-building in Sicily: an aristocratic remedy for the crisis of the 1590s", in *The European Crisis of the 1590s: Essays in Comparative History*, ed. Peter Clark (London, 1985), pp. 191–208.

21. Marcello Verga, *La Sicilia dei grani: Gestione dei feudi e cultura economica fra Sei e Settecento* (Florence, 1993), pp. 23–35.

22. Maurice Aymard and Henri Bresc, "Nourritures et consommation en Sicile entre XIVᵉ et XVIIIᵉ siècle", *Annales: Economies, Sociétés, Civilisations* (1975), 592–9.

23. Fernand Braudel, *The Mediterranean and the Mediterranean World in the Age of Philip II* (New York, 1976), p. 146.

24. Maurice Aymard, *Venise, Raguse et le commerce du blé pendant la seconde moitié du XVIᵉ siècle* (Paris, 1966), p. 14.

25. Silvio Zotta, "Agrarian crisis and feudal politics in the kingdom of Naples: the Doria at Melfi (1585–1615)", in *Good Government in Spanish Naples*, ed. A. Calabria and J. A. Marino (New York, 1990), pp. 128–203.

26. Jean Delumeau, *Vie économique et sociale de Rome dans la seconde moitié du XVIe siècle* (Paris, 1959) vol. 2, pp. 570–98.

27. Barsanti, *Allevamento e transumanza*, p. 54; Fabio Bertini, *Feudalità e servizio del Principe nella Toscana del '500: Federigo Barbolani da Montauto, Governatore di Siena* (Siena, 1996), p. 15.

28. John A. Marino, *Pastoral Economics in the Kingdom of Naples* (Baltimore, 1988).

29. Alberto Guenzi, "La politica annonaria in età moderna", in *Il pane: Antropologia e storia dell' alimentazione*, ed. Cristina Papa (Perugia, 1992), pp. 83–8; Gian Luigi Basini, *L'uomo e il pane: risorse, consumi e carenze alimentari della popolazione modenese nel Cinque e Seicento* (Milan, 1970); Monique Martinat, "Le blé du pape: système annonaire et logiques économiques à Rome à l'époque moderne", *Annales: Histoire, Sciences sociales*, 54 (1999), 219–44.

30. Delumeau, *Vie économique et sociale de Rome*, vol. 2.

31. Anna Maria Pult Quaglia, "Controls over food supplies in Florence", *Journal of European Economic History* (1980), 449–57; and *"Per provvedere ai popoli": Il sistema annonario nella Toscana dei Medici* (Florence, 1990); Licata, "Il problema del grano".

32. Aymard, *Venise, Raguse et le commerce du blé*, p. 74.

33. Alberto Guenzi, "La tutela del consumatore nell' antico regime. I 'vittuali di prima necessità' a Bologna", in *Disciplina dell' anima, disciplina del corpo e disciplina della società tra medioevo ed età moderna* (Bologna, 1994), pp. 733–56.

34. Giuseppe Galasso, "Economia e finanze nel Mezzogiorno tra XVI e XVII secolo", in *Finanze e ragion di Stato in Italia e in Germania nella prima età moderna*, ed. Aldo De Maddalena and Hermann Kellenbenz (Bologna, 1984), pp. 45–88.

Notes to Chapter 8: Traditional Catholicism and its Persistence

1. Renata Ago, *Carriere e clientele nella Roma barocca* (Bari, 1990), p. 16.

2. Cesarina Casanova, "Da 'parziale' a 'buono ecclesiastico'. Continuità o rottura?", in *Persistenze feudali e autonomie comunitative in stati padani fra Cinque e Settecento*, ed. G. Tocci (Bologna, 1988), pp. 247–61.

3. Enrico Stumpo, "Un mito da sfatare? Immunità ed esenzioni fiscali

della proprietà ecclesiastica negli stati italiani fra '500 e '600", in *Studi in onore di Gino Barbieri: Problemi e metodi di storia ed economia*, vol. 3 (Milan, 1983), pp. 1419–66.

4. Jean-Claude Waquet, "Politique, institutions et société dans l'Italie du 'Seicento' ", in *L'Italie au XVIIe siècle* (Paris, 1989), p. 40.

5. Gaetano Greco, "Fra disciplina e sacerdozio: il clero secolare nella società italiana dal Cinquecento al Settecento", in *Clero e società nell' Italia moderna*, ed. Mario Rosa (Bari, 1992), pp. 45–113; and "Istituzioni ecclesiastiche e vita religiosa nella diocesi di Colle in epoca medicea", in *Colle di Val d'Elsa: diocesi e città tra '500 e '600*, ed. Pietro Nencini (Castelfiorentino, 1994), pp. 139–71; Rosa Martucci, " 'De vita et honestate clericorum': la formazione del clero meridionale fra Sei e Settecento", *Archivio Storico Italiano* (1986), 423–67.

6. Martucci, "De vita et honestate clericorum".

7. Greco, "Fra disciplina e sacerdozio", in *Clero e società*, p. 55.

8. Oscar Di Simplicio, "Le diable de Montorgiali", in *Le clergé délinquant (XIIIe–XVIIIe siècle)*, ed. Benoît Garnot (Dijon, 1995), pp. 155–72.

9. Gentilcore, *From Bishop to Witch: the System of the Sacred in Early Modern Terra d'Otranto* (Manchester, 1992), p. 5.

10. Roberto Rusconi, "Gli ordini religiosi maschili dalla Controriforma alle soppressioni settecentesche", in *Clero e società*, pp. 207–74.

11. Maria Mariotti, "Rapporti tra vescovi e religiosi in Calabria (attraverso i sinodi diocesani, 1574–1795)", in *Ordini religiosi e società nel Mezzogiorno moderno: Atti del seminario di studio (Lecce 1986)* (Galatino, 1987), pp. 269–337; Gabriella Zarri, "Dalla profezia alla disciplina (1450–1650)", in *Donne e fede: Santità e vita religiosa in Italia*, ed. G. Zarri and L. Scaraffia (Bari, 1994), pp. 177–225.

12. Zarri, "Dalla profezia alla disciplina", in *Donne e fede*, pp. 177–225; Judith Brown, *Immodest Acts: The Life of a Lesbian Nun in Renaissance Italy* (New York), 1986; Greco, "Istituzioni ecclesiastiche e vita religiosa", in *Colle di Val d'Elsa*, p. 162ff.

13. Raimondo Turtas, "La Chiesa", in *Storia dei Sardi e della Sardegna*: vol. 3, *L'età moderna: dagli Aragonesi alla fine del dominio spagnolo* (Milan, 1989), p. 285.

14. Christopher Black, *Italian Confraternities in the Sixteenth Century* (Cambridge, 1989).

15. Angelo Torre, "Il consumo di devozioni: rituali e potere nelle campagne piemontesi nella prima metà del Settecento", *Quaderni Storici,* 20 (1985), 181–223; and "Politics cloaked in worship: state, church and local power in Piedmont, 1570–1770", *Past and Present*, 134 (1992), 42–92.

16. Robert Scribner, *The German Reformation* (Atlantic Highlands, N.J., 1986), pp. 10ff.

17. Ernesto de Martino, *Sud e Magia* (Milan, 1980; first pub. 1959); Jean-Michel Sallmann, *Naples et ses saints à l'âge baroque* (Paris, 1994); Gentilcore, *From Bishop to Witch*; Gérard Labrot, "Images, tableaux et statuaire dans les testaments napolitains", *Revue Historique*, 268 (1982), 131–66.

18. Mary O'Neil, "Sacerdote ovvero strione: Ecclesiastical and superstitious

remedies in 16th-century Italy", in *Understanding Popular Culture*, ed. Steven Kaplan (Berlin, 1984), pp. 53–83.

19. Sallmann, *Naples et ses saints*, pp. 333–47.

20. Michael Carroll, *Madonnas that Maim: Popular Catholicism in Italy since the Fifteenth Century* (Baltimore, 1991).

21. Jean Delumeau, *Le Catholicisme entre Luther et Voltaire* (Paris, 1971).

22. Sallmann, *Naples et ses saints*, p. 21.

23. Simon Ditchfield, "Sanctity in early modern Italy", *Journal of Ecclesiastical History*, 47 (1996), 98–112.

24. O'Neil, "Sacerdote ovvero strione".

25. Ernesto de Martino, *La Terre du remords* (Paris, 1966); and *Sud e Magia*.

26. Guido Ruggiero, *Binding Passions: Tales of Magic, Marriage and Power at the End of the Renaissance* (New York, 1995), p. 148.

27. Sallmann, *Chercheurs de trésors et jeteuses de sorts: La quête du surnaturel à Naples au XVIᵉ siècle* (Paris, 1986); Thomas Cohen and Elizabeth Cohen, *Words and Deeds in Renaissance Rome: Trials before Papal Magistrates* (Toronto, 1993).

28. Ruggiero, *Binding Passions*, pp. 75ff.

29. Sallmann, *Chercheurs de trésors*, p. 12.

30. Giovanni Romeo, *Inquisitori, esorcisti e streghe nell' Italia della Controriforma* (Florence, 1990).

Notes to Chapter 9: The Tridentine Church

1. Anne Jacobson Schutte, "Periodization of sixteenth-century Italian religious history: the post-Cantimori paradigm shift", *Journal of Modern History*, 61 (1989), 269–84; Delio Cantimori, *Prospettive di storia ereticale italiana del Cinquecento* (Bari, 1960).

2. Giovanni Miccoli, "Crisi e restaurazione cattolica nel Cinquecento", in *Storia d'Italia Einaudi*, vol. 2 (Turin, 1974), pp. 975–1079.

3. Ludwig von Pastor, *The History of the Popes* (London, 1952), vol. 24, pp. 222–30, and vol. 25, pp. 226–7.

4. Daniele Montanari, *Disciplinamento in terra veneta: La diocesi di Brescia nella seconda metà del XVI secolo* (Bologna, 1987), pp. 165–72.

5. M. Antonio Buchicchio, "Conventi e ordini religiosi mendicanti maschili in Basilicata dal XVI al XVII secolo: Vita materiale e rapporti col popolo", in *Società e religione in Basilicata nell' età moderna: Atti del Convegno di Potenza-Matera, 1975* (n.p., 1977), pp. 71–120.

6. Maria Antonietta Rinaldi, "La presenza francescana nella Basilicata moderna", in *Ordini religiosi e società nel Mezzogiorno moderno* (Galatina, 1987), pp. 189–202; Francesco Russo, "Presenza francescana in Calabria in età moderna (sec. XVI–XVIII)", ibid., pp. 257–67.

7. Emanuele Boaga, "I Carmelitani in Terra d'Otranto e di Bari in epoca moderna", in *Ordini religiosi e società*, pp. 113–87.

8. Charmarie J. Blaisdell, "Angela Merici and the Ursulines", in *Religious Orders of the Catholic Reformation*, ed. R. L. De Molen (New York, 1994), pp. 98–136.

9. Gian-Mario Anselmi, "Per un archeologia della 'Ratio': Dalla 'peda-

gogia' al 'governo'", *La "Ratio studiorum": modelli culturali e pratiche educative dei Gesuiti in Italia tra Cinque e Seicento*, ed. Gian Paolo Brizzi (Rome, 1981), pp. 11–42.

10. John Patrick Donnelly SJ, "The congregration of the Oratory", in *Religious Orders of the Catholic Reformation*, pp. 188–215.

11. Claudio Donati, "Vescovi e diocesi d'Italia dall' età post-Tridentina alla caduta dell' Antico Regime", in *Clero e società nell' Italia moderna*, ed. Mario Rosa (Bari, 1992), pp. 321–89; and Adriano Prosperi, "L'Inquisizione in Italia", ibid., pp. 275–320.

12. Christopher Black, *Italian Confraternities in the Sixteenth Century* (Cambridge, 1989).

13. David Gentilcore, "'Adapt yourself to the people's capabilities': missionary strategies, methods and impact in the kingdom of Naples", *Journal of Ecclesiastical History*, 45 (1994), 269–96; Luigi Mezzadri, "Le missioni popolari dei lazzaristi nell' Umbria (1675–1797)", in *Vincent de Paul: Actes du colloque international d'études vincentiennes, Paris, septembre 1981* (Rome, 1981), pp. 310–61.

14. Emanuele Boaga, *La soppressione innocenziana dei piccoli conventi in Italia* (Rome, 1971), pp. 46–56.

15. Gérard Labrot, *Quand l'histoire murmure: Villages et campagnes du royaume de Naples, XVIᵉ–XVIIIᵉ siècles* (Rome, 1995), pp. 416–37.

16. Boaga, *La soppressione innocenziana dei piccoli conventi in Italia*.

17. Gaetano Greco, "Istituzioni ecclesiastiche e vita religiosa nella diocesi di Colle in epoca medicea", in *Colle di Val d'Elsa: Diocesi e città tra '500 e '600* (Castelfiorentino, 1994), pp. 162ff.

18. Fiamma Lussana, "Rivolta e misticismo nei chiostri femminili del Seicento", *Studi Storici* (1987), 243–60.

19. Judith C. Brown, *Immodest Acts: The Life of a Lesbian Nun in Renaissance Italy* (New York, 1986), pp. 45ff.

20. Gérard Labrot, "Le comportement collectif de l'aristocratie de Naples à l'époque moderne", *Revue Historique* (1977), 45–71.

21. Gabriella Zarri, "Dalla profezia alla disciplina (1450–1650)", in *Donne e fede: Santità e vita religiosa in Italia*, ed. L. Scaraffia and G. Zarri (Bari, 1994), pp. 177–225; Marina Caffiero, "Dall' esplosione mistica tardo-barocca all' apostolato sociale (1650–1850)", ibid., pp. 327–73; Greco, "Istituzioni ecclesiastiche e vita religiosa nella diocesi di Colle in epoca medicea", in *Colle di Val d'Elsa*, pp. 162ff.

22. Donati, "Vescovi e diocesi d'Italia", in *Clero e società*, p. 362; Oscar Di Simplicio, *Peccato, penitenza, perdono, Siena, 1575–1800: La formazione della coscienza moderna* (Milan, 1994).

23. Paul Grendler, *Schooling in Renaissance Italy: Literacy and Learning, 1300–1600* (Baltimore, 1988); Richard De Molen, "The first century of the Barnabites (1533–1633)", in *Religious Orders of the Catholic Reformation*, pp. 58–96.

24. Gian-Mario Anselmi, "Per un' archeologia della 'Ratio': Dalla 'pedagogia' al 'governo'", in *La "Ratio Studiorum": modelli culturali e pratiche educative dei Gesuiti in Italia tra Cinque e Seicento*, ed. Gian Paolo Brizzi (Rome, 1981), pp. 11–42.

25. Ottavia Niccoli, "Creanza e disciplina: buone maniere per i fanciulli

nell' Italia della controriforma", in *Disciplina dell' anima, disciplina del corpo e disciplina della società tra medioevo ed età moderna* (Bologna, 1994), pp. 929–63; Dilwyn Knox, "Disciplina: le origini monastiche e clericali del buon comportamento nell' Europa cattolica del Cinquecento e primo Seicento", ibid.; pp. 63–99.

26. Claudio Donati, "Vescovi e diocesi d'Italia dall' età post-Tridentina alla caduta dell' antico regime", in *Clero e società nell' Italia moderna*, ed. Mario Rosa (Bari, 1992), pp. 321–70.

27. Ildebrando Imberciadori, "Spedale, scuola e chiesa in popolazioni rurali dei secoli XVI–XVII", *Economia e Storia*, 3 (1959), 423–49.

28. Paul Grendler, *Schooling in Renaissance Italy*.

29. Jean-Michel Sallmann, "Alphabétisation et hiérarchie sociale à Naples à la fin du XVIe siècle et au début du XVIIe siècle", in *Sulle vie della scrittura: alfabetizzazione, cultura scritta e istituzioni in età moderna*, ed. Maria Rosaria Pelizzari (Naples, 1989), pp. 79–98; Angela Frascadore, "Livelli di alfabetizzazione e cultura grafica a Lecce intorno alla metà del XVII secolo (1640–1659)", ibid., pp. 177–226.

30. Donati, "Vescovi e diocesi d'Italia", in *Clero e società*, p. 330.

31. Montanari, *Disciplinamento in terra veneta*; Christopher Black, "Perugia and post-Tridentine church reform", *Journal of Ecclesiastical History*, 35 (1984), 429–51; Janet Southorn, *Power and Display in the Seventeenth Century: The Arts and their Patrons in Modena and Ferrara* (New York, 1988), pp. 102ff.

32. Thomas Deutscher, "The growth of the secular clergy and the development of educational institutions in the diocese of Novara (1563–1772)", *Journal of Ecclesiastical History*, 40 (1989), 381–97.

33. Rosa Martucci, "'De vita et honestate clericorum': la formazione del clero meridionale fra Sei e Settecento", *Archivio Storico Italiano* (1986), 423–67.

34. Di Simplicio, *Peccato, penitenza, perdono*; and *Storia di un Anticristo: avidità, amore e morte nella Toscana medicea* (Siena, 1996), summarized as "Le diable de Montorgiali", in *Le Clergé délinquant (XIIIe–XVIIIe siècle)*, ed. Benoît Garnot (Dijon, 1995), pp. 155–72.

35. Frascadore, "Livelli di alfabetizzazione", in *Sulle vie della scrittura*, pp. 177–226.

36. Black, *Italian Confraternities*, pp. 103–8; Samuel Cohn Jr, *Death and Property in Siena, 1205–1800: Strategies for the Afterlife* (Baltimore, 1988); Brian Pullan, *Rich and Poor in Renaissance Venice: The Social Institutions of a Catholic State, to 1620* (Cambridge, Mass., 1971), p. 44.

37. Imberciadori, "Spedale, scuola e chiesa", *Economia e Storia* (1959), 423–49.

38. Pullan, *Rich and Poor in Renaissance Venice*, pp. 585ff.; Montanari, *Disciplinamento in terra veneta*, pp. 226ff.

39. Giuseppe Giarrizzo and Vincenzo d'Alessandro, *La Sicilia dal Vespro all' Unità d'Italia* (Turin, 1989), p. 307.

40. Gentilcore, *From Bishop to Witch*; Martucci, "'De vita et honestate clericorum'"; Giovanni Colangelo, "La diocesi di Marsico dal Concilio di Trento al 1656", in *Società e religione in Basilicata nell' età moderna*,

pp. 163–98; Maria Antonietta de Cristofaro, "La diocesi di Muro Lucano nei secoli XVII e XVIII", ibid., pp. 287–330.

41. Adriano Prosperi, "L'Inquisizione: verso una nuova immagine?", *Critica Storica* (1988), 119–45.

42. E. W. Monter and John Tedeschi, "Towards a statistical profile of the Italian Inquisitions, 16th–18th centuries", in *The Inquisition in Early Modern Europe: Studies on Sources and Methods*, ed. G. Henningsen and J. Tedeschi (Dekalb, Ill., 1986), pp. 130–57.

43. Donatella Calabi, "Les quartiers juifs en Italie entre 15e et 17e siècle: quelques hypothèses de travail", *Annales: Histoire, Sciences sociales*, 52 (1997), 777–97.

44. Adriano Prosperi, *Tribunali della coscienza: Inquisitori, confessori, missionari* (Turin, 1996).

45. John Martin, *Venice's Hidden Enemies: Italian Heretics in a Renaissance City* (Berkeley, 1993), p. 12.

46. Guido Ruggiero, *Binding Passions: Tales of Magic, Marriage and Power at the End of the Renaissance* (New York, 1995), p. 143.

47. John Tedeschi, "The organization and procedures of the Roman Inquisition: a sketch", in *The Spanish Inquisition and the Inquisitorial Mind*, ed. Alcala (New York, 1987), pp. 187–215.

48. Jean-Michel Sallmann, *Chercheurs de trésors et jeteuses de sorts: la quête du surnaturel à Naples au XVIe siècle* (Paris, 1986).

49. Giovanni Romeo, *Inquisitori, esorcisti e streghe nell' Italia della Controriforma* (Florence, 1990); Oscar Di Simplico, "L'inquisizione di Siena dal 1580 al 1700: prima analisi quantitativa", *L'Inquisizione Romana: Metodologia delle fonti e storia istituzionale: Convegno di Montreale, 1999* (forthcoming). I wish to thank the author for graciously permitting me to examine his graphics and to cite his unpublished conference paper.

Notes to Chapter 10: The Rebirth of Rome

1. Laurie Nussdorfer, *Civic Politics in the Rome of Urban VIII* (Princeton, 1992).

2. Giorgio Simoncini, *Città e società nel Rinascimento*, 2 vols (Turin, 1974); Paolo Portoghesi, *Roma Barocca: The History of an Architectonic Culture* (Cambridge, Mass., 1970).

3. Gigliola Fragnito, "Cardinals' courts in sixteenth-century Rome", *Journal of Modern History*, 65 (1993), 26–56.

4. Enrico Stumpo, "Un mito da sfatare? Immunità ed esenzioni fiscali della proprietà ecclesiastica negli stati italiani fra '500 e '600", in *Studi in onore di Gino Barbieri: Problemi e metodi di Storia ed Economia*, vol. 3 (Milan, 1983), pp. 1419–66.

5. Jean Delumeau, *Vie économique et sociale de Rome dans la seconde moitié du XVIe siècle*, vol. 2 (Paris, 1959).

6. Richard Krautheimer, *The Rome of Alexander VII, 1655–1667* (Princeton, 1985).

7. Torgil Magnuson, *Rome in the Age of Bernini*, 2 vols (New Jersey, 1982).

8. Paolo Prodi, *The Papal Prince: One Body and Two Souls: the Papal Monarchy in Early Modern Europe* (Cambridge, 1987), p. 40.
9. Victor-Lucien Tapié, *The Age of Grandeur: Baroque Art and Architecture* (New York, 1966; first pub. 1957).
10. Fragnito, "Cardinals' courts".
11. Owen Chadwick, *The Popes and European Revolution* (Oxford, 1981), p. 81; Clare Robertson, *Il Gran Cardinale* (Princeton, 1992).
12. Christopher Hibbert, *The Grand Tour* (London, 1974).
13. Krautheimer, *The Rome of Alexander VII*.
14. Francis Haskell, *Patrons and Painters: A Study in the Relations between Italian Art and Society in the Age of the Baroque*, revised and enlarged edition (London, 1980), p. 27.
15. Hanns Gross, *Rome in the Age of Enlightenment: The Post-Tridentine Syndrome and the Ancien Régime* (Cambridge, 1990), p. 310.
16. Christopher Johns, *Papal Art and Cultural Politics: Rome in the Age of Clement XI* (New York, 1993), p. 13.
17. Janet Southorn, *Power and Display in the Seventeenth Century: The Arts and their Patrons in Modena and Ferrara* (New York, 1988), p. 40.
18. Thomas V. Cohen and Elizabeth S. Cohen, *Words and Deeds in Renaissance Rome: Trials before the Papal Magistrates* (Toronto, 1993).
19. Fragnito, "Cardinals' courts".
20. Georg Lutz, "L'Esercito pontificio nel 1677: camera apostolica, bilancio militare dello Stato della Chiesa e nepotismo nel primo evo moderno", in *Miscellanea in onore di Monsignor Martino Giusti, Prefetto dell' Archivio Segreto Vaticano*, vol. 2 (Vatican City, 1978), pp. 33–95.
21. Prodi, *The Papal Prince*, p. 72.
22. Nussdorfer, *Civic Politics*, p. 32.
23. Giorgio Cosmacini, *Soigner et réformer: médecine et santé en Italie de la grande peste à la première guerre mondiale* (Paris, 1992).
24. Gross, *Rome in the Age of Enlightenment*, p. 215.
25. Jacques Revel, "Les privilèges d'une capitale: l'approvisionnement de Rome", *Annales: Economies, Sociétés, Civilisations* (1975), 563–73.

Notes to Chapter 11: Bella Figura: the Baroque Era

1. Victor-Lucien Tapié, *The Age of Grandeur: Baroque Art and Architecture* (New York, 1966; first pub. 1957).
2. Silvia Carandini, *Teatro e spettacolo nel Seicento* (Bari, 1990).
3. Harold Acton, *The Bourbons of Naples (1734–1825)* (London, 1956), p. 43.
4. William Heywood, *Palio and Ponte: An Account of the Sports of Central Italy from the Age of Dante to the XXth Century* (London, 1904); Alberto Fiorini, *Metamorfosi di una festa: Dalle "Pugna" al "Palio alla tonda" (1581–1720)* (Siena, 1986); Gregory Hanlon, "Glorifying war in a peaceful city", in *Self and Society in the Renaissance*, ed. W. Connell (forthcoming).
5. Iain Fenlon, "Lepanto: the arts of celebration in Renaissance Venice", *Proceedings of the British Academy*, 73 (1987), 201–36.
6. Christopher Black, *Italian Confraternities in the Sixteenth Century* (Cambridge, 1989).

7. Robert C. Davis, *The War of the Fists: Popular Culture and Public Violence in Renaissance Venice* (Oxford, 1994).
8. Horst Bredekamp, *Le Football florentin: Les jeux et le pouvoir à la Renaissance* (Paris, 1995).
9. Deanna Lenzi, "Teatri e anfiteatri a Bologna nei secoli XVI e XVII", in *Barocco romano e barocco italiano: Il teatro, l'effimero, l'allegoria*, ed. M. Fagiolo and M. L. Madonna (Rome, 1985), pp. 174–91.
10. Mario Praz, *Studies in Seventeenth-century Imagery*, 2nd edn (Rome, 1964).
11. Riccardo Pacciani, "Temi e strutture narrative dei festeggiamenti nuziali estensi a Modena nel seicento", in *Barocco romano*, pp. 204–16.
12. Giovanni Muto, "'I segni d'onore': rappresentazioni delle dinamiche nobiliari a Napoli in età moderna", in *Signori, patrizi, cavalieri in Italia centro-meridionale nell' età moderna*, ed. M. A. Visceglia (Bari, 1992), pp. 171–92.
13. Tim Carter, *Music in Late Renaissance and Early Baroque Italy* (Portland, Oreg., 1992), p. 40; Lorenzo Bianconi, *Music in the Seventeenth Century* (Cambridge, 1987); Patrick Barbier, *The World of the Castrati: The History of an Extraordinary Operatic Phenomenon* (London, 1996).
14. Bianconi, *Music in the Seventeenth Century*, p. 18.
15. Gérard Labrot, "Images, tableaux et statuaire dans les testaments napolitains, XVIIe–XVIIIe siècle", *Revue Historique*, 268 (1982), 131–66; Gérard Labrot and Renato Ruotolo, "Pour une étude historique de la commande aristocratique dans le royaume de Naples espagnol", *Revue Historique*, 264 (1980), 25–48; Janet Southorn, *Power and Display in the Seventeenth Century: The Arts and their Patrons in Modena and Ferrara* (New York, 1988); Françoise Point-Waquet, "Les Botti: fortunes et culture d'une famille florentine (1550–1621)", *Melanges de l'Ecole Française de Rome* (1978), 689–713.
16. Francis Haskell, *Patrons and Painters: A Study in the Relations between Italian Art and Society in the Age of the Baroque*, revised and enlarged edition (London, 1980), p. 11.
17. Haskell, *Patrons and Painters*, pp. 126–30.
18. Labrot and Ruotolo, "Pour une étude historique de la commande aristocratique".
19. Claude-Gilbert Dubois, *Le Baroque: profondeurs de l'apparence* (Paris, 1973), p. 39.
20. Heinrich Wölfflin, *Principles of Art History: The Problem of the Development of Style in Later Art* (New York, 1950; first pub. 1915), pp. 1–17.
21. M. Jack, "The Accademia del Disegno in late Renaissance Florence", *Sixteenth Century Journal* (1976), 3–20.
22. Charles Dempsey, "Some observations on the education of artists in Florence and Bologna during the later sixteenth century", *Art Bulletin*, 62 (1980), 552–69.
23. Charles Dempsey, "The Carracci reform of painting", in *The Age of Correggio and the Carracci: Emilian Painting of the Sixteenth and Seventeenth Centuries* (New York, 1986), pp. 237–54; Giuseppe Olmi and Paolo Prodi, "Art, science and nature in Bologna circa 1600", ibid.,

pp. 213–36; Federico Zeri, *Pittura e Controriforma: L'"arte senza tempo" di Scipione da Gaeta* (Turin, 1957).

24.   S. J. Freedberg, *Circa 1600: A Revolution of Style in Italian Painting* (Cambridge, Mass., 1983), p. 60.
25.   Haskell, *Patrons and Painters*, p. 27.
26.   Paolo Portoghesi, *Roma Barocca: The History of an Architectonic Culture* (Cambridge, Mass., 1970); Torgil Magnuson, *Rome in the Age of Bernini*, 2 vols (New Jersey, 1982).
27.   Haskell, *Patrons and Painters*, p. 6.
28.   Olivier Bonfait, "Le livre de comptes, la mémoire et le monument: la carrière des artistes à Bologne durant l'époque moderne", *Annales: Economies, Sociétés, Civilisations* (1993), 1497–1518.
29.   Magnuson, *Rome in the Age of Bernini*, vol. 2, p. 288.
30.   Christopher M. S. Johns, *Papal Art and Cultural Politics: Rome in the Age of Clement XI* (New York, 1993).
31.   Krzysztof Pomian, *Collectionneurs, amateurs et curieux: Paris, Venise, XVIᵉ–XVIIIᵉ siècle* (Paris, 1987), p. 131.
32.   See the brilliantly unorthodox article by D. Burrows, "Style in culture: Vivaldi, Zeno and Ricci", *Journal of Interdisciplinary History* (1973), 1–23.
33.   Hugh Honour, *Neo-Classicism* (Harmondsworth, 1968).
34.   Pierre Chaunu, *La Civilisation de l'Europe des Lumières* (Paris, 1981), p. 412.

Notes to Chapter 12: Aristocracy

1.   Claudio Donati, *L'idea di nobiltà in Italia (secoli XIV–XVIII)* (Bari, 1988).
2.   Marino Berengo, "Patriziato e nobiltà: il caso Veronese", *Rivista Storica Italiana* (1975), 493–517.
3.   Franco Angiolini, "La nobiltà 'imperfetta': cavalieri e commende di S. Stefano nella Toscana moderna", in *Signori, patrizi, cavalieri in Italia centro-meridionale nell' età moderna*, ed. M. A. Visceglia (Bari, 1992), pp. 146–70.
4.   Giulio Vismara, "Il patriziato milanese del Cinque-Seicento", in *Potere e società negli stati regionali italiani fra '500 e '600*, ed. E. Fasano Guarini (Bologna, 1978), pp. 153–72.
5.   Dante Zanetti, "The patriziato of Milan from the domination of Spain to the Unification of Italy", *Social History* (1977), 745–60.
6.   Renata Ago, *La feudalità in età moderna* (Bari, 1994), p. 144.
7.   Domenico Sella, *Crisis and Continuity: The Economy of Spanish Lombardy in the Seventeenth Century* (New York, 1979), pp. 151–61.
8.   Giorgio Doria, *Uomini e terre di un borgo collinare, dal XVI al XVIII secolo* (Milan, 1968); Maria Teresa Bobbioni, "Conflittualità e amministrazione della giustizia in un feudo padano tra la fine del '500 e il primo trentennio del '600", in *Persistenze feudali e autonomie comunitative in stati padani fra Cinque e Seicento*, ed. G. Tocci (Bologna, 1988), pp. 151–66.
9.   Giorgio Borelli, *Un patriziato della Terraferma veneta tra 17 e 18 secolo: Ricerche sulla nobiltà veronese* (Milan, 1974).

10. Raymond Burr Litchfield, *Emergence of a Bureaucracy: The Florentine Patricians, 1530–1790* (Princeton, 1986), pp. 205–12.

11. Jean-Claude Waquet, *Le Grand-Duché de Toscane sous les derniers Medicis* (Rome, 1990), p. 175.

12. Gregory Hanlon, "The demilitarization of a provincial military aristocracy: Siena, 1570–1740", *Past and Present*, 155 (1997), 64–108; and *The Twilight of a Military Tradition: Italian Aristocrats and European Conflicts, 1560–1800* (London, 1998).

13. Angel Antonio Spagnoletti, *Stato, aristocrazie e Ordine di Malta nell' Italia moderna* (Rome, 1988).

14. Gregory Hanlon, "The demilitarization of a military provincial aristocracy".

15. Françoise Point-Waquet, "Les Botti: Fortunes et culture d'une famille florentine (1550–1621)", *Mélanges de l'Ecole Française de Rome* (1978), 689–713.

16. Marcello Fantoni, *La corte del Granduca: Forme e simboli del potere mediceo fra Cinque e Seicento* (Rome, 1994), pp. 58–66.

17. Oscar Di Simplicio, "Sulla 'nobiltà povera' a Siena nel Seicento", *Bollettino Senese di Storia Patria*, 89 (1982), 71–94.

18. Jean-Claude Waquet, *Corruption: Ethics and Power in Florence, 1600–1770* (University Park, Penn., 1992).

19. Joanne Ferraro, *Family and Public Life in Brescia (1580–1650)* (New York, 1993), pp. 108ff.

20. Renata Ago, "Ecclesiastical careers and the destiny of cadets", *Continuity and Change* (1992), 272–82.

21. Giulia Calvi, *Il contratto morale: Madri e figli nella Toscana moderna* (Bari, 1994), p. 5.

22. R. Burr Litchfield, "Demographic characteristics of Florentine patrician families, 16th–19th centuries", *Journal of Economic History* (1969), 191–205.

23. Edoardo Grendi, *La repubblica aristocratica dei genovesi: Politica, carità e commercio fra Cinque e Seicento* (Bologna, 1987), p. 25.

24. Raffaele Colapietra, "Prestigio sociale e potere reale nell' Aquila d'Antico regime (1525-1800)", *Critica Storia* (1979), 370–86.

25. Angelantonio Spagnoletti, *L'inconstanza delle umane cose: il patriziato di Terra di Bari tra egemonia e crisi, XVI–XVIII secolo* (Bari, 1981); Aurelio Musi, "Il patriziato a Salerno in età moderna', in *Signori, patrizi, cavalieri*, pp. 122–45.

26. Gérard Labrot, *Quand l'histoire murmure: Villages et campagnes du royaume de Naples, XVIᵉ–XVIIIᵉ siècle* (Rome, 1995).

27. Aurelio Lepre, *Storia del Mezzogiorno d'Italia*, 2 vols (Naples, 1986), vol. 1, p. 115.

28. Rosario Villari, *The Anti-Spanish Revolt in Naples* (Cambridge, 1991), ch. 6.

29. Gérard Delille, *Famille et propriété dans le royaume de Naples, XVᵉ–XIXᵉ siècles* (Paris, 1985), pp. 23–75; Maria Antonietta Visceglia, *Il bisogno di eternità: I comportamenti aristocratici a Napoli in età moderna* (Naples, 1988).

30. Giovanni Muto, "'I segni d'honore': rappresentazioni delle dinamiche

nobiliari a Napoli in età moderna", in *Signori, patrizi, cavalieri*, pp. 171–92.

31. Tommaso Astarita, *The Continuity of Feudal Power: The Caracciolo di Brienza in Spanish Naples* (New York, 1992), pp. 40ff.
32. Ago, *La feudalità*, pp. 8–16.
33. Gérard Labrot, "Le comportement collectif de l'aristocratie de Naples à l'époque moderne", *Revue Historique* (1977), 45–71; Giuseppe Galasso, "La feudalità napoletana nel secolo XVI", in *Potere e società*, pp. 241–57.
34. Michèle Benaiteau, "Una nobiltà di lunga durata: Strategie e comportamenti dei Tocco di Montemiletto", in *Signori, patrizi, cavalieri*, pp. 193–213.
35. Visceglia, *Il bisogno di eternità*, pp. 15ff.
36. Richard Goldthwaite, *Wealth and the Demand for Art in Italy, 1300–1600* (Baltimore, 1992), p. 202.
37. Peter Burke, *Venice and Amsterdam: A Study of Seventeenth Century Elites* (London, 1974).
38. J. R. Hale, "Military academies on the Venetian Terraferma in the early seventeenth century", *Studi Veneziani* (1973), 273–96.
39. Giorgio Politi, *Aristocrazia e potere politico nella Cremona di Filippo II* (Milan, 1976), pp. 223ff.
40. Labrot, "Le comportement collectif".
41. Isabella Bigazzi, "Il 'bel palazzo' come immagine di un' ascesa sociale. I Castelli e il palazzo di via S. Gallo", *Archivio Storico Italiano* (1987), 203–28.
42. Claudio Donati, "L'evoluzione della coscienza nobiliare", in *Patriziati e aristocrazie nobiliari: ceti dominanti e organizzazione del potere nell' Italia centro-settentrionale dal XVI al XVIII secolo: seminario di Trento, 1977*, ed. C. Mozzarelli and P. Schiera (Trento, 1978), pp. 13–36.
43. Marzio Barbagli, *Sotto lo stesso tetto: Mutamenti della famiglia in Italia dal XV al XX secolo* (Bologna, 1984).
44. Frederick Robertson Bryson, *The Point of Honor in Sixteenth-century Italy: An Aspect of the Life of the Gentleman* (New York, 1935).
45. Renata Ago, *Carriere e clientele nella Roma barocca* (Bari, 1990), pp. 61–7.

Notes to Chapter 13: Italy and Islam in the Mediterranean

1. John Francis Guilmartin, *Gunpowder and Galleys: Changing Technology and Mediterranean Warfare at Sea in the Sixteenth Century* (New York, 1974); Franco Gay, "Considerazioni sulle navi dell' ordine di Santo Stefano", in *Le Imprese e i simboli: Contributi alla storia del Sacro Militare Ordine di S. Stefano, secoli XVI–XIX* (Pisa, 1989), pp. 99–122.
2. Maurice Aymard, "Chiourmes et galères dans la seconde moitié du XVIᵉ siècle", in *Il Mediterraneo nella seconda metà del '500 alla luce di Lepanto*, ed. G. Benzoni (Florence, 1974), pp. 71–94.
3. I. A. A. Thompson, *War and Government in Habsburg Spain, 1560–1620* (London, 1976); Guilmartin, *Gunpowder and Galleys*, pp. 18–34.

4. Charles Monchicourt, *L'Expédition espagnole de 1560 contre l'île de Djerba* (Paris, 1913).

5. John Hale, "From peacetime establishment to fighting machine: the Venetian army and the war of Cyprus and Lepanto", in *Il Mediterraneo nella seconda metà del '500 alla luce di Lepanto*, ed. G. Benzoni (Florence, 1974), pp. 163–84.

6. Marco Morin, "La battaglia di Lepanto", in *Venezia e i Turchi: Scontri e confronti di due civiltà* (Milan, 1985), pp. 210–31.

7. Andrew C. Hess, "The battle of Lepanto and its place in Mediterranean history", *Past and Present*, 57 (1972), 53–73.

8. Guilmartin, *Gunpowder and Galleys*, p. 54.

9. Maurice Aymard, "Chiourmes et galères", in *Il Mediterraneo*, pp. 71–94.

10. Bartolome Bennassar and Lucile Bennassar, *Les Chrétiens d'Allah: l'histoire extraordinaire des rénégats (XVIe–XVIIe siècles)* (Paris, 1989).

11. Salvatore Bono, *Corsari nel Mediterraneo: Cristiani e musulmani fra guerra, schiavitù e commercio* (Milan, 1993), pp. 191–200.

12. Antonello Mattone, "La Sardegna nel mondo mediterraneo", in *Storia dei Sardi e della Sardegna*: vol. 3, *L'età moderna: dagli Aragonesi alla fine del dominio spagnolo* (Milan, 1989), p. 48.

13. Gino Benzoni, "Il 'farsi turco', ossia l'ombra del rinnegato", in *Venezia e i Turchi*, pp. 91–133.

14. Bennassar & Bennassar, *Les Chrétiens d'Allah*, p. 374.

15. P. Alberto Guglielmotti, *Storia della marina pontificia*, 8 vols (Rome, 1892).

16. Michel Fontenay, "Corsaires de la foi ou rentiers du sol? Les chevaliers de Malte dans le 'corso' méditerranéen au XVIIe siècle", *Revue d'Histoire Moderne et Contemporaine* (1988), 361–84; Angelantonio Spagnoletti, *Stato, aristocrazie e Ordine di Malta nell' Italia moderna* (Rome, 1988).

17. Silvano Burgalassi, "La 'Religione' di Santo Stefano P.E.M.: saggio di sociologia religiosa", in *Le imprese e i simboli*, pp. 145–77.

18. Camillo Manfroni, *La marina militare del Granducato mediceo* (Rome, 1895); Niccolò Giorgetti, *Le armi toscane e le occupazioni straniere in Toscana (1537–1860)*, 3 vols (Città di Castello, 1916), vol. 1.

19. Peter Earle, *Corsairs of Malta and Barbary* (London, 1970), p. 53.

20. Fontenay, "Corsaires de la foi ou rentiers du sol?"

21. Peter Earle, *Corsairs*; Michel Fontenay, "La Place de la course dans l'économie portuaire: l'exemple de Malte et des ports barbaresques", *Annales: Economies, Sociétés, Civilisations* (1988), 1321–47.

22. Gregory Hanlon, *The Twilight of a Military Tradition: Italian Aristocrats and European Conflicts, 1560–1800* (London, 1997), pp. 42–3.

23. Francisco-Felipe Olesa Muñido, *La organizacion naval de los estados mediterraneos y en especial de España durante los siglos XVI y XVII*, 2 vols (Madrid, 1968), vol. 1, p. 378.

24. Bono, *Corsari nel Mediterraneo*, pp. 61–7.

25. Gian Carlo Calcagno, "La navigazione convogliata a Genova nella seconda metà del Seicento", in *Guerra e commercio nell' evoluzione della marina genovese tra XV e XVII secolo* (Genoa, n.d.), pp. 265–392.

26. Alberto Tenenti, *Piracy and the Decline of Venice, 1580–1615* (London, 1967), p. 25.
27. Mattone, *Storia dei Sardi e della Sardegna*, vol. 3, p. 31.
28. C. Randaccio, *Storia delle marine militari italiane, dal 1750 al 1860, e della marina militare Italiana dal 1860 al 1870* (Rome, 1886), vol. 1.
29. Charles Carrière and Marcel Courdurié, "Les grandes heures de Livourne au XVIIIe siècle", *Revue Historique*, 254 (1975), 39–80.

Notes to Chapter 14: Fifty Years of War, 1610–59

1. Giorgio Spini, "La congiura degli Spagnoli contro Venezia del 1618", *Archivio Storico Italiano* (1949), 17–53.
2. Romolo Quazza, *Storia politica d'Italia: la preponderanza spagnola (1559–1700)* (Milan, 1950; first pub. 1938), pp. 409–20.
3. Niccolò Brancaccio, *L'esercito del vecchio Piemonte:* vol. 1, *Gli ordinamenti* (Rome, 1923), pp. 81ff.
4. Ruth Kleinman, "Charles Emanuel I of Savoy and the Bohemian election of 1619", *European Studies Review* (1975), 3–29.
5. Gregory Hanlon, *The Twilight of a Military Tradition: Italian Aristocrats and European Conflicts, 1560–1800* (London, 1998), ch. 3.
6. Jonathan Israel, "A conflict of empires: Spain and the Netherlands, 1618–1648", *Past and Present*, 76 (1979), 34–74.
7. Romolo Quazza, *Mantova e Monferrato nella politica europea alla vigilia della guerra per la successione (1624–1627)* (Mantua, 1922); Charles Dufayard, *Le connétable de Lesdiguières* (Paris, 1892); Hubert Reade, *Sidelights on the Thirty Years' War*, 3 vols (London, 1924); Romolo Quazza, *La guerra per la successione di Mantova e del Monferrato (1628–1631)*, 2 vols (Mantua, 1926).
8. Gaston Zeller, "Saluces, Pignerol et Strasbourg: la politique des frontières au temps de la préponderance espagnole", *Revue Historique*, 193 (1942–3), 97–110; David Parrott, "The Mantuan Succession, 1627–1631: a sovereignty dispute in Early Modern Europe", *English Historical Review*, 112 (1997), 20–65.
9. Parker, *The Thirty Years' War*, pp. 154–61.
10. Yves-Marie Bercé, "Les guerres dans l'Italie du XVIIe siècle", *Le XVIIe siècle en Italie* (Paris, 1989), p. 322.
11. Romolo Quazza, *Tommaso di Savoia-Carignano, nelle campagne di Fiandre e di Francia, 1635–38* (Turin, n.d., 1941?); Guido Quazza, *Guerra civile in Piemonte, 1637–1642 (nuove ricerche)* (Turin, 1960).
12. Enrico Dalla Rosa, *Le milizie del Seicento nello Stato di Milano* (Milan, 1991); Mario Rizzo, "Istituzioni militari e strutture socio-economiche in un città di antico regime: la milizia urbana di Pavia nell' età moderna", *Cheiron* (1995), 157–85.
13. Gianvittorio Signorotti, "Il marchese di Caracena al governo di Milano (1648–1656)", *Cheiron: L'Italia degli Austrias*, 17–18, (1993), 135–81.
14. Antonio Calabria, *The Cost of Empire: The Finances of the Kingdom of Naples in the Time of Spanish Rule* (New York, 1991), p. 90.
15. Rosario Villari, *The Anti-Spanish Revolt in Naples* (Cambridge, 1991).

16. Luigi De Rosa, "Property rights, institutional change and economic growth in Southern Italy in the eighteenth and nineteenth centuries", pp. 531–51; Luigi De Rosa, "L'ultima fase della guerra dei trent' anni e il regno di Napoli: inflazione, tassazione, speculazioni e drenaggio di capitali", *Nuova Rivista Storica* (1983), 367–86; Giuseppe Galasso, "Economia e finanze nel Mezzogiorno tra XVI e XVII secolo", in *Finanze e ragion di stato in Italia e in Germania nella prima età moderna*, ed. Aldo De Maddalena and Hermann Kellenbenz (Bologna, 1984), pp. 45–88.
17. Romualdo Giuffrida, "La politica finanziaria spagnola da Filippo II a Filippo IV (1556–1665)", *Rivista Storica Italiana*, 88 (1976), 310–41.
18. Vittorio Sciuti Russi, "Aspetti della venalità degli uffici in Sicilia (secoli XVII–XVIII)", *Rivista Storica Italiana*, 87 (1976), 342–55.
19. H. G. Koenigsberger, "The revolt of Palermo in 1647", *Cambridge Historical Journal*, 8 (1944), 129–44; Antonio Cutrera, *Cronologia dei giustiziati di Palermo, 1541–1819* (Palermo, 1917).
20. Giovanni Colangelo, "La diocesi di Marsico dal Concilio di Trento al 1656", in *Società e religione in Basilicata nell' età moderna: Atti del Convegno di Potenza-Matera, 1975* (Rome, 1977), pp. 163–98.
21. Aurelio Musi, *La rivolta di Masaniello nella scena politica barocca* (Naples, 1989), p. 52.
22. Luigi Simeoni, *Francesco d'Este e la politica italiana del Mazarino* (Bologna, 1922).
23. Giovanni Muto, "Come leggere il Mezzogiorno spagnolo. Fonti e problemi storiografici in studi recenti", *Cheiron: L'Italia degli Austrias*, 9 (1993), 55–80.
24. Gaetano Demaria, "La guerra di Castro, e la spedizione de' Presidi (1639–1649)", *Miscellanea di Storia Italiana*, 3 ser., vol. 4 (Turin, 1898), 191–256; Yves-Marie Bercé, "Rome et l'Italie au XVIIe siècle: les dernières chances temporelles de l'état ecclésiastique, 1641–1649", in *Etudes réunies en l'honneur du doyen G. Livet* (Strasbourg, 1986), pp. 229–37.

Notes to Chapter 15: Economic Collapse

1. Carlo Cipolla, "The decline of Italy; the case of a fully matured economy", *Economic History Review* (1952), 178–87.
2. Giovanni Vigo, "Real wages of the working class in Italy, XIVth–XVIIIth centuries", *Journal of European Economic History* (1974), 378–99.
3. Richard T. Rapp, "The unmaking of the Mediterranean trade hegemony: International trade rivalry and the commercial revolution", *Journal of Economic History*, 35 (1975), 499–525.
4. Ugo Tucci, "Venetian ship-owners of the sixteenth century", *Journal of European Economic History* (1987), 277–96.
5. Gigliola Pagano de Divitiis, "Il Mediterraneo nel XVII secolo: l'espansione commerciale inglese e l'Italia", *Studi Storici*, 27 (1986), 109–48.
6. Michel Carmona, "Aspects du capitalisme toscan aux XVIe et XVIIe siècles; les sociétés en commandite à Florence et à Lucques", *Revue d'Histoire Moderne et Contemporaine* (1964), 81–108.

7. Rita Mazzei, *La società lucchese del Seicento* (Lucca, 1977).

8. Claudio Rotelli, "Indici della crisi economica della Toscana nel Seicento", in *Studi in onore di Gino Barbieri: Problemi e metodi di storia ed economia*, vol. 3 (Milan, 1983), pp. 1325–43.

9. Francesco Caracciolo, *Sud, debiti e gabelle. Gravami, potere e società nel Mezzogiorno* (Naples, 1984).

10. Luigi De Rosa, "The de-industrialization of the kingdom of Naples in the sixteenth and seventeenth centuries", in *The Rise and Decline of Urban Industries in Italy and the Low Countries*, ed. H. Van der Wee (Louvain, 1988), pp. 121–37.

11. Gigliola Pagano de Divitiis, "Il Mediterraneo nel XVII secolo: l'espansione commerciale inglese e l'Italia", *Studi Storici*, 27 (1986), 109–48; and *Il commercio inglese nel Mediterraneo dal '500 al '700: corrispondenza consolare e documentazione britannica tra Napoli e Londra* (Naples, 1984).

12. Fernand Braudel, *Civilization and Capitalism, 15th–18th Centuries*: vol. 3, *The Perspective of the World* (London, 1982), pp. 175–276.

13. Paolo Malanima, *Il lusso dei contadini: consumi e industrie nelle campagne toscane del Sei e Settecento* (Bologna, 1990), p. 83.

14. Judith Brown and Jordan Goodman, "Women and industry in Florence", *Journal of Economic History* (1980), 73–80.

15. Rita Mazzei, "Continuità e crisi nella Toscana di Ferdinando II (1621–1670)", *Archivio Storico Italiano* (1987), 61–80; Paolo Malanima, "An example of industrial reconversion: Tuscany in the sixteenth and seventeenth centuries", in *The Rise and Decline of Urban Industries in Italy and the Low Countries*, pp. 63–74; Claudio Rotelli, "Indici della crisi economica della Toscana nel Seicento", in *Studi in onore di Gino Barbieri*, vol. 3, pp. 1325–43.

16. A. M. L. Trezzi, "A case-study of de-industrialization of the city: the silk mills of the city and duchy of Milan from the seventeenth to the eighteenth century", in *The Rise and Decline of Urban Industries in Italy and the Low Countries*, pp. 129–51; A. Moioli, "De-industrialization in Lombardy during the seventeenth century", ibid., pp. 75–119.

17. Salvatore Ciriacono, "Mass consumption goods and luxury goods: the de-industrialization of the Republic of Venice from the sixteenth to the eighteenth century", in *The Rise and Decline of Urban Industries in Italy and the Low Countries*, pp. 41–61.

18. Suraiya Faroqhi, "The Venetian presence in the Ottoman Empire (1600–1630)", *Journal of European Economic History*, 15 (1986), 345–84.

19. Robert Mantran, "La navigation vénitienne et ses concurrentes en Mediterranée orientale aux XVIIᵉ et XVIIIᵉ siècles", in *Mediterraneo e Oceano indiano*, ed. M. Cortelazzo (Florence, 1970), pp. 375–91.

20. Salvatore Ciriacono, "Silk manufacturing in France and Italy in the XVIIth century: two models compared", *Journal of European Economic History* (1981), 167–200.

21. Mazzei, *La società lucchese del Seicento*, pp. 66ff.

22. Salvatore Ciriacono, "The Venetian economy and its place in the world economy of the 17th and 18th centuries", in *The Early Modern World-system in Geographical Perspective*, p. 126.

23. Carlo Marco Belfanti, "Rural manufactures and rural proto-industries

in the 'Italy of the cities' from the sixteenth to the eighteenth centuries", *Continuity and Change*, 8 (1993), 253–80.

24. Malanima, *Il lusso dei contadini: Consumi e industrie nelle campagne toscane del Sei e Settecento* (Bologna, 1990).
25. Sella, *Crisis and Continuity*, p. 137.
26. Jordan Goodman, "Financing pre-modern European industry: an example from Florence, 1580–1660", *Journal of European Economic History* (1981), 415–35.
27. Alexander F. Cowan, *The Urban Patriciate: Lubeck and Venice, 1580–1700* (Cologne, 1986), p. 197.
28. Luciano Pezzolo, "Elogio della rendita. Sul debito pubblico degli stati italiani nel Cinque e Seicento", *Rivista di Storia Economica*, 12 (1995), 283–328.
29. Fernand Braudel, *Civilization and Capitalism, 15th–18th Century:* vol. 1, *The Structures of Everyday Life: The Limits of the Possible* (London, 1981), p. 463.

Notes to Chapter 16: Rural Crisis, 1630–1740

1. Domenico Sella, "Coping with famine in the 1590s", *Sixteenth Century Journal*, 22 (1991), 185–97.
2. Giovanni Zalin, "Il pane e la fame. Mondo rurale e crisi alimentare nel Bresciano del Sei e Settecento", *Nuova Rivista Storica*, 72 (1988), 245–82.
3. Lucia Bonelli-Connena, *Il contado senese alla fine del XVII secolo: Poderi, rendite e proprietari* (Siena, 1990), pp. 20ff.; Marco Cattini, *I contadini di San Felice: Metamorfosi di un mondo rurale nell' Emilia dell' età moderna* (Turin, 1984), pp. 75ff.; Henri Desplanques, *Campagnes ombriennes: Contribution à l'étude des paysages ruraux en Italie centrale* (Paris, 1969), p. 498.
4. Domenico Sella, *Crisis and Continuity: The Economy of Spanish Lombardy in the Seventeenth century* (Cambridge, Mass., 1979), p. 66.
5. Aurelio Lepre, *Storia del Mezzogiorno d'Italia*, 2 vols (Naples, 1986), vol. 2, p. 17.
6. Giorgio Borelli, "Brescia tra recessione e decadenza (1630–1766)", *Nuova Rivista Storica*, 71 (1987), 587–96.
7. Pietro Castiglione, *Storia di un declino: il Seicento siciliano* (Siracusa, 1987), p. 173.
8. Aurelio Lepre, *Storia del Mezzogiorno d'Italia*, vol. 2, p. 21.
9. Merzario, *Signori e contadini di Calabria: Corigliano Calabro dal XVI al XIX secolo*, p. 20.
10. Borelli, "Brescia tra recessione e decadenza"; Carlo Marco Belfanti, "Dalla città alla campagna: industrie tessili a Mantova tra carestie ed epidemie (1550–1630)", *Critica Storica* (1988), 429–56.
11. Maria Teresa Bobbioni, "Aspetti del paesaggio agrario e della proprietà terriera nel ducato di Parma tra '500 e '600", *Rivista di Storia dell' Agricoltura* (1980), 107–24; for Montefollonico, Archivio comunale di Torrita di Siena, Montefollonico 160, Gabella dei contratti.

400 NOTES

12. Cattini, *I Contadini di San Felice*, p. 191.
13. Frank McArdle, *Altopascio: A Study in Tuscan Rural Society, 1587–1784* (Cambridge, 1978), pp. 71ff.
14. Jean Georgelin, *Venise au siècle des Lumières* (Paris, 1978), p. 215; Richard T. Rapp, "Real estate and rational investment in early modern Venice", *Journal of European Economic History* (1979), 269–90.
15. Bonelli-Connena, *Il contado senese alla fine del XVII secolo*, p. 48.
16. Giovanni Colangelo, "La diocesi di Marsico dal Concilio di Trento al 1656", in *Società e religione in Basilicata nell' età moderna: atti del Convegno di Potenza-Matera 1975* (Rome, 1977), pp. 163–98; Oscar Di Simplicio, "Sulla 'nobiltà povera' a Siena nel Seicento", *Bollettino Senese di Storia Patria* (1982), pp. 71–92.
17. Bonelli-Connena, *Il contado senese alla fine del XVII secolo*, pp. 28–30.
18. Marco della Pina, "Famiglia mezzadrile e celibato: le campagne di Prato nei secoli XVII e XVIII", in *Popolazione, società e ambiente: Temi di demografia storica italiana, secc. XVII–XIX* (Bologna, 1990), pp. 125–40.
19. Peter Musgrave, *Land and Economy in Baroque Italy: Valpolicella, 1630–1797* (London, 1992), pp. 85–91; Vito Caiati, "Peasant household; Sienese mezzadri, 1591–1641", *Journal of Family History* (1984), 111–26.
20. Renata Ago, *La feudalità in età moderna* (Bari, 1994), p. 87.
21. Sella, *Crisis and Continuity*, pp. 105ff.
22. Giovanni Levi, *Centro e periferia di uno stato assoluto. Tre saggi su Piemonte e Liguria in età moderna* (Turin, 1985).
23. Jean-Jacques Hemardinquer, "Les débuts du maïs en Mediterranée (premier aperçu)", in *Histoire économique du monde mediterranéen* (Toulouse, 1973), pp. 227–33.
24. Sella, *Crisis and Continuity*, p. 117.
25. Fernand Braudel, *Civilization and Capitalism, 15th–18th Century*: vol. 1, *The Structures of Everyday Life*, p. 120.
26. Paolo Malanima, "L'economia toscana nell' età di Cosimo III", in *La Toscana nell' età di Cosimo III* (Florence, 1993), pp. 3–19; Ildebrando Imberciadori, *Campagna toscana nel '700: dalla Reggenza alla Restaurazione* (Florence, 1953), p. 73.
27. Desplanques, *Campagnes ombriennes*, p. 183.
28. Andrea Menzione, "Riordinamenti colturali e mutamenti strutturali nelle campagne toscane fra XVII e XVIII secolo", in *La Toscana nell' età di Cosimo III* (Florence, 1993), pp. 19–32.
29. McArdle, *Altopascio*, pp. 152ff.
30. Emmanuel Todd, "Mobilité géographique et cycle de vie en Artois et en Toscane au XVIIIᵉ siècle", *Annales: Economies, Sociétés, Civilisations* (1975), 726–44.
31. Gérard Delille, "Agricultural systems and demographic structures in the kingdom of Naples", *Good Government in Spanish Naples*, ed. A. Calabria and J. A. Marino (New York, 1990), pp. 81–126.
32. Merzario, *Signori e contadini di Calabria*, p. 58.
33. Giulio Fenicia, "Esportazione di prodotti alimentari dal Regno di Napoli nella seconda metà del XVII secolo", *Nuova Rivista Storica*, 71 (1987), 269–92.

34. Giuseppe Tricoli, *Un periodo del governo spagnolo di Sicilia nella relazione del Vicerè Uzeda (1687–1696)* (Palermo, 1980).

35. Luigi Bonazzi, *Storia di Perugia, dalle origini al 1860* (Città di Castello, 1960; first pub. 1879), p. 296.

36. Fernand Braudel, *Civilization and Capitalism, 15th–18th Century*: vol. 3, *The Perspective of the World* (New York, 1982), p. 44.

37. Lorenzo Del Panta, "Dalla mortalità epidemica alla mortalità controllata", in *Vita, morte e miracoli di gente comune: appunti per una storia della popolazione della Toscana fra XIII e XX secolo*, ed. C. Corsini (Florence, 1989), pp. 66–94.

38. McArdle, *Altopascio*, p. 58.

39. Cattini, *I contadini di San Felice*, p. 89.

40. Doria, *Uomini e terre di un borgo collinare*, p. 241.

41. N. L. Adler, "Noto: a city rebuilt", *History Today* (September 1983), 39–42.

42. Lucia Carle, *La patria locale: L'identità dei Montalcinesi dal XVI al XX secolo* (Venice, 1996), pp. 127–50; Paolo Malanima, *Il lusso dei contadini: consumi e industrie nelle campagne toscane del Sei e Settecento* (Bologna, 1990); Stuart Woolf, *The Poor in Western Europe in the Eighteenth and Nineteenth Centuries* (London, 1986), pp. 6ff.

Notes to Chapter 17: Epidemics and Assistance

1. Carlo Cipolla, *Public Health and the Medical Profession in the Renaissance* (Cambridge, 1976).

2. Hilde de Ridder-Symoens, "Management and resources", in *A History of Universities in Europe*, vol. 2: *Universities in Early Modern Europe (1500–1800)*, ed. Hilde de Ridder-Symoens (Cambridge, 1996), p. 194.

3. Clelia Pighetti, *L'influsso scientifico di Robert Boyle nel tardo '600 italiano* (Milan, 1988), p. 161.

4. Giorgio Cosmacini, *Soigner et réformer: médecine et santé en Italie de la grande peste à la première guerre mondiale* (Paris, 1992), p. 107.

5. Piero Camporesi, *Les Effleuves du temps jadis* (Paris, 1995), p. 182.

6. Gérard Labrot, *Quand l'histoire murmure: villages et campagnes du Royaume de Naples, XVIe-XVIIIe siècles* (Rome, 1995), pp. 468–89.

7. Carlo Cipolla, *Contro un nemico invisibile: Epidemie e strutture sanitarie nell' Italia del Rinascimento* (Bologna, 1985), pp. 68–70; see also Camporesi, *Les Effleuves*, pp. 96ff.

8. Massimo Livi Bacci, *La Société italienne devant les crises de mortalité* (Florence, 1978), p. 13.

9. Cosmacini, *Soigner et réformer*, pp. 112–20.

10. Paolo Preto, *Epidemie, paura e politica nell' Italia moderna* (Bari, 1987).

11. Sandra Cavallo, *Charity and Power in Early Modern Italy: Benefactors and their Motives in Turin, 1541–1789* (Cambridge, 1995), pp. 41–53.

12. Carlo Cipolla, *Cristofano and the Plague: A Study of Public Health in the Age of Galileo* (Cambridge, 1973); Giulia Calvi, *Histories of a Plague Year* (Berkeley, 1989); Cipolla, *Faith, Reason and the Plague* (Cambridge, 1977).

13. Alessandro Pastore, *Crimine e giustizia in tempo di peste nell' Europa moderna* (Bari, 1991).
14. Giulia Calvi, "A metaphor for social exchange: the Florentine plague of 1630", *Representations*, 13 (1986), 139–63.
15. Pastore, *Crimine e giustizia*, p. 131.
16. Torgil Magnuson, *Rome in the Age of Bernini* (New Jersey, 1982), vol. 2, p. 134.
17. Giuseppe Galasso, *Napoli spagnola dopo Masaniello: Politica, cultura, società* (Florence, 1982), pp. 42ff.
18. Livi Bacci, *La Société italienne*, p. 121.
19. Lorenzo Del Panta, "Dalla mortalità epidemica alla mortalità controllata", in *Vita, morte e miracoli di gente comune: Appunti per una storia della popolazione della Toscana fra XIII e XX secolo* (Florence, 1989), pp. 66–94.
20. Cipolla, "I pidocchi e il Granduca", in *Contro un nemico invisibile*, pp. 31–75.
21. Ibid., pp. 51–64; Richard M. Smith, "Periods of 'Feast and Famine': food supply and long-term changes in European mortality, *c.* 1200 to 1800", *Alimentazione e nutrizione, secc. XII–XVIII: Atti delle Settimane di Studi*, vol. 28, Istituto di Storia Economica F. Datini di Patro, ed. Simonetta Cavaciocchi (Florence, 1997), pp. 159–86.
22. Livi Bacci, *La Société italienne*, p. 108.
23. Ibid., p. 54.
24. Cosmacini, *Soigner et réformer*, p. 137.
25. Maurice Le Lannou, *Pâtres et paysans de la Sardaigne* (Tours, 1941), p. 72.
26. Braudel, *Civilization and Capitalism 15th–18th Centuries*, vol. 1: *The Structures of Everyday Life*, p. 81; Yves-Marie Bercé, "Influence de la malaria sur l'histoire événementielle du Latium (XVIe–XIXe siècles)", in *Maladie et Société (XIIe–XVIIIe siècles): actes du Colloque de Bielefeld* (Paris, 1989), pp. 235–45.
27. Mario Breschi, "L'evoluzione della mortalità infantile", in *Vita, morte e miracoli della gente comune: Appunti per una storia della popolazione della Toscana fra XIV e XX secolo* (Florence, 1988), pp. 95–107.
28. Brian Pullan, *Rich and Poor in Renaissance Venice: The Social Institutions of a Catholic State, to 1620* (Cambridge, Mass., 1971); Giovanni Assereto, "Pauperismo e assistenza: messa a punto di studi recenti", *Archivio Storico Italiano*, 141 (1983), 253–71.
29. Sandra Cavallo, "Conceptions of poverty and poor-relief in Turin in the second half of the eighteenth century", in *Domestic Strategies: Work and Family in France and Italy, 1600–1800*, ed. Stuart Woolf (Cambridge, 1991), pp. 148–99.
30. Cavallo, *Charity and Power*, pp. 5–40.
31. Daniela Lombardi, *Povertà maschile, povertà femminile: l'Ospedale dei Mendicanti nella Firenze dei Medici* (Bologna, 1988); Jon Arrizabalaga, John Henderson and Roger French, *The Great Pox: The French Disease in Renaissance Europe* (New Haven, 1997), p. 178..
32. Stuart Woolf, *The Poor in Western Europe in the Eighteenth and Nineteenth Centuries* (London, 1986), pp. 24–30.

Notes to Chapter 18: Philosophy and Science, 1550–1700

1. Jean-Michel Sallmann, *Naples et ses saints à l'âge baroque* (Paris, 1994), p. 38.
2. Andrea Battistini, "I manuali di retorica dei Gesuiti", in *La "Ratio Studiorum": Modelli culturali e pratiche educative dei Gesuiti in Italia tra Cinque e Seicento*, ed. Gian Paolo Brizzi (Rome, 1981), pp. 77–120.
3. Gian Paolo Brizzi, *La formazione della classe dirigente nel Sei-Settecento. I Seminaria nobilium nell' Italia centro-settentrionale* (Bologna, 1976); Jean Boutier, "L'Accademia dei Nobili' di Firenze. Sociabilità ed educazione dei giovani nobili negli anni di Cosimo III", in *La Toscana nell' età di Cosimo III* (Florence, 1993), pp. 205–24.
4. Willem Frijhoff, "Patterns", in *A History of the University in Europe*, vol. 2: *Universities in Early Modern Europe (1500–1800)*, ed. Hilde de Ridder-Symoens (Cambridge, 1996), pp. 54ff.
5. Giuseppe Olmi and Paolo Prodi, "Art, science and nature in Bologna circa 1600", in *The Age of Correggio and the Carracci: Emilian Painting of the Sixteenth and Seventeenth Centuries* (New York, 1986), pp. 213–36.
6. Maria Rosa di Simone, "Students", in *A History of the University in Europe*, vol. 2: pp. 294–308.
7. Amedeo Quondam, "La scienza e l'accademia", in *Università, accademie e società scientifiche in Italia e in Germania dal Cinquecento al Settecento* (Bologna, 1981), pp. 21–69.
8. Eric Cochrane, *Tradition and Enlightenment in the Tuscan Academies, 1690–1800* (Chicago, 1961), p. 8.
9. Alessandro Lazzeri, "Agostino Coltellini e l'Accademia degli Apatisti di Firenze", in *Università, accademie e società*, pp. 237–44.
10. Christopher Johns, *Papal Art and Cultural Politics: Rome in the Age of Clement IX* (Cambridge, 1992).
11. Gino Benzoni, "Aspetti della cultura urbana nella società veneta del '500 e '600. Le accademie", *Archivio Veneto*, 198 (1977), 87–159; John Martin, *Venice's Hidden Enemies: Italian Heretics in a Renaissance City* (Berkeley, 1993), p. 76.
12. Krzysztof Pomian, *Collectionneurs, amateurs et curieux: Paris, Venise, XVIᵉ–XVIIIᵉ siècle* (Paris, 1987), pp. 85ff.; Haskell, *History and its Images* (New Haven, 1993).
13. Olmi and Prodi, "Art, science and nature in Bologna", in *The Age of Correggio*, pp. 213–36.
14. Hugh Kearney, *Science and Change, 1500–1700* (New York, 1971), pp. 17–48.
15. Allen G. Debus, *Man and Nature in the Renaissance* (New York, 1978), p. 21.
16. Hélène Védrine, *Philosophie et magie à la Renaissance* (Paris, 1996), pp. 8ff.
17. Jean-Michel Sallmann, *Chercheurs de trésors et jeteuses de sorts: La quête du surnaturel à Naples au XVIᵉ siècle* (Paris, 1986).
18. William Eamon, *Science and the Secrets of Nature: Books of Secrets in Medieval and Early Modern Culture* (Princeton, 1994), pp. 194–209.
19. Giovanni Romeo, *Inquisitori, esorcisti e streghe nell' Italia della Controriforma* (Florence, 1990), p. 249.

20.   E. Barnavi and M. Eliav-Feldon, *Le Périple de Francesco Pucci: Utopie, hérésie et vérité religieuse dans la Renaissance tardive* (Paris, 1988).

21.   Emile Namer, *La Vie et l'oeuvre de J. C. Vanini, prince des libertins, mort à Toulouse sur le bûcher en 1619* (Paris, 1980); Nicholas Davidson, "Unbelief and atheism in Italy, 1500–1700", in *Atheism from the Reformation to the Enlightenment*, ed. Michael Hunter and David Wootton (Oxford, 1992), pp. 55–86; Carlo Ginzburg, *Il formaggio e i vermi: il cosmo di un mugnaio del '500* (Turin, 1976); William Monter, *Frontiers of Heresy: The Spanish Inquisition from the Basque Lands to Sicily* (New York, 1990), p. 165.

22.   Ginzburg, *Il formaggio e i vermi.*

23.   Lorenzo Bianchi, "Il Libertinismo in Italia nel XVII secolo: Aspetti e problemi", *Studi Storici* (1984), 659–77.

24.   Hélène Vérin, *La Gloire des ingénieurs: L'intelligence technique du XVIe au XVIIIe siècle* (Paris, 1993), p. 96.

25.   David C. Goodman, *Power and Penury: Government, Technology and Science in Philip II's Spain* (Cambridge, 1988), pp. 100–29.

26.   Martha Pollak, *Turin, 1564–1680: Urban Design, Military Culture and the Creation of the Absolutist Capital* (Chicago, 1991).

27.   Mario Biagioli, "Scientific Revolution, social bricolage and etiquette", in *The Scientific Revolution in National Context*, ed. Roy Porter and Mikulas Teich (Cambridge, 1992), pp. 11–54; Charles B. Schmitt, "Science in the Italian universities in the sixteenth and early seventeenth centuries", *The Aristotelian Tradition and Renaissance Universities* (London, 1984), n.p.

28.   Giorgio Cosmacini, *Soigner et réformer: médecine et santé en Italie de la grande peste à la première guerre mondiale* (Paris, 1992; first pub. 1987), p. 84.

29.   Charles B. Schmitt, "Philosophy and science in sixteenth-century Italian universities", in *The Aristotelian Tradition*, n.p.

30.   Gabriele Baroncini, "L'insegnamento della filosofia naturale nei collegi italiani dei Gesuiti (1610–1670): un esempio di nuovo aristotelismo', in *La "Ratio Studiorum"*, pp. 163–215.

31.   Robert Mandrou, *Des Humanistes aux hommes de science, XVIe–XVIIe siècles* (Paris, 1973), p. 155.

32.   Emile Namer, *L'Affaire Galilée* (Paris, 1975); Mario Biagioli, *Galileo, Courtier* (Chicago, 1993).

33.   Pierre Chaunu, *La Civilisation de l'Europe classique* (Paris, 1984; first pub. 1966), p. 340.

34.   W. E. Knowles Middleton, *The Experimenters: A Study of the Accademia del Cimento* (Baltimore, 1971).

35.   Torgil Magnuson, *Rome in the Age of Bernini* (New Jersey, 1982), pp. 140ff.

36.   Maurizio Torrini, *Dopo Galileo: Una polemica scientifica (1684–1711)* (Florence, 1979), p. 180.

37.   John Stoye, *Marsigli's Europe, 1680–1730: The Life and Times of Luigi Ferdinando Marsigli, Soldier and Virtuoso* (New Haven, 1994).

38.   Marta Cavazza, "Riforma dell' università e nuove accademie nella politica culturale dell' Arcidiacono Marsili", in *Università, accademie e società*, pp. 245–82.

39. Clelia Pighetti, *L'influsso scientifico di Robert Boyle nel tardo '600 italiano* (Milan, 1988).
40. Maurizio Torrini, "L'Accademia degli Investiganti: Napoli, 1663–1670", *Quaderni Storici*, 16 (1981), 845–83.
41. Quondam, "La scienza e l'Accademia", in *Università, accademie e società*, p. 39.
42. Mario Biagioli, "Baroque Italy", in *The Scientific Revolution in National Context*.
43. Françoise Waquet, *Le Modèle français et l'Italie savante: conscience de soi et perception de l'autre dans la République des Lettres (1660–1750)* (Rome, 1989), p. 132.
44. Schmitt, "Science in the Italian universities", in *The Aristotelian Tradition*.
45. Renata Ago, *Carriere e clientele nella Roma barocca* (Bari, 1990), p. 173.
46. Waquet, *Le Modèle français et l'Italie savante*, p. 287.
47. Paul Grendler, *Schooling in Renaissance Italy: Literacy and Learning, 1300–1600* (Baltimore, 1989), p. 389.
48. Torrini, *Dopo Galileo*, p. 82.
49. Luciano Osbat, *L'Inquisizione a Napoli: Il processo agli ateisti (1688–1697)* (Rome, 1974), p. 12; Torrini, *Dopo Galileo*, pp. 18–28; Giuseppe Galasso, *Napoli spagnola dopo Masaniello: Politica, cultura, società* (Florence, 1982), pp. 394ff.
50. Cosmacini, *Soigner et réformer*, p. 182.
51. Carla Righi, "L'Inquisizione ecclesiastica a Modena nel '700", in *Formazione e controllo dell' opinione pubblica a Modena nel '700*, ed. A. Biondi (Modena, 1986), pp. 51–95.
52. Giovanna Solari, *The House of Farnese* (New York, 1968), p. 259.
53. Marcello Fantoni, "Il bigottismo di Cosimo III: Da leggenda storiografica ad oggetto storico", in *La Toscana nell' età di Cosimo III*, pp. 389–402.
54. Eric Cochrane, *Florence in the Forgotten Centuries* (Chicago, 1973), pp. 231–313.

Notes to Chapter 19: Venice: Twilight of Empire

1. Michael Mallett and John R. Hale, *The Military Organization of a Renaissance State: Venice, 1400–1617* (Cambridge, 1984).
2. Luciano Pezzolo, "Esercito e stato nella prima età moderna. Alcune considerazioni preliminari per una ricerca sulla Repubblica di Venezia", in *Guerre, stati e città: Mantova e l'Italia padana dal secolo XIII al XIX* (Mantua, 1988), pp. 13–30.
3. Richard Davis, "Arsenal and Arsenalotti: Workplace and community in seventeenth-century Venice", in *The Workplace before the Factory: Artisans and Proletarians, 1500–1800*, ed. T. Safley and L. N. Rosenband (Ithaca, 1993), pp. 180–203.
4. Gregory Hanlon, *The Twilight of a Military Tradition: Italian Aristocrats and European Conflicts, 1560–1800* (London, 1998), p. 237.
5. Ennio Concina, *Le Trionfanti e invittissime armate venete: le milizie della serenissima dal 16 al 18 secolo* (Venice, 1971).

6. Pedro Marrades, *El Camino del Imperio: Notas para el Estudio de Cuestión de la Valtelina* (Madrid, 1943), p. 20.

7. Gaetano Cozzi, *Venezia barocca: Conflitti di uomini e idee nella crisi del Seicento veneziano* (Venice, 1995), pp. 67–90.

8. Silvio Babudieri, "Gli Uscocchi. Loro formazione e loro attività a terra ed in mare", in *Le genti del Mare Mediterraneo*, ed. Rosalba Ragosta (Naples, 1981), vol. 1, pp. 445–98.

9. Jack Alden Clarke, *Huguenot Warrior: The Life and Times of Henri de Rohan, 1579–1638* (The Hague, 1966), pp. 183ff; ed. Giovanni Treccani degli Alfieri, *Storia di Brescia*, vol. 3: *La dominazione veneta (1576–1797)* (Brescia, 1964), p. 38.

10. Kenneth M. Setton, *Venice, Austria and the Turks in the Seventeenth Century* (Philadelphia, 1991), pp. 107ff.

11. D. Raines, "Pouvoir ou privilèges nobiliaires. Le dilemme du patriciat vénitien face aux agrégations du XVIIe siècle", *Annales: Economies, Sociétés, Civilisations* (1991), 827–48.

12. *Venezia e la difesa del Levante, da Lepanto a Candia, 1570–1670* (Venice, 1986).

13. Catherine W. Bracewell, "Uskoks in Venetian Dalmatia before the Venetian–Ottoman War of 1714–1718", in *East-Central European Society and War in the Pre-Revolutionary Eighteenth Century*, ed. G. E. Rothenberg, B. K. Kiràly and P. F. Sugar (Boulder, Colo., 1982), pp. 431–47.

14. Omer Lufti Barkan, "L'empire ottoman face au monde chrétien au lendemain de Lépante", in *Il Mediterraneo nella seconda metà del '500 alla luce di Lepanto*, ed. G. Benzoni (Florence, 1974), pp. 95–108.

15. Charles Terlinden, *Le Pape Clément IX et la guerre de Candie, 1667–1669, d'après les archives secrètes du Saint-Siège* (Louvain, 1904).

16. *L'Italie en 1671: relation d'un voyage du marquis de Seignelay*, ed. Pierre Clement (Paris, 1867), pp. 232–6.

17. Carlo Maria Belfanti, "Rural manufactures and rural proto-industries in the 'Italy of the cities' from the sixteenth to the eighteenth centuries", *Continuity and Change*, 8 (1993), 253–80.

18. Philip P. Argenti, *The Occupation of Chios by the Venetians (1694)* (London, 1935).

19. C. Randaccio, *Storia delle marine militari italiane, dal 1750 al 1860, e della marina militare Italiana dal 1860 al 1870*, vol. 1 (Rome, 1886), pp. 134–43.

20. Norbert Jonard, *La Vie quotidienne à Venise au XVIIIe siècle* (Geneva, 1978), pp. 33–44.

21. Jean Georgelin, *Venise au siècle des Lumières* (Paris, 1978), p. 453.

22. Alfieri (ed.), *Storia di Brescia*, vol.3; Joanne Ferraro, *Family and Public Life in Brescia, 1580–1650* (New York, 1993).

23. Georgelin, *Venise au siècle des Lumières*, p. 626.

24. James C. Davis, *The Decline of the Venetian Nobility as a Ruling Class* (Baltimore, 1962).

25. Andrea Zannini, "Un ceto di funzionari amministrativi: i cittadini originari veneziani, 1569–1730", *Studi Veneziani*, 23 (1992), 1312–45.

26. Georgelin, *Venise au siècle des Lumières*, p. 534; Brendan Dooley, "Crisis and survival in eighteenth-century Italy: the Venetian patriciate fights back", *Journal of Social History* (1986), 323–34.

Notes to Chapter 20: The Piedmontese Absolutist State

1. Nicola Brancaccio, *L'esercito del vecchio Piemonte: gli Ordinamenti*, vol. 1: *1560–1814* (Rome, 1923).
2. Pierpaolo Merlin, *Tra guerre e tornei: La corte sabauda nell' età di Carlo Emanuele I* (Turin, 1991).
3. Norbert Elias, *La Société de cour* (Paris, 1985; first pub. 1969).
4. Gregory Hanlon, *The Twilight of a Military Tradition: Italian Aristocrats and European Conflicts, 1560–1800* (London, 1998), pp. 238–41.
5. Martha Pollak, *Turin, 1564–1680: Urban Design, Military Culture and the Creation of the Absolutist Capital* (Chicago, 1991), pp. 84ff.
6. Brancaccio, *L'esercito del vecchio Piemonte*, pp. 74–81.
7. Roger Devos and Bernard Grosperrin, *La Savoie de la Réforme à la Révolution* (Rennes, 1985), p. 136.
8. Brancaccio, *L'esercito del vecchio Piemonte*, p. 133.
9. Geoffrey Symcox, *Victor Amadeus II: Absolutism in the Savoyard State, 1675–1730* (Berkeley, 1983).
10. Geoffrey Symcox, "Two forms of popular resistance in the Savoyard state of the 1680s: the rebels of Mondovì and the Vaudois", in *La guerra del sale (1680–1699)*, ed. Giorgio Lombardi, 2 vols (Milan, 1986), pp. 275–90; Romolo Quazza, *Storia politica d'Italia: Preponderanza spagnola*, p. 47.
11. Symcox, *Victor Amadeus II*, pp. 119–21.
12. Angelo Torre, "Politics cloaked in worship: state, church and local power in Piedmont, 1570–1770", *Past and Present*, 134 (1992), 43–92; and "Il consumo di devozioni: rituali e potere nelle campagne piemontesi nella prima metà del Settecento", *Quaderni Storici*, 20 (1985), 181–223.
13. Giovanni Levi, *Centro e periferia di uno stato assoluto: tre saggi su Piemonte e Liguria in età moderna* (Turin, 1985), pp. 15–25.
14. Emmanuel de Broglie, *Catinat: l'homme et la vie (1637–1712)* (Paris, 1902), pp. 40–3.
15. Giovanni Levi, *Inheriting Power: The Story of an Exorcist* (Chicago, 1988), pp. 131–4.
16. Geoffrey Symcox, *Victor Amadeus II*, pp. 39–62.
17. Devos and Grosperrin, *La Savoie*, pp. 401ff.
18. Enrico Stumpo, "Guerra ed economia: Spese e guadagni militari nel Piemonte del Seicento", *Studi Storici* (1986), 371–95.
19. Symcox, *Victor Amadeus II*, pp. 200ff.
20. Levi, *Inheriting Power*, pp. 72–4.
21. Devos and Grosperrin, *La Savoie*.
22. Geoffrey Symcox, *Victor Amadeus II*, p. 206.
23. Denis Mack Smith, *A History of Sicily*, vol. 3: *Modern Sicily after 1713* (London, 1968), pp. 243–5.
24. Vittorio Sciuti Russi, "Aspetti della venalità degli uffici in Sicilia (secoli XVII–XVIII)", *Rivista Storica Italiana*, 87 (1976), 342–55.
25. Brancaccio, *L'esercito del vecchio Piemonte*, p. 276.
26. Spenser Wilkinson, *The Defence of Piedmont, 1742–1748* (Oxford, 1927); Gaston-E. Broche, *La République de Gênes et la France pendant la guerre de la Succession d'Autriche (1740–1748)*, 3 vols (Paris, 1936).

27. Sabina Loriga, *Soldats. Un laboratoire disciplinaire: l'armée piémontaise au XVIIIe siècle* (Paris, 1991); Walter Barberis, *Le Armi del Principe: la tradizione militare sabauda* (Turin, 1988).
28. Stuart J. Woolf, *Studi sulla nobiltà piemontese nell' epoca dell' assolutismo* (Turin, 1963), pp. 136–59.
29. Vincenzo Ferrone, "Tecnocratici militari e scienziati nel Piemonte dell' Antico regime alle origini della Reale Accademia delle Scienze di Torino", *Rivista Storica Italiana* (1984), 414–509.
30. Enrico Stumpo, " 'Vel domi vel belli': arte della pace e strategie di guerra fra Cinque e Seicento. Casi del Piemonte sabaudo, e della Toscana medicea", in *Guerre, stati e città: Mantova e l'Italia padana del secolo XIII al XIX* (Mantua, 1988), pp. 53–68.
31. Jean Georgelin, *L'Italie à la fin du XVIIIe siècle* (Paris, 1989), p. 98.

Notes to Chapter 21: Italy as a Great Power Pawn, 1660–1760

1. Michel Devèze, *L'Espagne de Philippe IV (1621–1665)*, 2 vols (Paris, 1971); R. A. Stradling, *Philip IV and the Government of Spain, 1621–1665* (Cambridge, 1988).
2. R. A. Stradling, *Europe and the Decline of Spain: A Study of the Spanish System, 1580–1720* (London, 1981).
3. Antonio Dominguez Ortiz, "La crise intérieure de la monarchie des Habsbourgs espagnols", in *The Peace of Nijmegen, 1676–1678/9: La Paix de Nimègue* (Amsterdam, 1980), pp. 157–68; Henry Kamen, *Spain in the Later Seventeenth Century, 1665–1700* (London, 1980).
4. Gregory Hanlon, *The Twilight of a Military Tradition: Italian Aristocrats and European Conflicts, 1560–1800* (London, 1998), pp. 187–92.
5. Giuseppe Galasso, *Napoli spagnola dopo Masaniello: Politica, cultura, società* (Florence, 1982), p. 22.
6. Tommaso Astarita, *Aspetti dell' organizzazione militare del regno di Napoli alla fine del Viceregno spagnolo*, unpublished *Tesi di laurea*, Università degli Studi di Napoli, 1982–3.
7. Francesca Gallo, "Le gabelle e le mete dell' università di Siracusa", in *Il governo della città: Patriziati e politica nella Sicilia moderna* (Catania, 1990), pp. 71–172; Giuseppe Tricoli, *Un periodo del governo spagnolo di Sicilia nella relazione del Viceré Uzeda (1687–1696)* (Palermo, 1980), p. 19.
8. Emile Laloy, *La Révolte de Messine, l'expédition de Sicile, et la politique française en Italie (1674–1678)*, 3 vols (Paris, 1929).
9. Pierre Clément (ed.), *L'Italie en 1671: Relation d'un voyage du marquis de Seignelay* (Paris, 1867).
10. Jean Meuvret, "Louis XIV et l'Italie", *XVIIe Siècle* (1960), 84–102.
11. Luigi Simeoni, *L'assorbimento austriaco del ducato estense e la politica dei duchi Rinaldo e Francesco III* (Modena, 1986; first pub. 1919), p. 7.
12. Carlo Bitossi, " 'Il piccolo sempre succombe al grande': la Repubblica di Genova tra Francia e Spagna, 1684–1685", in *Il bombardamento di Genova nel 1684* (Genoa, 1988), pp. 39–69; Gianni Galliani, "Il 'Bombardamento' come atto militare: alcuni interrogativi e considerazioni", ibid., pp. 95–107.

13. Salvatore Pugliese, *Le prime strette dell' Austria in Italia* (Milan–Rome, 1932), pp. 1–46.

14. Karl Otmar von Aretin, "L'ordinamento feudale in Italia nel XVI e XVII secolo e le sue ripercussioni sulla politica europea: un contributo alla storia del tardo feudalesimo in Europa", *Annali dell' Istituto Storico Italo-Germanico in Trento*, 4 (1978), 51–94.

15. Angelantonio Spagnoletti, *Stato, aristocrazie e Ordine di Malta nell' Italia moderna* (Rome, 1988), pp. 5–27.

16. John P. Spielman, *Leopold I of Austria* (London, 1977); Jean Bérenger, *Finances et absolutisme autrichien dans la seconde moitié du XVIIe siècle* (Paris, 1975), vol. 1, p. 28.

17. Jean Nouzille, *Le Prince Eugène de Savoie et les problèmes des confins militaires autrichiens, 1699–1739*, unpublished thèse de doctorat, Université de Strasbourg, 1979, pp. 185ff.

18. Henry Frederick Schwarz, *The Imperial Privy Council in the Seventeenth Century* (Cambridge, Mass., 1943), p. 152.

19. Pugliese, *Le prime strette dell' Austria in Italia*, pp. 165ff.

20. Marcello Fantoni, *La Corte del Granduca: Forme e simboli del portere medico fra Cinque e Seicento* (Rome, 1994), pp. 69–91 and 180–215; Fausto Niccolini, "Cosimo III de' Medici e Antonio Carafa", *Archivio Storico Italiano*, (1938), 69–91 and 180–215.

21. Bérenger, *Finances et absolutisme autrichien*, vol. 1, p. 391.

22. Henry Kamen, *The War of Succession in Spain, 1700–1715* (London, 1969).

23. Derek McKay, *Prince Eugene of Savoy* (London, 1977).

24. von Aretin, "L'ordinamento feudale in Italia".

25. Christopher Duffy, *The Army of Maria Theresa: The Armed Forces of Imperial Austria, 1740–1780* (New York, 1977); Claudio Donati, "Esercito e società civile nella Lombardia del secolo XVIII", *Società e Storia*, 17 (1982), 527–54.

26. Guido Quazza, *Il problema italiano e l'equilibrio europeo, 1720–1738* (Turin, 1965), pp. 394ff.

27. Pugliese, *Le prime strette dell' Austria in Italia*, p. 273; Quazza, *Il problema italiano*; Karl A. Roider, *The Reluctant Ally: Austria's Policy in the Austro-Turkish War, 1737–1739* (Baton Rouge, La., 1972).

28. André Le Glay, *Theodore de Neuhoff, roi de Corse* (Monaco–Paris, 1907).

Notes to Chapter 22: Justice, Order and Social Control

1. Renata Ago, *Un feudo esemplare: immobilismo padronale e astuzia contadina nel Lazio del '700* (Fasano, 1988), p. 128.

2. Jean-Michel Sallmann, *Chercheurs de trésors et jeteuses de sorts: la quête du surnaturel à Naples au XVIe siècle* (Paris, 1986), p. 131.

3. Guido Ruggiero, *Binding Passions: Tales of Magic, Marriage and Power at the End of the Renaissance* (New York, 1995), p. 75.

4. Marino Berengo, *Nobili e mercanti nella Lucca del Cinquecento* (Turin, 1974), p. 342.

5. Stephen Wilson, *Feuding, Conflict and Banditry in Nineteenth-century*

Corsica (Cambridge, 1988), p. 415; Madeleine-Rose Marin-Muracciole, *L'honneur des femmes en Corse, du XIIIe siècle à nos jours* (Paris, 1964).

6. Paul Arrighi (ed.), *Histoire de la Corse* (Toulouse, 1971), pp. 279–81; and *La Vie quotidienne en Corse au XVIIIe siècle* (Paris, 1970), p. 123.

7. Osvaldo Raggio, *Faide e parentele: lo stato genovese visto dalla Fontanabuona* (Turin, 1990), pp. 10ff.; Maria Desiderata Floris, "La repressione della criminalità organizzata nella repubblica di Genova tra Cinque e Seicento. Aspetti e cronologia della prassi legislativa", in G. Ortalli (ed.), *Bande armate banditi, banditisimo, e repressione di giustizia negli stati europei di antico regime* (Rome, 1986) pp. 87–106.

8. Marco Cattini and Marzio Romani, "Tra faida familiare e rivolta politica: banditi e banditismo nella Montagna Estense (secolo XVII)", in *Bande armate, banditi, banditismo e repressione di giustizia negli stati europei di antico regime* (Rome, 1986), pp. 53–66.

9. Giorgio Politi, *Aristocrazia e potere politico nella Cremona di Filippo II* (Milan, 1976), pp. 374ff.

10. Joanne M. Ferraro, *Family and Public Life in Brescia, 1580–1650* (New York, 1993), p. 134; Cesarina Casanova, "Da 'parziale' a 'buono ecclesiastico'. Continuità o rottura?", in *Persistenze feudali e autonomie comunitative in stati padani fra Cinque e Settecento*, ed. G. Tocci (Bologna, 1988), pp. 247–61; Irene Polverini Fosi, *La società violenta: il banditismo nello stato pontificio nella seconda metà del Cinquecento* (Rome, 1985), pp. 29ff. Edward Muir, *Mad Blood Stirring: Vendetta and Factions in Friuli during the Renaissance* (Baltimore, 1992); Gérard Delille, "La Paix par les femmes", *Alla Signorina: Mélanges offerts à Noëlle de la Blanchardière* (Rome, 1995), pp. 99–121.

11. William Monter, *Frontiers of Heresy: The Spanish Inquisition from the Basque Lands to Sicily* (New York, 1990), p. 183.

12. Castiglione, *Storia di un declino*, p. 14.

13. Carmelo Trasselli, "Du fait divers à l'histoire sociale: criminalité et moralité en Sicile au début de l'époque moderne", *Annales: Economies, Sociétés, Civilisations* (1973), 226–46; Dennis Mack Smith, *A History of Sicily*, vol. 1: *Medieval Sicily, 800–1713* (London, 1968), pp. 146–51; Giovanni Marrone, *Città, campagna e criminalità nella Sicilia moderna* (Palermo, 1995).

14. Raggio, *Faide e parentele*, pp. 197–209.

15. Claudio Donati, "Vescovi e diocesi d'Italia dall' età post-Tridentina alla caduta dell' Antico regime", in *Clero e società nell' Italia moderna* ed. Mario Rosa (Bari, 1992), pp. 321–89.

16. Stephen Hughes, "Fear and loathing in Bologna and Rome: the papal police in perspective", *Journal of Social History* (1987), 97–116.

17. Francesco Caracciolo, *Sud, debiti e gabelle: Gravami, potere e società nel Mezzogiorno in età moderna* (Naples, 1983), pp. 282–4.

18. Polverini Fosi, *La società violenta*, pp. 66ff. On Catena, see pp. 109ff.

19. Rosario Villari, *La rivolta antispagnola a Napoli: le origini (1585–1647)* (Bari, 1976), p. 59.

20. Antonia Vanzulli, "Il banditismo", in *Architettura e politica, da Cosimo I a Ferdinando I* (Florence, 1976), pp. 423–60.

21. Jean Delumeau, *Vie économique et sociale de Rome dans la seconde moitié du*

XVIᵉ siècle, 2 vols (Paris, 1957–59), vol. 1, p. 81 and vol. 2, pp. 544ff.; on the jurisprudence bandits inspired, Luigi Lacchè, *Latrocinium: Giustizia, scienza penale e repressione* del banditisimo in Antico Regime (Milan, 1988); Gabriella Santoncini, "La legislazione premiale dello stato fiorentino nei secoli XVI–XVIII", *Le politiche criminali nel XVIII secolo*, vol. 11: *"La Leopoldina": Criminalità e giustizia criminale nelle riforme del '700 europeo*, ed. L. Berlinguer (Milan, 1990), pp. 3–42.

22. Polverini Fosi, *La società violenta*, p. 212.
23. Raggio, *Faide e parentele*, p. 28.
24. Furio Bianco, "Sbirri, contrabbandieri e le 'rie sette di malfattori' nel '700 friulano", in *Emarginazione, criminalità e devianza in Italia fra '600 e '900: Problemi e indicazioni di ricerca*, ed. A. Pastore and P. Sorcinelli (Milan, 1990), pp. 51–75.
25. Doria, *Uomini e terre di un borgo collinare*, p. 278.
26. Maria Teresa Bobbioni, "Conflittualità e amministrazione della giustizia in un feudo padano tra la fine del '500 e il primo trentennio del '600", in *Persistenze feudali e autonomie comunitative in stati padani fra Cinque e Seicento*, ed. G. Tocci (Bologna, 1988), pp. 151–66; and Ago, *Un feudo esemplare*, pp. 128–34.
27. Luciano Allegra, *La città verticale: Usurai, mercanti e tessitori nella Chieri del Cinquecento* (Milan, 1987), pp. 84 & 183.
28. Elena Fasano Guarini, "Produzione di leggi e disciplinamento nella Toscana granducale tra Cinque e Seicento. Spunti di ricerca", in *Disciplina dell' anima, disciplina del corpo e disciplina della società tra medioevo ed età moderna* (Bologna, 1994), pp. 659–90; Andrea Zorzi, "La politique criminelle en Italie (XIIIᵉ–XVIIᵉ siècle)", *Crime, histoire et sociétés*, 2 (1998), 91–110.
29. Luciano Allegra, "Stato e monopolio del controllo sociale: il caso del Piemonte fra '700 e '800", in *Emarginazione, criminalità e devianza*, pp. 77-84; Brian Pullan, *Rich and Poor in Renaissance Venice: The Social Institutions of a Catholic State, to 1620* (Cambridge, Mass., 1971), p. 349; Richard Mackenney, "In place of strife: the guilds and the law in Renaissance Venice", *History Today* (May 1984), 17–22.
30. Sallmann, *Chercheurs de trésors et jeteuses de sorts*, pp. 72ff.
31. Owen Chadwick, *The Popes and European Revolution* (Oxford, 1981), pp. 48–53.
32. Marrone, *Città, campagna e criminalità*, p. 150; Giovanni Liva, "Pena detentiva e carcere: il caso della Milano 'spagnola' ", in *Emarginazione, criminalità e devianza*, pp. 9–24.
33. Claudio Povolo, "Entre la force de l'honneur et le pouvoir de la justice: le délit de viol en Italie (XIVᵉ–XIXᵉ siècles)", in *L'Infrajudiciaire du Moyen Age à l'époque contemporaine: Actes du Colloque de Dijon, Octobre 1995* (Dijon, 1996), pp. 155–64; Bobbioni, 'Conflittualità e amministrazione della giustizia", in *Persistenze feudali e autonomie comunitative*, pp. 151–66.
34. Elena Fasano Guarini, "Le istituzioni di Siena e del suo stato nel ducato mediceo", in *I Medici e lo stato senese, 1555–1609: storia e territorio* (Rome, 1980), pp. 49-62; Marzio A. Romani, "Criminalità e giustizia nel ducato di Mantova alla fine del Cinquecento", *Rivista Storica Italiana* (1980), pp. 680–99.

35. Antonio Cutrera, *Cronologia dei giustiziati di Palermo, 1541–1819,* (Palermo, 1917), pp. 115–312.

36. Allegra, *La città verticale,* pp. 199ff.; Doria, *Uomini e terre di un borgo collinare,* pp. 241ff.; Bobbioni, "Conflittualità e amministrazione della giustizia", in *Persistenze feudali e autonomie comunitative,* pp. 151–66.

37. Thomas V. Cohen and Elizabeth S. Cohen, *Words and Deeds in Renaissance Rome: Trials before the Papal Magistrates* (Toronto, 1993).

38. John K. Brackett, *Criminal Justice and Crime in Late Renaissance Florence, 1537–1609* (New York, 1992), p. 62; Paolo Marchetti, *Testis contra se: L'imputato come fonte di prova nel processo penale dell' età moderna* (Milan, 1994), pp. 64–75; Aurelio Lepre, *Storia del Mezzogiorno d'Italia,* 2 vols (Naples, 1986), vol. 1, p. 126.

39. Brackett, *Criminal Justice and Crime,* p. 90.

40. Gross, *Rome in the Age of Enlightenment,* p. 217.

41. Gaetano Sabatini, "Fiscalità e banditismo in Abruzzo alla fine del Seicento", *Nuova Rivista Storica,* 79 (1995), 77–112.

42. Donati, "Vescovi e diocesi d'Italia", in *Clero e società nell' Italia moderna,* p. 362; Alfred Soman, "Deviance and criminal justice", in *Sorcellerie et justice criminelle,* p. 21.

43. Daniele Montanari, *Disciplinamento in terra veneta: La diocesi di Brescia nella seconda metà del XVI secolo,* (Bologna, 1987), pp. 165–84.

44. Oscar Di Simplicio, *Storia di un Anticristo: Avidità, amore e morte nella Toscana medicea* (Siena, 1996).

45. Oscar Di Simplicio, *Peccato, penitenza, perdono: Siena 1575–1800. La formazione della coscienza nell' Italia moderna* (Milan, 1994).

46. Gaetano Greco, "Istituzioni ecclesiastiche e vita religiosa nella diocesi di Colle in epoca medicea", *Colle di Val d'Elsa: diocesi e città tra '500 e '600,* ed. P. Nencini (Castelfiorentino, 1994), pp. 139–71; Luigi Mezzadri, "Le missioni popolari dei lazzaristi nell' Umbria (1675–1797), *Vincent de Paul: Actes du Colloque International d'Etudes Vincentiennes, Paris 1981* (Rome, 1981), pp. 310–61.

47. David Gentilcore, *From Bishop to Witch: The System of the Sacred in Early Modern Terra d'Otranto* (Manchester, 1992), pp. 45–8; and "'Adapt yourselves to the people's capabilities': Missionary strategies, methods and impact in the kingdom of Naples, 1600–1800", *Journal of Ecclesiastical History* (1994), 269–96.

48. Carla Zarrilli, "Lo stato ed i contrabbandieri: la violazione del monopolio del sale nel Senese all' inizio del XVIII secolo", *Bollettino Senese di Storia Patria* (1991), 195–214; Jean-Claude Waquet, "Aux marges de l'impôt: fraudeurs et contrebandiers dans la Toscane du XVIIIe siècle", in *La Fiscalité et ses implications sociales en Italie et en France aux XVIIe et XVIIIe siècles: Actes du Colloque de Florence, 1978* (Rome, 1980), pp. 75–94.

49. Bianco, "Sbirri, contrabbandieri e le 'rie sette di malfattori'", in *Emarginazione, criminalità e devianza,* pp. 51–75.

50. Giampiero Brunelli, "Poteri e privilegi. L'istituzione degli ordinamenti delle milizie nello stato pontificio tra Cinque e Seicento", *Cheiron* (1995), 105–29.

51. Mario Sbriccoli, "Fonti giudiziarie e giuridiche. Riflessioni sulla fase attuale degli studi", *Studi Storici,* 29 (1988) 491–501; Edoardo Grendi,

"Sulla 'storia criminale': risposta a Mario Sbriccoli", *Quaderni Storici*, 73, (1990), 269–75; Liva, "Pena detentiva e carcere", in *Emarginazione, criminalità e devianza in Italia fra '600 e '900*, pp. 9–24.

Notes to Chapter 23: The Italian Enlightenment

1. Françoise Waquet, *Le Modèle français et l'Italie savante: Conscience de soi et perception de l'autre dans la République des Lettres (1660–1750)* (Rome, 1989), p. 290; Pierre Chaunu, *La Civilisation de l'Europe des Lumières* (Paris, 1982), p. 26.
2. Christopher M. S. Johns, *Papal Art and Cultural Politics: Rome in the Age of Clement XI* (New York, 1993), pp. 33ff.
3. Claudio Donati, "Scipione Maffei e la 'Scienza Chiamata Cavalleresca': saggio sull' ideologia nobiliare al principio del Settecento", *Rivista Storica Italiana*, 90 (1978), 30–71.
4. Brendan Dooley, "The 'Giornale de' Letterati d'Italia"; Jouralism and 'modern' culture (1710–1740)", *Studi Veneziani* (1982), 229–70.
5. Owen Chadwick, *The Popes and European Revolution* (Oxford, 1981), p. 396.
6. Dino Carpanetto & Giuseppe Ricuperati, *Italy in the Age of Reason, 1685–1789* (London, 1987), pp. 106–13.
7. Romeo De Maio, "Il problema del quietismo napoletano", *Rivista Storica Italiana*, 81 (1969), 721–44.
8. Thomas Deutscher, "The growth of the secular clergy and the development of educational institutions in the diocese of Novara (1563–1772)", *Journal of Ecclesiastical History*, 40 (1989), 381–97.
9. Chadwick, *The Popes and European Revolution*, pp. 325, 76.
10. Carlo Francovich, *Storia della Massoneria in Italia, dalle origini alla Rivoluzione francese* (Florence, 1974), p. 50.
11. Geoffrey Symcox, *Victor Amadeus II: Absolutism in the Savoyard State, 1675–1730* (Berkeley, 1983), pp. 217ff.
12. Augusto Placanica, "Chiesa e società nel Settecento meridionale: clero, istituti e patrimoni nel quadro delle Riforme", in *Società e religione in Basilicata: Atti del convegno di Potenza-Matera, 1975*, 2 vols. (n.p., 1977), vol. 1, pp. 222–320.
13. Waquet, *Le modèle français et l'Italie savante*, p. 185; Brendan Dooley, "Social control and the Italian universities", *Journal of Modern History* (1989), 205–39.
14. Françoise Waquet and Jean-Claude Waquet, "Le Livre florentin dans la culture toscane: les enseignements du registre de la censure, 1743–1767", *Bibliothèque de l'Ecole des Chartes* (1980), 217–29; Anne Machet, "Censure et librairie en Italie au XVIIIe siècle", *Revue des Études Sud-est Européennes*, 10 (1972), 459–90.
15. Denis Mack Smith, *A History of Sicily*, vol. 3: *Modern Sicily after 1713* (London, 1968), p. 301.
16. Marina Caffiero, "Dall' esplosione mistica tardo-barocca all' apostolato sociale (1650–1850)", in *Donne e fede: Santità e vita religiosa in Italia*, ed. L. Scaraffia and G. Zarri (Bari, 1994), pp. 327–73.

17. Chadwick, *The Popes and European Revolution*, p. 148; Carla Righi, "L'Inquisizione ecclesiastica a Modena nel '700", in *Formazione e controllo dell' opinione pubblica a Modena nel '700*, ed. A. Biondi (Modena, 1986), pp. 51–95.
18. Chadwick, *The Popes and European Revolution*, p. 160; Harold Acton, *The Bourbons of Naples (1734–1825)* (London, 1956), pp. 83–4.
19. Maria Antonietta de Cristofaro, "La diocesi di Muro Lucano nei secoli XVII e XVIII", in *Società e religione in Basilicata*, pp. 287–330.
20. Rita Librandi, "La grammatica di Alfonso de' Liguori e il contributo dei Liguorini alla diffusione della lingua e della cultura nel secolo XVIII", in *Sulle vie della scrittura: Alfabetizzazione, cultura scritta e istituzioni in età moderna*, ed. M. R. Pelizzari (Naples, 1989), pp. 391–421.
21. Susan V. Nicassio, "'For the benefit of my soul': a preliminary study of the persistence of tradition in eighteenth-century mass obligations", *Catholic Historical Review*, 78 (1992), 175–96; Xenio Toscani, "Ecclesiastici e società civile nel '700: Un problema di storia sociale e religiosa", *Società e Storia* (1982), 683–716.
22. Samuel Cohn Jr, *Death and Property in Siena, 1205–1800: Strategies for the Afterlife* (Baltimore, 1988), pp. 210ff.
23. Cesare Mozzarelli, *Sovrano, società e amministrazione locale nella Lombardia teresiana (1749–1758)* (Bologna, 1982), pp. 220ff.
24. Jean Boutier, "L''Accademia dei Nobili' di Firenze: sociabilità ed educazione dei giovani nobili negli anni di Cosimo III", in *La Toscana nell' età di Cosimo III* (Florence, 1993), pp. 205-24.
25. Eric Cochrane, *Tradition and Enlightenment in the Tuscan Academies, 1690–1800* (Chicago, 1961).
26. Giorgio Montecchi, "La censura di stato nel ducato estense dalle origini alla fine del Settecento", in *Formazione e controllo dell' opinione pubblica*, pp. 23–49.
27. Eric Cochrane, *Florence in the Forgotten Centuries, 1527–1800* (Chicago, 1973), p. 331.
28. Françoise Waquet, "Le livre florentin", pp. 217–29; Jean Georgelin, *Venise au siècle des Lumières* (Paris, 1978), pp. 713ff.
29. Machet, "Censure et librairie".
30. Waquet, *Le Modèle français et l'Italie savante*, p. 146.
31. Dooley, The "Giornale de' Letterati d'Italia' ".
32. Françoise Waquet & Jean-Claude Waquet, "Presse et société. Le public des 'Novelle letterarie' de Florence, 1749–1769", *Revue Française d'Histoire du Livre* (1979), 39–60.
33. Miriam Levy, *Governance and Grievance: Habsburg Policy and Italian Tyrol in the Eighteenth Century* (Purdue, 1988).
34. Norbert Jonard, *La Vie quotidienne à Venise au XVIIIe siècle* (Geneva, 1978; first pub. 1965), p. 181.
35. Sabina Loriga, *Soldats: Un laboratoire disciplinaire. L'armée piémontaise au XVIIIe siècle* (Paris, 1991), p. 60.
36. Francovich, *Storia della Massoneria in Italia*, pp. 50 and 87.
37. Jonard, *La Vie quotidienne à Venise*, p. 150.
38. Elvira Chiosi, "Nobiltà e massoneria a Napoli. Il regno di Carlo di

Borbone", in *Signori, patrizi, cavalieri in Italia centro-meridionale nell' età moderna*, ed. M. A. Visceglia (Bari, 1992), pp. 326–39.

39. Daniel Klang, "Economics and political economy in eighteenth-century Lombardy", *Italian Quarterly* (Fall 1988), 37–53.

40. Mack Smith, *A History of Sicily*, vol. 3, p. 262.

41. Antonio Mazzarosa, *Storia di Lucca, dalla sua origine fino al MDCCCXIV*, 2 vols (Lucca, 1833), vol. 2, p. 124.

42. Edoardo Grendi, *La repubblica aristocratica dei genovesi: Politica, carità e commercio fra Cinque e Seicento* (Bologna, 1987), p. 39.

43. Claudio Donati, "Organizzazione militare e carriera delle armi nell' Italia d'antico regime", in *Ricerche di storia in onore di Franco Della Paruta: Politica e istituzioni*, ed. M. L. Betri and D. Bigazzi (Milan, 1996), pp. 9–39; Vincenzo Ferrone, "Tecnocratici militari e scienziati nel Piemonte dell' antico regime alle origini della Reale Accademia delle Scienze di Torino", *Rivista Storica Italiana*, (1984), 414–509; Loriga, *Soldats* (Paris, 1991).

44. Marzio Barbagli, *Sotto lo stesso tetto: Mutamenti della famiglia in Italia dal XV al XX secolo* (Bologna, 1984), pp. 320ff.

45. Dante Zanetti, "The patriziato of Milan from the domination of Spain to the unification of Italy: an outline of the social and demographic history", *Social History* (1977), 745–60.

46. Sandra Cavallo and Simona Cerutti, "Onore femminile e controllo sociale della riproduzione in Piemonte, tra '600 e '700", *Quaderni Storici*, 15 (1980), 346–83.

47. Jean-Michel Sallmann, "Alphabétisation et hiérarchie sociale à Naples à la fin du XVIᵉ siècle et au début du XVIIᵉ siècle", in *Sulle vie della scrittura*, pp. 79–98; Peter Burke, "The uses of literacy in early modern Italy", in *The Social History of Language*, ed. Peter Burke and Roy Porter (Cambridge, 1987), pp. 21–42; Piero Lucchi, "La prima istruzione. Idee, metodi, libri", in *Il catechismo e la grammatica: Istruzione e controllo sociale nell' area emiliana e romagnola* (Bologna, 1985), pp. 25–81.

48. Jean-Michel Sallmann, 'Les niveaux d'alphabétisation en Italie au XIXe siècle', *Mélanges de l'Ecole française de Rome; Italie et Méditerranée*, 101 (1989) 183–337.

49. Daniele Marchesini, "La fatica di scrivere. Alfabetismo e sottoscrizioni matrimoniali in Emilia tra Sette e Ottocento", in *Il catechismo e la grammatica*, pp. 83–169; and *Il bisogno di scrivere. Usi della scrittura nell' Italia moderna* (Bari, 1992); François Furet and Jacques Ozouf (eds), *Lire et écrire*, 2 vols (Paris, 1977).

50. Roger Devos and Bernard Grosperrin, *La Savoie de la Réforme à la Révolution* (Rennes, 1985), p. 441.

51. Gerard Delille, "Livelli di alfabetizzazione nell' Italia meridionale a metà '700: problemi di ricerca e primi risultati", in *Sulle vie della scrittura*, pp. 153–7; Maria Rosaria Pelizzari, "Alfabeto e fisco. Tra cultura scritta e oralità nel regno di Napoli a metà Settecento", ibid., pp. 99–152; Elvira Chiosi, "Intellettuali e plebe: il problema dell' istruzione elementare nel Settecento napoletano", ibid., pp. 353–74; Carlo Romeo, "Servi e scrittura: Scandagli nella Roma barocca", ibid., pp. 619–27; Angela Frascadore, "Livelli d'alfabetizzazione e cultura

grafica a Lecce intorno alla metà del XVII secolo (1640–1659)", ibid.,
pp. 177–226; Sallmann, "Les niveaux d'alphabétisation en Italie".

Notes to Chapter 24: An Equivocal Recovery

1. Paolo Malanima, *Il lusso dei contadini: Consumi e industrie nelle campagne
    toscane del Sei e Settecento* (Bologna, 1990), p. 151; Aurelio Lepre, *Storia
    del Mezzogiorno d'Italia*, 2 vols (Naples, 1986), vol. 2, pp. 52–4.
2. Marco Cattini, *I contadini di San Felice: Metamorfosi di un mondo rurale
    nell' Emilia nell' età moderna* (Turin, 1984); Claudio Bargelli, *Pauperismo,
    economia e società a Modena nei secoli XVII–XVIII* (Parma, 1997), pp. 49ff.
3. Massimo Livi Bacci, *La Société italienne devant les crises de mortalité*
    (Florence, 1978), p. 54.
4. Henri Desplanques, *Campagnes ombriennes: Contribution à l'étude des
    paysages ruraux en Italie centrale* (Paris, 1969).
5. Jean Georgelin, *Venise au siècle des Lumières*, (Paris, 1978), p. 369.
6. Ibid., p. 356; Georgelin, *L'Italie à la fin du XVIIIe siècle* (Paris, 1989) p. 76.
7. Jean Georgelin, *L'Italie à la fin du XVIIIe siècle*, p. 28.
8. Eric Cochrane, *Tradition and Enlightenment in the Tuscan Academies*
    (Chicago, 1961), p. 152.
9. Franco Venturi, "The Enlightenment in the Papal States", and "The
    Enlightenment in Southern Italy", in *Italy and the Enlightenment: Studies
    in a Cosmopolitan Century* (New York, 1972), pp. 198–264.
10. Tommaso Astarita, *The Continuity of Feudal Power: The Caracciolo di
    Brienza in Spanish Naples* (New York, 1992), p. 72.
11. Fernand Braudel, *Civilization and Capitalism, 15th–18th Century*, vol. 2:
    The Wheels of Commerce (New York, 1982), pp. 284–8.
12. Marcello Verga, *La Sicilia dei grani: Gestione dei feudi e cultura economica
    fra Sei e Settecento* (Florence, 1993), p. 84n., and p. 90.
13. Renata Ago, *Un feudo esemplare: Immobilismo padronale e astuzia contadina
    nel Lazio del '700* (Fasano, 1988), p. 121.
14. Rosalba Davico, "Baux, exploitations, techniques agricoles en Piémont
    dans la deuxième moitié du XVIIIe siècle', *Etudes Rurales* (1972),
    76–101.
15. Raul Merzario, *Signori e contadini di Calabria: Corigliano Calabro dal XVI
    al XIX secolo*, p. 38.
16. Patrick Chorley, *Oil, Silk and Enlightenment: Economic Problems in XVIIIth
    century Naples* (Naples, 1965).
17. Harold Acton, *The Bourbons of Naples (1734–1825)* (London, 1956),
    pp. 105ff.
18. Ildebrando Imberciadori, *Campagna toscana nel '700: Dalla reggenza alla
    restaurazione* (Florence, 1953), pp. 13 and 62.
19. Eric Cochrane, *Florence in the Forgotten Centuries, 1527–1800* (Chicago,
    1973), p. 437.
20. Franco Venturi, "The Enlightenment in southern Italy", in *Italy and the
    Enlightenment*, pp. 198–224.
21. John A. Marino, *Pastoral Economics in the Kingdom of Naples* (Baltimore,
    1988).

22. Georgelin, *L'Italie à la fin du XVIIIe siècle*, p. 126; Xenio Toscani, "Ecclesiastici e società civile nel '700: Un problema di storia sociale e religiosa", *Società e Storia* (1982), 683–716.

23. Malanima, *Il lusso dei contadini*, pp. 139–60.

24. Bargelli, *Pauperismo, economia e società a Modena*, p. 103.

25. Roland Sarti, *Long Live the Strong: A History of Rural Society in the Apennine Mountains* (Amherst, Mass., 1985).

26. Fernand Braudel, *Civilization and Capitalism 15th–18th Centuries*, vol. 3: *The Perspective of the World*, pp. 162–9.

27. Lucia Frattarelli Fischer, "Città fondata e sviluppo demografico: Livorno dal 1427 al 1750", in *Vita, morte e miracoli di gente comune: Appunti per una storia della popolazione della Toscana fra XIV e XX secolo* (Florence, 1988), pp. 118–33.

28. Charles Carrière and Marcel Coudurié, "Les grandes heures de Livourne au XVIIIe siècle: l'exemple de la guerre de sept ans", *Revue Historique*, 254 (1975), 39–80.

29. Gigliola Pagano de Divitiis, *Il commercio inglese nel Mediterraneo dal '500 al '700: Corrispondenza consolare e documentazione britannica tra Napoli e Londra* (Naples, 1984).

30. Georgelin, *Venise au siècle des Lumières*, pp. 95ff.

31. Anna Maria Rao, *Il regno di Napoli nel Settecento* (Naples, 1983), p. 97.

32. Ruggiero Romano, "Il commercio franco-napoletano nel secolo XVIII", in *Napoli: Dal Viceregno al regno: Storia economica* (Turin, 1976), pp. 67–122; Denis Mack Smith, *A History of Sicily*, vol. 3: *Modern Sicily after 1713* (London, 1968), p. 272.

33. Simona Cerutti, "Giustizia e località a Torino in età moderna: una ricerca in corso", *Quaderni Storici*, 30 (1995), 445–86.

34. Daniel Klang, "Economics and political economy in eighteenth-century Lombardy", *Italian Quarterly* (Fall 1988), 37–53.

35. Antonio di Vittorio, "Un caso di correlazione tra guerre, spese militari e cambiamenti economici: le guerre asburgiche della prima metà del XVIII secolo e le loro ripercussioni sulla finanza e l'economia dell' Impero", *Nuova Rivista Storica* (1982), 59–81.

36. Miriam Levy, *Governance and Grievance: Habsburg Policy and Italian Tyrol in the Eighteenth Century* (West Lafayette, Ind., 1988), pp. 24–8.

37. Bruno Caizzi, *Storia dell' industria italiana dal XVIII secolo ai nostri giorni* (Turin, 1965), pp. 88, 150.

38. Carlo Marco Belfanti, "Rural manufactures and rural proto-industries in the 'Italy of the Cities' from the 16th to the 18th century", *Continuity and Change*, 8 (1993), 253–80.

39. Salvatore Ciriacono, "The Venetian economy and its place in the world economy of the 17th and 18th centuries: a comparison with the Low Countries", in *The Early Modern World-system in Geographical Perspective*, ed. H. J. Nitz (Stuttgart, 1993), 120–35.

40. Giorgio Borelli, "Brescia tra recessione e decadenza (1630–1766)", *Nuova Rivista Storica*, 71 (1987), 587–96.

41. Caizzi, *Storia dell' industria italiana*.

42. Caizzi, *Storia dell' industria italiana*, pp. 9ff.; Carlo Poni, "Norms and disputes: the shoemakers' guild in eighteenth century Bologna", *Past and*

Present, 123 (1989), 80–108; and "Local market rules and practices: three guilds in the same line of production in early modern Bologna", in *Domestic Strategies: Work and Family in France and Italy, 1600–1800*, pp. 69–102.

43. Angelo Massafra, "En Italie méridionale: déséquilibres régionaux et réseaux de transport du milieu du XVIIIe siècle à l'unité italienne", *Annales: Economies, Sociétés, Civilisations* (1988), 1045–80.

44. Sandra Cavallo, "Conceptions of poverty and poor-relief in Turin in the second half of the eighteenth century", in *Domestic Strategies: Work and Family in France and Italy, 1600–1800*, ed. Stuart Woolf (Cambridge, 1991), pp. 148-99; Bargelli, *Pauperismo, economia e società*.

45. Malanima, *Il lusso dei contadini*, p. 123.

46. Christopher Hibbert, *The Grand Tour* (London, 1974).

47. Salvatore Ciriacono, "Echecs et réussites de la proto-industrialisation dans la Vénétie: le cas du Haut-Vicentin, XVIIe–XIXe siècles", *Revue d'Histoire Moderne et Contemporaine* (1985), 311–23.

48. Pierre Chaunu, *La Civilisation de l'Europe des Lumières* (Paris, 1982), p. 20.

Notes to Chapter 25: Absolutist Reforms in Bourbon Italy

1. Aurelio Musi, "Stato moderno e mediazione burocratica", *Archivio Storico Italiano* (1986), 75–96.

2. Harold Acton, *The Bourbons of Naples (1734–1825)* (London, 1963), pp. 27–65.

3. Gregory Hanlon, *Twilight of a Military Tradition: Italian Aristocrats and European Conflicts, 1560–1800* (London, 1998), ch. 8.

4. Owen Chadwick, *The Popes and European Revolution* (Oxford, 1981), p. 53.

5. Mario Spedicato, "Capacità contributiva ed articolazione patrimoniale dei regolari in Terra d'Otranto alla fine dell' Antico Regime", in *Ordini religiosi e società nel Mezzogiorno moderno: Atti del seminario di studio, Lecce 1986* (Galatina, 1987), pp. 361–79.

6. Michèle Benaiteau, "Una nobiltà di lunga durata: Strategie e comportamenti dei Tocco di Montemiletto", in *Signori, patrizi, cavalieri in Italia centro-meridionale nell' età moderna*, ed. M. A. Visceglia (Bari, 1992), pp. 193–213.

7. Anna Maria Rao, "Esercito e società a Napoli nelle riforme del secondo settecento", *Studi Storici* (1987), 623–77; and, "Antiche storie e autentiche scritture: prove di nobiltà a Napoli nel Settecento", in *Signori, patrizi, cavalieri*, pp. 279–308; Maria Grazia Maiorini, "Nobiltà napoletana e cariche amministrative: i presidi provinciali nel Settecento", ibid., pp. 309–25; Giuseppe Ferrarelli, *Memorie militari del Mezzogiorno d'Italia* (Bari, 1911), pp. 12–17.

8. Alessandra Bulgarelli Lukacs, "Le 'Universitates' meridionali all' inizio del regno di Carlo di Borbone", *Clio*, 17 (1981) pp. 208–26.

9. Anna Maria Rao, *Il regno di Napoli nel Settecento* (Naples, 1983), p. 106.

10. Luigi De Rosa, "Immobility and change in public finance in the

Kingdom of Naples, 1694–1806", *Journal of European Economic History,* 27 (1998), 9–28.

11. Patrick Chorley, *Oil, Silk and Enlightenment: Economic Problems in XVIIIth Century Naples* (Naples, 1965), p. 65.
12. Francesco Russo, "Presenza francescana in Calabria in età moderna (secoli XVI-XVIII)", in *Ordini religiosi e società,* pp. 257–67.
13. Luigi De Rosa, "Property rights, institutional changes and economic growth in southern Italy in the eighteenth and nineteenth centuries", *Journal of European Economic History,* 8 (1979), 531–51.
14. Rao, *Il regno di Napoli nel Settecento,* p. 116.
15. Denis Mack Smith, *A History of Sicily,* vol. 3: *Modern Sicily after 1713* (London, 1968), pp. 258–320.
16. Henri Bedarida, *Parme et la France de 1748 à 1789* (Geneva, 1977; first pub. 1928); Chadwick, *The Popes and European Revolution,* p. 363.

Notes to Chapter 26: The Habsburg Revolution

1. Salvatore Pugliese, *Le prime strette dell' Austria in Italia* (Milan, Rome, 1932), p. 314.
2. Antonio di Vittorio, "Un caso di correlazione tra guerre, spese militari e cambiamenti economici: le guerre asburgiche della prima metà del XVIII secolo e le loro ripercussioni sulla finanza e l'economia dell' Impero", *Nuova Rivista Storica* (1982), 59–81.
3. Francesca Gallo, "La Sicilia di Carlo VI: riforma amministrativa e ricerca del consenso (1719–1734)", *Cheiron: Dilattare l'impero,* 21 (1995), 187–226.
4. Denis Mack Smith, *A History of Sicily,* vol. 3: *Modern Sicily after 1713* (London, 1968), pp. 254ff.
5. Antonio Calabria, "Per la storia della dominazione austriaca a Napoli, 1707–1734", *Archivio Storico Italiano,* 139 (1981), 459–78; Antonio Di Vittorio, "Ancora a proposito di storia della dominazione austriaca a Napoli, 1707–1734", *Archivio Storico Italiano* (1984), 607–22.
6. Anna Maria Rao, *Il regno di Napoli nel Settecento* (Naples, 1983), pp. 38ff.
7. Alexander Grab, "Enlightened despotism and state building: the case of Austrian Lombardy", *Austrian History Yearbook* (1983–4), 43–72; J. M. Roberts, "Lombardy", in *The European Nobility in the Eighteenth Century,* ed. A. Goodwin (London, 1967), pp. 60–82.
8. Cesare Mozzarelli, "Sovrano, aristocrazia e amministrazione: un profilo costituzionale", in *La dinamica statale austriaca nel XVIII e XIX secolo: Strutture e tendenze di storia costituzionale,* ed. P. Schiera (Bologna, 1981), pp. 127–60.
9. Eric Cochrane, *Florence in the Forgotten Centuries, 1527–1800* (Chicago, 1973), p. 358.
10. Cesare Mozzarelli, *Sovrano, società e amministrazione locale nella Lombardia teresiana (1749–1758)* (Bologna, 1982).
11. Stuart Woolf, *A History of Italy, 1700–1860: The Social Constraints of Political Change* (London, 1979), p. 74.
12. Carlo Capra, "Riforme finanziarie e mutamento istituzionale nello

stato di Milano: gli anni sessanta del secolo XVIII", *Rivista Storica Italiana* (1979), 313–68.

13. John Spielman, *The City and the Crown: Vienna and the Imperial Court, 1600–1740* (West Lafayette, Ind., 1993); Christopher Duffy, *The Army of Maria Theresa: The Armed Forces of Imperial Austria, 1740–1780* (New York, 1977), p. 25; Claudio Donati, "Esercito e società civile nella Lombardia del secolo XVIII", *Società e Storia* (1982), 527–54.

14. F. Szabo, *Kaunitz and Enlightened Absolutism, 1753–1780* (Cambridge, 1994), p. 28.

15. Capra, "Riforme finanziarie e mutamento istituzionale", p. 332.

16. Daniel Klang, "Economics and political economy in eighteenth-century Lombardy", *Italian Quarterly* (Fall 1988), 37–53.

17. Woolf, *A History of Italy, 1700-1860*, pp. 99–104; Grab, "Enlightened despotism and state building", pp. 63–8.

18. Miriam J. Levy, *Governance and Grievance: Habsburg Policy and Italian Tyrol in the Eighteenth Century* (West Lafayette, Ind., 1988), pp. 47ff.

19. Owen Chadwick, *The Popes and European Revolution*, pp. 414–17; Levy, *Governance and Grievance*, p. 47.

20. Woolf, *A History of Italy, 1700–1860*, p. 108; Dino Carpanetto and Giuseppe Ricuperati, *Italy in the Age of Reason, 1685–1789* (London, 1987), pp. 174–7.

21. Susan V. Nicassio, " 'For the benefit of my soul': a preliminary study of the persistence of tradition in eighteenth-century mass obligations", *Catholic Historical Review*, 78 (1992), 175–96; Giorgio Montecchi, "La censura di stato nel ducato estense dalle origini alla fine del Settecento", in *Formazione e controllo dell' opinione pubblica a Modena nel '700*, ed. A. Biondi (Modena, 1986), pp. 23–49.

22. R. Burr Litchfield, *Emergence of a Bureaucracy: The Florentine Patricians, 1530–1790* (Princeton, 1986), p. 65.

23. Jean-Claude Waquet, *Le Grand-Duché de Toscane sous les derniers Medicis* (Rome, 1990), pp. 224–30.

24. Jean-Claude Waquet, *Corruption: Ethics and Power in Florence, 1600–1770* (University Park, Penn., 1992).

25. Waquet, *Le Grand-Duché de Toscane*; Hanns Gross, *Rome in the Age of Enlightenment: The Post-Tridentine Syndrome and the Ancien Regime* (Cambridge, 1990), pp. 126–7.

26. Cochrane, *Florence*, pp. 344ff.

27. Giuseppe Pansini, "Les réformes de François-Etienne de Lorraine en Toscane (1737–1765)", in *La Lorraine dans l'Europe des Lumières: Actes du Colloque de Nancy, 1966* (Nancy, 1968), pp. 359–66.

28. Niccolo Giorgetti, *Le Armi toscane e le occupazioni straniere in Toscana (1537–1860)*, 3 vols (Città di Castello, 1916), see vol. 2, pp. 16ff.

29. Danilo Marrara, *Riseduti e nobiltà: Profilo storico-istituzionale di un' oligarchia toscana nei secoli XVI–XVIII* (Pisa, 1976).

30. Levy, *Governance and Grievance*, p. 68; Cochrane, *Florence*, pp. 400ff.

31. Litchfield, *Emergence of a Bureaucracy*, pp. 305ff.

32. Ildebrando Imberciadori, *Campagna toscana nel '700: Dalla Reggenza alla Restaurazione* (Florence, 1953).

33. Cochrane, *Florence*, pp. 400–98.

Glossary

Agonistic society   The term applies to tight-knit families competing inamicably with each other, for status, reputation and wealth.

Agrotown   A large agglomeration in which the great majority of the population consisted of peasants, constrained to travel kilometres to work in the fields. These lacked a wide array of artisanal activities, services and cultural institutions common in Early Modern towns.

Amoral familism   The ethic whereby one was bound to act strictly in the short-term interest of the immediate family, and to expect other families to do likewise, even if the result was deleterious to the common good.

Annona   A name for the array of government intervention mechanisms and regulations in the sector of provisioning and distributing food and essential items to the population, indispensable because of frequent dearth.

Arcadia   A literary academy founded at Rome in 1690, whose members cultivated stylistic simplicity and clarity in poetry and prose, as a reaction against "baroque" extravagance.

Aristocratic republic   Like all republics, a political entity in which ultimate sovereignty belongs to the people, but in which only those born noble have access to political functions and have the right to express political opinions.

Arsenal (Venice)   A vast manufacturing complex, perhaps Europe's largest, for the construction and maintenance of galleys and ships, and their outfitting with naval stores, and for casting cannon and smaller weapons.

Asiento   A contract signed between the Spanish Crown and an individual, a company or even a country giving them a commercial monopoly during the term of the agreement. The *asiento* often opened the door to more lucrative side operations for those undertaking them, including contraband.

Bank of St. George   A financial institution in Genoa dating from the twelfth century, and the leading lending institution, managing state revenues of the Republic by the fifteenth century, and fulfilling banking operations of all kinds.

Bella figura   An outward aspect of a person or object that produces a sentiment of admiration, or which elicits a favourable impression. A cultivation of outward appearances universal in Italy.

Benefice   A judicial entity consisting of lands or rents intended to finance an ecclesiastical office. The person holding the title to it only has the right to enjoy the revenues and has no power to dispose of the property itself, except to resign it to a person of his choice.

Bonification   Works intending to permit cultivation of land by removing the causes impeding it, principally by draining marsh lands with canals, often financed or regulated by the state.

Cadaster   An inventory of real estate, land or buildings, compiled to certify ownership, to evaluate wealth and to calculate taxable income.

Canon law   A compilation of laws and decrees governing the discipline of the Roman Catholic Church, drafted originally in the thirteenth century and reviewed and reissued between 1560 and 1582.

Cardinal-nephew   A pope's nephew elevated to the rank of cardinal upon his uncle's election, and entrusted with the management of the Papal Curia, along with the attribution of offices and functions. A *de facto* "prime minister" of the papal monarchy.

Casa or "house"   The term designates a dynasty rather than a building, often noble, but even peasants often had a strong sense of family identity and dynastic tradition.

Casale   A small group of houses isolated in the countryside, distant from an agglomeration. In some areas it designated a large but isolated farmhouse with its attendant buildings.

Castello   A group of houses surrounded by a wall, placed most often in a perched site. It was typical of grouped rural habitat in much of central Italy.

Chiesa ricettizia   A parish church governed by a college of local priests who administered the church's property amongst themselves, and delegated parish and religious functions to a junior member amongst them.

Cicisbeo   A gentleman or noble attendant who accompanies a married noble woman, not his wife, on public and private occasions. Common in aristocratic circles in the eighteenth century.

Citadel   A stout fort, usually positioned along a town wall, whose primary function was to hold the townspeople in obedience. The defence of the place against external enemies was a secondary function.

Civil society   A non-institutional entity composed of educated and urbane citizens, distinct from servants of the Church or of the State, whose activities and whose opinions underpin social trends.

Classicism   A recurrent artistic and literary movement that proposes the imitation of models from Greek and Roman antiquity, and which involves elaborating and teaching the rules governing that genre.

Commenda   The commenda, or commanditary contract was an instrument whereby investors placed money in the hands of a merchant or artisan, who managed it for them. The rate of return was generally lower than in cases where the investor managed the use of his capital.

Concordat   An agreement between the papacy and a state that establishes regulations for ecclesiastics and church institutions with respect to the state's jurisdiction – like the Church's tax immunities, its disciplinary and hierarchical prerogatives, the administration of sacred places, etc.

Conservatory   An institution established to protect orphans and children of poor parents as a work of Christian charity. Educated according to their status, apprenticed and married, the wards were often taught music in urban conservatories in the early modern period.

Coppice   Woods subject to systematic cutting to provide charcoal, firewood and fodder for domestic animals. A vital part of the rural economy.

Council of Italy   A permanent committee in Madrid of six high officials, three Italians, and three Spaniards, dealing with matters and petitions from Milan, Naples and Sicily, and presenting the matters for the king's information and ultimate decision.

Curia   The jurisdiction of a pope or bishop in administrative, judicial or executive matters. The Roman Curia is the Pope's administration.

Devolution (fief)   In feudal law, the judicial process by which rights and jurisdictions passed from the family or dynasty that possessed them, back to the sovereign when the direct inheriting line ended.

Dogana of Foggia   A customs administration founded by the Aragonese crown, with its seat in Foggia in Apulia, governing the movement of transhumant sheep through the Capitanata plain, with an eye to raising revenue.

Doge   Supreme elected magistrate of the republic of Venice, and of Genoa. Elected by a patrician assembly, the doges had little direct influence over the administration, and were rather chief dignitaries than power brokers.

Dominante   The term signifies the privileged capital city, whose patricians attributed to themselves the monopoly of important positions and a decisive say in government over the elites of subject towns

Ex voto   A memento of some kind, left in a sanctuary, bearing witness to the receipt of some kind of miraculous intervention from the Virgin Mary or a saint.

Fattoria   In central Italy, an agricultural complex with control over a number of separate farms all owned by the same landlord. It concentrated special machinery like grape and olive presses, had storehouses for grain, wine and oil, all under the administration of a superintendent (*fattore*).

Fedecommesso   A judicial legal clause, granted by the prince to noble families, allowing the family head to place constraints on the enjoyment of the estate by future heirs.

Feud   A state of private war between two or more families, which could continue until all the menfolk of one of the families were exterminated, or until the parties accepted a settlement.

Fratellanza   An association of brothers who pooled the property inherited from their father and managed it jointly, often with more than one married couple under one roof.

Freemasonry   A group of notables, operating in autonomous lodges, promoting philanthropy, charity and congenial debate on social issues. Apart from expressing a belief in God and insisting on strict morality, Freemasons advocated religious tolerance and equality among members.

Free port   A port into which one could import merchandise without paying duties, if the goods were subsequently re-exported. Goods were subject to tariffs only when moved from the port to a point inland.

Gabelles   A term signifying various types of taxes placed on consumer items like salt, sometimes forcing individuals to buy a specific quota annually.

Gabellotti (Sicily)   Agricultural agents who rented large estates from absentee landlords, paying an advance sum in money, and then managing the estate by suballotment to family farms, or directly through hired labour.

Golden Book or **Libro d'oro**   A register into which were inscribed the names of families eligible to hold political and senior administrative functions in city and state government, first in Venice and later in most major cities.

Guilds   Corporations of merchants and artisans who held a city-wide monopoly over the production and distribution of their products, enforced by local government. They regulated all aspects of their trade, and guild officers served as intermediaries between their members and government.

Hagiography   The history of the lives of the saints, a biographical-historical genre aiming to edify the reader rather than recount an objective history.

Holy Office of the Inquisition   One of the sacred congregations of the Roman Curia, this was a tribunal entrusted with investigating persons suspected of not believing in Catholic doctrines. The inquisitors investigated as crimes not only heresy, but also magic, obscenity, blasphemy and some sexual misdemeanours.

Humanism   A series of ideas exalting the "discovery of man" based on ideas and imitating the forms of expression of Greek and Latin literature.

The term "humanists" designated those who gave themselves to the study of the humanities.

Index One of the cardinal congregations of the Papal Curia, and closely linked with the Inquisition, it investigated published books for their doctrinal content.

Intendant (Piedmont) Inspired by the French institution, the *intendant* was a high central functionary, dispatched to a specific territory to oversee the functioning of local officials. The *intendant* had very wide powers of intervention.

Interdict In canon law, a papal censure against a person or against a place, prohibiting the celebration of, or the participation in, ecclesiastic rites. Used with mixed success against Venice (1606), Lucca (1641), Sicily (1718).

Italian trace A revolutionary innovation in fortifications in which a place was protected by a ring of angular platforms, called bastions, set low in the ground behind a deep ditch to reduce its exposure to artillery.

Jurisdictionalism or **anticurialism** The concern by the state to defend its prerogatives and its jurisdiction from the Church.

Latifundia Very extensive landed property, generally given over to extensive culture by absentee landlords.

Lazaret More a holding pen than a hospital, the lazaret was a quarantine area near a city originally intended for lepers.

Lazzaroni A term initially signifying leper, or a beggar covered with scabs. It was eventually applied to the urban poor in Naples who crowded the streets and markets, living at the edge of legality.

Legation The legate was a representative of the pope to foreign governments, but by extension he was a kind of papal governor overseeing autonomous regions of the Papal States, called legations.

Libertine Initially a derogatory term designating those who led a debauched lifestyle, the term was applied to thinkers who put received truths into doubt, and who demanded the right of disbelief.

Macchia A vegetative association typical of temperate Mediterranean regions, derived from evergreens. Low *macchia* consisted of shrubs 1 metre high, and tall *macchia* consisted of small trees about 3 metres high.

Macinato A widespread tax levied on flour. Easy to assess, the *macinato* was levied on the miller, who paid a tax based on the weight of the flour. This was essentially a tax on bread, the staple food of the poor.

Mercantilism An economic doctrine in which government (both state and local) reserved the right to regulate the manufacture, distribution and consumption of economic goods in order to achieve economic stability and generate fiscal returns.

Mero e misto imperio The legal status giving feudal lords the right to dispense justice in their own name, in the first instance and on appeal, both civil and criminal.

Mezzadria   The Italian form of sharecropping by which a peasant family leases a self-sufficient farm from a landlord (a *podere*), splitting the crops and the profits in two with the landlord.

Monte di Pietà   An early credit institution, emitting transferable interest-bearing bonds redeemable for cash or letters of exchange. A *Monte Pio* was a pawnshop permitting the poor to withdraw grain for food or seed, or money for loans for dowries and modest investments at nominal rates of interest.

Mortmain   A term designating property belonging to an entity considered perpetual and which is not subject to normal circulation from person to person. Applies especially to property belonging to the Church.

Nuncio   A papal messenger and ambassador, both a diplomatic representative for the papacy, and a dignitary of the church in countries where they were posted. They enjoyed wide influence.

Patriciate   A group of families, either "de facto" or "de jure" noble, who shared by inheritance the principal administrative and judicial offices of a city, usually bound by a strong corporate sense.

Pellagra   A nutritional disorder caused by a niacin (vitamin B) deficiency, characterized by skin lesions, alternating constipation and diarrhoea, depression, apathy and even delirium.

Philology   Erudition of a literary nature, to determine the sense of texts and the context in which they were written, with an interest in the development of language.

Physiocracy   An eighteenth-century economic doctrine, promoting private property and the free disposal of it. By implication it advocated the circulation of harvests free of customs tolls and regulations.

Podere   See *Mezzadria.*

Prepotenza   The desire to impose one's will at the harm and expense of others. Usually applied to nobles who were inclined to display their power and safeguard their interests through force.

Presides   The name for Spain's garrison outposts in the Mediterranean, which included bases in Africa and Italy. The presidial state, administered from Naples, consisted of the garrison enclaves along the south Tuscan coast and on the island of Elba.

primogeniture   A practice of succession generally restricted to nobles, by which the eldest son inherited the family estate and its titles, apart from a pension for the cadets, and substantial dowries for his sisters.

Promiscuous culture   Sometimes termed "interculture", this entails the combination of tree crops (olives, figs, vines) with cereals and legumes on the same parcel of land, generally by spacing the vines and trees wide apart and sowing the interval with seed.

Proto-industry   A form of manufacturing, in which articles of common quality were produced in the off-season by families of peasants, for regional markets. Urban merchants controlled the flow of raw materials and commercialized the finished product.

Quietism   A religious sensitivity characterized by an extreme emphasis on interior reflection on grace and salvation, simultaneously casting off ritual or community requirements of outward devotion.

Ratio studiorum   The Latin term for "study plan", a coherent set of pedagogical rules governing the teaching activity of the Jesuits, extended to the entire order in 1599 and remaining unchanged until the order's suppression in 1773.

Regular clergy   Clergy living apart from lay society, in closed communities governed by an immutable "rule" granted to the order's founder; characteristic of both wealthy and mendicant orders, masculine and feminine.

Rettore (Venice)   A Venetian patrician functionary elected to watch over the government of one of the subject towns in the Terraferma, to arbitrate local conflicts of interest, and to cultivate good relations between the local population and the capital city.

Sacred congregations   Permanent departments of the Papal Curia dealing with specific sectors of business, each composed of a handful of cardinals, their technical advisers and subalternate personnel.

Sbirro   The policeman of early modern Italy, employed by the local magistrate to serve summonses and to make seizures of people and goods. Many had criminal pasts and proclivities, considered an employment asset.

Scienza cavalleresca   A body of lore dealing with the point of honour, that is, the nature of honour, how to defend it, under which conditions and with whom.

Secular clergy   Clerics who live in close contact with lay society, to which they administer the sacraments. It includes the parish clergy and others holding benefices, as well as the tonsured but unordained minor clerics without church revenues.

Spanish Inquisition   A church tribunal created by the Spanish Crown (1487) and under its direction, whose aim was to root out beliefs and practices not part of Catholic orthodoxy. Its jurisdiction included Sardinia and Sicily, but not Naples or Milan.

Taille   The standard head-tax levied on each hearth by European monarchs. Local government had the responsibility for apportioning it, according to the estimated wealth of each non-exempted household.

Tax farmer   A tax farmer was a businessman, alone or part of a consortium, who paid a sum of money to a government entity, in exchange for the authority to levy and administer a specific tax, with a view to turning a profit.

Tercio Originally the administrative structure of a large Spanish infantry unit, designated by the place it was stationed, the tercio evolved into an operational force equivalent to a regiment, *circa* 1500 men, named after the aristocrat who raised and commanded it.

Terraces A form of agricultural landscaping by which arable land was extended onto steep slopes by constructing stone retaining walls, and filling the intervals with earth.

Terraferma The name for the mainland portion of the Venetian Republic, distinct from the lagoon. The Terraferma embraced Venice's possessions from Fruili, through the Veneto, to eastern Lombardy.

Thesaurization The act of hoarding wealth in the form of luxury objects or precious metals that could be either hidden or displayed in artistic form.

Transhumance The transfer of flocks of sheep from winter pasture in the plain to summer pasture in the mountains, and vice versa, according to the season.

Tratte The export licence which was purchased from government officials. It allowed government to control the flow of essential items out of the area while constituting an important revenue.

Università (Mezzogiorno) A term designating the corporate entity of a town or village, in either the royal domain or a feudal one.

Uskoks A Serbian term designating free resisters. Applied to a multi-ethnic population of Christian refugees, predominantly Serbs and Croats, inhabiting the eastern coast of the Adriatic sea, and given to piracy.

Veglia A winter evening when families congregated after supper before a single hearth to converse and relax. While people brought light work to do, the *veglia* was a place for stories and fables, music and dancing.

Viceroy A dignitary (always an important noble) chosen by the king of Spain to represent the king's person in one of the monarchy's dominions, to transmit Madrid's instructions and oversee their application.

Virtù Any good quality, a valour, talent or strength of character by which a man or woman achieved a goal or acclaim, raising them above the others.

Visitadore A senior functionary of the Spanish Crown, whose task was to review an administration's procedures and its personnel, and to propose changes, improvements and reforms.

Index

429

Brindisi, 15
Britain (Great) and British, 264,
    275, 276, 290, 292, 333, 350, 355
Bruno (Giordano), 180, 245, 248,
    252
Busto Arsizio, 214, 337

cadaster, 277, 343, 355–6, 363
Cadiz, 194, 211, 333
Cagliari, 21, 65
Calabria, 16, 18, 86, 121, 126, 186,
    187, 200, 218, 224, 228, 259, 300,
    325, 329, 336, 345
Caltagirone, 226
Cameralism, 335, 357
Campanella (Tommaso), 245–6, 248
Campania, 14, 16, 24, 33, 223, 245,
    301, 329, 338
Candia, 260–1, 262, 265
canon law, 26, 133, 303
canons and chapters, 107, 108, 109,
    129, 167
Capuchin order, 123, 124, 126, 307,
    316, 345
Caracciolo (Domenico), 349–50
Carafa (Antonio), 289
Caravaggio (Michelangelo Merisi),
    161
Cardano (Girolamo), 41
cardinal Congregations, 61, 101, 122
cardinal-nephew, 61, 140, 257
cardinals, 12, 41, 47, 59–61, 75, 106,
    120, 124, 137, 138, 140, 143, 145,
    148, 153, 162, 257, 312, 324
Carmelite order, 123, 126, 134, 246
carnival, 111, 148, 156, 307, 308, 349
Carracci (painters), 159, 161
Casale Monferrato, 56, 194, 195,
    196, 198, 200, 272, 275, 276, 286,
    289
casali, 14, 24, 224, 228
Caserta, 335, 340
Cassa Sacra, 345
castelli, 9
Castiglione (Baidassare), 40, 45
Castile, 63, 88, 89, 99, 202, 290
Castilian language, 65, 679 176, 321
castrati, 143, 153
Castro, 202–4

Catalonia, 65, 197, 284
Catania, 13, 19, 224, 226, 285, 321,
    348
Catanzaro, 13, 16, 86
catechism, 122, 128, 308, 317, 359
censorship, 313, 315, 318, 357
central Italy, 7–12, 46, 165–70, 218,
    221, 241, 307
Cesare d'Este (duke), 55
Chambery, 58, 277
charity, 12, 66, 102, 103, 112, 113,
    121, 131, 144, 145, 168, 207, 237,
    238–9, 277, 297, 329, 348, 352,
    358, 365
charlatans, 228
Charlemagne, 46, 353
Charles II (king), 289, 290
Charles V (emperor), 19, 47, 52, 53,
    57, 63, 66, 71, 75, 120, 121
Charles VI (archduke and
    emperor), 290, 291, 293, 335, 347,
    353–4
Charles III Bourbon (king), 291,
    293, 294, 314, 315, 335, 340–52
Charles-Emanuel I of Savoy (duke),
    59, 74, 191–6, 271–5
Charles-Emanuel II of Savoy (duke),
    273, 277
Charles-Emanuel III of Savoy
    (duke), 279, 280
Charles of Gonzaga-Nevers (duke),
    195–6
Chianti, 223
Chieri, 6, 81, 84, 85, 87, 337
chiese ricettizie, 111, 132
Chieti, 15, 306
chivalric orders, 75, 340
chivalry romance, 40, 44, 151, 174
christianization, 1, 37, 105, 243
Christina of Sweden (queen), 143,
    156, 162, 242, 251, 312
Church, 12, 27, 34, 39, 41, 42, 56,
    59–61,72, 75, 87, 104–19, 120–35,
    156, 168, 169, 173, 180, 220, 244,
    246, 253, 257, 257, 278, 311, 315,
    323, 331, 342, 354, 355, 359, 368
church jurisdiction, 68, 72, 107, 144,
    168, 203, 233, 303–4, 310–11, 341,
    361